# *Cases in Communication Law*

# Cases in Communication Law

**Paul Siegel**

*Gallaudet University*

**Allyn and Bacon**

*Boston • London • Toronto • Sydney • Tokyo • Singapore*

*Series Editor:* Molly Taylor
*Editorial Assistant:* Michael Kish
*Editorial-Production Service:* Omegatype Typography, Inc.
*Composition and Prepress Buyer:* Linda Cox
*Manufacturing Buyer:* Julie McNeill
*Cover Administrator:* Kristina Mose-Libon
*Electronic Composition:* Omegatype Typography, Inc.

**Library of Congress Cataloging-in-Publication Data**

Siegel, Paul
    Communication law in America / Paul Siegel.
      p.   cm.
    Includes index.
    ISBN 0-205-28987-8 (alk. paper)
    1. Mass media—Law and legislation—United States.   2. Press law—United States.   3.
Freedom of speech—United States.   I. Title.

    KF2750 .S53 2002
    343.7309'9—dc21

                                                          2001022105

    ISBN 0-205-28986-X

# *Contents*

# *Preface*

*Cases in Communication Law* is designed to be used as a supplementary text in courses focusing on media law and freedom of speech in the United States. The chapter sequence mirrors that found in my *Communication Law in America,* also published by Allyn and Bacon.

The vast majority of the cases presented here were decided by the United States Supreme Court and are binding precedents on all jurisdictions nationwide. But such "controlling legal precedent"—to borrow an oft-heard phrase from the 2000 presidential campaign—does not exist for every important principle in media law. Therefore, also examined here is provocative lower court case law, whether from federal or state courts.

Whenever possible, cases were selected for their recognized status as landmark decisions. Readability and comprehensibility were equally compelling criteria, however. Thus, some landmark cases were consciously excluded. For example, one of the most important cases in U.S. constitutional history is the famous Pentagon Papers case,* where the Court ruled that the *New York Times* and the *Washington Post* may not be enjoined from further publication of purloined government documents exposing much wrongdoing in the Vietnam War. As important as that case was in demonstrating the judiciary's unlikeliness to accept a government-imposed prior restraint on the press, the decision itself is a mess. Every single justice wrote a separate opinion, and the accompanying *per curiam* (anonymously written, "by the Court") opinion is short and uninformative. Therefore, in lieu of the Pentagon Papers case, we offer here as a more readable example of prior restraint *United States v. The Progressive,* a provocative federal district case involving a magazine article about how to build a hydrogen bomb.

Whether you are reading this book as part of a college course or on your own, it is hoped that you take from it a richer understanding of the complexities of this fascinating area of the law.

*New York Times v. U.S.,* 403 U.S. 713 (1971).

## *Acknowledgments*

Many thanks to the reviewers of this supplement, Carrie Anna Criado, Southern Methodist University; Dale Herbeck, Boston College; and Robert Jensen, University of Texas.

# *About the Author*

Paul Siegel is professor and formerly chairperson of communication studies at Gallaudet University in Washington, D.C., the world's only comprehensive university designed specifically for deaf and hard-of-hearing students. As an adjunct, he teaches journalism law classes at George Mason University and American University.

He has also taught at Illinois State University, St. Cloud State University, Catholic University, the University of Missouri at Kansas City, and Tulane University. He has published dozens of essays in journals of communication, sociology, and anthropology, as well as in law reviews and as book chapters. Sample titles include "Second-Hand Prejudice, Racial Analogies and Shared Showers: Why 'Don't Ask, Don't Tell' Won't Sell" (*Notre Dame Journal of Law, Ethics, and Public Policy*); "Smart Shopping as Patriotism: Avoidance, Denial and Advertising" (*Communications and the Law*); and "Privacy: Control over Stimulus Input, Stimulus Output, and Self-Regarding Conduct" (*Buffalo Law Review*). A long-time associate editor of the *Free Speech Yearbook,* Siegel also edited a collection of readings on the Clarence Thomas hearings (*Outsiders Looking In,* published by Hampton Press).

Siegel's bachelor's degree in speech and psychology was awarded by the University of New Mexico. He earned a master's degree in interpersonal communication from the University of Wisconsin; his doctoral degree in communication studies is from Northwestern University.

# *Cases in Communication Law*

# 1

# *Introduction*

There are many sources of communication law in the United States. Chief among the United States Constitution's relevant provisions are the Free Press and Free Speech clauses of the First Amendment, which tell the Congress that it shall "make no law" abridging either one. Individual state constitutions also have provisions that mirror the First Amendment, although sometimes these have been interpreted so as to give a state's residents more rights than Americans in general enjoy (such as a right to leaflet on the grounds of privately owned shopping malls).

The legislative branch of government, whether a city council, a state legislature, or Congress itself, also has an important role to play in the creation of communication law. This mechanism is the one that produces everything from federal copyright law and state libel and obscenity laws to local ordinances governing how many newspaper racks may be placed on public streets. Some areas of communication law involve more than one level of legislation. Advertising is regulated at both the federal and state levels. The cable television industry is regulated by a complicated mosaic of federal legislation and contracts entered into between cable franchises and local governments.

The executive branch also creates communication law in several ways. The president (with the consent of the Senate) appoints federal judges as well as the top officials at such agencies as the Federal Communications Commission (FCC) and the Federal Trade Commission. By the simple act of signing an executive order, presidents can greatly affect the flow of information, such as by creating new rules governing how aggressively and timely officials will declassify once-secret documents.

This book, however, focuses exclusively on published decisions from the judicial branch, mostly the United States Supreme Court, but also lower federal and state courts. That focus can be justified in two ways. First, judges are often called on to rule on the constitutionality of the other governmental branches' actions. In *Reno v. ACLU,* for example (see Chapter 13), the Supreme Court struck down amendments made by Congress to the

1

Telecommunications Act of 1996 concerning sexual imagery on the Internet. The Hawaii Supreme Court, in *Borreca v. Fasi* (see Chapter 7), told the mayor of Honolulu that his practice of excluding from his press conferences reporters who angered him was unconstitutional. By reading court opinions, then, we see the machinations of the other branches of government as well.

The second reason for focusing on court decisions is that they are the most revealing and rhetorical among legal documents. Judges have to make arguments just as much as do the opposing counsel who appear before them. Lower court judges have to word their decisions clearly and defensibly so as not to be overturned on appeal. Appellate courts, consisting as they do of anywhere from three to almost two dozen judges, especially must produce rhetorically compelling opinions to attract enough votes to form a majority. To a large extent, this is why court decisions are generally more comprehensible to nonlawyers than are statutes themselves.

## *The U.S. Judiciary*

We should first realize that there is not one judicial system in the United States, but rather a federal system, a system for each of the states, and one for the District of Columbia. That is fifty-two systems in all, without even counting the courts governing such places as Puerto Rico or the Virgin Islands.

The structure of the judiciary itself need not be a source of complete bewilderment, however. Indeed, the hierarchy of courts in the states is almost without exception modeled after the federal system. There are three layers. At the bottom are the trial courts. In the federal system, they are called federal district courts. The names of the trial courts vary greatly from state to state, but are most frequently called superior courts.

Litigants who are unhappy with the trial court result have the option of bringing an appeal to the next layer of the judiciary. In the federal system, and in that of most states, these are called, intuitively enough, appellate courts. In the federal system, these appellate courts govern a specific region of the country, called a federal circuit. There are thirteen such circuits. Eleven of them are given numbers. The Appellate Court for the Eighth Circuit, for example, governs the states of Arkansas, Iowa, Minnesota, Missouri, Nebraska, North Dakota, and South Dakota.

There is also an appellate court for the District of Columbia. That particular court has jurisdiction over most appeals from decisions of the FCC and other federal agencies. The thirteenth federal appellate court is the one for the Federal Circuit, a special court created by Congress in 1982 to handle such specialized appeals as patent and trademark cases.

Litigants who are not satisfied with an appellate ruling can sometimes take their grievance one step higher. The pinnacle of the judiciary in both the federal and state systems is also an appellate court, but it goes by a special name. The highest federal court is, of course, the U.S. Supreme Court. The highest court of almost all the states is also referred to as a supreme court, although there are some exceptions. New York's highest court, for example, is its Court of Appeals.

Although we often hear aggrieved parties vow that they will take their cases "all the way to the Supreme Court, if necessary," in fact this is romantic fancy because the justices of the Supreme Court have tremendous latitude about which of the thousands of appeals filed there annually will be heard. In recent years, the justices have chosen to hear only a hundred or fewer cases on average each term. Many state supreme courts have similar discretion to determine which cases they will hear. As such, often litigants are realistically limited to having their grievances heard in two, rather than three, rungs of the judicial system.

Of the fifty-seven cases represented in this volume, thirty-four are U.S. Supreme Court decisions, fifteen are federal appellate decisions, and six were decided at the federal district court level. The book also includes two state cases, one from the Supreme Court of Hawaii and the other from a lower court in New York.

## *Understanding Legal Citations*

Each of the court cases excerpted in this book has not only a name, but also a citation. The citation tells you a fair amount of information about the legal dispute, not the least of which is where you can find the full text of the opinion should you decide to read further.

Although there are several published (and online) sources for the full text of Supreme Court decisions, the citation format provided in this book refers to the case's original appearance in the Court's own official volumes, called *United States Reports* (abbreviated U.S.). The very first case appearing in these pages is *Brandenburg v. Ohio,* the citation for which is 395 U.S. 444 (1969). This tells us that the full text of the Court's opinion can be found in volume 395 of the *United States Reports,* beginning on page 444. The case was decided in 1969.

Federal district court opinions, when they are published at all, appear most conveniently in a series from the Saint Paul, Minnesota–based West Publishing Company, called *Federal Supplement* (or F. Supp.). Notice the citation associated with *Weinstein v. Bullick,* which appears in Chapter 3: 827 F. Supp. 1193 (E.D. Pa. 1993). This notation means that the full text of the opinion can be found in volume 827 of the *Federal Supplement,* beginning on page 1193. The information in parentheses tells us that the case was decided in 1993 by the federal district court for the Eastern District of Pennsylvania.

As of 1998, the *Federal Supplement* volume numbering system began anew (rather than climb higher than 999), and so the most recent federal district cases are found in the *Federal Supplement,* second edition (abbreviated F. Supp. 2d). Chapter 13 boasts such a newer case, *Mainstream Loudoun v. Loudoun County Library.* That 1998 decision from the federal district court of the Eastern District of Virginia appears in volume 2 of the second edition of the *Federal Supplement,* beginning on page 783. Its citation is thus 2 F. Supp. 2d 783 (E.D. Va. 1998).

Federal appellate decisions are found in another West publication called the *Federal Reporter* (abbreviated simply as F.). In 1924, after publishing volume number 300, the *Federal Reporter* began numbering anew, and from that date until 1993, cases were thus found in the *Federal Reporter,* second edition (F.2d). The most recent cases—generally from 1994 forward—appear in the *Federal Reporter,* third edition (F.3d). This book includes cases from both the second and the third editions of the *Federal Reporter.*

Each state's judiciary publishes its own case reports. Thus, we may see references, for example, to the *Wisconsin Reporter* or the *New York Supplement. Stein v. Trager,* a 1962 New York libel case excerpted in Chapter 3, can be found in its entirety in that latter publication. Academic libraries at most colleges without law schools do not bother to subscribe to each and every state's reporters. Rather, they tend to subscribe to yet another West series of publications. West's regional reporters conveniently break down the states into seven separate areas—the Atlantic (A.), the Pacific (P.), the Northeastern (N.E.), the Northwestern (N.W.), the Southern (So.), the Southeastern (S.E.), and the Southwestern (S.W.). Just as was the case with the reporting of federal appellate cases, when the volume number of a regional reporter gets very high, West will start numbering again in a new series. Some of the regional reporters are in their second editions, some in their third. The citation for *Acker v. Texas Water Commission,* excerpted in Chapter 7, indicates that it was decided by the Texas Supreme Court in 1990 and appeared in volume 790 of the second edition of the *Southwestern Reporter.*

## A Word about the Editing of This Volume

The editing of this volume could aptly be described as *purposefully heavy-handed* and necessarily so. Most of the court cases found in this volume, if read in their entirety, would take up five to ten times as many pages as the excerpts offered here. Yet the publisher's intention and my own were to expose you to a fair sampling of court cases within each chapter's area of case law.

How were the cases cut down to size? Several strategies were used. It was helpful to delete the footnotes from the original cases. In those few instances where the information found in the footnotes was essential to understanding the case, that information was moved up to the main text instead.

Whole lines of arguments deemed distracting from the main point of a court case were also deleted. Some of these were rather generic. Courts often have to consider whether one or more parties to a lawsuit are eligible to sue or can be excused from a lawsuit, or indeed whether they came to the right court to state their claims. These arguments of standing, immunity, and jurisdiction have been surgically removed from the cases here.

Sometimes issues that are related to communication law are nonetheless distractions from a case's main point. In *New York Times v. Sullivan,* for example—the landmark libel case—one of the plaintiff's arguments was based on the Supreme Court's not-yet-evolved doctrines applicable to commercial speech. That argument was excised. Similarly, it is hoped that the detailed excerpts offered here from *Branzburg v. Hayes*—involving a *Louisville Courier Journal* reporter's subpoena to appear in front of a grand jury—will suffice to teach the case's main lessons even though the Court's discussion of the facts surrounding two companion cases involving other media outlets has been deleted.

Beyond these strategies, a heavy hand was taken to any jurists' long-winded prose or unnecessary redundancy. Internal quotations to earlier cases were generally omitted. These interventions sometimes resulted in sentence fragments that had to be combined and to portions of text that had to be moved up several paragraphs. To aid readability, the use of ellipses and other printers' tools to alert readers of deletions has been eschewed.

Users of this volume—especially if they have occasion to compare one or more of the case excerpts offered here with the original, full-text versions—will be in the best position to assess whether the purposely heavy-handed editing succeeded.

# 2 *First Amendment Principles*

In this chapter, we examine decisions in which the courts have outlined the First Amendment's scope and meaning, starting with *Brandenburg v. Ohio,* a 1969 decision stemming from a prosecution for "criminal syndicalism" against a Ku Klux Klan speaker. The *Brandenburg* test, still good law, says that political speech is protected by the First Amendment unless it is likely to produce "imminent lawless action." Our second case, *Hess v. Indiana,* is an example of the test's application and suggests that the Court takes seriously the earlier decision's "imminence" requirement.

*Rice v. Paladin Enterprises* never reached the Supreme Court, but it created quite a stir in the popular press and among constitutional scholars. At issue was whether survivors of a "gun for hire" could sue the publishers of a book that seems to have taught this particular "hit man" all he needed to know.

The First Amendment protects not only the interests of speakers, but listeners (and readers) as well. This message is made clear in *Board of Education v. Pico,* which suggests that public school library books, once purchased and shelved, achieve a kind of "squatters' right" to that shelf space, at least in some circumstances.

Another issue fundamental to the First Amendment's scope is the posited right not to speak. *Wooley v. Maynard,* one of the Supreme Court's many statements on this issue, has often been cited as an elegant paean to silence.

*United States v. O'Brien* asks us to consider when is communicative conduct that does not involve the vocal cords to be counted as "speech"? The emerging "*O'Brien* test" tells courts how to evaluate government regulations that are aimed at the *non*communicative component of an agent's conduct, but that have an effect on that agent's message.

Next, we look at the question of when and how the state may unabashedly discriminate among categories of speech permitted to take place in government-created public forums. *Cornelius v. NAACP Legal Defense and Education Fund* teaches that such forums need not be literal places.

Finally, we examine the matter of prior restraints on the press by reading *United States v. The Progressive,* in which a U.S. district judge issued an injunction against publication of an article the government argued could lead to nuclear annihilation.

# ■ *Brandenburg v. Ohio*

### 395 U.S. 444 (1969)

*Per curiam opinion*

The appellant, a leader of a Ku Klux Klan group, was convicted under the Ohio Criminal Syndicalism statute for "advocat[ing] . . . the duty, necessity, or propriety of crime, sabotage, violence, or unlawful methods of terrorism as a means of accomplishing industrial or political reform" and for "voluntarily assembl[ing] with any society, group, or assemblage of persons formed to teach or advocate the doctrines of criminal syndicalism."

The record shows that [the appellant] telephoned an announcer-reporter on the staff of a Cincinnati television station and invited him to come to a Ku Klux Klan "rally" to be held at a farm in Hamilton County. With the cooperation of the organizers, the reporter and a cameraman attended the meeting and filmed the events. Portions of the films were later broadcast on the local station and on a national network.

One film showed 12 hooded figures, some of whom carried firearms. They were gathered around a large wooden cross, which they burned. No one was present other than the participants and the newsmen who made the film. Most of the words uttered during the scene were incomprehensible when the film was projected, but scattered phrases could be understood that were derogatory of Negroes and, in one instance, of Jews [such as "Bury the niggers," "This is what we are going to do to the niggers," and "Send the Jews back to Israel."]. Though some of the figures in the films carried weapons, the speaker did not.

The Ohio Criminal Syndicalism Statute was enacted in 1919. From 1917 to 1920, identical or quite similar laws were adopted by 20 States and two territories. In 1927, this Court sustained the constitutionality of California's Criminal Syndicalism Act, the text of which is quite similar to that of the laws of Ohio. *Whitney v. California,* 274 U.S. 357 (1927). The Court upheld the statute on the ground that, without more, "advocating" violent means to effect political and economic change involves such danger to the security of the State that the State may outlaw it. But *Whitney* has been thoroughly discredited by later decisions. See *Dennis v. United States,* 341 U.S. 494, at 507 (1951). These later decisions have fashioned the principle that the constitutional guarantees of free speech and free press do not permit a

State to forbid or proscribe advocacy of the use of force or of law violation except where such advocacy is directed to inciting or producing imminent lawless action and is likely to incite or produce such action.

Ohio's Criminal Syndicalism Act cannot be sustained. The Act punishes persons who "advocate or teach the duty, necessity, or propriety" of violence "as a means of accomplishing industrial or political reform"; or who publish or circulate or display any book or paper containing such advocacy; or who "justify" the commission of violent acts "with intent to exemplify, spread or advocate the propriety of the doctrines of criminal syndicalism"; or who "voluntarily assemble" with a group formed "to teach or advocate the doctrines of criminal syndicalism." Neither the indictment nor the trial judge's instructions to the jury in any way refined the statute's bald definition of the crime in terms of mere advocacy not distinguished from incitement to imminent lawless action.

Accordingly, we are here confronted with a statute which, by its own words and as applied, purports to punish mere advocacy and to forbid, on pain of criminal punishment, assembly with others merely to advocate the described type of action. Such a statute falls within the condemnation of the First and Fourteenth Amendments.

Reversed.

## Points for Discussion

1. Should incitement of violent illegal action (such as "Burying the niggers") be treated differently under the *Brandenburg* test from advocacy of nonviolent action (e.g., tax evasion) or even advocacy of "victimless" crimes (e.g., having an extramarital affair)?

2. The *Brandenburg* test requires courts to consider whether a speaker's utterance is "likely to produce" lawless action. Does this mean that an ineffectual leader incapable of delivering a rousing speech enjoys more First Amendment freedoms than does a dramatic and talented rhetor?

## ▇ *Hess v. Indiana*

**414 U.S. 105 (1973)**

*Per curiam opinion*

Gregory Hess appeals from his conviction in the Indiana courts for violating the State's disorderly conduct statute. Appellant contends that his conviction should be reversed because the statute is unconstitutionally vague, because the statute is overbroad in that it forbids activity that is protected under the First and Fourteenth Amendments, and because the statute, as applied here, abridged his constitutionally protected freedom of speech. These contentions were rejected in the City Court, where Hess was convicted, and in the Superior Court, which reviewed his conviction. The Supreme Court of Indiana, with one dissent, considered and rejected each of Hess' constitutional contentions, and accordingly affirmed his conviction.

The events leading to Hess' conviction began with an antiwar demonstration on the campus of Indiana University. In the course of the demonstration, approximately 100 to 150 of the demonstrators moved onto a public street and blocked the passage of vehicles. When the demonstrators did not respond to verbal directions from the sheriff to clear the street, the sheriff and his deputies began walking up the street, and the demonstrators in their path moved to the curbs on either side, joining a large number of spectators who had gathered. Hess was standing off the street as the sheriff passed him. The sheriff heard Hess utter the word "fuck" in what he later described as a loud voice and immediately arrested him on the disorderly conduct charge. It was later stipulated that what appellant had said was "We'll take the fucking street later," or "We'll take the fucking street again." Two witnesses who were in the immediate vicinity testified, apparently without contradiction, that they heard Hess' words and witnessed his arrest. They indicated that Hess did not appear to be exhorting the crowd to go back into the street, that he was facing the crowd and not the street when he uttered the statement, that his statement did not appear to be addressed to any particular person or group, and that his tone, although loud, was no louder than that of the other people in the area.

The Indiana Supreme Court placed primary reliance on the trial court's finding that Hess' statement "was intended to incite further lawless action on the part of the crowd in the vicinity of appellant and was likely to produce such action." At best, however, the statement could be taken as counsel for present moderation; at worst, it amounted to nothing more than advocacy of illegal action at some indefinite future time. This is not sufficient to permit the State to punish Hess' speech. Under our decisions, "the constitutional guarantees of free speech and free press do not permit a State to forbid or proscribe advocacy of the use of force or of law violation except where such advocacy is directed to inciting or producing imminent lawless action and is likely to incite or produce such action." *Brandenburg v. Ohio,* 395 U.S. 444, 447 (1969). Since the uncontroverted evidence showed that Hess' statement was not directed to any person or group of persons, it cannot be said that he was advocating, in the normal sense, any action. And since there was no evidence, or rational inference from the import of the language, that his words were intended to produce, and likely to produce, imminent disorder, those words could not be punished by the State on the ground that they had "a 'tendency to lead to violence.' "

Accordingly, the judgment of the Supreme Court of Indiana is reversed.

## Points for Discussion

1. Clearly, the *Hess* decision emphasizes *Brandenburg v. Ohio's* "imminence" requirement. But why should "imminence" make a difference? Is a speaker who directs audience members to loot the downtown *now* any less culpable than one who advises them to take a brief lunch break first? Is the real issue the presumed opportunity for intervention to stop the violence from taking place?

2. If you were trying to predict in advance whether Hess's utterance was likely to lead to unlawful action, what would your guess have been? After all, he was surrounded by over a hundred followers (unlike the mere dozen or so "hooded figures" who listened to Brandenburg's racist speech) who had already broken the law (by blocking traffic, for example). Are courts likely to use their own "20-20 hindsight" when applying *Brandenburg's* "likely to produce . . ." requirement (i.e., speeches that *did* result in illegality were therefore "likely to produce" illegality)?

## ◼ *Rice v. Paladin Enterprises*

### 123 F. 3d 238 (4th Cir. 1997)

*Judge Luttig:*

[Judge Luttig's opinion begins with several pages of direct quotes from the book *Hit Man: A Technical Manual for Independent Contractors,* giving readers excruciatingly detailed instructions for killing an intended victim with a knife, a gun, or explosives or by arson and how to dispose of the body.]

On the night of March 3, 1993, readied by these instructions and steeled by these seductive adjurations from *Hit Man: A Technical Manual for Independent Contractors,* a copy of which was subsequently found in his apartment, James Perry brutally murdered Mildred Horn, her eight-year-old quadriplegic son Trevor, and Trevor's nurse, Janice Saunders, by shooting Mildred Horn and Saunders through the eyes and by strangling Trevor Horn. Perry's despicable crime was not one of vengeance; he did not know any of his victims. Nor did he commit the murders in the course of another offense. Perry acted instead as a contract killer, a "hit man," hired by Mildred Horn's ex-husband, Lawrence Horn, to murder Horn's family so that Horn would receive the $2 million that his eight-year-old son had received in settlement for injuries that had previously left him paralyzed for life. At the time of the murders, this money was held in trust for the benefit of Trevor, and, under the terms of the trust instrument, the trust money was to be distributed tax-free to Lawrence in the event of Mildred's and Trevor's deaths.

In soliciting, preparing for, and committing these murders, Perry meticulously followed countless of *Hit Man*'s 130 pages of detailed factual instructions on how to murder and to become a professional killer. *Hit Man* instructs that a "beginner" should use an AR-7 rifle to kill his victims. James Perry used an AR-7 rifle to slay Mildred Horn and Janice Saunders. The manual instructs its readers to kill their "mark" at close range, from a distance of three to six feet. James Perry shot Mildred Horn and Janice Saunders from a distance of three feet. *Hit Man* specifically instructs its audience of killers to shoot the victim through the eyes if possible. James Perry shot Mildred Horn and Janice Saunders two or three times and through the eyes. Perry [also] followed many of *Hit Man*'s instructions for concealing his murders.

In this civil, state-law wrongful death action against defendant Paladin Enterprises—the publisher of *Hit Man*—the relatives and representatives of Mildred and Trevor Horn and Janice Saunders allege that Paladin aided and abetted Perry in the commission of his murders through its publication of *Hit Man*'s killing instructions.

The parties agree that the sole issue to be decided by the Court is whether the First Amendment is a complete defense, as a matter of law, to the civil action set forth in the plaintiffs' Complaint. All other issues of law and fact are specifically reserved for subsequent proceedings.

Paladin, for example, has stipulated for purposes of summary judgment that Perry followed the above-enumerated instructions from *Hit Man* as well as instructions from another Paladin publication, *How to Make a Disposable Silencer, Vol. II,* in planning, executing, and attempting to cover up the murders of Mildred and Trevor Horn and Janice Saunders.

Paladin has stipulated not only that, in marketing *Hit Man,* Paladin "intended to attract and assist criminals and would-be criminals who desire information and instructions on how to commit crimes," but also that it "intended and had knowledge" that *Hit Man* actually "would be used, upon receipt, by criminals and would-be criminals to plan and execute the crime of murder for hire." Indeed, the publisher has even stipulated that, through publishing and selling *Hit Man,* it assisted Perry in particular in the perpetration of the very murders for which the victims' families now attempt to hold Paladin civilly liable.

Notwithstanding Paladin's extraordinary stipulations, the district court granted Paladin's motion for summary judgment and dismissed plaintiffs' claims that Paladin aided and abetted Perry, holding that these claims were barred by the First Amendment as a matter of law.

Because long-established caselaw provides that speech—even speech by the press—that constitutes criminal aiding and abetting does not enjoy the protection of the First Amendment, and because we are convinced that such caselaw is both correct and equally applicable to speech that constitutes civil aiding and abetting of criminal conduct (at least where, as here, the defendant has the specific purpose of assisting and encouraging commission of such conduct and the alleged assistance and encouragement takes a form other than abstract advocacy), we hold that the First Amendment does not pose a bar to a finding that Paladin is civilly liable as an aider and abetter of Perry's triple contract murder.

We also hold that the plaintiffs have stated against Paladin a civil aiding and abetting claim under Maryland law sufficient to withstand Paladin's motion for summary judgment. For these reasons, which we fully explain below, the district court's grant of summary judgment in Paladin's favor is reversed and the case is remanded for trial.

In the seminal case of *Brandenburg v. Ohio,* the Supreme Court held that abstract advocacy of lawlessness is protected speech under the First Amendment. Although the Court provided little explanation for this holding in its brief *per curiam* opinion, it is evident the Court recognized from our own history that such a right to advocate lawlessness is, almost paradoxically, one of the ultimate safeguards of liberty. Even in a society of laws, one of the most indispensable freedoms is that to express in the most impassioned terms the most passionate disagreement with the laws themselves, the institutions of, and created by, law, and the individual officials with whom the laws and institutions are entrusted. Without the freedom to criticize that which constrains, there is no freedom at all.

However, while even speech advocating lawlessness has long enjoyed protections under the First Amendment, it is equally well established that speech which, in its effect, is tantamount to legitimately proscribable non-expressive conduct may itself be legitimately proscribed, punished, or regulated incidentally to the constitutional enforcement of generally applicable statutes. *Cohen v. Cowles Media Co.,* 501 U.S. 663, 669 (1991) (noting "well-established line of decisions holding that generally applicable laws do not offend the First Amendment simply because their enforcement against the press has incidental effects on its ability to gather and report the news"). [See also] *United States v. Varani,* 435 F.2d 758, 762 (6th Cir. 1970) ("Speech is not protected by the First Amendment when it is the very vehicle of the crime itself").

Were the First Amendment to bar or to limit government regulation of such "speech brigaded with action," the government would be powerless to protect the public from countless of even the most pernicious criminal acts and civil wrongs [such as perjury or threatening public officials].

Every court that has addressed the issue, including this court, has held that the First Amendment does not necessarily pose a bar to liability for aiding and abetting a crime, even when such aiding and abetting takes the form of the spoken or written word. Thus, in a case indistinguishable in principle from that before us, the Ninth Circuit expressly held in *United States v. Barnett,* 667 F.2d 835 (9th Cir. 1982), that the First Amendment does not provide publishers a defense as a matter of law to charges of aiding and abetting a crime through the publication and distribution of instructions on how to make illegal drugs.

The First Amendment does not provide a defense to a criminal charge simply because the actor uses words to carry out his illegal purpose. Crimes, including that of aiding and abetting, frequently involve the use of speech as part of the criminal transaction. The principle of *Barnett*, that the provision of instructions that aid and abet another in the commission of a criminal offense is unprotected by the First Amendment, has been uniformly accepted, and the principle has been applied to the aiding and abetting of innumerable crimes. Notably, then-Judge Kennedy, in express reliance upon *Barnett*, invoked the principle in *United States v. Freeman* to sustain convictions for the aiding and abetting of tax fraud. 761 F.2d 549, 552–53 (9th Cir. 1985), *cert. denied*, 476 U.S. 1120 (1986). In *Freeman*, the Ninth Circuit concluded that the defendant could be held criminally liable for counseling tax evasion at seminars held in protest of the tax laws, even though the speech that served as the predicate for the conviction "sprang from the anterior motive to effect political or social change." Our own circuit, and every other circuit to address the issue, has likewise concluded that the First Amendment is generally inapplicable to charges of aiding and abetting violations of the tax laws.

The cloak of the First Amendment envelops critical, but abstract, discussions of existing laws, but lends no protection to speech which urges the listeners to commit violations of current law. Indeed, as the Department of Justice recently advised Congress, the law is now well established that the First Amendment, and *Brandenburg*'s "imminence" requirement in particular, generally poses little obstacle to the punishment of speech that constitutes criminal aiding and abetting, because "culpability in such cases is premised, not on defendants' 'advocacy' of criminal conduct, but on defendants' successful efforts to assist others by detailing to them the means of accomplishing the crimes." Department of Justice, "Report on the Availability of Bombmaking Information, the Extent to Which Its Dissemination Is Controlled by Federal Law, and the Extent to Which Such Dissemination May Be Subject to Regulation Consistent with the First Amendment to the United States Constitution" 37 (April 1997).

We can envision only two possible qualifications to these general rules, neither of which, for reasons that we discuss more extensively below, is of special moment in the context of the particular aiding and abetting case before us.

The first, which obviously would have practical import principally in the civil context, is that the First Amendment may, at least in certain circumstances, superimpose upon the speech-act doctrine a heightened intent requirement in order that preeminent values underlying that constitutional provision not be imperiled. That is, in order to prevent the punishment or even the chilling of entirely innocent, lawfully useful speech, the First Amendment may in some contexts stand as a bar to the imposition of liability on the basis of mere foreseeability or knowledge that the information one imparts could be misused for an impermissible purpose. Where it is necessary, such a limitation would meet the quite legitimate, if not compelling, concern of those who publish, broadcast, or distribute to large, undifferentiated audiences, that the exposure to suit under lesser standards would be intolerable. At the same time, it would not relieve from liability those who would, for profit or other motive, intentionally assist and encourage crime and then shamelessly seek refuge in the sanctuary of the First Amendment. Like our sister circuits, at the very least where a speaker—individual or media—acts with the purpose of assisting in the commission of crime, we do not believe that the First Amendment insulates that speaker from responsibility for his actions simply because he may have disseminated his message to a wide audience. Were the First Amendment to offer protection even in these circumstances, one could publish, by traditional means or even on the internet, the necessary plans and instructions for assassinating the President, for poisoning a city's water supply, for blowing up a skyscraper or public building, or for similar acts of terror and mass destruction, with the specific, indeed even the admitted, purpose of assisting such crimes—all with impunity.

Paladin has stipulated that it provided its assistance to Perry with both the knowledge and the intent that the book would immediately be used by criminals and would-be criminals in the solicitation, planning, and commission of murder and murder for hire, and even absent the stipulations, a jury could reasonably find such specific intent. Thus, Paladin has stipulated to an intent, and a jury could otherwise reasonably find that Paladin acted with a kind and degree of intent, that would satisfy any heightened standard that might be required by the First Amendment prerequisite to the imposition of liability for aiding and abetting through speech conduct.

The second qualification is that the First Amendment might well (and presumably would) interpose the same or similar limitations upon the imposition of civil liability for abstract advocacy, without more, that it interposes upon the imposition of criminal punishment for such advocacy. In other words, the First Amendment might well circumscribe the power of the state to create and enforce a cause of action that would permit the imposition of civil liability, such as aiding and abetting civil liability, for speech that would constitute pure abstract advocacy, at least if that speech were not "directed to inciting or producing imminent lawless action, and . . . likely to incite or produce such action." *Brandenburg,* 395 U.S. at 447.

Here, it is alleged, and a jury could reasonably find, that Paladin aided and abetted the murders at issue through the quintessential speech act of providing step-by-step instructions for murder (replete with photographs, diagrams, and narration) so comprehensive and detailed that it is as if the instructor were literally present with the would-be murderer not only in the preparation and planning, but in the actual commission of, and follow-up to, the murder; there is not even a hint that the aid was provided in the form of speech that might constitute abstract advocacy. We are satisfied a jury could readily find that the provided instructions not only have no, or virtually no, noninstructional communicative value, but also that their only instructional communicative "value" is the indisputably illegitimate one of training persons how to murder and to engage in the business of murder for hire.

This detailed, focused instructional assistance to those contemplating or in the throes of planning murder is the antithesis of speech protected under *Brandenburg*. The murder instructions in *Hit Man* are, collectively, a textbook example of the type of speech that the Supreme Court has quite purposely left unprotected, and the prosecution of which, criminally or civilly, has historically been thought subject to few, if any, First Amendment constraints. Accordingly, we hold that the First Amendment does not pose a bar to the plaintiffs' civil aiding and abetting cause of action against Paladin Enterprises. If, as precedent uniformly confirms, the states have the power to regulate speech that aids and abets crime, then certainly they have the power to regulate the speech at issue here.

In concluding that *Hit Man* is protected "advocacy," the district court appears to have misperceived the nature of the speech that the Supreme Court held in *Brandenburg* is protected under the First Amendment. In particular, the district court seems to have misunderstood the Court in *Brandenburg* as having distinguished between "advocating or teaching" lawlessness on the one hand, and "inciting or encouraging" lawlessness on the other, any and all of the former being entitled to First Amendment protection. The district court thus framed the issue before it as "whether *Hit Man* merely advocates or teaches murder or whether it incites or encourages murder." And, finding that *Hit Man* "merely teaches" in technical fashion the fundamentals of murder, it concluded that "the book does not cross that line between permissible advocacy and impermissible incitation to crime or violence."

The Court in *Brandenburg*, however, did not hold that "mere teaching" is protected; the Court never even used this phrase. And it certainly did not hold, as the district court apparently believed, that all teaching is protected. Rather, however inartfully it may have done so, the Court fairly clearly held only that the "mere *abstract* teaching" of principles, and "*mere* advocacy," are protected. In the final analysis, it appears the district court simply failed to fully appreciate the import of the qualification to the kind of "teaching" that the Supreme Court held to be protected in *Brandenburg*.

Accordingly, we hold that plaintiffs have stated, sufficient to withstand summary judgment, a civil cause of action against Paladin Enterprises for aiding and abetting the murders of Mildred and Trevor Horn and Janice Saunders on the night of March 3, 1993, and that this cause of action is not barred by the First Amendment to the United States Constitution.

*Editor's Note:* The parties to this case reached an out-of-court settlement—providing for a cash payment and the destruction of all remaining copies of the book—so the Supreme Court never heard the case.

## Points for Discussion

1. Where *Brandenburg* itself dealt with incitement, *Rice* seems to deal with instruction. Yet Judge Luttig makes much of the publisher's stipulated *intent* to encourage (incite?) potential hit men. What should be done with a book that offers clear instructions for wrongdoing (for example, a crime novel that gives sufficient detail to help those inclined to slowly poison their spouses), but that is not intended to produce violence?

2. *Brandenburg's* imminence requirement emerged from a case involving a speaker addressing a live audience. Can that requirement ever be met by the publication of a book that presumably won't be read or acted on until many months or years after the writing is complete?

## ■ *Board of Education v. Pico*

### 457 U.S. 853 (1982)

*Justice Brennan announced the judgment of the Court.**

The principal question presented is whether the First Amendment imposes limitations upon the exercise by a local school board of its discretion to remove library books from high school and junior high school libraries.

The Board of Education of the Island Trees Union Free School District No. 26 in New York is a state agency charged with responsibility for the operation and administration of the public schools within the Island Trees School District, including the Island Trees High School and Island Trees Memorial Junior High School. [When this suit was brought], Steven Pico, Jacqueline Gold, Glenn Yarris, and Russell Rieger were students at the High School, and Paul Sochinski was a student at the Junior High School.

In September 1975, [Board members] attended a conference sponsored by Parents of New York United (PONYU), a politically conservative organization of parents concerned about education legislation in the State of New York. [There they] obtained lists of books described as "objectionable," and as "improper fare for school students." It was later determined

---

*The Brennan opinion is a plurality opinion rather than a majority opinion, commanding only four votes for most sections and only three votes for some sections.

that the High School library contained nine of the listed books, and that another listed book was in the Junior High School library.

[Among the books in question were] *Slaughter House Five,* by Kurt Vonnegut, Jr.; *The Naked Ape,* by Desmond Morris; *Down These Mean Streets,* by Piri Thomas; *Laughing Boy,* by Oliver LaFarge; *Black Boy,* by Richard Wright; *A Hero Ain't Nothin' But A Sandwich,* by Alice Childress; and *Soul On Ice,* by Eldridge Cleaver.

In February 1976, at a meeting with the Superintendent of Schools and the Principals of the High School and Junior High School, the Board gave an "unofficial direction" that the listed books be removed from the library shelves and delivered to the Board's offices, so that Board members could read them. When this directive was carried out, it became publicized, and the Board issued a press release justifying its action. It characterized the removed books as "anti-American, anti-Christian, anti-[Semitic], and just plain filthy," and concluded that "[it] is our duty, our moral obligation, to protect the children in our schools from this moral danger as surely as from physical and medical dangers."

A short time later, the Board appointed a "Book Review Committee," consisting of four Island Trees parents and four members of the Island Trees schools staff, to read the listed books and to recommend to the Board whether the books should be retained, taking into account the books' "educational suitability," "good taste," "relevance," and "appropriateness to age and grade level." In July, the Committee made its final report to the Board, recommending that five of the listed books be retained and that two others be removed from the school libraries. As for the remaining four books, the Committee could not agree on two, took no position on one, and recommended that the last book be made available to students only with parental approval. The Board substantially rejected the Committee's report later that month, deciding that only one book should be returned to the High School library without restriction, that another should be made available subject to parental approval, but that the remaining nine books should "be removed from elementary and secondary libraries and [from] use in the curriculum." As a result, the nine removed books could not be assigned or suggested to students in connection with school work. However, teachers were not instructed to refrain from discussing the removed books or the ideas and positions expressed in them. The Board gave no reasons for rejecting the recommendations of the Committee that it had appointed.

We emphasize at the outset the limited nature of the substantive question presented by the case before us. Our precedents have long recognized certain constitutional limits upon the power of the State to control even the curriculum and classroom. For example, *Meyer v. Nebraska,* 262 U.S. 390 (1923), struck down a state law that forbade the teaching of modern foreign languages in public and private schools, and *Epperson v. Arkansas,* 393 U.S. 97 (1968), declared unconstitutional a state law that prohibited the teaching of the Darwinian theory of evolution in any state-supported school. But the current action does not require us to re-enter this difficult terrain. For as this case is presented to us, it does not involve textbooks, or indeed any books that Island Trees students would be required to read. The students do not seek in this Court to impose limitations upon their school Board's discretion to prescribe the curricula of the Island Trees schools. On the contrary, the only books at issue in this case are library books, books that by their nature are optional rather than required reading. Our adjudication of the present case thus does not intrude into the classroom, or into the compulsory courses taught there. Furthermore, even as to library books, the action before us does not involve the acquisition of books. The students have not sought to compel their school Board to add to the school library shelves any books that students desire to read. Rather, the only action challenged in this case is the removal from school libraries of books originally placed there by the school authorities, or without objection from them.

The substantive question before us is still further constrained by the procedural posture of this case. The school board members were granted summary judgment by the District Court. The Court of Appeals reversed that judgment, and remanded the action for a trial on the merits. We can reverse the judgment of the Court of Appeals, and grant the Board's request for reinstatement of the summary judgment in their favor, only if we determine that "there is no genuine issue as to any material fact," that they are "entitled to a judgment as a matter of law."

In sum, the issue before us in this case is a narrow one, both substantively and procedurally. It may best be restated as two distinct questions. First, does the First Amendment impose any limitations upon the discretion of petitioners to remove library books from the Island Trees High School and Junior High School? Second, if so, do the affidavits and other evidentiary materials before the District Court, construed most favorably to respondents, raise a genuine issue of fact whether petitioners might have exceeded those limitations? If we answer either of these questions in the negative, then we must reverse the judgment of the Court of Appeals and reinstate the District Court's summary judgment for petitioners. If we answer both questions in the affirmative, then we must affirm the judgment below. We examine these questions in turn.

The Court has long recognized that local school boards have broad discretion in the management of school affairs, that, by and large, "public education in our Nation is committed to the control of state and local authorities," and that federal courts should not ordinarily "intervene in the resolution of conflicts which arise in the daily operation of school systems." We have also acknowledged that public schools are vitally important "in the preparation of individuals for participation as citizens," and as vehicles for "inculcating fundamental values necessary to the maintenance of a democratic political system." We are therefore in full agreement with petitioners that local school boards must be permitted "to establish and apply their curriculum in such a way as to transmit community values," and that "there is a legitimate and substantial community interest in promoting respect for authority and traditional values be they social, moral, or political."

At the same time, however, we have necessarily recognized that the discretion of the States and local school boards in matters of education must be exercised in a manner that comports with the transcendent imperatives of the First Amendment. In *West Virginia Board of Education v. Barnette,* 319 U.S. 624 (1943), we held that under the First Amendment a student in a public school could not be compelled to salute the flag. We reasoned:

> Boards of Education . . . have, of course, important, delicate, and highly discretionary functions, but none that they may not perform within the limits of the Bill of Rights. That they are educating the young for citizenship is reason for scrupulous protection of Constitutional freedoms of the individual, if we are not to strangle the free mind at its source and teach youth to discount important principles of our government as mere platitudes.

Later cases have consistently followed this rationale. *Tinker v. Des Moines School District* held that a local school board had infringed the free speech rights of high school and junior high school students by suspending them from school for wearing black armbands in class as a protest against the Government's policy in Vietnam; we stated there that the "comprehensive authority . . . of school officials" must be exercised "consistent with fundamental constitutional safeguards." In sum, students do not "shed their constitutional rights to freedom of speech or expression at the schoolhouse gate," and therefore local school boards must discharge their "important, delicate, and highly discretionary functions" within the limits and constraints of the First Amendment.

We have held that in a variety of contexts "the Constitution protects the right to receive information and ideas." This right is an inherent corollary of the rights of free speech and press that are explicitly guaranteed by the Constitution, in two senses. First, the right to receive ideas follows ineluctably from the sender's First Amendment right to send them. The right of freedom of speech and press embraces the right to distribute literature, and necessarily protects the right to receive it. The dissemination of ideas can accomplish nothing if otherwise willing addressees are not free to receive and consider them. It would be a barren marketplace of ideas that had only sellers and no buyers.

More importantly, the right to receive ideas is a necessary predicate to the recipient's meaningful exercise of his own rights of speech, press, and political freedom. Madison admonished us: "A popular Government, without popular information, or the means of acquiring it, is but a Prologue to a Farce or a Tragedy; or, perhaps both. Knowledge will forever govern ignorance: And a people who mean to be their own Governors, must arm themselves with the power which knowledge gives."

Students too are beneficiaries of this principle. In our system, students may not be regarded as closed-circuit recipients of only that which the State chooses to communicate. School officials cannot suppress expressions of feeling with which they do not wish to contend.

In sum, just as access to ideas makes it possible for citizens generally to exercise their rights of free speech and press in a meaningful manner, such access prepares students for active and effective participation in the pluralistic, often contentious society in which they will soon be adult members. Of course all First Amendment rights accorded to students must be construed in light of the special characteristics of the school environment. But the special characteristics of the school library make that environment especially appropriate for the recognition of the First Amendment rights of students.

A school library, no less than any other public library, is a place dedicated to quiet, to knowledge, and to beauty. Students must always remain free to inquire, to study and to evaluate, to gain new maturity and understanding. The school library is the principal locus of such freedom. In the school library a student can literally explore the unknown, and discover areas of interest and thought not covered by the prescribed curriculum. The student learns that a library is a place to test or expand upon ideas presented to him, in or out of the classroom.

The Board members emphasize the inculcative function of secondary education, and argue that they must be allowed unfettered discretion to transmit community values through the Island Trees schools. But that sweeping claim overlooks the unique role of the school library. It appears from the record that use of the Island Trees school libraries is completely voluntary on the part of students. Their selection of books from these libraries is entirely a matter of free choice; the libraries afford them an opportunity at self-education and individual enrichment that is wholly optional. Board members might well defend their claim of absolute discretion in matters of curriculum by reliance upon their duty to inculcate community values. But their reliance upon that duty is misplaced where, as here, they attempt to extend their claim of absolute discretion beyond the compulsory environment of the classroom, into the school library and the regime of voluntary inquiry that there holds sway.

We do not deny that local school boards have a substantial legitimate role to play in the determination of school library content. We thus must turn to the question of the extent to which the First Amendment places limitations upon their discretion to remove books from their libraries. In this inquiry we enjoy the guidance of several precedents. *West Virginia Board of Education v. Barnette* stated: "If there is any fixed star in our constitutional constellation, it is that no official, high or petty, can prescribe what shall be orthodox in politics, nationalism, religion, or other matters of opinion. If there are any circumstances which permit an exception, they do not now occur to us." This doctrine has been reaffirmed in later cases involving education. For example, [a 1977 case noted that] "the First Amendment does not tolerate laws that cast a pall of orthodoxy over the classroom"; [and another] recognized First Amendment limitations upon the discretion of a local school board to refuse to rehire a nontenured teacher.

With respect to the present case, the message of these precedents is clear. School boards rightly possess significant discretion to determine the content of their school libraries. But that discretion may not be exercised in a narrowly partisan or political manner. If a Democratic school board, motivated by party affiliation, ordered the removal of all books written by or in favor of Republicans, few would doubt that the order violated the constitutional rights of the students denied access to those books. The same conclusion would surely apply if an all-white school board, motivated by racial animus, decided to remove all books authored by blacks or advocating racial equality and integration. Our Constitution does not permit the official suppression of ideas. Thus whether the Board's removal of books from their school libraries denied students their First Amendment rights depends upon the motivation behind those actions. If the Board intended by the removal decision to deny access to ideas with which they disagreed, and if this intent was the decisive factor in their decision, then they have exercised their discretion in violation of the Constitution. On the other hand, the students implicitly concede that an unconstitutional motivation would not be demonstrated if it were shown that the Board had decided to remove the books at issue because those books were pervasively vulgar. If it were demonstrated that the removal decision was based solely upon the "educational suitability" of the books in question, then their removal would be perfectly permissible.

As noted earlier, nothing in our decision today affects in any way the discretion of a local school board to choose books to add to the libraries of their schools. Because we are concerned in this case with the suppression of ideas, our holding today affects only the discretion to remove books. In brief, we hold that local school boards may not remove books from school library shelves simply because they dislike the ideas contained in those books and seek by their removal to "prescribe what shall be orthodox in politics, nationalism, religion, or other matters of opinion." Such purposes stand inescapably condemned by our precedents.

[Justice Brennan then looks at the conflicting testimony and court documents in the case. He concludes that there were contradictory accounts of the school board's motivation in removing the books from the library. Therefore, the case is to be remanded back to the lower court to make this factual determination. Justice Blackmun wrote a separate concurring opinion, espousing a doctrine hardly distinguishable from that embraced by Brennan's plurality opinion. Justice White, the crucial fifth vote in favor of sending the case back to the lower court for further factual development, would have preferred that the Supreme Court not inject itself into the question whether the board's motivations were constitutional, at least not until the lower courts have a chance to determine what those motivations were.]

## *Points for Discussion*

1. If public school students *do* enjoy a constitutional right to read books their school boards think inappropriate for them, why should such a right be limited to library books? What should be done with a student who insists on fulfilling a book report assignment by reading a "forbidden" book?

2. Justice Brennan says that a school board composed entirely of Democrats could not systematically remove (or initially refuse to purchase?) all books written by or espousing Republican Party philosophies. Allotment of library space, however, is rarely an all-or-nothing proposition. Won't the relevant question more typically focus on the ratio of books espousing one view over another? What of a school library in a southern state that has a disproportionate number of history books sympathetic to the Confederate cause? Or a "majority minority" inner-city school whose library has a lot of Afrocentric histories but virtually no "traditional" Eurocentric works?

## *Wooley v. Maynard*

**430 U.S. 705 (1977)**

*Chief Justice Burger delivered the opinion of the Court.*

The issue on appeal is whether the State of New Hampshire may constitutionally enforce criminal sanctions against persons who cover the motto "Live Free or Die" on passenger vehicle license plates because that motto is repugnant to their moral and religious beliefs.

Since 1969 New Hampshire has required that noncommercial vehicles bear license plates embossed with the state motto, "Live Free or Die." Another New Hampshire statute makes it a misdemeanor "knowingly [to obscure] . . . the figures or letters on any number plate." The term "letters" in this section has been interpreted by the State's highest court to include the state motto. Appellees George Maynard and his wife Maxine are followers of the Jehovah's Witnesses faith. The Maynards consider the New Hampshire State motto to be repugnant to their moral, religious, and political beliefs, and therefore assert it objectionable to disseminate this message by displaying it on their automobiles. Pursuant to these beliefs, the Maynards began early in

1974 to cover up the motto on their license plates. In May or June 1974 Mr. Maynard actually snipped the words "or Die" off the license plates, and then covered the resulting hole, as well as the words "Live Free," with tape. This was done, according to Mr. Maynard, because neighborhood children kept removing the tape. The Maynards have since been issued new license plates, and have disavowed any intention of physically mutilating them.

On November 27, 1974, Mr. Maynard was issued a citation. On December 6, 1974, he appeared in Lebanon, N. H. District Court to answer the charge. After waiving his right to counsel, he entered a plea of not guilty and proceeded to explain his religious objections to the motto. The state trial judge expressed sympathy for Mr. Maynard's situation, but considered himself bound to hold Maynard guilty. [For this and subsequent violations, Maynard was fined $75 and served 15 days in jail.]

On March 4, 1975, appellees brought the present action, [seeking] injunctive and declaratory relief. Following a hearing on the merits, the District Court entered an order enjoining the State "from arresting and prosecuting [the Maynards] at any time in the future for covering over that portion of their license plates that contains the motto 'Live Free or Die.' "

The District Court held that by covering up the state motto "Live Free or Die" on his automobile license plate, Mr. Maynard was engaging in symbolic speech and that "New Hampshire's interest in the enforcement of its defacement statute is not sufficient to justify the restriction on [appellee's] constitutionally protected expression." We find it unnecessary to pass on the "symbolic speech" issue. We note [however] that appellees' claim of symbolic expression is substantially undermined by their prayer in the District Court for issuance of special license plates not bearing the state motto. This is hardly consistent with the stated intent to communicate affirmative opposition to the motto. Whether or not we view appellees' present practice of covering the motto with tape as sufficiently communicative to sustain a claim of symbolic expression, display of the "expurgated" plates requested by appellees would surely not satisfy that standard.

We find more appropriate First Amendment grounds to affirm the judgment of the District Court. We turn instead to what in our view is the essence of appellees' objection to the requirement that they display the motto "Live Free or Die" on their automobile license plates. This is succinctly summarized in the statement made by Mr. Maynard in his affidavit filed with the District Court: "I refuse to be coerced by the State into advertising a slogan which I find morally, ethically, religiously and politically abhorrent."

We are thus faced with the question of whether the State may constitutionally require an individual to participate in the dissemination of an ideological message by displaying it on his private property in a manner and for the express purpose that it be observed and read by the public. We hold that the State may not do so.

We begin with the proposition that the right of freedom of thought protected by the First Amendment against state action includes both the right to speak freely and the right to refrain from speaking at all. A system which secures the right to proselytize religious, political, and ideological causes must also guarantee the concomitant right to decline to foster such concepts. The right to speak and the right to refrain from speaking are complementary components of the broader concept of "individual freedom of mind."

The Court in *West Virginia Board of Education v. Barnette,* 319 U.S. 624 (1943), was faced with a state statute which required public school students to participate in daily public ceremonies by honoring the flag both with words and traditional salute gestures. The Court held that "a ceremony so touching matters of opinion and political attitude may [not] be imposed upon the individual by official authority under powers committed to any political organization under our Constitution." Compelling the affirmative act of a flag salute involved a more serious infringement upon personal liberties than the passive act of carrying the state motto on a license plate, but the difference is essentially one of degree. Here, as in *Barnette,* we are faced with a state measure which forces an individual, as part of his daily life—indeed constantly while his automobile is in public view—to be an instrument for fostering public adherence to an ideological point of view he finds unacceptable. In doing so, the State "invades the sphere of intellect and spirit which it is the purpose of the First Amendment to our Constitution to reserve from all official control." New Hampshire's statute in effect requires that appellees use their private property as a "mobile billboard" for the State's ideological message, or suffer a penalty, as Maynard already has. As a condition to driving an automobile—a virtual necessity for most Americans—the Maynards must display "Live Free or Die" to hundreds of people each day. The fact that most individuals agree with the thrust of New Hampshire's motto is not the test; most Americans also find the flag salute acceptable. The First Amendment protects the right of individuals to hold a point of view different from the majority and to refuse to foster, in the way New Hampshire commands, an idea they find morally objectionable.

Identifying the Maynards' interests as implicating First Amendment protections does not end our inquiry however. We must also determine whether the State's countervailing interest is sufficiently compelling to justify requiring appellees to display the state motto on their license plates. The two interests advanced by the State are that display of the motto (1) facilitates the identification of passenger vehicles, and (2) promotes appreciation of history, individualism, and state pride.

The State first points out that passenger vehicles, but not commercial, trailer, or other vehicles are required to display the state motto. Thus, the argument proceeds, officers of the law are more easily able to determine whether passenger vehicles are carrying the proper plates. However, the record here reveals that New Hampshire passenger license plates normally consist of a specific configuration of letters and numbers, which makes them readily distinguishable from other types of plates, even without reference to the state motto. Even were we to credit the State's reasons and even though the governmental purpose be legitimate and substantial, that purpose cannot be pursued by means that broadly stifle fundamental personal liberties when the end can be more narrowly achieved. The breadth of legislative abridgment must be viewed in the light of less drastic means for achieving the same basic purpose.

The State's second claimed interest is not ideologically neutral. The State is seeking to communicate to others an official view as to proper appreciation of history, state pride, and individualism. Of course, the State may legitimately pursue such interests in any number of ways. However, where the State's interest is to disseminate an ideology, no matter how acceptable to some, such interest cannot outweigh an individual's First Amendment right to avoid becoming the courier for such message.

We conclude that the State of New Hampshire may not require appellees to display the state motto upon their vehicle license plates; and, accordingly, we affirm the judgment of the District Court.

It has been suggested that today's holding will be read as sanctioning the obliteration of the national motto, "In God We Trust" from United States coins and currency. That question is not before us today but we note that currency, which is passed from hand to hand, differs in significant respects from an automobile, which is readily associated with its operator. Currency is generally carried in a purse or pocket and need not be displayed to the public. The bearer of currency is thus not required to publicly advertise the national motto.

## Points for Discussion

1. Should the right not to speak be dependent on how strongly one abhors the message? Suppose a Philadelphian covered up her license plate motto ("You have a friend in Pennsylvania") not because it offends her, but because she thinks it silly? What about an Anchorage resident who thinks that the cosmos, not the state of Alaska, is "the last frontier"?

2. Suppose that a state could demonstrate that its automobile license's color scheme is very similar to that of one or two other states and that the motto therefore helps to identify the driver as a local resident. Should the Court's result have then been different?

## ■ *United States v. O'Brien*

### 391 U.S. 367 (1968)

*Chief Justice Warren delivered the opinion of the Court.*

On the morning of March 31, 1966, David Paul O'Brien and three companions burned their Selective Service registration certificates on the steps of the South Boston Courthouse. A sizable crowd, including several agents of the Federal Bureau of Investigation, witnessed the event. Immediately after the burning, members of the crowd began attacking O'Brien and his companions. An FBI agent ushered O'Brien to safety inside the courthouse. After he was advised of his right to counsel and to silence, O'Brien stated to FBI agents that he had burned his registration certificate because of his beliefs, knowing that he was violating federal law. He produced the charred remains of the certificate, which, with his consent, were photographed.

For this act, O'Brien was indicted, tried, convicted, and sentenced in the United States District Court for the District of Massachusetts. He did not contest the fact that he had burned the certificate. He stated in argument to the jury that he burned the certificate publicly to influence others to adopt his antiwar beliefs, as he put it, "so that other people would reevaluate their positions with Selective Service, with the armed forces, and reevaluate their place in the culture of today, to hopefully consider my position."

The indictment upon which he was tried charged that he "willfully and knowingly did mutilate, destroy, and change by burning . . . [his] Registration Certificate (Selective Service System Form No. 2); in violation of Title 50, App., United States Code, Section 462(b)."

Section 462(b) is part of the Universal Military Training and Service Act of 1948. Section 462(b)(3), one of six numbered subdivisions of section 462(b), was amended by Congress in 1965, so that at the time O'Brien burned his certificate an offense was committed by any person "who forges, alters, knowingly destroys, knowingly mutilates, or in any manner changes any such certificate. . . ." In the District Court, O'Brien argued that the 1965 Amendment prohibiting the knowing destruction or mutilation of certificates was unconstitutional because it was enacted to abridge free speech, and because it served no legitimate legislative purpose. The District Court rejected these arguments, holding that the statute on its face did not abridge First Amendment rights, that the court was not competent to inquire into the motives of Congress in enacting the 1965 Amendment, and that the Amendment was a reasonable exercise of the power of Congress to raise armies.

On appeal, the Court of Appeals for the First Circuit held the 1965 Amendment unconstitutional as a law abridging freedom of speech. At the time the Amendment was enacted, a regulation of the Selective Service System required registrants to keep their registration certificates in their "personal possession at all times." Wilful violations of regulations promulgated pursuant to the Universal Military Training and Service Act were made criminal by statute. The Court of Appeals, therefore, was of the opinion that conduct punishable under the 1965 Amendment was already punishable under the nonpossession regulation, and consequently that the Amendment served no valid purpose; further, that in light of the prior regulation, the Amendment must have been "directed at public as distinguished from private destruction." On this basis, the court concluded that the 1965 Amendment ran afoul of the First Amendment by singling out persons engaged in protests for special treatment. The court ruled, however, that O'Brien's conviction should be affirmed under the statutory provision, 50 U.S.C. App., section 462(b)(6), which in its view made violation of the nonpossession regulation a crime, because it regarded such violation to be a lesser included offense of the crime defined by the 1965 Amendment.

The Government petitioned for certiorari, arguing that the Court of Appeals erred in holding the statute unconstitutional, and that its decision conflicted with decisions by the Courts of Appeals for the Second and Eighth Circuits upholding the 1965 Amendment against identical constitutional challenges. O'Brien cross-petitioned for certiorari, arguing that the Court of Appeals erred in sustaining his conviction on the basis of a crime of which he was neither charged nor tried. We granted the Government's petition to resolve the conflict in the circuits, and we also granted O'Brien's cross-petition. We hold that the 1965 Amendment is constitutional both as enacted and as applied. We therefore vacate the judgment of the Court of Appeals and reinstate the judgment and sentence of the District Court without reaching the issue raised by O'Brien.

When a male reaches the age of 18, he is required by the Universal Military Training and Service Act to register with a local draft board. He is assigned a Selective Service number, and within five days he is issued a registration certificate. Subsequently, and based on a questionnaire completed by the registrant, he is assigned a classification denoting his eligibility for induction, and "as soon as practicable" thereafter he is issued a Notice of Classification. This initial classification is not necessarily permanent, and if in the interim before induction the registrant's status changes in some relevant way, he may be reclassified. After such a reclassification, the local board "as soon as practicable" issues to the registrant a new Notice of Classification.

Both the registration and classification certificates are small white cards, approximately 2 by 3 inches. The registration certificate specifies the name of the registrant, the date of registration, and the number and address of the local board with which he is registered. Also inscribed upon it are the date and place of the registrant's birth, his residence at registration, his physical description, his signature, and his Selective Service number. The Selective Service number itself indicates his State of registration, his local board, his year of birth, and his chronological position in the local board's classification record.

The classification certificate shows the registrant's name, Selective Service number, signature, and eligibility classification. It specifies whether he was so classified by his local board, an appeal board, or the President. It contains the address of his local board and the date the certificate was mailed.

Both the registration and classification certificates bear notices that the registrant must notify his local board in writing of every change in address, physical condition, and occupational, marital, family, dependency, and military status, and of any other fact which might change his classification. Both also contain a notice that the registrant's Selective Service number should appear on all communications to his local board.

Congress demonstrated its concern that certificates issued by the Selective Service System might be abused well before the 1965 Amendment here challenged. Under the 1948 Act, it was unlawful (1) to transfer a certificate to aid a person in making false identification; (2) to possess a certificate not duly issued with the intent of using it for false identification; (3) to forge, alter, "or in any manner" change a certificate or any notation validly inscribed thereon; (4) to photograph or make an imitation of a certificate for the purpose of false identification; and (5) to possess a counterfeited or altered certificate. In addition, as previously mentioned, regulations of the Selective Service System required registrants to keep both their registration and classification certificates in their personal possession at all times.

By the 1965 Amendment, Congress added the provision here at issue, subjecting to criminal liability not only one who "forges, alters, or in any manner changes" but also one who "knowingly destroys, [or] knowingly mutilates" a certificate.

We note at the outset that the 1965 Amendment plainly does not abridge free speech on its face, and we do not understand O'Brien to argue otherwise. On its face [the Amendment] deals with conduct having no connection with speech. It prohibits the knowing destruction of certificates issued by the Selective Service System, and there is nothing necessarily expressive about such conduct. The Amendment does not distinguish between public and private destruction, and it does not punish only destruction engaged in for the purpose of expressing views. A law prohibiting destruction of Selective Service certificates no more abridges free speech on its face than a motor vehicle law prohibiting the destruction of drivers' licenses, or a tax law prohibiting the destruction of books and records.

O'Brien nonetheless argues that the 1965 Amendment is unconstitutional in its application to him, and is unconstitutional as enacted because what he calls the "purpose" of Congress was "to suppress freedom of speech." We consider these arguments separately.

O'Brien first argues that the 1965 Amendment is unconstitutional as applied to him because his act of burning his registration certificate was protected "symbolic speech" within the First Amendment. His argument is that the freedom of expression which the First Amendment guarantees includes all modes of "communication of ideas by conduct," and that his conduct is within this definition because he did it in "demonstration against the war and against the draft." We cannot accept the view that an apparently limitless variety of conduct can be labeled "speech" whenever the person engaging in the conduct intends thereby to express an idea. However, even on the assumption that the alleged communicative element in O'Brien's conduct is sufficient to bring into play the First Amendment, it does not necessarily follow that the destruction of a registration certificate is constitutionally protected activity. This Court has held that when "speech" and "nonspeech" elements are combined in the same course of conduct, a sufficiently important governmental interest in regulating the nonspeech element can justify incidental limitations on First Amendment freedoms. To characterize the quality of the governmental interest which must appear, the Court has employed a variety of descriptive terms: compelling; substantial; subordinating; paramount; cogent; strong. Whatever imprecision inheres in these terms, we think it clear that a government regulation is sufficiently justified if it is within the constitutional power of the Government; if it furthers an important or substantial governmental interest; if the governmental interest is unrelated to the suppression of free expression; and if the incidental restriction on alleged First Amendment freedoms is no greater than is essential to the furtherance of that interest.

We find that the 1965 Amendment meets all of these requirements, and consequently that O'Brien can be constitutionally convicted for violating it.

The constitutional power of Congress to raise and support armies and to make all laws necessary and proper to that end is broad and sweeping. The power of Congress to classify and conscript manpower for military service is beyond question. Pursuant to this power, Congress may establish a system of registration for individuals liable for training and service, and may require such individuals within reason to cooperate in the registration system. The issuance of certificates indicating the registration and eligibility classification of individuals is a legitimate and substantial administrative aid in the functioning of this system. And legislation to insure the continuing availability of issued certificates serves a legitimate and substantial purpose in the system's administration.

O'Brien's argument to the contrary is necessarily premised upon his unrealistic characterization of Selective Service certificates. He essentially adopts the position that such certificates are so many pieces of paper designed to notify registrants of their registration or classification, to be retained or tossed in the wastebasket according to the convenience or taste of the registrant. Once the registrant has received notification, according to this view, there is no reason for him to retain the certificates. O'Brien notes that most of the information on a registration certificate serves no notification purpose at all; the registrant hardly needs to be told his address and physical characteristics. We agree that the registration certificate contains much information of which the registrant needs no notification. This circumstance, however, does not lead to the conclusion that the certificate serves no purpose, but that, like the classification certificate, it serves purposes in addition to initial notification. Many of these purposes would be defeated by the certificates' destruction or mutilation. Among these are:

- The registration certificate serves as proof that the individual described thereon has registered for the draft. Voluntarily displaying the two certificates is an easy and painless way for a young man to dispel a question as to whether he might be delinquent in his Selective Service obligations. Further, it is in the interest of the just and efficient administration of the system that [the certificates] be continually available, in the event, for example, of a mix-up in the registrant's file.

- The information supplied on the certificates facilitates communication between registrants and local boards, simplifying the system and benefiting all concerned. To begin with, each certificate bears the address of the registrant's local board, an item unlikely to be committed to memory. Further, each card bears the registrant's Selective Service number, and a registrant who has his number readily available so that he can communicate it to his local board when he supplies or requests information can make simpler the board's task in locating his file. Finally, a registrant's inquiry, particularly through a local board other than his own, concerning his eligibility status is frequently answerable simply on the basis of his classification certificate; whereas, if the certificate were not reasonably available and the registrant were uncertain of his classification, the task of answering his questions would be considerably complicated.
- Both certificates carry continual reminders that the registrant must notify his local board of any change of address, and other specified changes in his status.
- The regulatory scheme involving Selective Service certificates includes clearly valid prohibitions against the alteration, forgery, or similar deceptive misuse of certificates. The destruction or mutilation of certificates obviously increases the difficulty of detecting and tracing abuses such as these. Further, a mutilated certificate might itself be used for deceptive purposes.

The many functions performed by Selective Service certificates establish beyond doubt that Congress has a legitimate and substantial interest in preventing their wanton and unrestrained destruction and assuring their continuing availability by punishing people who knowingly and willfully destroy or mutilate them.

We think it apparent that the continuing availability to each registrant of his Selective Service certificates substantially furthers the smooth and proper functioning of the system that Congress has established to raise armies. We think it also apparent that the Nation has a vital interest in having a system for raising armies that functions with maximum efficiency and is capable of easily and quickly responding to continually changing circumstances. For these reasons, the Government has a substantial interest in assuring the continuing availability of issued Selective Service certificates.

It is equally clear that the 1965 Amendment specifically protects this substantial governmental interest. We perceive no alternative means that would more precisely and narrowly assure the continuing availability of issued Selective Service certificates than a law which prohibits their wilful mutilation or destruction. The 1965 Amendment prohibits such conduct and does nothing more. In other words, both the governmental interest and the operation of the 1965 Amendment are limited to the noncommunicative aspect of O'Brien's conduct. The governmental interest and the scope of the 1965 Amendment are limited to preventing harm to the smooth and efficient functioning of the Selective Service System. When O'Brien deliberately rendered unavailable his registration certificate, he willfully frustrated this governmental interest. For this noncommunicative impact of his conduct, and for nothing else, he was convicted.

In conclusion, we find that because of the Government's substantial interest in assuring the continuing availability of issued Selective Service certificates, because [the law] is an appropriately narrow means of protecting this interest and condemns only the independent noncommunicative impact of conduct within its reach, and because the noncommunicative impact of O'Brien's act of burning his registration certificate frustrated the Government's interest, a sufficient governmental interest has been shown to justify O'Brien's conviction.

### Points for Discussion

1. The *O'Brien* Court says it "cannot accept the view that an apparently limitless variety of conduct can be labeled 'speech' whenever the person engaging in the conduct intends thereby to express an idea." When, if ever, *should* conduct be treated the same as speech? Are you exercising your right to free speech when you walk a picket line? What about the civil rights demonstrators of the 1960s who conducted sit-ins at lunch counters that refused to serve "Coloreds"?

2. O'Brien was charged with "willfully and knowingly" mutilating, destroying, and burning his draft card. Given the unlikelihood that a young man would take such actions in support of the Vietnam War, what are we to make of Chief Justice Warren's assertion that the statute at issue here was aimed at "the noncommunicative aspect of O'Brien's conduct"?

## ■ *Cornelius v. NAACP Legal Defense and Educational Fund*

### 473 U.S. 788 (1985)

*Justice O'Connor delivered the opinion of the Court.*

This case requires us to decide whether the Federal Government violates the First Amendment when it excludes legal defense and political advocacy organizations from participation in the Combined Federal Campaign (CFC), a charity drive aimed at federal employees. The United States District Court for the District of Columbia held that the respondent organizations could not be excluded from the CFC, and the Court of Appeals affirmed.

The CFC is an annual charitable fundraising drive conducted in the federal workplace during working hours largely through the voluntary efforts of federal employees. At all times relevant to this litigation, participating organizations confined their fundraising activities to a 30-word statement submitted by them for inclusion in the Campaign literature. Volunteer federal employees distribute to their co-workers literature describing the Campaign and the participants along with pledge cards. Contributions may take the form of either a payroll deduction or a lump-sum payment made to a designated agency or to the general Campaign fund. Undesignated contributions are distributed on the local level by a private umbrella organization to certain participating organizations. Designated funds are paid directly to the specified recipient. Through the CFC, the Government employees contribute in excess of $100 million to charitable organizations each year.

The CFC is a relatively recent development. Prior to 1957, charitable solicitation in the federal workplace occurred on an ad hoc basis. Federal managers received requests from dozens of organizations seeking endorsements and the right to solicit contributions from federal employees at their work sites. Because no systemwide regulations were in place to provide for orderly procedure, fundraising frequently consisted of passing an empty coffee can from employee to employee. Eventually, the increasing number of entities seeking access to federal buildings and the multiplicity of appeals disrupted the work environment and confused employees who were unfamiliar with the groups seeking contributions.

In 1957, President Eisenhower established the forerunner of the Combined Federal Campaign to bring order to the solicitation process and to ensure truly voluntary giving by federal employees. In 1982, President Reagan issued Executive Order No. 12353, to replace the 1961 Executive Order which had established the CFC. The new Order retained the original limitation to "national voluntary health and welfare agencies and such other national voluntary agencies as may be appropriate," and delegated to the Director of the Office of Personnel Management the authority to establish criteria for determining appropriateness. Shortly thereafter, the President amended Executive Order No. 12353 to specify the purposes of the CFC and to identify groups whose participation would be consistent with those purposes. The CFC was designed to lessen the Government's burden in meeting human health and welfare needs by providing a convenient, nondisruptive channel for federal employees to contribute to nonpartisan agencies that directly serve those needs. The Order limited participation to "voluntary, charitable, health and welfare agencies that provide or support direct health and welfare services to individuals or their families," and specifically excluded those "[agencies] that seek to influence the outcomes of elections or the determination of public policy through political activity or advocacy, lobbying, or litigation on behalf of parties other than themselves."

Respondents in this case are the NAACP Legal Defense and Educational Fund, Inc., the Sierra Club Legal Defense Fund, [and several other organizations that] attempt to influence public policy through one or more of the following means: political activity, advocacy, lobbying, or litigation on behalf of others.

Respondents brought this action challenging their threatened exclusion under the new Executive Order. They argued that the denial of the right to seek designated funds violates their First Amendment right to solicit charitable contributions and that the denial of the right to participate in undesignated funds violates their rights under the equal protection component of the Fifth Amendment. The District Court held that respondents' exclusion from the designated contribution portion of the CFC was unconstitutional. The court reasoned that the CFC was a "limited public forum" and that respondents' exclusion was content based. Finding that the regulation was not narrowly drawn to support a compelling governmental interest, the District Court granted summary judgment to respondents and enjoined the denial of respondents' pending or future applications to participate in the solicitation of designated contributions.

The judgment was affirmed by a divided panel of the United States Court of Appeals for the District of Columbia Circuit. The majority did not decide whether the CFC was a limited public forum or a nonpublic forum because in its view the Government restrictions were not reasonable and therefore failed even the least exacting scrutiny. The dissent disagreed with both the analysis used and the result reached by the majority. The dissent defined the relevant forum as the federal workplace and found that it was a nonpublic forum under our cases. Based on this characterization, the dissent argued that the Government must merely provide a rational basis for the exclusion, and that this standard was met here.

The issue presented is whether respondents have a First Amendment right to solicit contributions that was violated by their exclusion from the CFC. To resolve this issue we must first decide whether solicitation in the context of the CFC is speech protected by the First Amendment, for, if it is not, we need go no further. Assuming that such solicitation is protected speech, we must identify the nature of the forum, because the extent to which the Government may limit access depends on whether the forum is public or nonpublic. Finally, we must assess whether the justifications for exclusion from the relevant forum satisfy the requisite standard. Applying this analysis, we find that respondents' solicitation is protected speech occurring in the context of a nonpublic forum and that the Government's reasons for excluding respondents from the CFC appear, at least facially, to satisfy the reasonableness standard. We express no opinion on the question whether petitioner's explanation is merely a pretext for viewpoint discrimination. Accordingly, we reverse and remand for further proceedings consistent with this opinion.

Charitable solicitation of funds has been recognized by this Court as a form of protected speech. Soliciting financial support is undoubtedly subject to reasonable regulation but the latter must be undertaken with due regard for the reality that solicitation is characteristically intertwined with informative and perhaps persuasive speech seeking support for particular causes or for particular views and for the reality that without solicitation the flow of such information and advocacy would likely cease.

In a face-to-face encounter [our earlier cases dealt with such communications] there is a greater opportunity for the exchange of ideas and the propagation of views than is available in the CFC. The statements contained in the CFC literature are merely informative. Although prepared by the participants, the statements must conform to federal standards which prohibit persuasive speech and the use of symbols "or other distractions" aimed at competing for the potential donor's attention.

Notwithstanding the significant distinctions between in-person solicitation and solicitation in the abbreviated context of the CFC, we find that the latter deserves First Amendment protection. The brief statements in the CFC literature directly advance the speaker's interest in informing readers about its existence and its goals. Moreover, an employee's contribution in response to a request for funds functions as a general expression of support for the recipient and its views.

The conclusion that the solicitation which occurs in the CFC is protected speech merely begins our inquiry. Even protected speech is not equally permissible in all places and at all times. Nothing in the Constitution requires the Government freely to grant access to all who wish to exercise their right to free speech on every type of Government property without regard to the nature of the property or to the disruption that might be caused by the speaker's activities. Recognizing that the Government, no less than a private owner of property, has power to preserve the property under its control for the use to which it is lawfully dedicated, the Court has adopted a forum analysis as a means of determining when the Government's interest in limiting the use of its property to its intended purpose outweighs the interest of those wishing to use the property for other purposes. Accordingly, the extent to which the Government can control access depends on the nature of the relevant forum. Because a principal purpose of traditional public forum is the free exchange of ideas, speakers can be excluded from a public forum only when the exclusion is necessary to serve a compelling state interest and the exclusion is narrowly drawn to achieve that interest. Similarly, when the Government has intentionally designated a place or means of communication as a public forum speakers cannot be excluded without a compelling governmental interest. Access to a nonpublic forum, however, can be restricted as long as the restrictions are reasonable and are not an effort to suppress expression merely because public officials oppose the speaker's view.

To determine whether the First Amendment permits the Government to exclude respondents from the CFC, we must first decide whether the forum consists of the federal workplace, as petitioner contends, or the CFC, as respondents maintain. Having defined the relevant forum, we must then determine whether it is public or nonpublic in nature.

Petitioner contends that a First Amendment forum necessarily consists of tangible government property. Because the only "property" involved here is the federal workplace, in petitioner's view the workplace constitutes the relevant forum. Under this analysis, the CFC is merely an activity that takes place in the federal workplace. Respondents, in contrast, argue that the forum should be defined in terms of the access sought by the speaker. Under their view, the particular channel of communication constitutes the forum for First Amendment purposes. Because respondents seek access only to the CFC and do not claim a general right to engage in face-to-face solicitation in the federal workplace, they contend that the relevant forum is the CFC and its attendant literature.

We agree with respondents that the relevant forum for our purposes is the CFC. Although petitioner is correct that as an initial matter a speaker must seek access to public property or to private property dedicated to public use to evoke First Amendment concerns, forum analysis is not completed merely by identifying the government property at issue. Rather, in defining the forum we have focused on the access sought by the speaker. When speakers seek general access to public property, the forum encompasses that property. Here, respondents seek access to a particular means of communication. Consistent with the approach taken in prior cases, we find that the CFC, rather than the federal workplace, is the forum.

Having identified the forum as the CFC, we must decide whether it is nonpublic or public in nature. [This Court has] three types of fora: the traditional public forum, the public forum created by government designation, and the nonpublic forum. Traditional public fora are those places which by long tradition or by government fiat have been devoted to assembly and debate. Public streets and parks fall into this category. In addition to traditional public fora, a public forum may be created by government designation of a place or channel of communication for use by the public at large for assembly and speech, for use by certain speakers, or for the discussion of certain subjects.

Here the parties agree that neither the CFC nor the federal workplace is a traditional public forum. Respondents argue, however, that the Government created a limited public forum for use by all charitable organizations to solicit funds from federal employees. Petitioner contends, and we agree, that neither its practice nor its policy is consistent with an intent to designate the CFC as a public forum open to all tax-exempt organizations. In 1980, an estimated 850,000 organizations qualified for tax-exempt status. In contrast, only 237 organizations participated in the 1981 CFC of the

National Capital Area. The Government's consistent policy has been to limit participation in the CFC to "appropriate" voluntary agencies and to require agencies seeking admission to obtain permission from federal and local Campaign officials. Although the record does not show how many organizations have been denied permission throughout the 24-year history of the CFC, there is no evidence suggesting that the granting of the requisite permission is merely ministerial. The Civil Service Commission and, after 1978, the Office of Personnel Management developed extensive admission criteria to limit access to the Campaign to those organizations considered appropriate. Such selective access, unsupported by evidence of a purposeful designation for public use, does not create a public forum.

Nor does the history of the CFC support a finding that the Government was motivated by an affirmative desire to provide an open forum for charitable solicitation in the federal workplace when it began the Campaign. The historical background indicates that the Campaign was designed to minimize the disruption to the workplace that had resulted from unlimited ad hoc solicitation activities by lessening the amount of expressive activity occurring on federal property. Indeed, the OPM stringently limited expression to the 30-word statement included in the Campaign literature. The decision of the Government to limit access to the CFC is not dispositive in itself; instead, it is relevant for what it suggests about the Government's intent in creating the forum. The Government did not create the CFC for purposes of providing a forum for expressive activity. That such activity occurs in the context of the forum created does not imply that the forum thereby becomes a public forum for First Amendment purposes.

An examination of the nature of the Government property involved strengthens the conclusion that the CFC is a nonpublic forum. The federal workplace, like any place of employment, exists to accomplish the business of the employer. The Government, as an employer, must have wide discretion and control over the management of its personnel and internal affairs. It follows that the Government has the right to exercise control over access to the federal workplace in order to avoid interruptions to the performance of the duties of its employees. In light of the Government policy in creating the CFC and its practice in limiting access, we conclude that the CFC is a nonpublic forum.

Control over access to a nonpublic forum can be based on subject matter and speaker identity so long as the distinctions drawn are reasonable in light of the purpose served by the forum and are viewpoint neutral. Although a speaker may be excluded from a nonpublic forum if he wishes to address a topic not encompassed within the purpose of the forum, or if he is not a member of the class of speakers for whose especial benefit the forum was created, the government violates the First Amendment when it denies access to a speaker solely to suppress the point of view he espouses on an otherwise includible subject. The Court of Appeals found it unnecessary to resolve whether the government's denial of access to respondents was viewpoint based, because it determined that respondents' exclusion was unreasonable in light of the purpose served by the CFC.

Petitioner maintains that the purpose of the CFC is to provide a means for traditional health and welfare charities to solicit contributions in the federal workplace, while at the same time maximizing private support of social programs that would otherwise have to be supported by Government funds and minimizing costs to the Federal Government by controlling the time that federal employees expend on the Campaign. Petitioner posits that excluding agencies that attempt to influence the outcome of political elections or the determination of public policy is reasonable in light of this purpose. First, petitioner contends that there is likely to be a general consensus among employees that traditional health and welfare charities are worthwhile, as compared with the more diverse views concerning the goals of organizations like respondents. Limiting participation to widely accepted groups is likely to contribute significantly to employees' acceptance of the Campaign and consequently to its ultimate success. In addition, because the CFC is conducted largely through the efforts of federal employees during their working hours, any controversy surrounding the CFC would produce unwelcome disruption. Finally, the President determined that agencies seeking to affect the outcome of elections or the determination of public policy should be denied access to the CFC in order to avoid the reality and the appearance of Government favoritism or entanglement with particular viewpoints.

In respondents' view, the reasonableness standard is satisfied only when there is some basic incompatibility between the communication at issue and the principal activity occurring on the Government property. Respondents contend that the purpose of the CFC is to permit solicitation by groups that provide health and welfare services. By permitting such solicitation to take place in the federal workplace, respondents maintain, the Government has concluded that such activity is consistent with the activities usually conducted there. Because respondents are seeking to solicit such contributions and their activities result in direct, tangible benefits to the groups they represent, the Government's attempt to exclude them is unreasonable. Respondents reject petitioner's justifications on the ground that they are unsupported by the record.

We conclude that respondents may be excluded from the CFC. The Court of Appeals' conclusion to the contrary fails to reflect the nature of a nonpublic forum. The Government's decision to restrict access to a nonpublic forum need only be reasonable; it need not be the most reasonable or the only reasonable limitation. In contrast to a public forum, a finding of strict incompatibility between the nature of the speech or the identity of the speaker and the functioning of the nonpublic forum is not mandated. Even if some incompatibility with general expressive activity were required, the CFC would meet the requirement because it would be administratively unmanageable if access could not be curtailed in a reasonable manner. Nor is there a requirement that the restriction be narrowly tailored or that the Government's interest be compelling. The First Amendment does not demand unrestricted access to a nonpublic forum merely because use of that forum may be the most efficient means of delivering the speaker's message. Rarely will a nonpublic forum provide the only means of contact with a particular audience. Here, the speakers have access to alternative channels, including direct mail and in-person solicitation outside the workplace, to solicit contributions from federal employees.

The reasonableness of the Government's restriction of access to a nonpublic forum must be assessed in the light of the purpose of the forum and all the surrounding circumstances. Here the President could reasonably conclude that a dollar directly spent on providing food or shelter to the needy is more beneficial than a dollar spent on litigation that might or might not result in aid to the needy. Moreover, avoiding the appearance of political favoritism is a valid justification for limiting speech in a nonpublic forum. In furthering this interest, the Government is not bound by decisions of other executive agencies made in other contexts. Thus, respondents' tax status, while perhaps relevant, does not determine the reasonableness of the Government's conclusion that participation by such agencies in the CFC will create the appearance of favoritism.

Finally, the record amply supports an inference that respondents' participation in the CFC jeopardized the success of the Campaign. OPM submitted a number of letters from federal employees and managers, as well as from Chairmen of local Federal Coordinating Committees and Members of Congress expressing concern about the inclusion of groups termed "political" or "nontraditional" in the CFC. More than 80 percent of this correspondence related requests that the CFC be restricted to "non-political," "non-advocacy," or "traditional" charitable organizations. In addition, OPM received approximately 1,450 telephone calls complaining about the inclusion of respondents and similar agencies in the 1983 Campaign. Many Campaign workers indicated that extra effort was required to persuade disgruntled employees to contribute. The evidence indicated that the number of contributors had declined in some areas. Other areas reported significant declines in the amount of contributions. Although the avoidance of controversy is not a valid ground for restricting speech in a public forum, a nonpublic forum by definition is not dedicated to general debate or the free exchange of ideas. The First Amendment does not forbid a viewpoint-neutral exclusion of speakers who would disrupt a nonpublic forum and hinder its effectiveness for its intended purpose.

We conclude that the Government does not violate the First Amendment when it limits participation in the CFC in order to minimize disruption to the federal workplace, to ensure the success of the fundraising effort, or to avoid the appearance of political favoritism without regard to the viewpoint of the excluded groups. Accordingly, we reverse the judgment of the Court of Appeals that the exclusion of respondents was unreasonable, and we remand this case for further proceedings consistent with this opinion.

## Points for Discussion

1. Public forum analysis has often been criticized for its circularity. As Justice Blackmun wrote in his dissenting opinion in *Cornelius,* "the very fact that the Government denied access to the speaker indicates that the Government did not intend to provide an open forum for expressive activity, and under the [majority's] analysis that fact alone would demonstrate that the forum is not [even] a limited public forum." Should a history of denying access translate into a right to deny access?

2. The Court admits that, even in a nonpublic forum, the government should not discriminate on the basis of the speaker's viewpoint. Thus, for example, it could not permit prolife charities while excluding prochoice charities. Yet Justice O'Connor accepts the government's argument that "limiting participation to widely accepted groups is likely to contribute significantly to employees' acceptance of the [CFC] and consequently to its ultimate success." Do you perceive a contradiction here, and, if so, how might it be resolved?

## ■ United States v. The Progressive
### 467 F. Supp. 990 (W.D. Wis. 1979)

*Judge Warren:*

On March 9, 1979, this Court, at the request of the government, but after hearing from both parties, issued a temporary restraining order enjoining defendants, their employees, and agents from publishing or otherwise communicating or disclosing in any manner any restricted data contained in the article: "The H-Bomb Secret: How We Got It, Why We're Telling It."

In keeping with the Court's order that the temporary restraining order should be in effect for the shortest time possible, a preliminary injunction hearing was scheduled for one week later, on March 16, 1979. At the request of the parties and with the Court's acquiescence, the preliminary injunction hearing was rescheduled for 10:00 A.M. today in order that both sides might have additional time to file affidavits and arguments. The Court continued the temporary restraining order until 5:00 P.M. today.

In order to grant a preliminary injunction, the Court must find that plaintiff has a reasonable likelihood of success on the merits, and that the plaintiff will suffer irreparable harm if the injunction does not issue. In addition, the Court must consider the interest of the public and the balance of the potential harm to plaintiff and defendants.

In its argument and briefs, plaintiff relies on national security, as enunciated by Congress in The Atomic Energy Act of 1954, as the basis for classification of certain documents. Plaintiff contends that, in certain areas, national preservation and self-interest permit the retention and classification of government secrets. The government argues that its national security interest also permits it to impress classification and censorship upon information originating in the public domain, if when drawn together, synthesized and collated, such information acquires the character of presenting immediate, direct and irreparable harm to the interests of the United States.

Defendants argue that freedom of expression as embodied in the First Amendment is so central to the heart of liberty that prior restraint in any form becomes anathema. They contend that this is particularly true when a nation is not at war and where the prior restraint is based on surmise or conjecture. While acknowledging that freedom of the press is not absolute, they maintain that the publication of the projected article does not rise to the level of immediate, direct and irreparable harm which could justify incursion into First Amendment freedoms.

Both parties have already marshalled impressive opinions covering all aspects of the case. The Court has read all this material and has now heard extensive argument. It is time for decision.

From the founding days of this nation, the rights to freedom of speech and of the press have held an honored place in our constitutional scheme. The establishment and nurturing of these rights is one of the true achievements of our form of government. Because of the importance of these rights, any prior restraint on publication comes into court under a heavy presumption against its constitutional validity.

However, First Amendment rights are not absolute. They are not boundless. Free speech is not so absolute or irrational a conception as to imply paralysis of the means for effective protection of all the freedoms secured by the Bill of Rights.

In *Near v. Minnesota*, 283 U.S. 697 (1931), the Supreme Court specifically recognized an extremely narrow area, involving national security, in which interference with First Amendment rights might be tolerated and a prior restraint on publication might be appropriate. The Court stated: "When a nation is at war many things that might be said in time of peace are such a hindrance to its effort that their utterance will not be endured so long as men fight and that no Court could regard them as protected by any constitutional right. No one would question but that a government might prevent actual obstruction to its recruiting service or the publication of the sailing dates of transports or the number and location of troops."

Thus, it is clear that few things, save grave national security concerns, are sufficient to override First Amendment interests. A court is well admonished to approach any requested prior restraint with a great deal of skepticism.

Juxtaposed against the right to freedom of expression is the government's contention that the national security of this country could be jeopardized by publication of the article.

The Court is convinced that the government has a right to classify certain sensitive documents to protect its national security. The problem is with the scope of the classification system.

Defendants contend that the projected article merely contains data already in the public domain and readily available to any diligent seeker. They say other nations already have the same information or the opportunity to obtain it. How then, they argue, can they be in violation of [the relevant federal laws] which purport to authorize injunctive relief against one who would disclose restricted data "with reason to believe such data will be utilized to injure the United States or to secure an advantage to any foreign nation . . . "? Although the government states that some of the information is in the public domain, it contends that much of the data is not, and that the Morland article contains a core of information that has never before been published.

Furthermore, the government's position is that whether or not specific information is in the public domain or has been declassified at some point is not determinative. The government states that a court must look at the nature and context of prior disclosures and analyze what the practical impact of the prior disclosures are as contrasted to that of the present revelation.

The government feels that the mere fact that the author, Howard Morland, could prepare an article explaining the technical processes of thermonuclear weapons does not mean that those processes are available to everyone. They lay heavy emphasis on the argument that the danger lies in the exposition of certain concepts never heretofore disclosed in conjunction with one another.

In an impressive affidavit, Dr. Hans A. Bethe states that sizeable portions of the Morland text should be classified as restricted data because the processes outlined in the manuscript describe the essential design and operation of thermonuclear weapons. He later concludes that "the design and operational concepts described in the manuscript are not expressed or revealed in the public literature nor do I believe they are known to scientists not associated with the government weapons programs."

The Court has grappled with this difficult problem and has read and studied the affidavits and other documents on file. After all this, the Court finds concepts within the article that it does not find in the public realm, concepts that are vital to the operation of the hydrogen bomb.

Even if some of the information is in the public domain, due recognition must be given to the human skills and expertise involved in writing this article. The author needed sufficient expertise to recognize relevant, as opposed to irrelevant, information and to assimilate the information obtained. The right questions had to be asked or the correct educated guesses had to be made.

Does the article provide a "do-it yourself" guide for the hydrogen bomb? Probably not. A number of affidavits make quite clear that a *sine qua non* to thermonuclear capability is a large, sophisticated industrial capability coupled with a coterie of imaginative, resourceful scientists and technicians. One does not build a hydrogen bomb in the basement. However, the article could possibly provide sufficient information to allow a medium size nation to move faster in developing a hydrogen weapon. It could provide a ticket to by-pass blind alleys.

Although the defendants state that the information contained in the article is relatively easy to obtain, only five countries now have a hydrogen bomb. Yet the United States first successfully exploded the hydrogen bomb some twenty-six years ago.

The point has also been made that it is only a question of time before other countries will have the hydrogen bomb. That may be true. However, there are times in the course of human history when time itself may be very important. This time factor becomes critical when considering mass annihilation weaponry. Witness the failure of Hitler to get his V-1 and V-2 bombs operational quickly enough to materially affect the outcome of World War II.

Defendants have stated that publication of the article will alert the people of this country to the false illusion of security created by the government's futile efforts at secrecy. They believe publication will provide the people with needed information to make informed decisions on an urgent issue of public concern.

However, this Court can find no plausible reason why the public needs to know the technical details about hydrogen bomb construction to carry on an informed debate on this issue. Furthermore, the Court believes that the defendants' position in favor of nuclear non-proliferation would be harmed, not aided, by the publication of this article.

The Court is of the opinion that the government has shown that the defendants had reason to believe that the data in the article, if published, would injure the United States or give an advantage to a foreign nation. Extensive reading and studying of the documents on file lead to the conclusion that not all the data is available in the public realm in the same fashion, if it is available at all.

What is involved here is information dealing with the most destructive weapon in the history of mankind, information of sufficient destructive potential to nullify the right to free speech and to endanger the right to life itself. Stripped to its essence then, the question before the Court is a basic confrontation between the First Amendment right to freedom of the press and national security.

Our Founding Fathers believed, as we do, that one is born with certain inalienable rights which, as the Declaration of Independence intones, include the right to life, liberty and the pursuit of happiness. The Constitution, including the Bill of Rights, was enacted to make those rights operable in everyday life. The Court believes that each of us is born seized of a panoply of basic rights, that we institute governments to secure these rights and that there is a hierarchy of values attached to these rights which is helpful in deciding the clash now before us.

Certain of these rights have an aspect of imperativeness or centrality that make them transcend other rights. Somehow it does not seem that the right to life and the right to not have soldiers quartered in your home can be of equal import in the grand scheme of things. While it may be true in the long-run, as Patrick Henry instructs us, that one would prefer death to life without liberty, nonetheless, in the short-run, one cannot enjoy freedom of speech, freedom to worship or freedom of the press unless one first enjoys the freedom to live.

Faced with a stark choice between upholding the right to continued life and the right to freedom of the press, most jurists would have no difficulty in opting for the chance to continue to breathe and function as they work to achieve perfect freedom of expression.

Is the choice here so stark? Only time can give us a definitive answer. But considering another aspect of this panoply of rights we all have is helpful in answering the question now before us. This aspect is the disparity of the risk involved.

The destruction of various human rights can come about in differing ways and at varying speeds. Freedom of the press can be obliterated overnight by some dictator's imposition of censorship or by the slow nibbling away at a free press through successive bits of repressive legislation enacted by a nation's lawmakers. Yet, even in the most drastic of such situations, it is always possible for a dictator to be overthrown, for a bad law to be repealed or for a judge's error to be subsequently rectified. Only when human life is at stake are such corrections impossible. The case at bar is so difficult precisely because the consequences of error involve human life itself and on such an awesome scale.

A mistake in ruling against *The Progressive* will seriously infringe cherished First Amendment rights. If a preliminary injunction is issued, it will constitute the first instance of prior restraint against a publication in this fashion in the history of this country, to this Court's knowledge. Such notoriety is not to be sought. It will curtail defendants' First Amendment rights in a drastic and substantial fashion. It will infringe upon our right to know and to be informed as well. A mistake in ruling against the United States could pave the way for thermonuclear annihilation for us all. In that event, our right to life is extinguished and the right to publish becomes moot.

In the *Near* case, the Supreme Court recognized that publication of troop movements in time of war would threaten national security and could therefore be restrained. Times have changed significantly since 1931 when *Near* was decided. Now war by foot soldiers has been replaced in large part by war by machines and bombs. No longer need there be any advance warning or any preparation time before a nuclear war could be commenced.

In light of these factors, this Court concludes that publication of the technical information on the hydrogen bomb contained in the article is analogous to publication of troop movements or locations in time of war and falls within the extremely narrow exception to the rule against prior restraint.

Because the government has met its heavy burden of showing justification for the imposition of a prior restraint on publication of the objected-to technical portions of the Morland article, and because the Court is unconvinced that suppression of the objected-to technical portions of the Morland article would in any plausible fashion impede the defendants in their laudable crusade to stimulate public knowledge of nuclear armament and bring about enlightened debate on national policy questions, the Court finds that the objected-to portions of the article fall within the narrow area recognized by the Court in *Near v. Minnesota* in which a prior restraint on publication is appropriate.

However, the Court is acutely aware of the old legal adage that "bad cases make bad law." This case in its present posture will undoubtedly go to the Supreme Court because it does present so starkly the clash between freedom of press and national security. Does it go there with the blessing of the entire press? The Court thinks not. Many elements of the press see grave risk of permanent damage to First Amendment freedoms if this case goes forward. They feel appellate courts will find, as this Court has, that the risk is simply too great to permit publication.

Furthermore, if there is any one inescapable conclusion that one arrives at after wading through all these experts' affidavits, it is that many wise, intelligent, patriotic individuals can hold diametrically opposite opinions on the issues before us.

The government seeks only the deletion of certain technical material and, in the Court's opinion, would have an interest in settling this case out of court. On the other hand, the Court believes that *The Progressive* does not really require the objected-to material in order to ventilate its views on government secrecy and the hydrogen bomb.

The facts and circumstances as presented here fall within the extremely narrow recognized area, involving national security, in which a prior restraint on publication is appropriate. Issuance of a preliminary injunction does not, under the circumstances presented to the Court, violate defendants' First Amendment rights.

Plaintiff has proven all necessary prerequisites for issuance of a preliminary injunction restraining defendants from publishing or disclosing any Restricted Data contained in the Morland article until a final determination in this action has been made by the Court.

*Editor's Note:* As it turns out, the *Progressive* case never went to the Supreme Court. While an appeal was pending, a number of other publications—including campus newspapers at the University of Wisconsin and Stanford University—printed essays very similar to the Morland article. The case was therefore dismissed as moot in that there was no more damage that could be done by the Morland article itself.

## *Points for Discussion*

1. Suppose that a publication wanted to print an essay arguing that the U.S. government is inadequately preparing for the possibility of terrorism using biological weapons. Suppose further that the publisher felt that the point can only be made by showing how easy it would be to wage biologic warfare against this country. Upon the government's request, should a modern-day court do as Judge Warren did? Should publication of the article be stopped?

2. Judge Warren struggled with this case precisely because he was asked to impose a prior restraint on publication, and such restraints were viewed with special disdain by the Founders. He allows that a prior restraint is appropriate here because total annihilation of the human race may result, if he permits publication, and then determines if the Morland essay was in violation of the Atomic Energy Act. Are there other situations, beyond the possible end of humankind, that you think justify the use of prior restraints on communication?

# 3 *Libel: Common-Law Elements*

Libel law is designed to protect individuals' interest in their reputation, permitting aggrieved parties to sue those who make false and defamatory statements of fact about them. Generally plaintiffs must prove four things to prevail:

- *Identification* (that the utterances in question are about the plaintiff)
- *Publication* (that at least one third party has heard or read the charges)
- *Defamation* (that the utterance would tend to damage reputation)
- *Fault* (that the speaker or publisher was guilty, minimally, of negligence in disseminating the charges)

The court cases in this chapter were selected because they exemplify key principles of common law applied to libel, long before the Supreme Court ever suggested that the First Amendment itself places important limitations on the use of libel suits to squelch political debate.

In *Greenbelt Cooperative Publishing Association v. Bresler,* the Supreme Court says that language is complex and that utterances that seem to make false factual allegations may instead be expressions only of the speaker's opinion. What does it mean, the Court had to decide, to call someone a "blackmailer"? The answer, as you will see, is that "it depends . . . upon the context." Although the case was decided a few years after the Court had applied constitutional limitations to libel law, its holding is not dependent on First Amendment doctrine.

Next comes *Stein v. Trager,* a New York decision dependent on the common-law concept of *libel per se*, utterances so obviously defamatory that plaintiffs would not have to prove precisely how they were hurt. One of the questions raised by the case is whether an attribution of homosexuality falls into this category.

*Weinstein v. Bullick* serves as a cautionary tale, reminding us that we might be guilty of libeling another even if we never mention him or her by name. The court here tells us that we must consider the conjunction of the details presented by the defendant and whatever additional information is already known by readers. The element of identification is met if those two sources of data, together, make the plaintiff recognizable.

Finally, we look at a case involving Kato Kaelin, who achieved fame of sorts by dint of his status as O. J. Simpson's houseguest (*Kaelin v. Globe Communications Corporation*). Kaelin's suit against a tabloid newspaper emphasizes that a misleading headline can be defamatory, even if the article it introduces is not.

## ■ *Greenbelt Cooperative Publishing Association v. Bresler*

### 398 U.S. 6 (1970)

*Justice Stewart delivered the opinion of the Court.*

The petitioners are the publishers of a small weekly newspaper, the *Greenbelt News Review,* in the city of Greenbelt, Maryland. The respondent Bresler is a prominent local real estate developer and builder in Greenbelt, and was, during the period in question, a member of the Maryland House of Delegates from a neighboring district. In the autumn of 1965 Bresler was engaged in negotiations with the Greenbelt City Council to obtain certain zoning variances that would allow the construction of high-density housing on land owned by him. At the same time the city was attempting to acquire another tract of land owned by Bresler for the construction of a new high school. Extensive litigation concerning compensation for the school site seemed imminent, unless there should be an agreement on its price between Bresler and the city authorities, and the concurrent negotiations obviously provided both parties considerable bargaining leverage.

These joint negotiations evoked substantial local controversy, and several tumultuous city council meetings were held at which many members of the community freely expressed their views. The meetings were reported at length in the news columns of the *Greenbelt News Review.* Two news articles in consecutive weekly editions of the paper stated that at the public meetings some people had characterized Bresler's negotiating position as "blackmail." The word appeared several times, both with and without quotation marks, and was used once as a subheading within a news story.

Bresler reacted to these news articles by filing the present lawsuit for libel, seeking both compensatory and punitive damages. The primary thrust of his complaint was that the articles, individually and along with other items published in the petitioners' newspaper, imputed to him the crime of blackmail. The case went to trial, and the jury awarded Bresler $5,000 in compensatory damages and $12,500 in punitive damages. The Maryland Court of Appeals affirmed the judgment.

It is not disputed that the articles published in the petitioners' newspaper were accurate and truthful reports of what had been said at the public hearings before the city council. The contention is, rather, that the speakers at the meeting, in using the word "blackmail," and the petitioners in reporting the use of that word in the newspaper articles, were charging Bresler with the crime of blackmail, and that since the petitioners knew that Bresler had committed no such crime, they could be held liable for the knowing use of falsehood. It was upon this theory that the case was submitted to the jury, and upon this theory that the judgment was affirmed by the Maryland Court of Appeals. For the reasons that follow, we hold that the word "blackmail" in these circumstances was not slander when spoken, and not libel when reported in the *Greenbelt News Review.*

There can be no question that the public debates at the sessions of the city council regarding Bresler's negotiations with the city were a subject of substantial concern to all who lived in the community. The debates themselves were heated, as debates about controversial issues usually are. During the course of the arguments Bresler's opponents characterized the position he had taken in his negotiations with the city officials as "blackmail." The *Greenbelt News Review* was performing its wholly legitimate function as a community newspaper when it published full reports of these public debates in its news columns. If the reports had been truncated or distorted in such a way as to extract the word "blackmail" from the context in which it was used at the public meetings, this would be a different case. But the reports were accurate and full. Their headlines, "School Site Stirs Up Council—Rezoning Deal Offer Debated" and "Council Rejects By 4–1 High School Site Deal," made it clear to all readers that the paper was reporting the public debates on the pending land negotiations. Bresler's proposal was accurately and fully described in each article, along with the accurate statement that some people at the meetings had referred to the proposal as blackmail, and others had indicated they thought Bresler's position not unreasonable.

It is simply impossible to believe that a reader who reached the word "blackmail" in either article would not have understood exactly what was meant: it was Bresler's public and wholly legal negotiating proposals that were being criticized. No reader could have thought that either the speakers at the meetings or the newspaper articles reporting their words were charging Bresler with the commission of a criminal offense. On the contrary, even the most careless reader must have perceived that the word was no more than rhetorical hyperbole, a vigorous epithet used by those who considered Bresler's negotiating position extremely unreasonable. Indeed, the record is completely devoid of evidence that anyone in the city of Greenbelt or anywhere else thought Bresler had been charged with a crime.

To permit the infliction of financial liability upon the petitioners for publishing these two news articles would subvert the most fundamental meaning of a free press. Accordingly, we reverse the judgment and remand the case to the Court of Appeals of Maryland for further proceedings not inconsistent with this opinion.

## Points for Discussion

1. Does Justice Stewart's analysis suggest that readers will always "get the joke" when newspapers engage in exaggeration, irony, or "rhetorical hyperbole"? How would such an assumption square with the many times that news outlets have felt the need to apologize to individuals or to whole groups who have felt maligned by a *failed* attempt at humor?

2. The *Greenbelt News Review* escaped liability because the larger context made clear that it was not really accusing Bresler of criminal activity. What should happen in situations where the allegedly libelous words are vague on their face, but highly inflammatory if a larger context is known? For example, suppose that a state governor is accused in the press of having fashioned a "final solution" for prison unrest. If the governor sues for libel, could the media plausibly claim that very few of its readers know enough about contemporary history to recognize the phrase as a reference to the Nazis' program of genocide, that "final solution" could refer innocently to a solution that would not have to be revisited?

## ■ *Stein v. Trager*

### 232 N.Y.S.2d 363 (Sup. Ct., N.Y., Erie County, 1962)

*Judge Lawless:*

Plaintiff was a research fellow of the University of Buffalo and defendant was a professor in the Department of Anthropology and Linguistics at that university and was teaching the plaintiff. The complaint charges the defendant with having referred to plaintiff as "psychopath", "very destructive", "anti-social", "son-of-a-bitch", "intellectually incompetent", "immoral", "liar", "homosexual", and "made up all the data for his Master's thesis".

It is fundamental that in a complaint based upon slander there must be an allegation of special damage, or the words spoken must be slanderous per se. To be held slanderous per se, the words must charge a person with a punishable crime, or, they must tend to injure a person in his trade, occupation or profession.

In the complaint before this court, the only word spoken which might remotely constitute a punishable crime is the allegation that the plaintiff is a "homosexual". However, an examination of the New York Criminal Code and Penal Law fails to disclose any specific crime embraced in the phrase "homosexual". [The "Crimes Against Nature" section of the state Penal Law] relates to specific acts not necessarily embraced in the phrase "homosexual". We conclude, therefore, that the use of this phrase does not constitute words which charge a punishable crime and that this word is not slanderous per se.

The other group of words that have been held to be slanderous per se, are those which tend to injure a person in his trade, occupation or profession. The words must be spoken in relation to the profession or trade. Disparagement of a professional man will ipso facto be actionable per se.

In the complaint before us, there is no allegation that the plaintiff was pursuing a trade, business or profession at the time of the alleged slander. The claim is that he was a graduate student seeking to continue graduate study. The complaint before us is deficient because it fails to allege that the plaintiff was engaged in a trade, business or profession, and it fails further, for the reason that it does not allege that the words damaged plaintiff in his trade, business or profession.

### Points for Discussion

1.  If libel plaintiffs are treated differently depending on whether they are "pursuing a trade, business or profession," would this suggest that the law of defamation has a classist flavor to it, that poor people are less protected than more successful ones?

2.  The court's treatment of the "libel per se" issue rests on a posited distinction between being homosexual, which cannot be illegal, and performing specified homosexual acts, which, at least at the time, were illegal in New York. Can the same status versus conduct distinction apply to allegations of other kinds of criminal behavior? Is a "drug addict" someone who uses illicit drugs, or someone who only wants to use them?

### ■ *Weinstein v. Bullick*

**827 F. Supp. 1193 (E.D. Pa. 1993)**

*Judge Giles:*

The complaint alleges that Sarah Weinstein was abducted in November 1991 from a street in the City of Philadelphia by an unknown assailant who thereafter sexually assaulted her. Following her release by her abductor, plaintiff complained to the Philadelphia Police Department, giving officers of the Sex Crimes Unit a detailed description of the assault in a recorded interview.

Richard Bullick was commanding officer of the Sex Crimes Unit at the time of the above described events. In an on-camera interview with reporters from WCAU-TV, Bullick made statements which Weinstein alleges defamed her. She further alleges that Bullick knew that his statements were improper, erroneous, misleading, untrue, and defamatory. WCAU-TV broadcasted Bullick's remarks throughout the Philadelphia area on its evening news program. Weinstein alleges that Bullick's statements were broadcast by WCAU in spite of the fact that WCAU knew or should have known that the information contained in the broadcast was erroneous, misleading, untrue, and defamatory.

Based upon the above-described allegations, Weinstein brought the instant action against Bullick and WCAU, claiming defamation. Defendants have moved to dismiss the complaint, or in the alternative, for summary judgment.

Summary judgment is to be granted only if the pleadings, depositions, answers to interrogatories, and admissions on file, together with the affidavits, if any, show that there is no genuine issue as to any material fact and that the moving party is entitled to judgment as a matter of law. Where, as here, the non-moving party has the burden of proof at trial, the movant need not produce evidence negating the non-movant's case. Instead, the moving party need only demonstrate that there is a lack of any evidence to support the non-movant's claim. Once the movant satisfies this initial burden, the non-movant cannot rest solely upon the allegations of her pleadings. Instead, she must demonstrate that there is sufficient evidence for a jury to return a verdict in her favor. The court must determine whether the evidence presents a sufficient disagreement to require submission to a jury or whether it is so one-sided that one party must prevail as a matter of law. With these general considerations in mind, we will examine each count of the complaint.

Under Pennsylvania law, a plaintiff in a defamation action has the burden of proving: (1) the defamatory character of the communication; (2) its publication by the defendant; (3) its application to the plaintiff; (4) the understanding by the recipient of its defamatory meaning; (5) the understanding by the recipient of it as intended to be applied to the plaintiff. Defendants argue that the statements by Bullick were not defamatory because they were merely expressions of opinion. Defendants also assert that, even if the statements were defamatory, plaintiff cannot establish that they applied to her. Because there is a genuine issue of material fact with respect to each of these contentions, the motions for summary judgment on the defamation claim will be denied.

## The Defamatory Character of the Publication

The threshold question in a defamation action is whether the publication is capable of defamatory meaning. Whether a broadcast can be understood as defamatory is for the court to decide. If the court determines that a statement could be construed as defamatory, it is for the jury to determine if it was so understood by the recipient.

A communication is defamatory if it tends so to harm the reputation of another as to lower him in the estimation of the community or to deter third persons from associating or dealing with him. In determining whether a statement is capable of defamatory meaning, the court must look to the effect that it is fairly calculated to produce, the impression it would naturally engender, in the minds of the average persons among whom it is intended to circulate. The allegedly defamatory statement must be reviewed in the context of the entire broadcast. The words must be given by judges and juries the same signification that other people are likely to attribute to them.

Defendants argue that Bullick's statements are not capable of defamatory meaning because they are merely expressions of opinion. It is true that opinion without more does not create a cause of action in libel. However, this does not mean that there is a wholesale defamation exception for anything that might be labeled "opinion." Expressions of opinion may often imply an assertion of objective fact. Statements of opinion are actionable if the allegedly libeled party can demonstrate that the communicated opinion may reasonably be understood to imply the existence of undisclosed defamatory facts justifying the opinion. An opinion which is unfounded reveals its lack of merit when the opinion-holder discloses the factual basis for the idea. If the disclosed facts are true and the opinion is defamatory, a listener may choose to accept or reject it on the basis of an independent evaluation of the facts. However, if an opinion is stated in a manner that implies that it draws upon unstated facts for its basis, the listener is unable to make an evaluation of the soundness of the opinion.

With these general considerations in mind, we examine the content of the allegedly defamatory broadcast. It is undisputed that the following is the transcript of the November 7, 1991 broadcast in its entirety:

> **Jane Robelot [WCAU-TV Anchorperson]:**   And tonight authorities are investigating a complicated case of abduction and rape that allegedly occurred last Friday. Channel 10 News reporter Andrew Glassman has learned that while the Philadelphia Sex Crimes Division is actively investigating the case, some say they have reservations.
>
> **Andrew Glassman:**   The Bryn Mawr student told police a man forced his way into her car outside a party at the University of Pennsylvania, pulled what appeared to be a gun, forced her to

take off her clothes and have sex with him while he drove across the Walt Whitman Bridge, then stopped the car and raped her again. The woman had a plan: she told her attacker she'd bring him back here—to her dorm room at Bryn Mawr College. She said she'd get her instant teller card and get him cash. She was trying to lure him to a public place to get someone's attention—an officer or a security guard. But even after all that, she couldn't find anyone to help her out. Bryn Mawr Public Safety Chief Steven Heath was sorry his officers were not able to respond.

**Steven Heath:** There is a bright side of this whole tragic event is the fact that the victim really used her head. There could have been a textbook response to such a concern. She most certainly used it.

**Andrew Glassman:** But this was the reaction today from Captain Richard Bullick, Sex Crimes Division of the Philadelphia Police. He is investigating this case.

**Richard Bullick:** She's saying a lot of things that went on in the car—she's driving—she's driving 80 miles an hour having sex with the guy—in a little Nissan. I couldn't do it, maybe she could. I don't know. And even if there was sex, that doesn't mean it was forcible sex. So it's all of these things we have to look into before we come to a conclusion. But, you know, I'm skeptical at the beginning of the investigation.

**Andrew Glassman:** You're skeptical at the beginning of this investigation? Or?

**Richard Bullick:** Both. As we are now, I'm a little skeptical about it.

**Andrew Glassman:** Captain Bullick later phoned us to say he knew we were recording him but was uncomfortable with what he had said. He said he did not wish to appear insensitive to the alleged victim. This was his official statement on the case:

**Richard Bullick:** It's a very sensitive investigation as they all are. And we handle it just as we handle every other investigation that until it's proven to be factual or non-factual, we handle it as if it is factual.

**Andrew Glassman:** A source at Bryn Mawr College in contact with the alleged victim told us late tonight that she would be devastated if she heard that Philadelphia police did not believe her story. Officially the police department continues to seek this man in connection with the incident and Bullick says, he plans to interview the alleged victim again tomorrow. Andrew Glassman, Channel 10 News.

Read in the light most favorable to the plaintiff, Bullick's statements are at least expressions of skepticism about the truthfulness of plaintiff's account of the alleged abduction and rape. While his comments may be interpreted reasonably as an expression of opinion, the content and context of the broadcast allow a reasonable listener to conclude that Bullick's skeptical opinion is based upon undisclosed defamatory facts.

Bullick's comment that the plaintiff said "a lot of things that went on in the car," could reasonably lead a listener to believe that his skepticism about plaintiff's story was based upon more facts than those relayed in the rest of his statement or even in the rest of the broadcast as a whole. A listener to the broadcast could reasonably conclude that the police officer in charge of investigating an alleged abduction and rape knew much more about the case than the limited facts revealed in a television news broadcast. Thus, a reasonable listener could conclude that Bullick's statements of opinion imply the existence of undisclosed facts indicating that plaintiff engaged in consensual sexual intercourse with a stranger while driving at high speed, and then fabricated a story of abduction and rape for the police. Accordingly, we find that the broadcast is capable of a defamatory meaning. Therefore, there exists an issue of material fact as to whether the broadcast was understood by its recipients as defamatory. Summary judgment on this issue must be denied.

## The "Of and Concerning" Requirement

Defendants argue that Weinstein cannot establish the application of the allegedly defamatory statements to her, that is, the broadcast was not "of and concerning" her, and, therefore, her defamation claim fails as a matter of law. The court disagrees.

It is undisputed that plaintiff was not named in the allegedly defamatory broadcast. However, a defamed party need not be specifically named in a defamatory statement in order to recover, if she is pointed to by description or circumstances tending to identify her. When the plaintiff is not named in the broadcast, the court must determine if a viewer could reasonably conclude that the broadcast referred to the plaintiff. If the court decides in the affirmative, the jury must determine if the recipient actually concluded that the defamatory matter referred to the plaintiff.

The broadcast contains numerous details that would help a viewer identify the subject of the allegedly defamatory statements. The subject of the broadcast is identified as a female Bryn Mawr student who was the reported victim of a rape on a certain day. Some of the unusual details of the abduction leading to the rape are given. The victim is said to live in a dorm at Bryn Mawr College, to drive a Nissan, and to have attended a party at the University of Pennsylvania shortly before her abduction. All of these things are the types of description of or reference to the plaintiff that could lead those who saw the broadcast to reasonably understand the plaintiff to be the person intended.

The possibility that plaintiff would be identified by a viewer as the subject of the broadcast is heightened when we consider evidence submitted by defendants that Bryn Mawr is a small school, with approximately 1,200 undergraduate students and 550 graduate students. The defendants' own submission also indicates that "Bryn Mawr's size allows its students and faculty to work closely together and to know each other well." In this type of environment, it would not be surprising if some people could identify plaintiff from the information supplied in the broadcast.

Of course, we are not free to base our decision on speculation that someone might have identified plaintiff as the subject of the broadcast. Because the applicability of the defamatory matter to Weinstein depends upon extrinsic circumstances, rather than upon her being identified by name, the evidence must be able to support a conclusion that some person who saw the broadcast was familiar with the circumstances and reasonably believed that the broadcast referred to plaintiff. The court is satisfied that the evidence submitted by the parties does support such a conclusion.

Weinstein has submitted affidavits from two Bryn Mawr students stating that "news of Sarah Weinstein's rape spread quickly across the campus." The affiants further declare that when the broadcast was "aired lots of people on campus were talking about it." Read in the light most favorable to the plaintiff, these affidavits indicate that many Bryn Mawr students, faculty, and staff knew that a rape had allegedly occurred, could identify plaintiff as the alleged victim of the rape, and could reasonably have identified her as the subject of the broadcast.

Defendants argue that the affiants' assertion that "lots of people" knew about the rape is premised upon hearsay, and therefore not admissible as part of plaintiff's opposition to summary judgment. It is true that a court considering a motion for summary judgment has discretion to disregard those facts which would not be admissible in evidence and to rely upon only facts that would be admissible. [But] admissibility of testimony sometimes depends upon the form in which it is offered, the background which is laid for it, and perhaps on other factors as well. It is therefore possible that [evidence that seems to be hearsay] will be admissible at trial. We would be particularly hesitant to ignore hearsay-based evidence in plaintiff's affidavits at this stage of the proceedings, when discovery is still open and hearsay evidence might well lead to the discovery of evidence which is admissible at trial. Therefore, the court will consider affidavit claims that knowledge of plaintiff's abduction and rape was widespread on Bryn Mawr's campus.

Even if we were to ignore those portions of the affidavits which are arguably based upon hearsay, the affidavits show that the affiants had personal knowledge that could have led them to conclude reasonably that the broadcast was of and concerning plaintiff. The affidavits state that shortly after the alleged abduction and rape Weinstein told affiants about her ordeal. As a result, each of these Bryn Mawr students has sworn that "even though her

name was never mentioned, I knew that the broadcast was about [plaintiff]."
Because the information given in the broadcast was sufficient to make the
affiants' association of the broadcast with plaintiff a reasonable one, plaintiff's evidence is sufficient to withstand defendants' motions for summary
judgment as to the "of and concerning" requirement.

Defendants argue that affiants' claims that they knew the broadcast
was about plaintiff have no probative value since "the affiants cannot even
purport to have known that each and every other female student attending
Bryn Mawr was not the victim of a rape."

Plaintiff need only prove that viewers of the broadcast identified her as
its subject, and that the identification was reasonable. As described above,
plaintiff has submitted evidence sufficient for a jury to find that at least two
people identified her as the subject of the broadcast. The court must conclude, based upon the identifying information given in the broadcast, that
the affiants' identification of plaintiff was reasonable.

Defendants also seize upon evidence that plaintiff told others that she
had been the victim of a rape. Defendants argue that "the source of information about the identity of the alleged victim came not from the broadcast,
but from Weinstein herself. Had Weinstein not disclosed information about
her alleged assault, neither affiant could even purport to discern the identity of the putative victim referred to in the broadcast. Without the benefit
of extrinsic facts, which the plaintiff herself voluntarily chose to impart, reasonable viewers of the Broadcast could not have known that Weinstein was
the putative victim from the sparse identifying details disclosed by CBS."

Defendants ask the court to find that the broadcast was not of and concerning plaintiff because viewers could identify plaintiff only on the basis of
knowledge given by her to them. Defendants' argument is fatally flawed in two
ways. First, defendants' argument improperly reads the evidentiary submission
as asserting that all who may have identified plaintiff from the broadcast did
so only because of her own disclosure that she was the victim. In considering
a motion for summary judgment, all reasonable inferences from the evidence
must be made in favor of the party opposing the motion. The affidavits can
reasonably be read to assert that many people on campus identified plaintiff
as the subject of the broadcast, but are silent as to the means by which others than the affiants came to recognize her. We cannot make an inference
detrimental to plaintiff's case when a favorable inference is also possible.

In addition, and more fundamentally, defendants' argument confuses
nondefamatory information to the effect that one was a rape victim with
defamatory information to the effect that one has lied to the police and made
up false claims of abduction and sexual abuse. Under defendants' rationale,
had plaintiff announced to the entire campus that she had been abducted
and raped she could not sue for defamation if later someone announced that
the woman who claimed she was raped was a liar. Where a plaintiff has announced certain non-defamatory facts about herself, which later assist a rea-

sonable recipient of defamatory remarks in identifying their subject, it is irrelevant that those non-defamatory facts came from her mouth.

The court finds that a listener to the broadcast could reasonably conclude that plaintiff was its subject. In addition, plaintiff's submissions create a genuine issue of material fact as to whether some listeners actually did conclude that the broadcast referred to her. Therefore, summary judgment is not appropriate.

### Points for Discussion

1. As a result of this decision, Weinstein's suit can proceed against both the police chief and WCAU-TV. Would it be fair for the TV station to be held accountable for broadcasting the words of a high-ranking public official? After all, the station never suggested that Bullick's viewpoint was their own; indeed, the station's reporter questioned Bullick on air as to why he was skeptical about Weinstein's account.

2. For an utterance to be protected as "opinion," this court holds, speakers must not imply that they have certain unrevealed facts at their disposal that inform their opinions. Since police officers engaged in ongoing investigations will almost never be ready or willing to tell all the facts they know, what kinds of training would you suggest for police department spokespersons?

## ■ *Kaelin v. Globe Communications Corporation*

### 162 F.3d 1036 (9th Cir. 1998)

*Judge Silverman:*

Brian "Kato" Kaelin became known to the public during the course of the criminal trial of O.J. Simpson as the houseguest at Simpson's estate. Kaelin testified to various events surrounding the killings of Nicole Brown Simpson and Ronald Goldman. Simpson was acquitted of the double murders on October 3, 1995. One week later, the *National Examiner,* a weekly newspaper published by Globe Communications Corporation, featured the following headline on its cover:

> ### COPS THINK KATO DID IT!
> **He fears they want him for perjury, say pals**

Inside the paper, on page 17, in large, boldface, capital letters, [an almost identical] headline appeared. The first four paragraphs of the article read as follows:

> Kato Kaelin is still a suspect in the murder of Nicole Brown Simpson and Ron Goldman, friends fear.
> They are worried that LAPD cops are desperately looking for a way to put Kato behind bars for perjury.
> "We're sure the cops have been trying to prove that Kato didn't tell them everything he knows, that somehow he spoiled their case against O.J.," says one pal. "It's not true, but we think they're out to get even with Kato. I'm worried that Kato will get a persecution complex. He'll end up looking around every corner and thinking he sees a cop."

The remainder of the article contained other comments supposedly made by Kaelin's friends regarding the Simpson case. It also contained several references to a book about Kaelin by author Marc Eliot.

In a letter dated October 12, 1995, Kaelin demanded a retraction. Globe refused. Kaelin then filed this libel action against Globe in the Superior Court of California, and Globe removed it to federal court on the basis of diversity of citizenship.

During discovery, John Garton, the news editor of the *National Examiner* and Globe's designated representative, testified at deposition as follows:

**Q.**  Okay. Did you have any concerns when you saw this headline of September 22nd [the deadline for the article] about the way this headline was framed?

**A.**  I wasn't mad about it.

**Q.**  What do you mean by that?

**A.**  Journalistically I didn't think it was the best headline in the world.

**Q.**  Were you concerned that it implied that Kato had committed the murders or played some role in them?

**A.**  No, I just didn't think it was very accurate to the story. It could have been better.

\* \* \* \* \* \* \* \* \*

**Q.**  Other than what is actually written in Exhibit 2 [prior published articles], any of the things that are in those articles, did the *National Examiner* have in its possession on September 22nd, 1995 any information that a police officer anywhere thought that Kato Kaelin was involved in Nicole Brown Simpson's and Ronald Goldman's murders?

**A.**   No.

* * * * * * * * * *

**Q.**   What did you think, on September 22nd, 1995 about what the words "Cops Think He Did It" meant? What is the "it" to which this statement—

**A.**   Perjury.

**Q.**   Perjury?

**A.**   Mm-hmm.

**Q.**   Did you have any concern that a reader might connect the "Cops Think He Did It" with the other information in the article that refers to allegations that Mr. Kaelin was involved in the murders themselves?

**A.**   I was a bit concerned about it, yes, but in fact I thought the second part of the headline coped with that. . . .

Globe filed a motion for summary judgment. Focusing its analysis on the text of the article rather than on the headline, which was the heart of Kaelin's claim, the district court ruled that Kaelin " . . . has not submitted any evidence which tends to show that Defendants actually doubted the truth of the story . . . " With respect to the headline, the district court stated, "While Globe employees might not have acted with the professionalism that would be expected at a more reputable journalistic institution before running the article about Plaintiff, the failure to act reasonably is not enough to establish malice." [The District Court granted defendant's motion for summary judgment.]

We must decide, viewing the evidence in the light most favorable to the nonmoving party, whether there are any genuine issues of material fact and whether the district court correctly applied the relevant substantive law.

We must draw all justifiable inferences in favor of Kaelin, including questions of credibility and of the weight to be accorded particular evidence. The plaintiff, to survive the defendant's motion, need only present evidence from which a jury might return a verdict in his favor. If he does so, there is a genuine issue of fact that requires a trial.

Although Kaelin complains about the first sentence of the article on page 17, we assume for the purposes of this appeal that the text of the story is not defamatory. This case is about the headlines, especially the one appearing on the cover. The first issue is whether the headlines alone are susceptible of a false and defamatory meaning and, if so, whether they can be the basis of a libel action even though the accompanying story is not defamatory.

As already seen, the front page headline consists of two sentences. The first—"COPS THINK KATO DID IT!"—states what the cops supposedly think. The second—"He fears they want him for perjury, say pals"—is what Kato's pals supposedly said. These two sentences express two different thoughts and are not mutually exclusive. California courts in libel cases have emphasized that the publication is to be measured, not so much by its effect when subjected to the critical analysis of a mind trained in the law, but by the natural and probable effect upon the mind of the average reader. Since the publication occurred just one week after O.J. Simpson's highly publicized acquittal for murder, we believe that a reasonable person, at that time, might well have concluded that the "it" in the first sentence of the cover and internal headlines referred to the murders. Such a reading of the first sentence is not negated by or inconsistent with the second sentence as a matter of logic, grammar, or otherwise. In our view, an ordinary reader reasonably could have read the headline to mean that the cops think that Kato committed the murders and that Kato fears that he is wanted for perjury.

Globe argues that the "it" refers to perjury. Even assuming that such a reading is reasonably possible, it is not the only reading that is reasonably possible as a matter of law. So long as the publication is reasonably susceptible of a defamatory meaning, a factual question for the jury exists.

Globe argues that even if the front page headline could be found to be false and defamatory, the totality of the publication is not. Globe's position is that because the text of the accompanying story is not defamatory, the headline by itself cannot be the basis of a libel action under California law.

It is true that a defamatory meaning must be found, if at all, in a reading of the publication as a whole. This is a rule of reason. Defamation actions cannot be based on snippets taken out of context. By the same token, not every word of an allegedly defamatory publication has to be false and defamatory to sustain a libel action. The test of libel is not quantitative; a single sentence may be the basis for an action in libel even though buried in a much longer text.

Although California courts have not had occasion to opine on whether a headline alone can be the basis of a libel action, it is certainly clear under California law that headlines are not irrelevant, extraneous, or liability-free zones. They are essential elements of a publication. In *Selleck v. Globe International* (1985), for example, Globe published headlines, a caption to a photograph, and the text of an article, all of which created the false impression that the father of actor Tom Selleck had granted an interview to Globe. While not addressing whether any one element of the publication alone would support a libel claim, the court explained that "headlines and captions of an allegedly libellous article are regarded as a part of the article." The court concluded that "the article, including the headline and caption and taking into account the circumstances of its publication, is reasonably susceptible of a defamatory meaning on its face and therefore is libelous per se." In *Davis v. Hearst* (1911), the Supreme Court of California concerned itself with three headlines that read as follows:

---

**MAYOR INVESTIGATES THE BOARD OF EDUCATION'S ACTS**
**Exposures Made by *Examiner* Found to Be True**
Pasadena Council Will Act

---

Although the article explained that the mayor's investigation covered only one matter, the court found that the text did not negate the effect of the headlines, which implied that the mayor had discovered more than one impropriety. It stated that "the mere fact that in the body of the article the mayor's investigations are limited to a single charge is not controlling. The captions and headlines are themselves a part of the libel."

Globe argues that the entirety of the publication, including the story itself, clears up any false and defamatory meaning that could be found on the cover. Whether it does or not is a question of fact for the jury. The Kaelin story was located 17 pages away from the cover. In this respect, the *National Examiner*'s front page headline is unlike a conventional headline that immediately precedes a newspaper story, and nowhere does the cover headline reference the internal page where readers could locate the article. A reasonable juror could conclude that the Kaelin article was too far removed from the cover headline to have the salutary effect that Globe claims. In analyzing the totality of the circumstances of an allegedly defamatory publication, the effect of a front page headline is neither insignificant nor unprecedented. In any event, it is a fact question for a jury.

Viewing the facts in the light most favorable to Kaelin as we are required to do, we hold that Kaelin has come forward with clear and convincing evidence to get to a jury on the issue of whether the headlines are susceptible of a false and defamatory meaning.

Globe editor John Garton testified at his deposition that he saw the headline before it ran and did not think that it "was very accurate to the story." He stated that he was "a bit concerned" that readers might connect the "it" in the headline with the murders. This is direct evidence from which a reasonable juror could find that Globe knew that the headline was factually inaccurate or that Globe acted with reckless disregard for the truth. It is for a jury to decide whether, as Globe argues, it intended to clarify the sentence "COPS THINK KATO DID IT!" with the sentence that followed, " . . . he fears they want him for perjury, say pals." The editors' statements of their subjective intention are matters of credibility for a jury.

It is [also] undisputed that Globe ran the headline "COPS THINK KATO DID IT!" knowing that it had no reason to believe that Kaelin was a murder suspect. This is not a case where Globe relied in good faith on information that turned out to be false. It is undisputed that Globe never believed Kaelin to be a suspect in the murders.

Garton testified at his deposition that "the front page of the tabloid paper is what we sell the paper on, not what's inside it." That testimony permits a reasonable juror to draw the inference that Globe had a pecuniary motive for running a headline that, in Garton's words, was not "very accurate to the story."

Because the issue at this stage of the case is only whether Kaelin has come forward with evidence adequate to survive summary judgment, we analyze the facts and draw the inferences in the light most favorable to him. We hold today that a reasonable juror could find, by clear and convincing evidence, that the headlines are defamatory, and that Globe's editors acted with actual malice* in their decision to run a headline from which a reasonable juror could conclude that Kaelin was a murder suspect. Globe's motion for summary judgment should have been denied.

## *Points for Discussion*

1. John Garton, one of the *National Examiner*'s editors, admitted at trial that the headline at issue here was not "the best in the world" and that it may not have been 100 percent accurate. Does the way in which his words were used against the newspaper suggest that editors should be very careful about ever expressing doubts about their work product?

2. The court here makes much of the fact that the nondefamatory explanation of the headline does not show up until page 17 of the newspaper. What if the explanation appeared on the front page, but the plaintiff produced experts to show that most of these tabloids' "readers" never see much of anything beyond the headlines because they are only glancing at the papers while standing in line at the supermarket? Could such tabloids thus be less protected from libel suits than more "serious" newspapers, not because of the papers' contents, but because of the different ways that readers consume that content?

---

*See the excerpts from *New York Times v. Sullivan,* beginning on page 64, for an explanation of "actual malice."

# 4 Libel: Constitutional Considerations

For most of this country's history, the existence of libel law was not seen as at all inconsistent with the First Amendment's promise that "no law" should abridge freedom of the press. A dramatic change came in 1964, in *New York Times v. Sullivan*, when the U.S. Supreme Court concluded that to permit public officials to sue citizens who criticize their performance in office is hauntingly reminiscent of sedition laws that criminalized antigovernment speech. The Supreme Court's *New York Times* ruling, which begins this chapter, did not prohibit public officials from bringing suit for libel, but it did make such suits far more difficult to prove.

Ten years later, in *Gertz v. Welch, Inc.*, the Supreme Court fine-tunes its evolving libel doctrine and creates important new law. No longer would libel plaintiffs be able to prevail without proving that they were harmed in some way by a defendant's utterance; moreover, any plaintiff seeking punitive damages—those designed to punish the press more than to compensate for reputational harm—would have to overcome the same obstacles constitutionally mandated for public officials.

In the traditional common law of libel, plaintiffs did not have to prove that the defamations hurled against them were false. They were presumed false in that citizens' reputations were presumed unsullied until proven otherwise. In *Philadelphia Newspapers v. Hepps, Inc.* the Court considers whether this traditional rule can survive the application of First Amendment principles to libel law.

Libel law is aimed at defamatory factual allegations. Speakers are generally free to express their unadorned opinions about others with impunity. But how to know when an utterance is a pure opinion, or whether it at least implies a factual attribution? That issue is raised by the last two cases in this chapter. In *Ollman v. Evans*, the D.C. Circuit Court of Appeals suggests a four-part test to distinguish fact from opinion. The Supreme Court's more recent decision in *Milkovich v. Lorain Journal Co.* ostensibly rejects the notion that statements of opinion can never be the basis of a libel suit, thus also rejecting the need for *Ollman*-type tests to distinguish fact from opinion. Still, the Court does seem to set up its own test, a way of distinguishing "pure" opinion from opinions that imply factual statements.

## ■ *New York Times v. Sullivan*

### 376 U.S. 254 (1964)

*Justice Brennan delivered the opinion of the Court.*

We are required in this case to determine for the first time the extent to which the constitutional protections for speech and press limit a State's power to award damages in a libel action brought by a public official against critics of his official conduct. L. B. Sullivan is one of the three elected Commissioners of the City of Montgomery, Alabama. He brought this civil libel action against the four individual petitioners, who are Negroes and Alabama clergymen, and against petitioner the New York Times Company. A jury in the Circuit Court of Montgomery County awarded him damages of $500,000, the full amount claimed, against all the petitioners, and the Supreme Court of Alabama affirmed.

Respondent's complaint alleged that he had been libeled by statements in a full-page advertisement that was carried in the *New York Times* on March 29, 1960. Entitled "Heed Their Rising Voices," the advertisement began by stating that "As the whole world knows by now, thousands of Southern Negro students are engaged in widespread non-violent demonstrations in positive affirmation of the right to live in human dignity as guaranteed by the U.S. Constitution and the Bill of Rights." It went on to charge that "in their efforts to uphold these guarantees, they are being met by an unprecedented wave of terror by those who would deny and negate that document which the whole world looks upon as setting the pattern for modern freedom. . . ." Succeeding paragraphs purported to illustrate the "wave of terror" by describing certain alleged events. The text concluded with an appeal for funds for three purposes: support of the student movement, "the struggle for the right-to-vote," and the legal defense of Dr. Martin Luther King, Jr., leader of the movement, against a perjury indictment then pending in Montgomery.

The text appeared over the names of 64 persons, many widely known for their activities in public affairs, religion, trade unions, and the performing arts. Below these names, and under a line reading "We in the south who are struggling daily for dignity and freedom warmly endorse this appeal," appeared the names of the four individual petitioners and of 16 other persons, all but two of whom were identified as clergymen in various Southern cities. The advertisement was signed at the bottom of the page by the "Committee to Defend Martin Luther King and the Struggle for Freedom in the South," and the officers of the Committee were listed.

Of the 10 paragraphs of text in the advertisement, the third and a portion of the sixth were the basis of respondent's claim of libel. The third paragraph read:

> In Montgomery, Alabama, after students sang "My Country, 'Tis of Thee" on the State Capitol steps, their leaders were expelled from school, and truckloads of police armed with shotguns and tear-gas ringed the Alabama State College Campus. When the entire student body protested to state authorities by refusing to re-register, their dining hall was padlocked in an attempt to starve them into submission.

The sixth paragraph read:

> Again and again the Southern violators have answered Dr. King's peaceful protests with intimidation and violence. They have bombed his home almost killing his wife and child. They have assaulted his person. They have arrested him seven times—for "speeding," "loitering" and similar "offenses." And now they have charged him with "perjury"—a felony under which they could imprison him for ten years. . . .

Although neither of these statements mentions respondent by name, [respondent] contended that the word "police" in the third paragraph referred to him as the Montgomery Commissioner who supervised the Police Department, so that he was being accused of "ringing" the campus with police. He further claimed that the paragraph would be read as imputing to the police, and hence to him, the padlocking of the dining hall in order to starve the students into submission. As to the sixth paragraph, he contended that it [accused] the Montgomery police, and hence him, of answering Dr. King's protests with "intimidation and violence," bombing his home, assaulting his person, and charging him with perjury.

It is uncontroverted that some of the statements contained in the two paragraphs were not accurate descriptions of events which occurred in Montgomery. Although nine students were expelled by the State Board of Education, this was not for leading the demonstration at the Capitol, but for demanding service at a lunch counter in the Montgomery County Courthouse on another day. Not the entire student body, but most of it, had protested the expulsion, not by refusing to register, but by boycotting classes on a single day; virtually all the students did register for the ensuing semester. The campus dining hall was not padlocked on any occasion, and the only students who may have been barred from eating there were the few who had neither signed a preregistration application nor requested temporary meal tickets. Although the police were deployed near the campus in large numbers on three occasions, they did not at any time "ring" the campus, and they were not called to the campus in connection with the demonstration on the State Capitol steps, as the third paragraph implied. Dr. King had not been arrested seven times, but only four; and although he claimed to have been assaulted some years earlier in connection with his arrest for loitering outside a courtroom, one of the officers who made the arrest denied that there was such an assault.

On the premise that the charges in the sixth paragraph could be read as referring to him, respondent was allowed to prove that he had not participated in the events described. Although Dr. King's home had in fact been bombed twice when his wife and child were there, both of these occasions antedated respondent's tenure as Commissioner, and the police were not only not implicated in the bombings, but had made every effort to apprehend those who were. Three of Dr. King's four arrests took place before respondent became Commissioner. Although Dr. King had in fact been indicted (he was subsequently acquitted) on two counts of perjury, each of which carried a possible five-year sentence, respondent had nothing to do with procuring the indictment.

Respondent relies heavily, as did the Alabama courts, on statements of this Court to the effect that the Constitution does not protect libelous publications. Those statements do not foreclose our inquiry here. None of the cases sustained the use of libel laws to impose sanctions upon expression critical of the official conduct of public officials.

The general proposition that freedom of expression upon public questions is secured by the First Amendment has long been settled by our decisions. Thus we consider this case against the background of a profound national commitment to the principle that debate on public issues should be uninhibited, robust, and wide-open, and that it may well include vehement, caustic, and sometimes unpleasantly sharp attacks on government and public officials. The present advertisement, as an expression of grievance and protest on one of the major public issues of our time, would seem clearly to qualify for the constitutional protection. The question is whether it forfeits that protection by the falsity of some of its factual statements and by its alleged defamation of respondent. Authoritative interpretations of the First Amendment guarantees have consistently refused to recognize an exception for any test of truth—whether administered by judges, juries, or administrative officials—and especially one that puts the burden of proving truth on the speaker. Erroneous statement is inevitable in free debate, and it must be protected if the freedoms of expression are to have the breathing space that they need to survive.

Injury to official reputation affords no more warrant for repressing speech that would otherwise be free than does factual error. Where judicial officers are involved, this Court has held that concern for the dignity and reputation of the courts does not justify the punishment as criminal contempt of criticism of the judge or his decision. This is true even though the utterance contains half-truths and misinformation. Such repression can be justified, if at all, only by a clear and present danger of the obstruction of justice. If judges are to be treated as men of fortitude, able to thrive in a hardy climate, surely the same must be true of other government officials, such as elected city commissioners. Criticism of their official conduct does not lose its constitutional protection merely because it is effective criticism and hence diminishes their official reputations.

If neither factual error nor defamatory content suffices to remove the constitutional shield from criticism of official conduct, the combination of the two elements is no less inadequate. This is the lesson to be drawn from the great controversy over the Sedition Act of 1798, which first crystallized a national awareness of the central meaning of the First Amendment. Although the Sedition Act was never tested in this Court, the attack upon its validity has carried the day in the court of history. Fines levied in its prosecution were repaid by Act of Congress on the ground that it was unconstitutional. Jefferson, as President, pardoned those who had been convicted and sentenced under the Act and remitted their fines.

What a State may not constitutionally bring about by means of a criminal statute is likewise beyond the reach of its civil law of libel. The fear of damage awards under a rule such as that invoked by the Alabama courts here may be markedly more inhibiting than the fear of prosecution under a criminal statute. Alabama, for example, has a criminal libel law. Presumably a person charged with violation of this statute enjoys ordinary criminal-law safeguards such as the requirements of an indictment and of proof beyond a reasonable doubt. These safeguards are not available to the defendant in a civil action. The judgment awarded in this case—without the need for any proof of actual pecuniary loss—was one thousand times greater than the maximum fine provided by the Alabama criminal statute, and one hundred times greater than that provided by the Sedition Act. Whether or not a newspaper can survive a succession of such judgments, the pall of fear and timidity imposed upon those who would give voice to public criticism is an atmosphere in which the First Amendment freedoms cannot survive.

The state rule of law is not saved by its allowance of the defense of truth. A rule compelling the critic of official conduct to guarantee the truth of all his factual assertions—and to do so on pain of libel judgments virtually unlimited in amount—leads to self-censorship. Allowance of the defense of truth, with the burden of proving it on the defendant, does not mean that only false speech will be deterred. Under such a rule, would-be critics of official conduct may be deterred from voicing their criticism, even though it is believed to be true and even though it is in fact true, because of doubt whether it can be proved in court or fear of the expense of having to do so. The rule thus dampens the vigor and limits the variety of public debate.

The constitutional guarantees require, we think, a federal rule that prohibits a public official from recovering damages for a defamatory falsehood relating to his official conduct unless he proves that the statement was made with "actual malice"—that is, with knowledge that it was false or with reckless disregard of whether it was false or not. Such a privilege for criticism of official conduct is appropriately analogous to the protection accorded a public official when he is sued for libel by a private citizen. The reason for the official privilege is said to be that the threat of damage suits would otherwise inhibit the fearless, vigorous, and effective administration of policies of government and dampen the ardor of all but the most resolute, or the most irresponsible, in the unflinching discharge of their duties. Analogous considerations support the privilege for the citizen-critic of government. It is as much his duty to criticize as it is the official's duty to administer.

We have no occasion here to determine how far down into the lower ranks of government employees the "public official" designation would extend for purposes of this rule, or otherwise to specify categories of persons who would or would not be included. Nor need we here determine the boundaries of the "official conduct" concept. It is enough for the present case that respondent's position as an elected city commissioner clearly made him a public official, and that the allegations in the advertisement concerned what was allegedly his official conduct as Commissioner in charge of the Police Department.

We hold today that the Constitution delimits a State's power to award damages for libel in actions brought by public officials against critics of their official conduct. Since this is such an action, the rule requiring proof of actual malice is applicable. While Alabama law apparently requires proof of actual malice for an award of punitive damages, where general damages are concerned malice is "presumed." Such a presumption is inconsistent with the federal rule.

We consider that the proof presented to show actual malice lacks the convincing clarity which the constitutional standard demands, and hence that it would not constitutionally sustain the judgment for respondent under the proper rule of law. The case of the individual petitioners requires little discussion. Even assuming that they could constitutionally be found to have authorized the use of their names on the advertisement, there was no evidence whatever that they were aware of any erroneous statements or were in any way reckless in that regard. The judgment against them is thus without constitutional support. As to the *Times,* we similarly conclude that the facts do not support a finding of actual malice.

There is evidence that the *Times* published the advertisement without checking its accuracy against the news stories in the *Times'* own files. The mere presence of the stories in the files does not, of course, establish that the *Times* "knew" the advertisement was false, since the state of mind required for actual malice would have to be brought home to the persons in the *Times'* organization having responsibility for the publication of the advertisement. With respect to the failure of those persons to make the check, the record shows that they relied upon their knowledge of the good reputation of many of those whose names were listed as sponsors of the advertisement. There was testimony that the persons handling the advertisement saw nothing in it that would render it unacceptable under the *Times'* policy of rejecting advertisements containing "attacks of a personal character"; their failure to reject it on this ground was not unreasonable.

We think the evidence against the *Times* supports at most a finding of negligence in failing to discover the misstatements, and is constitutionally insufficient to show the recklessness that is required for a finding of actual malice.

We also think the evidence was constitutionally defective in another respect: it was incapable of supporting the jury's finding that the allegedly libelous statements were made "of and concerning" respondent. There was no reference to respondent in the advertisement, either by name or official position. A number of the allegedly libelous statements—the charges that the dining hall was padlocked and that Dr. King's home was bombed, his person assaulted, and a perjury prosecution instituted against him—did not even concern the police.

The judgment of the Supreme Court of Alabama is reversed and the case is remanded to that court for further proceedings not inconsistent with this opinion.

## Points for Discussion

1. Since very few libel defendants will ever admit that they went to press knowing that they would be printing falsehoods, public officials will need to prove that the defendant published with "reckless disregard of truth or falsity." What kinds of behaviors would or should constitute proof of such reckless disregard?

2. There is much talk these days about the importance of political candidates' "character." If the citizenry has a legitimate interest in their representatives' character, can there ever be criticisms of public officials that do *not* at least have important implications for their "official conduct"?

## ▉ *Gertz v. Welch, Inc.*

### 418 U.S. 323 (1974)

*Justice Powell delivered the opinion of the Court.*

In 1968 a Chicago policeman named Nuccio shot and killed a youth named Nelson. The state authorities prosecuted Nuccio for the homicide and ultimately obtained a conviction for murder in the second degree. The

Nelson family retained petitioner Elmer Gertz, a reputable attorney, to represent them in civil litigation against Nuccio.

Respondent publishes *American Opinion,* a monthly outlet for the views of the John Birch Society. In March 1969 respondent published [an] article under the title "FRAME-UP: Richard Nuccio And The War On Police." The article purports to demonstrate that the testimony against Nuccio at his criminal trial was false and that his prosecution was part of the Communist campaign against the police.

In his capacity as counsel for the Nelson family in the civil litigation, petitioner attended the coroner's inquest into the boy's death and initiated actions for damages, but he neither discussed Officer Nuccio with the press nor played any part in the criminal proceeding. Notwithstanding petitioner's remote connection with the prosecution of Nuccio, respondent's magazine portrayed him as an architect of the "frame-up." According to the article, the police file on petitioner took "a big, Irish cop to lift." The article stated that petitioner had been an official of the "Marxist League for Industrial Democracy, originally known as the Intercollegiate Socialist Society, which has advocated the violent seizure of our government." It labeled Gertz a "Leninist" and a "Communist-fronter." It also stated that Gertz had been an officer of the National Lawyers Guild, described as a Communist organization that "probably did more than any other outfit to plan the Communist attack on the Chicago police during the 1968 Democratic Convention."

These statements contained serious inaccuracies. The implication that petitioner had a criminal record was false. There was also no basis for the charge that petitioner was a "Leninist" or a "Communist-fronter." And he had never been a member of the "Marxist League for Industrial Democracy" or the "Intercollegiate Socialist Society."

Petitioner claimed that the falsehoods published by respondent injured his reputation as a lawyer and a citizen. Respondent asserted that petitioner was a public official or a public figure and that the article concerned an issue of public interest and concern. For these reasons, respondent argued, it was entitled to invoke the privilege enunciated in *New York Times Co. v. Sullivan,* under [which] respondent would escape liability unless petitioner could prove publication of defamatory falsehood with actual malice—that is, with knowledge that it was false or with reckless disregard of whether it was false or not.

The principal issue in this case is whether a newspaper or broadcaster that publishes defamatory falsehoods about an individual who is neither a public official nor a public figure may claim a constitutional privilege against liability for the injury inflicted by those statements.

We begin with the common ground. Under the First Amendment there is no such thing as a false idea. However pernicious an opinion may seem, we depend for its correction not on the conscience of judges and juries but on the competition of other ideas. But there is no constitutional value in false statements of fact. Neither the intentional lie nor the careless error materially advances society's interest in uninhibited, robust, and wide-open debate on public issues.

Although the erroneous statement of fact is not worthy of constitutional protection, it is nevertheless inevitable in free debate. And punishment of error runs the risk of inducing a cautious and restrictive exercise of the constitutionally guaranteed freedoms of speech and press. The need to avoid self-censorship by the news media is, however, not the only societal value at issue. If it were, this Court would have embraced long ago the view that publishers and broadcasters enjoy an unconditional and indefeasible immunity from liability for defamation. Such a rule would, indeed, obviate the fear that the prospect of civil liability for injurious falsehood might dissuade a timorous press from the effective exercise of First Amendment freedoms. Yet absolute protection for the communications media requires a total sacrifice of the competing value served by the law of defamation. The legitimate state interest underlying the law of libel is the compensation of individuals for the harm inflicted on them by defamatory falsehood. We would not lightly require the State to abandon this purpose.

Some tension necessarily exists between the need for a vigorous and uninhibited press and the legitimate interest in redressing wrongful injury. This Court has extended a measure of strategic protection to defamatory falsehood. The *New York Times* standard defines the level of constitutional protection appropriate to the context of defamation of a public person. Those who, by reason of the notoriety of their achievements or the vigor and success with which they seek the public's attention, are properly classed as public figures and those who hold governmental office may recover for injury to reputation only on clear and convincing proof that the defamatory falsehood was made with knowledge of its falsity or with reckless disregard for the truth. For the reasons stated below, we conclude that the state interest in compensating injury to the reputation of private individuals requires that a different rule should obtain with respect to them.

The first remedy of any victim of defamation is self-help—using available opportunities to contradict the lie or correct the error and thereby to minimize its adverse impact on reputation. Public officials and public figures usually enjoy significantly greater access to the channels of effective communication and hence have a more realistic opportunity to counteract false statements than private individuals normally enjoy. Private individuals are therefore more vulnerable to injury, and the state interest in protecting them is correspondingly greater.

More important than the likelihood that private individuals will lack effective opportunities for rebuttal, there is a compelling normative consideration underlying the distinction between public and private defamation plaintiffs. An individual who decides to seek governmental office must accept certain necessary consequences of that involvement in public affairs.

He runs the risk of closer public scrutiny than might otherwise be the case. Those classed as public figures stand in a similar position. Hypothetically, it may be possible for someone to become a public figure through no purposeful action of his own, but the instances of truly involuntary public figures must be exceedingly rare. For the most part those who attain this status have assumed roles of special prominence in the affairs of society. Some occupy positions of such persuasive power and influence that they are deemed public figures for all purposes. More commonly, those classed as public figures have thrust themselves to the forefront of particular public controversies in order to influence the resolution of the issues involved. In either event, they invite attention and comment.

A private individual has not accepted public office or assumed an influential role in ordering society, has relinquished no part of his interest in the protection of his own good name, and consequently he has a more compelling call on the courts for redress of injury inflicted by defamatory falsehood. Thus, private individuals are not only more vulnerable to injury than public officials and public figures; they are also more deserving of recovery.

For these reasons we conclude that the States should retain substantial latitude in their efforts to enforce a legal remedy for defamatory falsehood injurious to the reputation of a private individual. We hold that, so long as they do not impose liability without fault, the States may define for themselves the appropriate standard of liability for a publisher or broadcaster of defamatory falsehood injurious to a private individual.

The *New York Times* privilege [is not] wholly inapplicable to the context of private individuals. We hold that the States may not permit recovery of presumed or punitive damages, at least when liability is not based on a showing of knowledge of falsity or reckless disregard for the truth. The common law of defamation is an oddity of tort law, for it allows recovery of purportedly compensatory damages without evidence of actual loss. Under the traditional rules pertaining to actions for libel, the existence of injury is presumed from the fact of publication. Juries may award substantial sums as compensation for supposed damage to reputation without any proof that such harm actually occurred. The largely uncontrolled discretion of juries to award damages where there is no loss unnecessarily compounds the potential of any system of liability for defamatory falsehood to inhibit the vigorous exercise of First Amendment freedoms. Additionally, the doctrine of presumed damages invites juries to punish unpopular opinion rather than to compensate individuals for injury sustained by the publication of a false fact. More to the point, the States have no substantial interest in securing for plaintiffs such as this petitioner gratuitous awards of money damages far in excess of any actual injury.

It is necessary to restrict defamation plaintiffs who do not prove knowledge of falsity or reckless disregard for the truth to compensation for actual injury. We need not define "actual injury," as trial courts have wide experience in framing appropriate jury instructions in tort actions. Suffice it to say that actual injury is not limited to out-of-pocket loss. Indeed, the more customary types of actual harm inflicted by defamatory falsehood include impairment of reputation and standing in the community, personal humiliation, and mental anguish and suffering. There need be no evidence which assigns an actual dollar value to the injury.

We also find no justification for allowing awards of punitive damages against publishers and broadcasters held liable under state-defined standards of liability for defamation. In most jurisdictions jury discretion over the amounts awarded is limited only by the gentle rule that they not be excessive. Consequently, juries assess punitive damages in wholly unpredictable amounts bearing no necessary relation to the actual harm caused. And they remain free to use their discretion selectively to punish expressions of unpopular views. Punitive damages are not compensation for injury. Instead, they are private fines levied by civil juries to punish reprehensible conduct and to deter its future occurrence. In short, the private defamation plaintiff who establishes liability under a less demanding standard than that stated by *New York Times* may recover only such damages as are sufficient to compensate him for actual injury.

Notwithstanding our refusal to extend the *New York Times* privilege to defamation of private individuals, respondent contends that we should affirm the judgment below on the ground that petitioner is either a public official or a public figure. There is little basis for the former assertion. Several years prior to the present incident, petitioner had served briefly on housing committees appointed by the mayor of Chicago, but at the time of publication he had never held any remunerative governmental position. [The public figure] designation may rest on either of two alternative bases. In some instances an individual may achieve such pervasive fame or notoriety that he becomes a public figure for all purposes and in all contexts. More commonly, an individual voluntarily injects himself or is drawn into a particular public controversy and thereby becomes a public figure for a limited range of issues. In either case such persons assume special prominence in the resolution of public questions. Petitioner has long been active in community and professional affairs. He has served as an officer of local civic groups and of various professional organizations, and he has published several books and articles on legal subjects. Although petitioner was consequently well known in some circles, he had achieved no general fame or notoriety in the community. None of the prospective jurors called at the trial had ever heard of petitioner prior to this litigation, and respondent offered no proof that this response was atypical of the local population. We would not lightly assume that a citizen's participation in community and professional affairs rendered him a public figure for all purposes. Absent clear evidence of general fame or notoriety in the community, and pervasive involvement in the affairs of society, an individual should not be deemed a public personality for all aspects of his life. It is preferable to reduce the public-figure question to a more meaningful context by looking to the nature and extent of an individual's participation in the particular controversy giving rise to the defamation. In this context it is plain that petitioner was not a public figure. He played a minimal role at the coroner's inquest, and his participation related solely to his representation of a private client. He took no part in the criminal prosecution of Officer Nuccio. Moreover, he never discussed either the criminal or civil litigation with the press and was never quoted as having done so. He plainly did not thrust himself into the vortex of this public issue, nor did he engage the public's attention in an attempt to influence its outcome. We therefore conclude that the *New York Times* standard is inapplicable to this case.

### Points for Discussion

1. Justice Powell provides two reasons in support of making it very hard for public officials and public figures to win libel suits. One reason is that people choose to be public officials and typically become public figures as a result of their own actions. Clearly, one cannot become a public official involuntarily. But are instances of involuntary public figures as "exceedingly rare" as Justice Powell suggests?

2. The second reason Justice Powell offers for setting up obstacles to libel suits by public officials and public figures is that such persons have access to "self-help," that they can always call a press conference and the press will come. From the viewers' perspective, however, is there not a world of difference between seeing a public official's self-serving response to an allegedly defamatory article and learning that a neutral jury found that the article was libelous?

## ■ *Philadelphia Newspapers, Inc. v. Hepps*
### 475 U.S. 767 (1986)

*Justice O'Connor delivered the opinion of the court.*

This case requires us once more to struggle to define the proper accommodation between the law of defamation and the freedoms of speech and press protected by the First Amendment. In *Gertz v. Robert Welch, Inc.,* the Court held that a private figure who brings a suit for defamation cannot recover without some showing that the media defendant was at fault in publishing the statements at issue. Here, we hold that, at least where a newspaper publishes speech of public concern, a private-figure plaintiff cannot recover damages without also showing that the statements at issue are false.

Maurice S. Hepps is the principal stockholder of General Programming, Inc. (GPI), a corporation that franchises a chain of stores—known at the relevant time as "Thrifty" stores—selling beer, soft drinks, and snacks. Mr. Hepps, GPI, and a number of its franchises are the appellees here. Appellant Philadelphia Newspapers, Inc., owns the *Philadelphia Inquirer.* The *Inquirer* published a series of articles containing the statements at issue here. The general theme of the five articles, which appeared in the *Inquirer* between May 1975 and May 1976, was that appellees had links to organized crime and used some of those links to influence the State's governmental processes, both legislative and administrative. The articles discussed a state legislator, described as "a Pittsburgh Democrat and convicted felon," whose actions displayed "a clear pattern of interference in state government by [the legislator] on behalf of Hepps and Thrifty." The stories reported that federal "investigators have found connections between Thrifty and underworld figures," that "the Thrifty Beverage beer chain . . . had connections . . . with organized crime," and that Thrifty had "won a series of competitive advantages through rulings by the State Liquor Control Board." A grand jury was said to be investigating the "alleged relationship between the Thrifty chain and known Mafia figures," and "[whether] the chain received special treatment from the [state Governor's] administration and the Liquor Control Board."

Appellees brought suit for defamation against appellants in a Pennsylvania state court. Consistent with *Gertz,* Pennsylvania requires a private figure who brings a suit for defamation to bear the burden of proving negligence or malice by the defendant in publishing the statements at issue. As to falsity, Pennsylvania follows the common law's presumption that an individual's reputation is a good one. Statements defaming that person are therefore presumptively false, although a publisher who bears the burden of proving the truth of the statements has an absolute defense.

The parties first raised the issue of burden of proof as to falsity before trial, but the trial court reserved its ruling on the matter. Appellee Hepps testified at length that the statements at issue were false, and he extensively cross-examined the author of the stories as to the veracity of the statements at issue. After all the evidence had been presented by both sides, the trial court concluded that Pennsylvania's statute giving the defendant the burden of proving the truth of the statements violated the Federal Constitution. The trial court therefore instructed the jury that the plaintiffs bore the burden of proving falsity.

The Pennsylvania Supreme Court viewed *Gertz* as simply requiring the plaintiff to show fault in actions for defamation. It concluded that a showing of fault did not require a showing of falsity. We noted probable jurisdiction, and now reverse.

One can discern [from our prior decisions] two forces that may reshape the common-law landscape to conform to the First Amendment. The first is whether the plaintiff is a public official or figure, or is instead a private figure. The second is whether the speech at issue is of public concern. When the speech is of public concern and the plaintiff is a public official or public figure, the Constitution clearly requires the plaintiff to surmount a much higher barrier before recovering damages from a media defendant than is raised by the common law. When the speech is of public concern but the plaintiff is a private figure, as in *Gertz,* the Constitution still supplants the standards of the common law, but the constitutional requirements are, in at least some of their range, less forbidding than when the plaintiff is a public figure and the speech is of public concern. When the speech is of exclusively private concern and the plaintiff is a private figure, the constitutional requirements do not necessarily force any change in at least some of the features of the common-law landscape.

Here, as in *Gertz,* the plaintiff is a private figure and the newspaper articles are of public concern. In *Gertz,* as in *New York Times,* the common-law rule was superseded by a constitutional rule. We believe that the common law's rule on falsity—that the defendant must bear the burden of proving truth—must similarly fall here to a constitutional requirement that the plaintiff bear the burden of showing falsity, as well as fault, before recovering damages.

There will always be instances when the fact finding process will be unable to resolve conclusively whether the speech is true or false; it is in those cases that the burden of proof is dispositive. Under a rule forcing the plaintiff to bear the burden of showing falsity, there will be some cases in which plaintiffs cannot meet their burden despite the fact that the speech is in fact false. The plaintiff's suit will fail despite the fact that, in some abstract sense, the suit is meritorious. Similarly, under an alternative rule placing the burden of showing truth on defendants, there would be some cases in which defendants could not bear their burden despite the fact that the speech is in fact true. Those suits would succeed despite the fact that, in some abstract sense, those suits are unmeritorious. Under either rule, then, the outcome of the suit will sometimes be at variance with the outcome that we would desire if all speech were either demonstrably true or demonstrably false.

This dilemma stems from the fact that the allocation of the burden of proof will determine liability for some speech that is true and some that is false, but all of such speech is unknowably true or false. Because the burden of proof is the deciding factor only when the evidence is ambiguous, we cannot know how much of the speech affected by the allocation of the burden of proof is true and how much is false. In a case presenting a configuration of speech and plaintiff like the one we face here, and where the scales are in such an uncertain balance, we believe that the Constitution requires us to tip them in favor of protecting true speech. To ensure that true speech on matters of public concern is not deterred, we hold that the common-law presumption that defamatory speech is false cannot stand when a plaintiff seeks damages against a media defendant for speech of public concern. We note that our decision adds only marginally to the burdens that the plaintiff must already bear as a result of our earlier decisions in the law of defamation. The plaintiff must show fault. A jury is obviously more likely to accept a plaintiff's contention that the defendant was at fault in publishing the statements at issue if convinced that the relevant statements were false. As a practical matter, then, evidence offered by plaintiffs on the publisher's fault in adequately investigating the truth of the published statements will generally encompass evidence of the falsity of the matters asserted.

We have no occasion to consider the quantity of proof of falsity that a private-figure plaintiff must present to recover damages. Nor need we consider what standards would apply if the plaintiff sues a nonmedia defendant, or if a State were to provide a plaintiff with the opportunity to obtain a judgment that declared the speech at issue to be false but did not give rise to liability for damages.

For the reasons stated above, the judgment of the Pennsylvania Supreme Court is reversed, and the case is remanded for further proceedings not inconsistent with this opinion.

## Points for Discussion

1. The *Hepps* case tells us that three variables determine much of the First Amendment's impact on libel law: who is the plaintiff (public official/figure or private citizen?), who is the defendant (media or nonmedia?), and what was the topic of the allegedly libelous remark (a topic of public or private interest?). These variables create a 2 × 2 × 2 matrix of sorts, as if all libel scenarios can be sorted into eight "boxes." Which one of those eight boxes is most directly affected by the *Hepps* ruling itself?

2. Justice O'Connor suggests that libel plaintiffs who are already required to prove actual malice must thus surely also have proven falsity. After all, it makes no sense to publish the *truth* "with reckless disregard for truth or falsity." Can't the same also be said of the lesser burden of proof demanded of private plaintiffs? Does it make sense to be punished for "negligently" publishing the truth?

## ■ *Ollman v. Evans*

**750 F.2d 970 (D.C. Cir. 1984)**

*Judge Starr:*

This defamation action arises out of the publication of a syndicated column by Rowland Evans and Robert Novak in May 1978. The question before us is whether the allegedly defamatory statements set forth in the column are constitutionally protected expressions of opinion or, as appellant contends, actionable assertions of fact. We conclude, as did the District Court, that the challenged statements are entitled to absolute First Amendment protection as expressions of opinion.

Rowland Evans and Robert Novak are nationally syndicated columnists whose columns appear regularly in newspapers across the country. According to the complaint in this case, which was filed by plaintiff Bertell Ollman on February 15, 1979, an Evans and Novak column appeared on or about May 4, 1978 in The *Washington Post* and other newspapers across the Nation. Ollman is a professor of political science at New York University. In March 1978, Mr. Ollman was nominated by a departmental search committee to head the Department of Government and Politics at the University of Maryland. The committee's recommendation was duly approved by the Provost of the University and the Chancellor of the College Park campus.

The Evans and Novak column begins as follows: "What is in danger of becoming a frivolous public debate over the appointment of a Marxist to head the University of Maryland's department of politics and government has so far ignored this unspoken concern within the academic community: the avowed desire of many political activists to use higher education for indoctrination." It goes on to state that "the proposal to name Bertell Ollman, Professor at New York University, as department head has generated wrong-headed debate. Politicians who jumped in to oppose Ollman simply for his Marxist philosophy have received a justifiable going-over from defenders of academic freedom in the press and the university. Academic Prince Valiants seem arrayed against McCarthyite know-nothings."

With these opening two paragraphs as lead-in, the authors then pose what they deemed the pivotal issue in the debate: "But neither side approaches the crucial question: not Ollman's beliefs, but his intentions. His candid writings avow his desire to use the classroom as an instrument for preparing what he calls 'the revolution.' Whether this is a form of indoctrination that could transform the real function of a university and transcend limits of academic freedom is a concern to academicians who are neither McCarthyite nor know-nothing."

The columnists thus, in the first three paragraphs, articulated a view of what should be the central question in what they viewed as a fruitless debate. The authors then go on in the next paragraph to state: "to protect academic freedom, that question should be posed not by politicians but by professors. But professors throughout the country troubled by the nomination, clearly a minority, dare not say a word in today's campus climate."

With this observation, the authors turn in the following six paragraphs to a discussion of Mr. Ollman and his writings. Evans and Novak state that "while Ollman is described in news accounts as a 'respected Marxist scholar,' he is widely viewed in his profession as a political activist. Amid the increasingly popular Marxist movement in university life, he is distinct from philosophical Marxists. Rather, he is an outspoken proponent of 'political Marxism.' "

The authors next relate Mr. Ollman's two unsuccessful efforts to win election to membership on the council of the American Political Science Association. In these elections, the column states (and appellant does not dispute) that Professor Ollman ran as a candidate of the Caucus for a New Political Science and finished last out of sixteen candidates each time. "Whether or not that represents a professional judgment by his colleagues, as some critics contend, the verdict clearly rejected his campaign pledge: 'If elected . . . I shall use every means at my disposal to promote the study of Marxism and Marxist approaches to politics throughout the profession.' "

Evans and Novak then direct the four ensuing paragraphs of the column to a summary of an article by Mr. Ollman, entitled "On Teaching Marxism and Building the Movement" in the Winter 1978 issue of *New Political Science Record.* In this article, Mr. Ollman claims that most students conclude his political science course with a "Marxist outlook." The authors go on: "Ollman concedes that will be seen 'as an admission that the purpose of my course is to convert students to socialism.' That bothers him not at all because 'a correct understanding of Marxism (as indeed of any body of scientific truths) leads automatically to its acceptance.' The classroom is a place where the students' bourgeois ideology is being dismantled. 'Our prior task' before the revolution, he writes, 'is to make more revolutionaries.' "

Moving to a brief discussion of Mr. Ollman's principal work, *Alienation: Marx's Conception of Man in Capitalist Society,* the authors described the work as "a ponderous tome in adoration of the master." This brings the columnists to the last statement specifically identified in the complaint as defamatory: "Such pamphleteering is hooted at by one political scientist in a major eastern university, whose scholarship and reputation as a liberal are well known. 'Ollman has no status within the profession, but is a pure and simple activist,' he said. Would he say that publicly? 'No chance of it. Our academic culture does not permit the raising of such questions.' "

On May 19, 1978, Mr. Ollman's lawyer wrote to Evans and Novak demanding retraction of the allegedly defamatory statements in the column. This Evans and Novak refused to do. On May 8, however, only four days after the Evans and Novak column appeared, The *Washington Post* published a letter from Mr. Ollman. In this letter, Professor Ollman rejected the allegation that he used the classroom to indoctrinate students and set the column's quotations from his writings in what he viewed as their proper context.

The District Court granted Evans and Novak's motion for summary judgment, concluding that the column simply reflected the columnists' opinion and their "interpretation of [Mr. Ollman's] writings," absolutely protected by the First Amendment. This appeal followed.

This case presents us with the delicate and sensitive task of accommodating the First Amendment's protection of free expression of ideas with the common law's protection of an individual's interest in reputation. The judiciary's task in accommodating these competing interests is by no means new: at common law, the fair comment doctrine bestowed qualified immunity from libel actions as to certain types of opinions in order that writers could express freely their views about subjects of public interest.

In *Gertz,* the Supreme Court in dicta seemed to provide absolute immunity from defamation actions for all opinions and to discern the basis for this immunity in the First Amendment. The Court began its analysis of the case by stating: "Under the First Amendment there is no such thing as a false idea. However pernicious an opinion may seem, we depend for its correction not on the conscience of judges and juries but on the competition of other ideas." By this statement, *Gertz* elevated to constitutional principle the distinction between fact and opinion, which at common law had formed the basis of the doctrine of fair comment. However, the Supreme Court provided little guidance in *Gertz* itself as to the manner in which the distinction between fact and opinion is to be discerned. With largely uncharted seas having been left in *Gertz*'s wake, the lower federal courts and state courts have, not surprisingly, fashioned various approaches in attempting to articulate the *Gertz*-mandated distinction between fact and opinion. Some courts have, in effect, eschewed any effort to construct a theory and simply treated the distinction between fact and opinion as a judgment call. Other courts have concentrated on a single factor, such as the verifiability of the allegedly defamatory statement. Still others have adopted a multi-factor test, attempting to assess the allegedly defamatory proposition in the totality of the circumstances in which it appeared.

In formulating a test to distinguish between fact and opinion, courts are admittedly faced with a dilemma. Because of the richness and diversity of language, as evidenced by the capacity of the same words to convey different meanings in different contexts, it is quite impossible to lay down a bright-line or mechanical distinction. Judicial decisions, however, that represent mere ad hoc judgments or which, in contrast, lay down rules of excessive complexity may deter publication of the very opinions which the *Gertz*-mandated distinction is designed to protect, inasmuch as potential speakers or writers would, under such regimes, be at a loss to predict what courts will ultimately deem to be opinion. While this dilemma admits of no easy resolution, we think it obliges us to state plainly the factors that guide us in distinguishing fact from opinion and to demonstrate how these factors lead to a proper accommodation between the competing interests in free expression of opinion and in an individual's reputation.

While courts are divided in their methods of distinguishing between assertions of fact and expressions of opinion, they are universally agreed that the task is a difficult one. To be sure, paradigm examples of statements of fact, on the one hand, and paradigm examples of expressions of opinion, on the other, can be contrasted. Clearly, in the former category are assertions that describe present or past conditions capable of being known through sense impressions. It is rather hard to imagine a context in which the statement, "Mr. Jones had ten drinks at his office party and sideswiped two vehicles on his way home," could be deemed to be a statement of opinion. At the other extreme are evaluative statements reflecting the author's political, moral, or aesthetic views, not the author's sense perceptions. A statement such as, "Mr. Jones is a despicable politician," is a paradigm of opinion.

It is a fitting illustration of the complexity of language and communication that many statements from which actions for defamation arise do not clearly fit into either category. These statements pose more subtle problems and are the stuff of which litigation is made. The principal difficulty arises from statements that on first analysis seem to be based upon perceptions of events, but are not themselves simply a record of those perceptions. Such statements may imply in some contexts the existence of facts not disclosed by the author. An example of such a statement, is: "Mr. Jones is an alcoholic."

The degree to which such kinds of statements have real factual content can, of course, vary greatly. We believe, in consequence, that courts should analyze the totality of the circumstances in which the statements are made to decide whether they merit the absolute First Amendment protection enjoyed by opinion. To evaluate the totality of the circumstances of an allegedly defamatory statement, we will consider four factors in assessing whether the average reader would view the statement as fact or, conversely, opinion. While necessarily imperfect, these factors will, we are persuaded, assist in discerning as systematically as possible what constitutes an assertion of fact and what is, in contrast, an expression of opinion.

First, we will analyze the common usage or meaning of the specific language of the challenged statement itself. Our analysis of the specific language under scrutiny will be aimed at determining whether the statement has a precise core of meaning for which a consensus of understanding exists or, conversely, whether the statement is indefinite and ambiguous. Readers are, in our judgment, considerably less likely to infer facts from an indefinite or ambiguous statement than one with a commonly understood meaning.

Second, we will consider the statement's verifiability—is the statement capable of being objectively characterized as true or false? Insofar as a statement lacks a plausible method of verification, a reasonable reader will not believe that the statement has specific factual content. And, in the setting of litigation, the trier of fact obliged in a defamation action to assess the truth of an unverifiable statement will have considerable difficulty returning a verdict based upon anything but speculation.

Third, moving from the challenged language itself, we will consider the full context of the statement—the entire article or column, for example—inasmuch as other, unchallenged language surrounding the allegedly defamatory statement will influence the average reader's readiness to infer that a particular statement has factual content.

Finally, we will consider the broader context or setting in which the statement appears. Different types of writing have, as we shall more fully see, widely varying social conventions which signal to the reader the likelihood of a statement's being either fact or opinion.

The first factor of our inquiry is to analyze the common usage or meaning of the allegedly defamatory words themselves. We seek in this branch of our analysis to determine whether the allegedly defamatory statement has a precise meaning and thus is likely to give rise to clear factual implications. A classic example of a statement with a well-defined meaning is an accusation of a crime. To be sure, such accusations are not records of sense perceptions. Quite to the contrary, they depend for their meaning upon social normative systems. But those norms are so commonly understood that the statements are seen by the reasonable reader or hearer as implying highly damaging facts.

On the other hand, statements that are loosely definable or variously interpretable cannot in most contexts support an action for defamation. In one case, a writer in his book on the political right in the United States accused columnist and author William F. Buckley, Jr., of being a "fellow traveler" of "fascists." Noting that Mr. Buckley and the author of this particular tome embraced widely different definitions of "fascism" and different views as to which journals could be described as "fascist," the court declined to develop a "correct" definition of this pivotal term.

Courts should, secondly, consider the degree to which the statements are verifiable—is the statement objectively capable of proof or disproof? The reason for this inquiry is simple: a reader cannot rationally view an unverifiable statement as conveying actual facts. Moreover, insofar as a statement is unverifiable, the First Amendment is endangered when attempts are made to prove the statement true or false. Lacking a clear method of verification with which to evaluate a statement, the trier of fact may improperly tend to render a decision based upon approval or disapproval of the contents of the statement, its author, or its subject. In making this observation, we imply no criticism of a jury's ability to find facts, if facts are to be found. The rule against allowing unverifiable statements to go to the jury is, in actuality, merely one of many rules in tort law that prevent the jury from rendering a verdict based on speculation.

Needless to say, it will often be difficult to assay whether a statement is verifiable. But even if the principle of inquiring as to verifiability provides no panacea, this approach will nonetheless aid trial judges in assessing whether a statement should have the benefit of the absolute privilege conferred upon expressions of opinion.

Courts should, thirdly, examine the context in which the statement occurs. Readers will inevitably be influenced by a statement's context, and the distinction between fact and opinion can therefore be made only in context. The degree to which a statement is laden with factual content or can be read to imply facts depends upon the article or column, taken as a whole, of which the statement is a part. The language of the entire column may signal that a specific statement which, standing alone, would appear to be factual is in actuality a statement of opinion.

Courts should examine, finally, the broader social context into which the statement fits. Some types of writing or speech by custom or convention signal to readers or listeners that what is being read or heard is likely to be opinion, not fact. It is one thing to be assailed as a corrupt public official by a soapbox orator and quite another to be labeled corrupt in a research monograph detailing the causes and cures of corruption in public service. This observation reflects no novel principle. The Supreme Court [once said of] the word "traitor" as applied to an employee who crossed a picket line, that "such exaggerated rhetoric was commonplace in labor disputes." In the same vein, [other courts have] observed that statements [appearing] on the editorial page [will more likely be seen as opinions than if they] appeared on the front page.

After deciding that a particular statement is opinion rather than fact, courts often undertake a second mode of analysis before wrapping the statement in the mantle of the First Amendment's opinion privilege—whether the opinion implies the existence of undisclosed facts as the basis for the opinion. If the opinion implied factual assertions, courts have held that it should not receive the benefit of First Amendment protection as an opinion. In our view, however, the tests already articulated are a sufficient aid in determining whether a statement implies the existence of undisclosed facts. The definiteness and verifiability of a statement (factors one and two) clearly bear on the ability of a statement to carry factual implications. The linguistic and social context of the statement (factors three and four) will also influence the average reader's readiness to infer from the statement the existence of undisclosed facts. Thus, once our inquiry into whether the statement is an assertion of fact or expression of opinion has concluded, the factors militating either in favor of or against the drawing of factual implications from any statement have already been identified.

Now we turn to the case at hand to apply the foregoing analysis. As we have seen, Mr. Ollman alleges various instances of defamation in the Evans and Novak column. Before analyzing each such instance, we will first examine the context (the third and fourth factors in our approach) in which the alleged defamations arise. We will then assess the manner in which this context would influence the average reader in interpreting the alleged defamations as an assertion of fact or an expression of opinion.

The reasonable reader who peruses an Evans and Novak column on the editorial or Op-Ed page is fully aware that the statements found there are not "hard" news like those printed on the front page or elsewhere in the news sections of the newspaper. Readers expect that columnists will make strong statements, sometimes phrased in a polemical manner that would hardly be considered balanced or fair elsewhere in the newspaper. That proposition is inherent in the very notion of an "Op-Ed page." Because of obvious space limitations, it is also manifest that columnists or commentators will express themselves in condensed fashion without providing what might be considered the full picture. Columnists are, after all, writing a column, not a full-length scholarly article or a book. Of course, we do not hold that any statement on an editorial or Op-Ed page is constitutionally privileged opinion. While such a rule would have the advantage of simplicity and clarity, it could too readily become a license to libel. Even when situated on the editorial page the statement "Mr. Jones had ten drinks at his office party and sideswiped two vehicles on his way home" would obviously be construed as a factual statement.

A reader of this particular Evans and Novak column would also have been influenced by the column's express purpose. The columnists laid squarely before the reader their interest in ending what they deemed a "frivolous" debate among politicians over whether Mr. Ollman's political beliefs should bar him from becoming head of the Department of Government and Politics at the University of Maryland. Instead, the authors plainly intimated in the column's lead paragraph that they wanted to spark a more appropriate debate within academia over whether Mr. Ollman's purpose in teaching was to indoctrinate his students. Later in the column, they openly questioned the measure or method of Professor Ollman's scholarship. Evans and Novak made it clear that they were not purporting to set forth definitive conclusions, but instead meant to ventilate what in their view constituted the central questions raised by Mr. Ollman's prospective appointment.

We turn next to the alleged defamation that, in our view, is most clearly opinion, namely that "[Ollman] is an outspoken proponent of political Marxism." This is unmistakably a loosely definable, variously interpretable statement of opinion. It is obviously unverifiable. Since Mr. Ollman concedes that he is a Marxist, the trier of fact in assessing the statement would have the dubious task of trying to distinguish "political Marxism" from "nonpolitical Marxism," whatever that may be.

Nor is the statement that "[Mr. Ollman] is widely viewed in his profession as a political activist" a representation or assertion of fact. "Political activist" is a term, like "political Marxism," that is hopelessly imprecise and indefinite. While Mr. Ollman argues that this assertion is defamatory since it implies that he has no reputation as a scholar, we are rather skeptical of the strength of that implication, particularly in the context of this column. It does not appear the least bit evident that "scholarship" and "political activism" are generally understood to be incompatible.

Next we turn to Mr. Ollman's complaints about the column's quotations from and remarks about his writings, and specifically his article, "On Teaching Marxism and Building the Movement." When a critic is commenting about a book, the reader is on notice that the critic is engaging in interpretation, an inherently subjective enterprise, and therefore realizes that others, including the author, may utterly disagree with the critic's interpretation. The average reader further understands that because of limitations of space, not to mention those limitations imposed by the patience of the prospective audience, the critic as a practical matter will be able to support his opinion only by rather truncated quotations from the book or work under scrutiny. The reader is thus predisposed to view what the critic writes as opinion.

Mr. Ollman also complains of the statement: "His candid writings avow his desire to use the classroom as an instrument for preparing what he calls the 'revolution'." It is clear from the context that the statement represents Evans' and Novak's interpretation of Mr. Ollman's writing. It does not have a well-defined meaning or admit of a method of proof or disproof. What to one person is a patently improper use of the classroom for political purposes may represent to another no more than the imparting of ideas, in the faith that ideas have consequences.

Finally, we turn to the most troublesome statement in the column. In the third-to-last paragraph, an anonymous political science professor is quoted as saying: "Ollman has no status within the profession but is a pure and simple activist." Certainly a scholar's academic reputation among his peers is crucial to his or her career. Like the peripatetic philosophers of ancient Greece, modern scholars depend upon their reputation to enable them to pursue their chosen calling. We are of the view, however, that under the constitutionally based opinion privilege announced in *Gertz,* this quotation, under the circumstances before us, is protected. Inasmuch as the column appears on the Op-Ed page, the average reader will be influenced by the general understanding of the functions of such columns and read the remark to be opinion. In addition, the thrust of the column, taken as a whole, is to raise questions about Mr. Ollman's scholarship and intentions, not to state conclusively from Evans' and Novak's first-hand knowledge that Professor Ollman is not a scholar or that his colleagues do not regard him as such. Moreover, the anonymous professor's unflattering comment appears only after the columnists expressly state that Mr. Ollman is a professor at New York University, a highly respected academic institution, a fact which provides objective evidence of Mr. Ollman's "status." So too, the controversy itself was occasioned by Professor Ollman's nomination by the departmental search committee as chairman of an academic department at the University of Maryland, a fact stated in the column's opening paragraph which also plainly suggested to the average reader that Professor Ollman did in fact enjoy some considerable status in academia. Finally in this regard, the column expressly states that Professor Ollman's imminent ascension to the departmental chairmanship at Maryland was troubling only to a clear minority of academics. Thus, the charge of "no status" in this context would plainly appear to the average reader to be "rhetorical hyperbole," and which in turn would lead the reader to treat the statement as one of opinion.

The judgment of the District Court is therefore affirmed.

### Points for Discussion

1. Evans and Novak attributed to a liberal political scientist the belief that Ollman has "no status" in his field. Judge Starr concluded this was a matter of opinion. But might it be seen as a factual, empirical statement concerning how many political scientists respect or disparage Ollman's research? What if a survey were conducted of the American Political Scientists Association's membership on this issue?

2. The last of Judge Starr's four criteria for distinguishing facts from opinions is the larger social context surrounding the alleged libel. Thus, assertions appearing in editorials and op-ed pieces are more likely to be seen as opinions than they would if printed on the front page. Does this also mean that supermarket tabloids are or should be more protected from libel suits than more "serious" newspapers? After all, we *expect* to find outlandish charges in the tabloids.

### ■ *Milkovich v. Lorain Journal Co.*

**497 U.S. 1 (1990)**

*Chief Justice Rehnquist delivered the opinion of the Court.*

Respondent J. Theodore Diadiun authored an article in an Ohio newspaper implying that petitioner Michael Milkovich, a local high school wrestling coach, lied under oath in a judicial proceeding about an incident involving petitioner and his team which occurred at a wrestling match. Petitioner sued Diadiun and the newspaper for libel, and the Ohio Court of Appeals affirmed a lower court entry of summary judgment against petitioner. This judgment was based in part on the grounds that the article constituted an "opinion" protected from the reach of state defamation law by the First Amendment to the United States Constitution. We hold that the First Amendment does not prohibit the application of Ohio's libel laws to the alleged defamations contained in the article.

Milkovich, now retired, was the wrestling coach at Maple Heights High School in Maple Heights, Ohio. In 1974, his team was involved in an altercation at a home wrestling match with a team from Mentor High School. Several people were injured. In response to the incident, the Ohio High School Athletic Association (OHSAA) held a hearing at which Milkovich and H. Don Scott, the Superintendent of Maple Heights Public Schools, testified. Following the hearing, OHSAA placed the Maple Heights team on probation for a year and declared the team ineligible for the 1975 state tournament. OHSAA also censured Milkovich for his actions during the altercation. Thereafter, several parents and wrestlers sued OHSAA in the Court of Common Pleas of Franklin County, Ohio, seeking a restraining order against OHSAA's ruling on the grounds that they had been denied due process in the OHSAA proceeding. Both Milkovich and Scott testified in that proceeding. The court overturned OHSAA's probation and ineligibility orders on due process grounds.

The day after the court rendered its decision, respondent Diadiun's column appeared in the *News-Herald,* a newspaper which circulates in Lake County, Ohio, and is owned by respondent Lorain Journal Co. The column bore the heading "Maple beat the law with the 'big lie,' " beneath which appeared Diadiun's photograph and the words "TD Says." The carryover page headline announced " . . . Diadiun says Maple told a lie." The column contained the following:

> [A] lesson was learned (or relearned) yesterday by the student body of Maple Heights High School, and by anyone who attended the Maple-Mentor wrestling meet of last Feb. 8. A lesson which, sadly, in view of the events of the past year, is well they learned early. It is simply this: If you get in a jam, lie your way out. If you're successful enough, and powerful enough, and can sound sincere enough, you stand an excellent chance of making the lie stand up, regardless of what really happened. The teachers responsible were mainly head Maple wrestling coach, Mike Milkovich, and former superintendent of schools H. Donald Scott.
>
> Anyone who attended the meet, whether he be from Maple Heights, Mentor, or impartial observer, knows in his heart that Milkovich and Scott lied at the hearing after each having given his solemn oath to tell the truth. Is that the kind of lesson we want our young people learning from their high school administrators and coaches?

Respondents would have us recognize First-Amendment-based protection for defamatory statements which are categorized as "opinion" as opposed to "fact." For this proposition they rely principally on the following dictum from our opinion in *Gertz v. Welch:* "Under the First Amendment there is no such thing as a false idea. However pernicious an opinion may seem, we depend for its correction not on the conscience of judges and juries but on the competition of other ideas." Read in context, though, the fair meaning of the passage is to equate the word "opinion" in the second sentence with the word "idea" in the first sentence. We do not think this passage from *Gertz* was intended to create a wholesale defamation exemption for anything that might be labeled "opinion." Not only would such an interpretation be contrary to the tenor and context of the passage, but it would also ignore the fact that expressions of "opinion" may often imply an assertion of objective fact.

If a speaker says, "In my opinion John Jones is a liar," he implies a knowledge of facts which lead to the conclusion that Jones told an untruth. Even if the speaker states the facts upon which he bases his opinion, if those facts are either incorrect or incomplete, or if his assessment of them is erroneous, the statement may still imply a false assertion of fact. Simply couching such statements in terms of opinion does not dispel these implications; and the statement, "In my opinion Jones is a liar," can cause as much damage to reputation as the statement, "Jones is a liar."

Respondents contend that in every defamation case the First Amendment mandates an inquiry into whether a statement is "opinion" or "fact," and that only the latter statements may be actionable. But we [see no need to create] an artificial dichotomy between "opinion" and fact. Foremost, we think [*Philadelphia Newspapers, Inc. v.*] *Hepps* stands for the proposition that a statement on matters of public concern must be provable as false before there can be liability under state defamation law, at least in situations, like the present, where a media defendant is involved. Thus, unlike the statement, "In my opinion Mayor Jones is a liar," the statement, "In my opinion Mayor Jones shows his abysmal ignorance by accepting the teachings of Marx and Lenin," would not be actionable. *Hepps* ensures that a statement of opinion relating to matters of public concern which does not contain a provably false factual connotation will receive full constitutional protection. [And later precedents] provide protection for statements that cannot reasonably be interpreted as stating actual facts about an individual. [Also], where a statement of "opinion" on a matter of public concern reasonably implies false and defamatory facts regarding public figures or officials, those individuals must show that such statements were made with knowledge of their false implications or with reckless disregard of their truth. Similarly, where such a statement involves a private figure on a matter of public concern, a plaintiff must show that the false connotations were made with some level of fault.

We are not persuaded that, in addition to these protections, an additional separate constitutional privilege for "opinion" is required to ensure the freedom of expression guaranteed by the First Amendment. The dispositive question in the present case then becomes whether a reasonable fact finder could conclude that the statements in the Diadiun column imply an assertion that petitioner Milkovich perjured himself in a judicial proceeding. We think this question must be answered in the affirmative. As the Ohio Supreme Court itself observed: "The clear impact in some nine sentences and a caption is that [Milkovich] lied at the hearing after . . . having given his solemn oath to tell the truth." This is not the sort of loose, figurative, or hyperbolic language which would negate the impression that the writer was seriously maintaining that petitioner committed the crime of perjury. Nor does the general tenor of the article negate this impression.

We also think the connotation that petitioner committed perjury is sufficiently factual to be susceptible of being proved true or false. A determination whether petitioner lied in this instance can be made on a core of objective evidence by comparing, *inter alia,* petitioner's testimony before the OHSAA board with his subsequent testimony before the trial court.

The judgment of the Ohio Court of Appeals is reversed, and the case is remanded for further proceedings not inconsistent with this opinion.

## Points for Discussion

1. A speaker who says, "In my opinion Jones is a liar," Chief Justice Rehnquist says, implies that she has some factual basis (not disclosed to us) for this belief. What if that factual basis were disclosed? Suppose, for example, a person said, "I think Jones just lied to me. He claims he is thirty-nine, but to me he looks well over fifty." Should such an utterance be protected opinion? Can it be, under the rules Rehnquist gives us in the *Milkovich* case?

2. When the *Lorain Journal* columnist surmised that Milkovich likely had perjured himself, is that conclusion based on any facts undisclosed to the column's readers? If not, and if the columnist is merely expressing a hunch, a conjecture, based on facts that he openly discloses to readers, should the accusation be an actionable libel? What if the columnist had simply reminded readers about the sanctions against the wrestling team (and that they were lifted soon after Milkovich's testimony) and then claimed only to "wonder what the coach said to the grand jury." Would this not at least imply that Milkovich had perjured himself? Should the subtlety of the accusation make a difference?

# 5

## *Invasions of Privacy*

Compared with libel, invasion of privacy cases are relative newcomers to the American scene. Their birth is often attributed to an 1890 *Harvard Law Review* article written by Boston attorney Samuel Warren and his law partner, Louis Brandeis (later to achieve fame as a U.S. Supreme Court justice). Seventy years later, Dean William Prosser of the University of California Law School reviewed the development of privacy law and determined that it had grown into four distinct civil actions, or torts.

- The *false light* tort is highly similar to libel except that the revelation about the plaintiff need not be defamatory. The first case in this chapter—*Time, Inc. v. Hill,* a 1967 Supreme Court decision—emphasizes this feature of the tort.
- The *public disclosure* tort is distinguishable from libel in that the revelations are true (although embarrassing). The plaintiff in *Neff v. Time, Inc.* complains of being "revealed" not through prose but through a candid photograph of him in a state of partial undress. The case also involves elements of the misappropriation tort, described below.
- The *intrusion* tort is the only one of the four that does not require publication to be actionable. The action, similar to trespass, typically alleges that the defendant has intruded on the plaintiff's personal space, her zone of privacy (such as in following her around incessantly, camera in hand). The radio news reporter in *Holman v. Central Arkansas Broadcasting Company* did not use a roving microphone. He did not need to because his subject, being held in jail on a DUI charge, could not escape.
- The *misappropriation* tort involves the unauthorized use of another's name or "likeness" (e.g., his or her voice, or photo) for commercial purposes. When the plaintiff's main grievance is not having been paid for the use, the tort is sometimes referred to as the **right of publicity.** This chapter concludes with two such cases. *Zacchini v. Scripps-Howard Broadcasting Company* is the Supreme Court's only foray into this area

of law, and commentators have generally agreed that the unusual facts of the case make its precedential value limited. Finally, in *White v. Samsung Electronics America, Inc.,* TV game show personality Vanna White expressed her displeasure with a TV commercial's homage to her on-screen persona.

## *Time, Inc. v. Hill*

385 U.S. 374 (1967)

*Justice Brennan delivered the opinion of the Court.*

The question in this case is whether appellant, publisher of *Life* Magazine, was denied constitutional protections of speech and press by the application of the New York Civil Rights Law to award appellee damages on allegations that *Life* falsely reported that a new play portrayed an experience suffered by appellee and his family.

The article appeared in *Life* in February 1955. It was entitled "True Crime Inspires Tense Play," with the subtitle, "The ordeal of a family trapped by convicts gives Broadway a new thriller, '*The Desperate Hours.*'" The text of the article reads as follows:

> Three years ago Americans all over the country read about the desperate ordeal of the James Hill family, who were held prisoners in their home outside Philadelphia by three escaped convicts. Later they read about it in Joseph Hayes' novel, *The Desperate Hours,* inspired by the family's experience. Now they can see the story re-enacted in Hayes's Broadway play based on the book, and next year will see it in his movie, which has been filmed but is being held up until the play has a chance to pay off.
>
> The play, directed by Robert Montgomery and expertly acted, is a heart-stopping account of how a family rose to heroism in a crisis. LIFE photographed the play during its Philadelphia tryout, transported some of the actors to the actual house where the Hills were besieged.

The pictures on the ensuing two pages included an enactment of the son being "roughed up" by one of the convicts, entitled "brutish convict," a picture of the daughter biting the hand of a convict to make him drop a gun, entitled "daring daughter," and one of the father throwing his gun through the door after a "brave try" to save his family is foiled.

The James Hill referred to in the article is the appellee. He and his wife and five children involuntarily became the subjects of a front-page news story after being held hostage by three escaped convicts in their suburban,

Whitemarsh, Pennsylvania, home for 19 hours on September 11–12, 1952. The family was released unharmed. In an interview with newsmen after the convicts departed, appellee stressed that the convicts had treated the family courteously, had not molested them, and had not been at all violent. The convicts were thereafter apprehended in a widely publicized encounter with the police which resulted in the killing of two of the convicts. Shortly thereafter the family moved to Connecticut. The appellee discouraged all efforts to keep them in the public spotlight through magazine articles or appearances on television.

In the spring of 1953, Joseph Hayes' novel, *The Desperate Hours,* was published. The story depicted the experience of a family of four held hostage by three escaped convicts in the family's suburban home. But, unlike Hill's experience, the family of the story suffer violence at the hands of the convicts; the father and son are beaten and the daughter subjected to a verbal sexual insult. The book was made into a play, also entitled *The Desperate Hours,* and it is *Life*'s article about the play which is the subject of appellee's action. The complaint sought damages on allegations that the *Life* article was intended to, and did, give the impression that the play mirrored the Hill family's experience, which, to the knowledge of defendant "was false and untrue." Appellant's defense was that the article was "a subject of legitimate news interest." [Hill was awarded $30,000 in compensatory damages.]

In *New York Times v. Sullivan,* we held that the Constitution delimits a State's power to award damages for libel in actions brought by public officials against critics of their official conduct. Factual error, content defamatory of official reputation, or both, are insufficient for an award of damages for false statements unless actual malice—knowledge that the statements are false or in reckless disregard of the truth—is alleged and proved. We hold that the constitutional protections for speech and press preclude the application of the New York statute to redress false reports of matters of public interest in the absence of proof that the defendant published the report with knowledge of its falsity or in reckless disregard of the truth. The guarantees for speech and press are not the preserve of political expression or comment upon public affairs, essential as those are to healthy government. One need only pick up any newspaper or magazine to comprehend the vast range of published matter which exposes persons to public view, both private citizens and public officials. Exposure of the self to others in varying degrees is a concomitant of life in a civilized community. The risk of this exposure is an essential incident of life in a society which places a primary value on freedom of speech and of press.

We have no doubt that the subject of the *Life* article, the opening of a new play linked to an actual incident, is a matter of public interest. The line between the informing and the entertaining is too elusive for the protection of freedom of the press. Erroneous statement is no less inevitable in such a case than in the case of comment upon public affairs, and in both, if innocent or merely negligent, it must be protected if the freedoms of expression are to have the breathing space that they need to survive. We held in *New York Times* that calculated falsehood enjoyed no immunity in the case of alleged defamation of a public official concerning his official conduct. Similarly, calculated falsehood should enjoy no immunity in the situation here presented us. This is neither a libel action by a private individual nor a statutory action by a public official. Therefore, although the First Amendment principles pronounced in *New York Times* guide our conclusion, we reach that conclusion only by applying these principles in this discrete context.

Turning to the facts of the present case, the proofs reasonably would support either a jury finding of innocent or merely negligent misstatement by *Life*, or a finding that *Life* portrayed the play as a re-enactment of the Hill family's experience reckless of the truth or with actual knowledge that the portrayal was false.

Joseph Hayes, author of the book, also wrote the play. His story was not shaped by any single incident, but by several, including incidents which occurred in California, New York, and Detroit. [Still], the Hill family's experience "triggered" the writing of the book and the play.

The *Life* article was prepared at the direction and under the supervision of its entertainment editor (Prideaux), who learned of the production of the play from a news story. The play's director, Robert Montgomery, later suggested to him that its interesting stage setting would make the play a worthwhile subject for an article in *Life*. Hayes [told Prideaux] that an incident somewhat similar to the play had occurred in Philadelphia, and agreed to find out whether the former Hill residence would be available for the shooting of pictures for a *Life* article. Prideaux drove with Hayes to the former Hill residence to test its suitability for a picture story.

Prideaux's first draft made no mention of the Hill name except for the caption of one of the photographs. The text related that the play was a "somewhat fictionalized" account of the family's heroism in time of crisis. Prideaux's research assistant, whose task it was to check the draft for accuracy, put a question mark over the words "somewhat fictionalized." Prideaux testified that the question mark "must have been" brought to his attention, although he did not recollect having seen it. The draft was also brought before the copy editor, who, in the presence of Prideaux, made several changes in emphasis and substance. The first sentence was changed to focus on the Hill incident, using the family's name; the novel was said to have been "inspired" by that incident, and the play was referred to as a "re-enactment." The words "somewhat fictionalized" were deleted.

The jury might reasonably conclude from this evidence—particularly that the *New York Times* article was in the story file, that the copy editor deleted "somewhat fictionalized" after the research assistant questioned its accuracy, and that Prideaux admitted that he knew the play was "between a little bit and moderately fictionalized"—that *Life* knew the falsity of, or was reckless of the truth in, stating in the article that "the story re-enacted" the Hill family's experience. On the other hand, the jury might reasonably predicate a finding of innocent or only negligent misstatement on the testimony that a statement was made to Prideaux by the free-lance photographer that linked the play to an incident in Philadelphia, that the author Hayes cooperated in arranging for the availability of the former Hill home, and that Prideaux thought beyond doubt that the "heart and soul" of the play was the Hill incident.

We do not think, however, that the instructions confined the jury to a verdict of liability based on a finding that the statements in the article were made with knowledge of their falsity or in reckless disregard of the truth. The jury was instructed that liability could rest only on findings that (1) *Life* published the article, "not to disseminate news, but was using plaintiffs' names, in connection with a fictionalized episode as to plaintiffs' relationship to *The Desperate Hours"*; and that (2) the article was published to advertise the play or "for trade purposes." The court also instructed the jury that an award of punitive damages was justified if the jury found that the appellant falsely connected appellee to the play "knowingly or through failure to make a reasonable investigation," if you find "a reckless or wanton disregard of the plaintiffs' rights."

We [note] the marked contrast in the instructions on compensatory and punitive damages. The element of "knowingly" is mentioned only in the instruction that punitive damages must be supported by a finding that *Life* falsely connected the Hill family with the play "knowingly or through failure to make a reasonable investigation." Moreover, even as to punitive damages, the instruction that such damages were justified on the basis of "failure to make a reasonable investigation" is an instruction that proof of negligent misstatement is enough, and we have rejected the test of negligent misstatement as inadequate.

The requirement that the jury also find that the article was published "for trade purposes," as defined in the charge, cannot save the charge from constitutional infirmity. That books, newspapers, and magazines are published and sold for profit does not prevent them from being a form of expression whose liberty is safeguarded by the First Amendment.

The judgment of the Court of Appeals is set aside and the case is remanded for further proceedings not inconsistent with this opinion. It is so ordered.

## Points for Discussion

1. The main difference between libel and false light privacy cases is that, in the latter, plaintiffs need not prove that the falsehoods were defamatory. Presuming that Hill could prove the requisite degree of fault (the "actual malice" test from *New York Times v. Sullivan*), could the facts of *Time, Inc. v. Hill* have produced a libel suit? Were the falsehoods defamatory?

**2.** The Court's holding, requiring application of the "actual malice" test to false light privacy cases, is limited to "false reports of *matters of public interest.*" This case involved a popular magazine—likely better known for its photography than for its prose—not a serious newspaper with a tight deadline. The article itself dealt with the arts (the opening of a play), not political events, and the Hill family's ordeal had been years ago. With all that in mind, what likelihood is there that the Court would ever find an article that appears in a mainstream media outlet to be *not* "of public interest"?

# ■ *Neff v. Time, Inc.*

### 406 F. Supp. 858 (W.D. Pa. 1976)

*Judge Marsh:*

A complaint filed by John W. Neff, the plaintiff, against Time, Inc., the defendant, alleges that the defendant is the owner of a magazine known as *Sports Illustrated,* that in its issue of August 5, 1974, the defendant's magazine used Neff's picture without his prior knowledge and consent to illustrate an article entitled "A Strange Kind of Love;" that the photograph shows Neff with the front zipper of his trousers completely opened implying that he is a "crazy, drunken slob," and combined with the title of the article, "a sexual deviate." Neff alleges that the unauthorized publication and circulation of his picture to illustrate the article invaded his right of privacy and subjected him to public ridicule and contempt.

The undenied facts contained in affidavits filed by defendant establish beyond peradventure that the picture was taken with Neff's knowledge and with his encouragement; that he knew he was being photographed by a photographer for *Sports Illustrated* and thereby impliedly consented to its publication.

The photograph was taken about 1:00 o'clock P.M. November 25, 1973, while Neff was present on a dugout with a group of fans prior to a professional football game at Cleveland between the Cleveland Browns and the Pittsburgh Steelers. The photographer was on the field intending to take pictures of the Steeler players as they entered the field from the dugout. Neff and the others were jumping up and down in full view of the fans in the stadium; they were waving Steeler banners and drinking beer; they all seemed to be slightly inebriated. One of the group asked the photographer for whom he was working and was told *Sports Illustrated,* whereupon the group began to act as if a television camera had been put on them; as the pictures were taken they began to react even more, screaming and howling and imploring the photographer to take more pictures. The more pictures taken of the group, the more they hammed it up.

During the period from July through December, 1973, this photographer took 7,200 pictures pursuant to his assignment to cover the Steelers. As part of his duty he edited the pictures and submitted one hundred to the magazine for selection by a committee of five employees. After several screenings of the thirty pictures of the group on the dugout, the committee selected Neff's picture with his fly open. Although Neff's fly was not open to the point of being revealing, the selection was deliberate and surely in utmost bad taste; subjectively, as to Neff, the published picture could have been embarrassing, humiliating and offensive to his sensibilities. Without doubt the magazine deliberately exhibited Neff in an embarrassing manner.

It appears that the pictures were taken to illustrate a book being written by one Blount about the Steeler fans, and three excerpts from the book were published in the magazine. Only three pictures, including Neff's, accompanied the article of August 5, 1974. The title to this article "A Strange Kind of Love" could convey to some readers a derogatory connotation. Neff is not mentioned by name in the article; the Steeler-Cleveland game of November 1974, is not mentioned in the article; Neff's photograph was not selected on the basis of its relationship to that game. The caption appearing adjacent to the photograph reads: "In the fading autumn Sundays at Three Rivers, the fans joined the players in mean pro dreams." Three Rivers is the name of the stadium in Pittsburgh. Neff's photograph was selected because "it represented the typical Steeler fan: a rowdy, strong rooter, much behind his team, having a good time at the game," and "it fitted in perfectly with the text of the story."

It seems to us that art directors and editors should hesitate to deliberately publish a picture which most likely would be offensive and cause embarrassment to the subject when many other pictures of the same variety are available. Notwithstanding, the courts are not concerned with establishing canons of good taste for the press or the public.

The right of privacy is firmly established in Pennsylvania despite the fact that its perimeter is not yet clearly defined and its contours remain amorphous. In Pennsylvania, invasion of privacy is actionable under any one of four distinct, but coordinate, torts.

Plaintiff's claim is based on "appropriation of name or likeness" and "publicity given to private life." [An appropriation suit cannot stand] when a person's picture is used in a non-commercial article dealing with an accident, or the picture of a bystander at a political convention, or parade, or generally in the reporting of news. We think actions of excited fans at a football game are news as is a story about the fans of a professional football team. The fact that *Sports Illustrated* is a magazine published for profit does not constitute a "commercial appropriation of Neff's likeness." The fact that Neff was photographed in a public place for a newsworthy article entitles the defendant to the protection of the First Amendment.

[As to Neff's "publicity" action,] the article about Pittsburgh Steeler fans was of legitimate public interest; the football game in Cleveland was of legitimate public interest; Neff's picture was taken in a public place with his knowledge and with his encouragement; he was catapulted into the news by his own actions; nothing was falsified; a photograph taken at a public event which everyone present could see, with the knowledge and implied consent of the subject, is not a matter concerning a private fact. A factually accurate public disclosure is not tortious when connected with a newsworthy event even though offensive to ordinary sensibilities. The constitutional privilege protects all truthful publications relevant to matters of public interest.

Of course, we are concerned that Neff's picture was deliberately selected by an editorial committee from a number of similar pictures and segregated and published alone. If his picture had appeared as part of the general crowd scene of fans at a game, even though embarrassing, there would be no problem. Although we have some misgivings, it is our opinion that the publication of Neff's photograph taken with his active encouragement and participation, and with knowledge that the photographer was connected with a publication, even though taken without his express consent, is protected by the Constitution.

## Points for Discussion

1. Judge Marsh makes much of the fact that Neff and his friends were keenly aware of the *Sports Illustrated* photographer's presence. But what if Neff and company were acting drunk and rowdy only for their own pleasure, completely unaware that they were being photographed? Should the judgment be different?

2. Suppose that the offensive photo were more revealing, at least partially exposing Neff's genitalia. Would the added degree of offensiveness inherent in publishing such a photo in a popular magazine outweigh the publisher's First Amendment interests?

## ■ *Holman v. Central Arkansas Broadcasting Company*

### 610 F.2d 542 (8th Cir. 1979)

*Judge Lay:*

Summary judgment was granted defendants Central Arkansas Broadcasting Company, Inc. [and news reporter] Carl Connerton, in a suit brought by Marvin Holman for alleged invasion of Holman's right of privacy. We affirm.

On November 20, 1975, Holman and his wife were stopped on the highway at approximately 3:56 A.M., and taken to the Russellville, Arkansas police station. Holman was charged with the offense of driving while intoxicated, second offense, and using profane and abusive language; Mrs. Holman was charged with public drunkenness. Holman, an attorney, had formerly served as municipal judge.

Holman was allowed to privately confer with his retained counsel, Robert Hays Williams, at 4:30 A.M. in a private lounge. Williams later represented Holman at his trial in municipal court. Holman's young associate, an attorney named Roderick Weaver, came to the jail shortly after 5:30 A.M. to secure the release of Holman and his wife on bond. The police informed him they would not release the Holmans until 9:00 A.M. Upon his return he observed at least two persons who were not police officers, one of whom he later learned was Mr. Connerton, a news reporter. When he went to Holman's cell he noticed Connerton was in the cell block a short distance behind him and had a tape recorder in his hand. Weaver told Connerton not to record any conversation between himself and Holman. According to Weaver, Connerton appeared to walk away. At this time, Holman's wife was taken from her cell for fingerprinting and photographing. According to the affidavits of three police officers, Holman was hitting and banging on his cell door, hollering and cursing from the time of his arrest until his release at approximately 9:00 A.M. The police communications operator stated Holman became abusive and refused to cooperate when she tried to give him a gas chromatograph test. When placed in the holding cell, he started hollering, cussing and screaming.

No credible evidence appears in the record that Connerton recorded any confidential information. It is obvious that the words broadcast could be heard by others in the police station. Holman argues the Fourth and Sixth Amendments create a "zone" of privacy which was violated by Connerton's recording and publishing of Holman's statements. The simple answer to this contention is that the boisterous complaints which were recorded were not made with the expectation of privacy or confidentiality. Neither Weaver nor Holman asserts confidential legal advice was given. The evidence demonstrates unequivocally that Holman was simply complaining loudly while Weaver tried to quiet him down in order to arrange his release.

Even assuming the police called the news reporter to the station and allowed him to enter the cell block, no right to privacy is invaded when state officials allow or facilitate publication of an official act such as an arrest. Although Weaver asked Connerton not to record Holman's statements, they were made loudly and in such a manner as to attract attention. Connerton could not be prevented from reporting the statements he could so easily overhear aurally; use of a device to record them cannot create a claim for invasion of privacy when one would not otherwise exist.

We recognize the important and vital right to private consultation that is basic to effective representation by counsel flows from the confidential relationship between an accused and his counsel. However, the undisputed facts distinguish this case from those in which that right is protected. Here there was no attempt to record or overhear statements made with an expectation of privacy. Holman's boisterous complaints were obviously not intended for Weaver's ears alone. The tape demonstrates this.

### Points for Discussion

1. The reporter, we learn here, "appeared to walk away" when instructed by Holman's attorney not to record his conversations with his client. Might the case have come out differently if the reporter had explicitly *promised* not to record the conversation?

2. As you likely know, conversations between attorney and client generally enjoy a great deal of confidentiality in the U.S. legal system. Attorneys can almost never be compelled to testify as to what their clients have told them, and the American Bar Association's code of ethics makes clear that attorneys must keep to themselves that which they learn from their clients. Should the client's loudness (because he is drunk and presumably not thinking clearly) be sufficient to waive any rights to confidentiality?

## Zacchini v. Scripps-Howard Broadcasting Company

### 433 U.S. 562 (1977)

*Justice White delivered the opinion of the Court.*

Petitioner, Hugo Zacchini, is an entertainer. He performs a "human cannonball" act in which he is shot from a cannon into a net some 200 feet away. Each performance occupies some 15 seconds. In August and September 1972, petitioner was engaged to perform his act on a regular basis at the Geauga County Fair in Burton, Ohio. Members of the public attending the fair were not charged a separate admission fee to observe his act.

On August 30, a free-lance reporter for Scripps-Howard Broadcasting Co., the operator of a television broadcasting station, attended the fair. He carried a small movie camera. Petitioner noticed the reporter and asked him not to film the performance. The reporter did not do so on that day; but on the instructions of the producer of his daily newscast, returned the following day and videotaped the entire act. This film clip, approximately 15 seconds in length, was shown on the 11 o'clock news program that night, together with favorable commentary ("The great Zacchini is about the only human cannonball around, these days. Although it's not a long act, it's a thriller, and you really need to see it in person to appreciate it.")

Petitioner then brought this action for damages, alleging that respondent showed and commercialized the film of his act without his consent, and that such conduct was an unlawful appropriation of plaintiff's professional property. Respondent answered and moved for summary judgment, which was granted by the trial court.

The Court of Appeals of Ohio reversed. The Supreme Court of Ohio [reinstated the granting of summary judgment]. We granted certiorari to consider whether the First and Fourteenth Amendments immunized respondent from damages for its alleged infringement of petitioner's state-law right of publicity. Insofar as the Ohio Supreme Court held that the First and Fourteenth Amendments of the United States Constitution required judgment for respondent, we reverse the judgment of that court.

The Ohio Supreme Court held that respondent is constitutionally privileged to include in its newscasts matters of public interest that would otherwise be protected by the right of publicity, absent an intent to injure or to appropriate for some nonprivileged purpose. If under this standard respondent had merely reported that petitioner was performing at the fair and described or commented on his act, with or without showing his picture on television, we would have a very different case. But petitioner is not contending that his appearance at the fair and his performance could not be reported by the press as newsworthy items. His complaint is that respondent filmed his entire act and displayed that film on television for the public to see and enjoy. This, he claimed, was an appropriation of his professional property.

The Ohio Supreme Court held that the challenged invasion was privileged, that the press "must be accorded broad latitude in its choice of how much it presents of each story or incident, and of the emphasis to be given to such presentation." Under this view, respondent was thus constitutionally free to film and display petitioner's entire act. The Ohio Supreme Court relied heavily on *Time, Inc. v. Hill,* but that case does not mandate a media privilege to televise a performer's entire act without his consent. It is also abundantly clear that *Time, Inc. v. Hill,* [a "false light" privacy case], did not involve a performer, a person with a name having commercial value, or any claim to a "right of publicity."

The differences between these two torts are important. First, the State's interests in providing a cause of action in each instance are different. The interest protected in permitting recovery for placing the plaintiff in a false light is clearly that of reputation, with the same overtones of mental distress as in defamation. By contrast, the State's interest in permitting a right of publicity is in protecting the proprietary interest of the individual in his act in part to encourage such entertainment.

Second, the two torts differ in the degree to which they intrude on dissemination of information to the public. In "false light" cases the only way to protect the interests involved is to attempt to minimize publication of the damaging matter, while in "right of publicity" cases the only question is who gets to do the publishing. An entertainer such as petitioner usually has no objection to the widespread publication of his act as long as he gets the commercial benefit of such publication. Indeed, in the present case petitioner did not seek to enjoin the broadcast of his act; he simply sought compensation for the broadcast in the form of damages.

Wherever the line in particular situations is to be drawn between media reports that are protected and those that are not, we are quite sure that the First and Fourteenth Amendments do not immunize the media when they broadcast a performer's entire act without his consent. The Constitution no more prevents a State from requiring respondent to compensate petitioner for broadcasting his act on television than it would privilege respondent to film and broadcast a copyrighted dramatic work without liability to the copyright owner.

The broadcast of a film of petitioner's entire act poses a substantial threat to the economic value of that performance. [Zacchini's] act is the product of his own talents and energy, the end result of much time, effort, and expense. Much of its economic value lies in the right of exclusive control over the publicity given to his performance; if the public can see the act free on television, it will be less willing to pay to see it at the fair. The effect of a public broadcast of the performance is similar to preventing petitioner from charging an admission fee. Moreover, the broadcast of petitioner's entire performance, unlike the unauthorized use of another's name for purposes of trade or the incidental use of a name or picture by the press, goes to the heart of petitioner's ability to earn a living as an entertainer.

Of course, [there is more involved here] than a desire to compensate the performer for the time and effort invested in his act; the protection provides an economic incentive for him to make the investment required to produce a performance of interest to the public. This same consideration underlies the patent and copyright laws long enforced by this Court.

There is no doubt that entertainment, as well as news, enjoys First Amendment protection. It is also true that entertainment itself can be important news. But it is important to note that neither the public nor respondent will be deprived of the benefit of petitioner's performance as long as his commercial stake in his act is appropriately recognized. Petitioner does not seek to enjoin the broadcast of his performance; he simply wants to be paid for it. Respondent knew that petitioner objected to televising his act but nevertheless displayed the entire film. We conclude that although the

State of Ohio may as a matter of its own law privilege the press in the circumstances of this case, the First and Fourteenth Amendments do not require it to do so.

Reversed.

## Points for Discussion

1. Justice White's opinion makes much of the fact that the TV station broadcast Zacchini's "entire act." But did it really? Do not carnival stunts such as this one usually begin with some fanfare (introduction of the performer, description of the uniqueness and danger of that which is to come, perhaps a last-minute check of the equipment) designed to heighten the audience's anticipation? If Zacchini's "act" included such moments, which were not broadcast, is doubt cast on White's analysis?

2. Was Zacchini really hurt by the station's conduct? Note that the commentator went out of his way to advise viewers that to really appreciate the act, they should see it *in person*. Is it not at least therefore arguable that the TV story increased the live attendance?

## White v. Samsung Electronics America, Inc.

### 971 F.2d 1395 (9th Cir. 1992)

*Judge Goodwin:*

This case involves a promotional "fame and fortune" dispute. In running a particular advertisement without Vanna White's permission, defendants Samsung Electronics America, Inc. (Samsung) and David Deutsch Associates, Inc. (Deutsch) attempted to capitalize on White's fame to enhance their fortune. White sued, alleging infringement of various intellectual property rights.

Plaintiff Vanna White is the hostess of "Wheel of Fortune," one of the most popular game shows in television history. An estimated forty million people watch the program daily. Capitalizing on the fame which her participation in the show has bestowed on her, White markets her identity to various advertisers.

The dispute in this case arose out of a series of advertisements prepared for Samsung by Deutsch. The series ran in at least half a dozen publications with widespread, and in some cases national, circulation. Each of the advertisements in the series followed the same theme. Each depicted a current item from popular culture and a Samsung electronic product. Each was set in the twenty-first century and conveyed the message that the Samsung product would still be in use by that time.

The advertisement which prompted the current dispute was for Samsung video-cassette recorders (VCRs). The ad depicted a robot, dressed in a wig, gown, and jewelry consciously selected to resemble White's hair and dress. The robot was posed next to a game board which is instantly recognizable as the Wheel of Fortune game show set, in a stance for which White is famous. The caption of the ad read: "Longest-running game show. 2012 A.D." Defendants referred to the ad as the "Vanna White" ad. Unlike the other celebrities used in the campaign, White neither consented to the ads nor was she paid.

Following the circulation of the robot ad, White sued Samsung and Deutsch in federal district court under the California common law right of publicity. The district court granted summary judgment against White on each of her claims. White now appeals.

The common law right of publicity cause of action may be pleaded by alleging (1) the defendant's use of the plaintiff's identity; (2) the appropriation of plaintiff's name or likeness to defendant's advantage, commercially or otherwise; (3) lack of consent; and (4) resulting injury.

The district court dismissed White's claim for failure to [establish that] defendants had appropriated White's "name or likeness" with their robot ad. We agree that the robot ad did not make use of White's name or likeness. However, the common law right of publicity is not so confined. The "name or likeness" formulation originated not as an element of the right of publicity cause of action, but [in Dean William Prosser's famous] description of the types of cases in which the cause of action had been recognized. It is not impossible that there might be appropriation of the plaintiff's identity, as by impersonation, without the use of either his name or his likeness, and that this would be an invasion of his right of privacy. Since Prosser's early formulation, the case law has borne out his insight that the right of publicity is not limited to the appropriation of name or likeness. The common law right of publicity reaches means of appropriation other than name or likeness; [moreover], the specific means of appropriation are relevant only for determining whether the defendant has in fact appropriated the plaintiff's identity. The right of publicity does not require that appropriations of identity be accomplished through particular means to be actionable.

The right of publicity has developed to protect the commercial interest of celebrities in their identities. The theory of the right is that a celebrity's identity can be valuable in the promotion of products, and the celebrity has an interest that may be protected from the unauthorized commercial exploitation of that identity. If the celebrity's identity is commercially exploited, there has been an invasion of his right whether or not his "name or likeness" is used. It is not important how the defendant has appropriated the plaintiff's identity, but whether the defendant has done so. A rule which says that the right of publicity can be infringed only through the use of nine different methods of appropriating identity merely challenges the clever advertising strategist to come up with the tenth.

Indeed, if we treated the means of appropriation as dispositive in our analysis of the right of publicity, we would not only weaken the right but effectively eviscerate it. The right would fail to protect those plaintiffs most in need of its protection. Advertisers use celebrities to promote their products. The more popular the celebrity, the greater the number of people who recognize her, and the greater the visibility for the product. The identities of the most popular celebrities are not only the most attractive for advertisers, but also the easiest to evoke without resorting to obvious means such as name, likeness, or voice.

Viewed separately, the individual aspects of the advertisement in the present case say little. Viewed together, they leave little doubt about the celebrity the ad is meant to depict. The female-shaped robot is wearing a long gown, blond wig, and large jewelry. Vanna White dresses exactly like this at times, but so do many other women. The robot is in the process of turning a block letter on a game-board. Vanna White dresses like this while turning letters on a game-board but perhaps similarly attired Scrabble-playing women do this as well. The robot is standing on what looks to be the Wheel of Fortune game show set. Vanna White dresses like this, turns letters, and does this on the Wheel of Fortune game show. She is the only one. Indeed, defendants themselves referred to their ad as the "Vanna White" ad. We are not surprised.

Television and other media create marketable celebrity identity value. Considerable energy and ingenuity are expended by those who have achieved celebrity value to exploit it for profit. The law protects the celebrity's sole right to exploit this value whether the celebrity has achieved her fame out of rare ability, dumb luck, or a combination thereof. We decline Samsung and Deutsch's invitation to permit the evisceration of the common law right of publicity through means as facile as those in this case. Because White has alleged facts showing that Samsung and Deutsch had appropriated her identity, the district court erred by rejecting, on summary judgment, White's common law right of publicity claim.

## *Points for Discussion*

1. If a group of comics, such as NBC's *Saturday Night Live* cast, wanted to make fun of Vanna White's on-air persona, they could surely imitate White visually and vocally far more closely than the Samsung robot did, yet they would not have to ask White's permission to do the sketch. If Samsung's purpose in creating the Vanna White commercial

was also to make fun of the game show cohost, should their ultimate purpose of selling VCRs count against them?

2. Judge Goodwin claims that Samsung appropriated White's "identity" by creating a robot with the physical proportions of an attractive woman, posed gracefully, dressed in a blond wig, an evening gown, and jewelry. But are not these characteristics of countless numbers of young women in the entertainment industry? Is not the only feature of the commercial that is uniquely attributable to White the replication of the *Wheel of Fortune* set (to which, presumably, she does not own the rights)? Why, then, should White be able to sue for damages for Samsung's "taking" from her that which never belonged to her?

# 6 Copyright and Trademark

The constitutional basis for federal copyright law is found in Article I, Section 8, which tells Congress that it may create laws to protect "for limited times to authors . . . the exclusive right to their respective writings and discoveries." Under current law, individuals who create literary, musical, or similar works will enjoy the exclusive right to profit from their creations throughout their lives, after which their heirs may inherit that protection for an additional 70 years.

Not all works are copyrightable in the first place, however. They must manifest at least a modicum of creativity, of originality. Such is the lesson of the first case in this chapter, the 1991 *Feist Publications v. Rural Telephone Service Company* decision.

Who owns a copyright when an individual creates a work at the behest of an employer has been a complicated matter, generating conflicting appellate case law. The Supreme Court's 1989 decision in *Community for Creative Non-Violence v. Reid,* which includes the Court's interpretation of the Copyright Act's "work for hire" doctrine, is an attempt to clarify the difference between an employee and a contractor.

Not every taking of another's work is an actionable infringement. Section 107 of the Copyright Act, the text of which you likely have seen reproduced above self-service copy machines at commercial shops such as Kinko's, seeks to establish a balance between the interests of the original author and those who wish to comment on, or otherwise build on, the original. One often-litigated issue has been the special role of the parodist in the context of fair use analysis. The Supreme Court's 1994 decision in *Campbell v. Acuff-Rose Music* tells us what it means to be a parodist.

Closely related to copyright is the law of trademarks, which is aimed at protecting words, logos, and the like designed to make us think of a specific company's products or services. In *Lyons Partnership v. Giannoulas,* the Fifth Circuit Court of Appeals reminds us that trademark law also provides for the interests of parodists. This 1999 decision involves an unusual plaintiff: Barney, the purple dinosaur.

# *Feist Publications v. Rural Telephone Service Company*

### 499 U.S. 340 (1991)

*Justice O'Connor delivered the opinion of the Court.*

Rural Telephone Service Company, Inc., is a certified public utility that provides telephone service to several communities in northwest Kansas. It is subject to a state regulation that requires all telephone companies operating in Kansas to issue annually an updated telephone directory. Accordingly, as a condition of its monopoly franchise, Rural publishes a typical telephone directory, consisting of white pages and yellow pages. The white pages list in alphabetical order the names of Rural's subscribers, together with their towns and telephone numbers. The yellow pages list Rural's business subscribers alphabetically by category and feature classified advertisements of various sizes. Rural distributes its directory free of charge to its subscribers, but earns revenue by selling yellow pages advertisements. Feist Publications, Inc., is a publishing company that specializes in area-wide telephone directories. Unlike a typical directory, which covers only a particular calling area, Feist's area-wide directories cover a much larger geographical range, reducing the need to call directory assistance or consult multiple directories. The Feist directory that is the subject of this litigation covers 11 different telephone service areas in 15 counties and contains 46,878 white pages listings—compared to Rural's approximately 7,700 listings. Like Rural's directory, Feist's is distributed free of charge and includes both white pages and yellow pages. Feist and Rural compete vigorously for yellow pages advertising.

As the sole provider of telephone service in its service area, Rural obtains subscriber information quite easily. Persons desiring telephone service must apply to Rural and provide their names and addresses; Rural then assigns them a telephone number. Feist is not a telephone company, let alone one with monopoly status, and therefore lacks independent access to any subscriber information. To obtain white pages listings for its area-wide directory, Feist approached each of the 11 telephone companies operating in northwest Kansas and offered to pay for the right to use its white pages listings. Of the 11 telephone companies, only Rural refused to license its listings to Feist. Rural's refusal created a problem for Feist, as omitting these listings would have left a gaping hole in its area-wide directory, rendering it less attractive to potential yellow pages advertisers. Unable to license Rural's white pages listings, Feist used them without Rural's consent. Feist began by removing several thousand listings that fell outside the geographic range of its area-wide directory, then hired personnel to investigate the 4,935 that remained. These employees verified the data reported by Rural and sought to obtain additional information.

As a result, a typical Feist listing includes the individual's street address; most of Rural's listings do not. Notwithstanding these additions, however, 1,309 of the 46,878 listings in Feist's 1983 directory were identical to listings in Rural's 1982–1983 white pages. Four of these were fictitious listings that Rural had inserted into its directory to detect copying.

Rural sued for copyright infringement in the District Court for the District of Kansas taking the position that Feist, in compiling its own directory, could not use the information contained in Rural's white pages. Rural asserted that Feist's employees were obliged to travel door-to-door or conduct a telephone survey to discover the same information for themselves. Feist responded that such efforts were economically impractical and, in any event, unnecessary because the information copied was beyond the scope of copyright protection.

This case concerns the interaction of two well-established propositions. The first is that facts are not copyrightable; the other, that compilations of facts generally are. There is an undeniable tension between these two propositions. Many compilations consist of nothing but raw data—i.e., wholly factual information not accompanied by any original written expression. On what basis may one claim a copyright in such a work? Common sense tells us that 100 uncopyrightable facts do not magically change their status when gathered together in one place. Yet copyright law seems to contemplate that compilations that consist exclusively of facts are potentially within its scope. The key to resolving the tension lies in understanding why facts are not copyrightable. The sine qua non of copyright is originality. Original, as the term is used in copyright, means only that the work was independently created by the author (as opposed to copied from other works), and that it possesses at least some minimal degree of creativity. To be sure, the requisite level of creativity is extremely low; even a slight amount will suffice. Originality does not signify novelty; a work may be original even though it closely resembles other works so long as the similarity is fortuitous, not the result of copying. To illustrate, assume that two poets, each ignorant of the other, compose identical poems. Neither work is novel, yet both are original and, hence, copyrightable.

It is this bedrock principle of copyright that mandates the law's seemingly disparate treatment of facts and factual compilations. No one may claim originality as to facts, facts do not owe their origin to an act of authorship. The distinction is one between creation and discovery: The first person to find and report a particular fact has not created the fact; he or she has merely discovered its existence. Census takers, for example, do not "create" the population figures that emerge from their efforts; in a sense, they copy these figures from the world around them.

Factual compilations, on the other hand, may possess the requisite originality. The compilation author typically chooses which facts to include, in what order to place them, and how to arrange the collected data so that they may be used effectively by readers. These choices as to selection and arrangement, so long as they are made independently by the compiler and entail a minimal degree of creativity, are sufficiently original that Congress may protect such compilations through the copyright laws. Thus, even a directory that contains absolutely no protectible written expression, only facts, meets the constitutional minimum for copyright protection if it features an original selection or arrangement. This protection is subject to an important limitation. The mere fact that a work is copyrighted does not mean that every element of the work may be protected. Originality remains the sine qua non of copyright; accordingly, copyright protection may extend only to those components of a work that are original to the author. Thus, if the compilation author clothes facts with an original collocation of words, he or she may be able to claim a copyright in this written expression. Others may copy the underlying facts from the publication, but not the precise words used to present them. Where the compilation author adds no written expression but rather lets the facts speak for themselves, the expressive element is more elusive. The only conceivable expression is the manner in which the compiler has selected and arranged the facts. Thus, if the selection and arrangement are original, these elements of the work are eligible for copyright protection. No matter how original the format, however, the facts themselves do not become original through association.

This inevitably means that the copyright in a factual compilation is thin. Notwithstanding a valid copyright, a subsequent compiler remains free to use the facts contained in another's publication to aid in preparing a competing work, so long as the competing work does not feature the same selection and arrangement. It may seem unfair that much of the fruit of the compiler's labor may be used by others without compensation. However, this is not some unforeseen byproduct of a statutory scheme. It is, rather, the essence of copyright, and a constitutional requirement.

There is no doubt that Feist took from the white pages of Rural's directory a substantial amount of factual information. At a minimum, Feist copied the names, towns, and telephone numbers of 1,309 of Rural's subscribers. Not all copying, however, is copyright infringement. To establish infringement, two elements must be proven: (1) ownership of a valid copyright, and (2) copying of constituent elements of the work that are original. The first element is not at issue here; Feist appears to concede that Rural's directory, considered as a whole, is subject to a valid copyright because it contains some foreword text, as well as original material in its yellow pages advertisements. The question is whether Rural has proved the second element. In other words, did Feist, by taking 1,309 names, towns, and telephone numbers from Rural's white pages, copy anything that was "original" to Rural? Certainly, the raw data does not satisfy the originality requirement. Rural may have been the first to discover and report the names, towns, and telephone numbers of its subscribers, but this data does not

" 'owe its origin' " to Rural. Rather, these bits of information are uncopyrightable facts; they existed before Rural reported them and would have continued to exist if Rural had never published a telephone directory.

The question that remains is whether Rural selected, coordinated, or arranged these uncopyrightable facts in an original way. As mentioned, originality is not a stringent standard; it does not require that facts be presented in an innovative or surprising way. It is equally true, however, that the selection and arrangement of facts cannot be so mechanical or routine as to require no creativity whatsoever. The standard of originality is low, but it does exist. The selection, coordination, and arrangement of Rural's white pages do not satisfy the minimum constitutional standards for copyright protection. As mentioned at the outset, Rural's white pages are entirely typical. Persons desiring telephone service in Rural's service area fill out an application and Rural issues them a telephone number. In preparing its white pages, Rural simply takes the data provided by its subscribers and lists it alphabetically by surname. The end product is a garden-variety white pages directory, devoid of even the slightest trace of creativity.

Rural's selection of listings could not be more obvious: It publishes the most basic information—name, town, and telephone number—about each person who applies to it for telephone service. This is "selection" of a sort, but it lacks the modicum of creativity necessary to transform mere selection into copyrightable expression. Rural expended sufficient effort to make the white pages directory useful, but insufficient creativity to make it original.

We note in passing that the selection featured in Rural's white pages may also fail the originality requirement for another reason. Feist points out that Rural did not truly "select" to publish the names and telephone numbers of its subscribers; rather, it was required to do so by the Kansas Corporation Commission as part of its monopoly franchise. Accordingly, one could plausibly conclude that this selection was dictated by state law, not by Rural. Nor can Rural claim originality in its coordination and arrangement of facts. The white pages do nothing more than list Rural's subscribers in alphabetical order. This arrangement may, technically speaking, owe its origin to Rural; no one disputes that Rural undertook the task of alphabetizing the names itself. But there is nothing remotely creative about arranging names alphabetically in a white pages directory. It is an age-old practice, firmly rooted in tradition and so commonplace that it has come to be expected as a matter of course. It is not only unoriginal, it is practically inevitable.

We conclude that the names, towns, and telephone numbers copied by Feist were not original to Rural and therefore were not protected by the copyright in Rural's combined white and yellow pages directory. As a constitutional matter, copyright protects only those constituent elements of a work that possess more than a de minimis quantum of creativity. Rural's white pages, limited to basic subscriber information and arranged alphabetically, fall short of the mark. Because Rural's white pages lack the requisite originality, Feist's use of the listings cannot constitute infringement. This decision should not be construed as demeaning Rural's efforts in compiling its directory, but rather as making clear that copyright rewards originality, not effort.

The judgment of the Court of Appeals is reversed.

## Points for Discussion

1. Early copyright cases had suggested that the law should protect works that, although not very creative, were born from much "sweat of the brow." How much of Justice O'Connor's decision seems based on the fact that the Rural Telephone Service Company did not even decide independently to expend its sweat in that it was required by the state regulatory agency to compile a phone book annually?

2. More and more, we tend to look to the Internet rather than printed telephone books to obtain the numbers we need. Web sites may differ in the strategies they permit searchers to use. Some may require us to know the target individual's home town, and others do not; some are slightly "forgiving" should we misspell the name, and others may demand exactitude. Should these variations be themselves considered creative enough to justify copyright protection (apart from any patent protection that may accrue to the underlying technology)? What happens if, at some future date, the organization of such data becomes so routine as to resemble yesterday's printed, alphabetical listings? To the extent that the logic of organizing data becomes "garden-variety," "obvious," and even "inevitable" (borrowing Justice O'Connor's language), should it then lose copyright protection?

## ■ *Community for Creative Non-Violence v. Reid*

### 490 U.S. 730 (1989)

*Justice Marshall delivered the opinion for the Court.*

In this case, an artist and the organization that hired him to produce a sculpture contest the ownership of the copyright in that work. To resolve this dispute, we must construe the "work made for hire" provisions of the Copyright Act of 1976, which defines as a "work made for hire" a "work prepared by an employee within the scope of his or her employment." Petitioners are the Community for Creative Non-Violence, a nonprofit unincorporated association dedicated to eliminating homelessness in America, and Mitch Snyder, a member and trustee of CCNV. In the fall of 1985, CCNV decided to participate in the annual Christmastime Pageant of Peace in Washington, D.C., by sponsoring a display to dramatize the plight of the homeless. Snyder and fellow CCNV members conceived the idea for the nature of the display: a sculpture of a modern Nativity scene in which, in lieu of the traditional Holy Family, the two adult figures and the infant would appear as contemporary homeless people huddled on a street side steam grate. The family was to be black (most of the homeless in Washington being black); the figures were to be life-sized, and the steam grate would be positioned atop a platform pedestal, or base, within which special-effects equipment would be enclosed to emit simulated 'steam' through the grid to swirl about the figures. They also settled upon a title for the work—"Third World America"—and a legend for the pedestal: "And still there is no room at the inn." Snyder was referred to respondent James Earl Reid, a Baltimore, Maryland, sculptor. In the course of two telephone calls, Reid agreed to sculpt the three human figures. CCNV agreed to make the steam grate and pedestal for the statue. Reid proposed that the work be cast in bronze, at a total cost of approximately $100,000 and taking six to eight months to complete. Snyder rejected that proposal because CCNV did not have sufficient funds, and because the statue had to be completed by December 12 to be included in the pageant. Reid then suggested, and Snyder agreed, that the sculpture would be made of a material known as "Design Cast 62," a synthetic substance that could meet CCNV's monetary and time constraints, could be tinted to resemble bronze, and could withstand the elements. The parties agreed that the project would cost no more than $15,000, not including Reid's services, which he offered to donate. The parties did not sign a written agreement. Neither party mentioned copyright.

After Reid received an advance of $3,000, he made several sketches of figures in various poses. At Snyder's request, Reid sent CCNV a sketch of a proposed sculpture showing the family in a creche-like setting: the mother seated, cradling a baby in her lap; the father standing behind her, bending over her shoulder to touch the baby's foot. Reid testified that Snyder asked for the sketch to use in raising funds for the sculpture. Snyder testified that it was also for his approval. Reid sought a black family to serve as a model for the sculpture. Upon Snyder's suggestion, Reid visited a family living at CCNV's Washington shelter but decided that only their newly born child was a suitable model. While Reid was in Washington, Snyder took him to see homeless people living on the streets. Snyder pointed out that they tended to recline on steam grates, rather than sit or stand, in order to warm their bodies. From that time on, Reid's sketches contained only reclining figures.

Throughout November and the first two weeks of December 1985, Reid worked exclusively on the statue, assisted at various times by a dozen different people who were paid with funds provided in installments by

CCNV. On a number of occasions, CCNV members visited Reid to check on his progress and to coordinate CCNV's construction of the base. CCNV rejected Reid's proposal to use suitcases or shopping bags to hold the family's personal belongings, insisting instead on a shopping cart. Reid and CCNV members did not discuss copyright ownership on any of these visits.

On December 24, 1985, 12 days after the agreed-upon date, Reid delivered the completed statue to Washington. There it was joined to the steam grate and pedestal prepared by CCNV and placed on display near the site of the pageant. Snyder paid Reid the final installment of the $15,000. The statue remained on display for a month. In late January 1986, CCNV members returned it to Reid's studio in Baltimore for minor repairs. Several weeks later, Snyder began making plans to take the statue on a tour of several cities to raise money for the homeless. Reid objected, contending that the Design Cast 62 material was not strong enough to withstand the ambitious itinerary. He urged CCNV to cast the statue in bronze at a cost of $35,000, or to create a master mold at a cost of $5,000. Snyder declined to spend more of CCNV's money on the project. In March 1986, Snyder asked Reid to return the sculpture. Reid refused. He then filed a certificate of copyright registration for "Third World America" in his name and announced plans to take the sculpture on a more modest tour than the one CCNV had proposed. Snyder, acting in his capacity as CCNV's trustee, immediately filed a competing certificate of copyright registration. Snyder and CCNV then commenced this action against Reid, seeking return of the sculpture and a determination of copyright ownership. The District Court granted a preliminary injunction, ordering the sculpture's return. After a 2-day bench trial, the District Court declared that "Third World America" was a "work made for hire" under §101 of the Copyright Act and that Snyder, as trustee for CCNV, was the exclusive owner of the copyright in the sculpture. The Court of Appeals for the District of Columbia Circuit reversed and remanded. We granted certiorari to resolve a conflict among the Courts of Appeals over the proper construction of the "work made for hire" provisions of the Act.

The Copyright Act of 1976 provides that copyright ownership "vests initially in the author or authors of the work." As a general rule, the author is the party who actually creates the work. The Act carves out an important exception, however, for "works made for hire." If the work is for hire, the employer or other person for whom the work was prepared is considered the author and owns the copyright, unless there is a written agreement to the contrary. The contours of the work for hire doctrine therefore carry profound significance for freelance creators—including artists, writers, photographers, designers, composers, and computer programmers—and for the publishing, advertising, music, and other industries which commission their works.

The dispositive inquiry in this case is whether "Third World America" is "a work prepared by an employee within the scope of his or her employment" under §101(1). The starting point for our interpretation of a statute is always its language. The Act nowhere defines the terms "employee" or "scope of employment." It is, however, well established that where Congress uses terms that have accumulated settled meaning under the common law, a court must infer, unless the statute otherwise dictates, that Congress means to incorporate the established meaning of these terms. In the past, when Congress has used the term "employee" without defining it, we have concluded that Congress intended to describe the conventional master-servant relationship as understood by common-law agency doctrine. Nothing in the text of the work for hire provisions indicates that Congress used the words "employee" and "employment" to describe anything other than the conventional relation of employer and employee. In past cases of statutory interpretation, when we have concluded that Congress intended terms such as "employee," "employer," and "scope of employment" to be understood in light of agency law, we have relied on the general common law of agency, rather than on the law of any particular State, to give meaning to these terms. This practice reflects the fact that federal statutes are generally intended to have uniform nationwide application. Establishment of a federal rule of agency, rather than reliance on state agency law, is particularly appropriate here given the Act's express objective of creating national, uniform copyright law by broadly pre-empting state statutory and common-law copyright regulation. We thus agree with the Court of Appeals that the term "employee" should be understood in light of the general common law of agency. To determine whether a work is for hire under the Act, a court first should ascertain, using principles of general common law of agency, whether the work was prepared by an employee or an independent contractor. After making this determination, the court can apply the appropriate subsection of §101.

We turn, finally, to an application of §101 to Reid's production of "Third World America." In determining whether a hired party is an employee under the general common law of agency, we consider the hiring party's right to control the manner and means by which the product is accomplished. Among the other factors relevant to this inquiry are the skill required; the source of the instrumentalities and tools; the location of the work; the duration of the relationship between the parties; whether the hiring party has the right to assign additional projects to the hired party; the extent of the hired party's discretion over when and how long to work; the method of payment; the hired party's role in hiring and paying assistants; whether the work is part of the regular business of the hiring party; whether the hiring party is in business; the provision of employee benefits; and the tax treatment of the hired party. No one of these factors is determinative.

Examining the circumstances of this case in light of these factors, we agree with the Court of Appeals that Reid was not an employee of CCNV but an independent contractor. True, CCNV members directed enough of Reid's work to ensure that he produced a sculpture that met their specifications. But the extent of control the hiring party exercises over the details of the product is not dispositive. Indeed, all the other circumstances weigh heavily against finding an employment relationship. Reid is a sculptor, a skilled occupation. Reid supplied his own tools. He worked in his own studio in Baltimore, making daily supervision of his activities from Washington practicably impossible. Reid was retained for less than two months, a relatively short period of time. During and after this time, CCNV had no right to assign additional projects to Reid. Apart from the deadline for completing the sculpture, Reid had absolute freedom to decide when and how long to work. CCNV paid Reid $15,000, a sum dependent on completion of a specific job, a method by which independent contractors are often compensated. Reid had total discretion in hiring and paying assistants. Creating sculptures was hardly 'regular business' for CCNV. Indeed, CCNV is not a business at all. Finally, CCNV did not pay payroll or Social Security taxes, provide any employee benefits, or contribute to unemployment insurance or workers' compensation funds. For the aforestated reasons, we affirm the judgment of the Court of Appeals for the District of Columbia Circuit. It is so ordered.

## Points for Discussion

1. Justice Marshall's opinion tells that there are several factors courts should weigh when determining whether a worker is an employee or a contractor. Look again at those factors and consider how they play out in the typical relationship between university professors and their employers. Typically, professors at research universities know that they must regularly produce publishable research (or similarly scholarly output) if they are to retain their jobs and obtain promotions. Moreover, universities can have a hand in determining what kinds of publications will be produced. A history department that hoped to hire a specialist in twentieth-century American political history will look more favorably if a faculty member seeking tenure has published a book on FDR than one on Saint Augustine. Still, there is a longstanding tradition in academe for individual professors to retain the copyrights to their works. Do you think this tradition is a wise one? Can you envision circumstances in which exceptions should be made?

2. There is nothing in the Court's interpretation of the work-for-hire doctrine that would prevent a media company from demanding that all its freelance contractors (reporters, photographers, etc.) sign contracts relinquishing their copyrights to the company. Is the matter of who controls a copyright, then, really reduced to a question of power?

# ■ *Campbell v. Acuff-Rose Music*

## 510 U.S. 569 (1994)

*Justice Souter delivered the opinion of the Court.*

In 1964, Roy Orbison and William Dees wrote a rock ballad called "Oh, Pretty Woman" and assigned their rights in it to respondent Acuff-Rose Music, Inc. Acuff-Rose registered the song for copyright protection. Petitioners Luther R. Campbell, Christopher Wongwon, Mark Ross, and David Hobbs are collectively known as 2 Live Crew, a popular rap music group. In 1989, Campbell wrote a song entitled "Pretty Woman," which he later described in an affidavit as intended, "through comical lyrics, to satirize the original work." In June or July 1989, 2 Live Crew released records, cassette tapes, and compact discs of "Pretty Woman" in a collection of songs entitled "As Clean As They Wanna Be." Almost a year later, after nearly a quarter of a million copies of the recording had been sold, Acuff-Rose sued 2 Live Crew and its record company, Luke Skyywalker Records, for copyright infringement. The District Court granted summary judgment for 2 Live Crew, reasoning that the commercial purpose of 2 Live Crew's song was no bar to fair use; that 2 Live Crew's version was a parody, which "quickly degenerates into a play on words, substituting predictable lyrics with shocking ones" to show "how bland and banal the Orbison song" is; that 2 Live Crew had taken no more than was necessary to "conjure up" the original in order to parody it; and that it was "extremely unlikely that 2 Live Crew's song could adversely affect the market for the original." The Court of Appeals for the Sixth Circuit reversed; concluding that its "blatantly commercial purpose" prevents [2 Live Crew's] parody from being a fair use. We granted certiorari to determine whether 2 Live Crew's commercial parody could be a fair use.

The first factor in a fair use enquiry is "the purpose and character of the use, including whether such use is of a commercial nature or is for nonprofit educational purposes." The enquiry here looks to whether the use is for criticism, or comment, or news reporting, and the like. The central purpose of this investigation is to see whether the new work merely supersedes the objects of the original creation or instead adds something new, with a further purpose or different character, altering the first with new expression, meaning, or message; it asks, in other words, whether and to what extent the new work is "transformative." Parody has an obvious claim to transformative value, by shedding light on an earlier work, and, in the process, creating a new one. The heart of any parodist's claim to quote from existing material is the use of some elements of a prior author's composition to create a new one that, at least in part, comments on that author's works. If, on the contrary, the commentary has no critical bearing on the substance or style of the original composition, which the alleged infringer merely uses to get attention or to avoid the drudgery in working up something fresh, the claim to fairness in borrowing from another's work diminishes accordingly (if it does not vanish).

The fact that parody can claim legitimacy for some appropriation does not, of course, tell either parodist or judge much about where to draw the line. Like a book review quoting the copyrighted material criticized, parody may or may not be fair use, and petitioners' suggestion that any parodic use is presumptively fair has no more justification in law or fact than the equally hopeful claim that any use for news reporting should be presumed fair.

Here, the District Court held, and the Court of Appeals assumed, that 2 Live Crew's "Pretty Woman" contains parody, commenting on and criticizing the original work, whatever it may have to say about society at large. As the District Court remarked, the words of 2 Live Crew's song copy the original's first line, but then "quickly degenerate into a play on words, substituting predictable lyrics with shocking ones that derisively demonstrate how bland and banal the Orbison song seems to them." The 2 Live Crew song "was clearly intended to ridicule the white-bread original" and "reminds us that sexual congress with nameless streetwalkers is not necessarily the stuff of romance and is not necessarily without its consequences. The singers (there are several) have the same thing on their minds as did the lonely man with the nasal voice, but here there is no hint of wine and roses." While we might not assign a high rank to the parodic element here, we think it fair to say that 2 Live Crew's song reasonably could be perceived as commenting on the original or criticizing it, to some degree.

The Court of Appeals, however, immediately cut short the enquiry into 2 Live Crew's fair use claim by confining its treatment of the first factor essentially to one relevant fact, the commercial nature of the use. The court then inflated the significance of this fact by applying a presumption ostensibly that "every commercial use of copyrighted material is presumptively . . . unfair." In giving virtually dispositive weight to the commercial nature of the parody, the Court of Appeals erred.

The language of the statute makes clear that the commercial or nonprofit educational purpose of a work is only one element of the first factor enquiry into its purpose and character. Accordingly, the mere fact that a use is educational and not for profit does not insulate it from a finding of infringement, any more than the commercial character of a use bars a finding of fairness. If, indeed, commerciality carried presumptive force against a finding of fairness, the presumption would swallow nearly all of the illustrative uses listed in the [Copyright Act], including news reporting, comment, criticism, teaching, scholarship, and research, since these activities are generally conducted for profit in this country.

The second statutory factor, "the nature of the copyrighted work," calls for recognition that some works are closer to the core of intended copyright protection than others, with the consequence that fair use is more difficult to establish when the former works are copied. We agree with both the District Court and the Court of Appeals that the Orbison original's creative expression for public dissemination falls within the core of the copyright's protective purposes. This fact, however, is not much help in this case, or ever likely to help much in separating the fair use sheep from the infringing goats in a parody case, since parodies almost invariably copy publicly known, expressive works.

The third factor asks whether "the amount and substantiality of the portion used in relation to the copyrighted work as a whole" are reasonable in relation to the purpose of the copying. Here, attention turns to the persuasiveness of a parodist's justification for the particular copying done, and the enquiry will harken back to the first of the statutory factors, for we recognize that the extent of permissible copying varies with the purpose and character of the use. The facts bearing on this factor will also tend to address the fourth, by revealing the degree to which the parody may serve as a market substitute for the original or potentially licensed derivatives.

The District Court considered the song's parodic purpose in finding that 2 Live Crew had not helped themselves overmuch. The Court of Appeals disagreed, stating that "while it may not be inappropriate to find that no more was taken than necessary, the copying was qualitatively substantial. Taking the heart of the original and making it the heart of a new work was to purloin a substantial portion of the essence of the original." The Court of Appeals is of course correct that this factor calls for thought not only about the quantity of the materials used, but about their quality and importance, too. Where we part company with the court below is in applying this guide to parody, and in particular to parody in the song before us. Parody presents a difficult case. Parody's humor, or in any event its comment, necessarily springs from recognizable allusion to its object through distorted imitation. Its art lies in the tension between a known original and its parodic twin. When parody takes aim at a particular original work, the parody must be able to "conjure up" at least enough of that original to make the object of its critical wit recognizable. What makes for this recognition is quotation of the original's most distinctive or memorable features, which the parodist can be sure the audience will know. Once enough has been taken to assure identification, how much more is reasonable will depend, say, on the extent to which the song's overriding purpose and character is to parody the original or, in contrast, the likelihood that the parody may serve as a market substitute for the original. But using some characteristic features cannot be avoided.

We think the Court of Appeals was insufficiently appreciative of parody's need for the recognizable sight or sound when it ruled 2 Live Crew's use unreasonable as a matter of law. It is true, of course, that 2 Live Crew copied the characteristic opening bass riff (or musical phrase) of the original, and true that the words of the first line copy the Orbison lyrics. But if quotation of the opening riff and the first line may be said to go to the "heart" of the original, the heart is also what most readily conjures up the song for parody, and it is the heart at which parody takes aim. Copying does not become excessive in relation to parodic purpose merely because the portion taken was the original's heart. If 2 Live Crew had copied a significantly less memorable part of the original, it is difficult to see how its parodic character would have come through. This is not, of course, to say that anyone who calls himself a parodist can skim the cream and get away scot free. Context is everything, and the question of fairness asks what else the parodist did besides go to the heart of the original. It is significant that 2 Live Crew not only copied the first line of the original, but thereafter departed markedly from the Orbison lyrics for its own ends. 2 Live Crew not only copied the bass riff and repeated it, but also produced otherwise distinctive sounds, interposing "scraper" noise, overlaying the music with solos in different keys, and altering the drum beat. This is not a case, then, where "a substantial portion" of the parody itself is composed of a "verbatim" copying of the original. It is not, that is, a case where the parody is so insubstantial, as compared to the copying, that the third factor must be resolved as a matter of law against the parodists. Suffice it to say here that, as to the lyrics, we think the Court of Appeals correctly suggested that "no more was taken than necessary," but just for that reason, we fail to see how the copying can be excessive in relation to its parodic purpose, even if the portion taken is the original's "heart." As to the music, we express no opinion whether repetition of the bass riff is excessive copying, and we remand to permit evaluation of the amount taken, in light of the song's parodic purpose and character, its transformative elements, and considerations of the potential for market substitution sketched more fully below.

The fourth fair use factor is "the effect of the use upon the potential market for or value of the copyrighted work." It requires courts to consider not only the extent of market harm caused by the particular actions of the alleged infringer, but also "whether unrestricted and widespread conduct of the sort engaged in by the defendant would result in a substantially adverse impact on the potential market" for the original. The enquiry "must take account not only of harm to the original but also of harm to the market for derivative works." Since fair use is an affirmative defense, its proponent would have difficulty carrying the burden of demonstrating fair use without favorable evidence about relevant markets. In moving for summary judgment, 2 Live Crew left themselves at just such a disadvantage when they failed to address the effect on the market for rap derivatives, and confined themselves to uncontroverted submissions that there was no likely effect on the market for the original. The [appellate] court resolved the fourth factor against 2 Live Crew, just as it had the first, by applying a presumption about the effect of commercial use, a presumption which as applied here we hold to be error. As to parody pure and simple, it is likely that the new work will not affect the market for the original in a way cognizable under this factor, that is, by acting as a substitute for it. This is so because the parody and the original usually serve different market functions. We do not, of course, suggest that a parody may not harm the market at all, but when a lethal parody, like a scathing theater review, kills demand for the original, it does not produce a harm cognizable under the Copyright Act. The role of the courts is to distinguish between biting criticism that merely suppresses demand and copyright infringement, which usurps it.

2 Live Crew's song comprises not only parody but also rap music, and the derivative market for rap music is a proper focus of enquiry. Evidence of substantial harm to it would weigh against a finding of fair use, because the licensing of derivatives is an important economic incentive to the creation of originals. Of course, the only harm to derivatives that need concern us, as discussed above, is the harm of market substitution. The fact that a parody may impair the market for derivative uses by the very effectiveness of its critical commentary is no more relevant under copyright than the like threat to the original market. Although 2 Live Crew submitted uncontroverted affidavits on the question of market harm to the original, neither they, nor Acuff-Rose, introduced evidence or affidavits addressing the likely effect of 2 Live Crew's parodic rap song on the market for a nonparody, rap version of "Oh, Pretty Woman." The District Court essentially passed on this issue, observing that Acuff-Rose is free to record "whatever version of the original it desires," and the Court of Appeals went the other way by erroneous presumption. Contrary to each treatment, it is impossible to deal with the fourth factor except by recognizing that a silent record on an important factor bearing on fair use disentitled the proponent of the defense, 2 Live Crew, to summary judgment. The evidentiary hole will doubtless be plugged on remand.

We reverse the judgment of the Court of Appeals and remand the case for further proceedings consistent with this opinion.

## Points for Discussion

1. Justice Souter makes clear that parodies enjoy special protection only when they make fun of the original, but do most artists we think of as musical parodists—from Mark Russell to the Capitol Steps to the late Alan Sherman—really accomplish that? The Capitol Steps' "Breaking Knees Is Hard to Do" is aimed straight at controversial ice-skater Tonya Harding, not at songwriter Neil Sedaka ("Breaking Up Is Hard to Do"), and their "The Fools on the Hill" is a critique of Congress, not of the similarly titled Lennon-McCartney tune. With these examples in mind, how much protection does the *Campbell* decision really provide to such parodists?

**2.** What do you think *should* be the proper balance between the interests of the original artists and those of parodists? The typical musical parodist takes an entire melody from a familiar tune and writes comedic lyrics for the tune. If audiences appreciate the new work and if that new work will not by its very structure dampen the market for the original, what harm is there in protecting the parodist? On the other hand, why should parodists have the right to borrow others' melodies without permission?

## *Lyons Partnership v. Giannoulas*

### 179 F.3d 384 (5th Cir. 1999)

*Judge E. Grady Jolly:*

This case involves a dispute over the use of the likeness of "Barney," a children's character who appears in a number of products marketed to children. Barney, a six-foot tall purple "tyrannosaurus rex," entertains and educates young children. His awkward and lovable behavior, good-natured disposition, and renditions of songs like "I love you, you love me," have warmed the hearts and captured the imaginations of children across the United States. According to Lyons, the owner of the intellectual property rights for Barney and the plaintiff in the suit below, the defendants—Ted Giannoulas d/b/a The Famous Chicken and TFC, Inc., the owner of the intellectual property rights to the Chicken—sought to manipulate Barney's wholesome image to accomplish their own nefarious ends.

The Chicken, a sports mascot conceived of and played by Giannoulas, targets a more grown-up audience. While the Chicken does sell marketing merchandise, it is always sold either by direct order or in conjunction with one of the Chicken's appearances. Thus, the Chicken's principal means of income could, perhaps loosely, be referred to as "performance art." Catering to the tastes of adults attending sporting events, most notably baseball games, the Chicken is renowned for his hard hitting satire. Fictional characters, celebrities, ball players, and, yes, even umpires, are all targets for the Chicken's levity. Hardly anything is sacred. And so, perhaps inevitably, the Chicken's beady glare came to rest on that lovable and carefree icon of childhood, Barney. Lyons argues that the Chicken's motivation was purely mercenary. Seeing the opportunity to hitch his wagon to a star, the Chicken incorporated a Barney look-alike into his acts. The character, a person dressed in a costume (sold with the title "Duffy the Dragon") that had a remarkable likeness to Barney's appearance, would appear next to the Chicken in an extended performance during which the Chicken would flip, slap, tackle, trample, and generally assault the Barney look-alike.

The results, according to Lyons, were profound. Lyons regales us with tales of children observing the performance who honestly believed that the real Barney was being assaulted. In one poignant account related by Lyons, a parent describes how the spectacle brought his two-year-old child to tears. Giannoulas offers a slightly different perspective on what happened. True, he argues, Barney, depicted with his large, rounded body, never changing grin, giddy chuckles, and exclamations like "Super-dee-Dooper!," may represent a simplistic ideal of goodness. Giannoulas, however, also considers Barney to be a symbol of what is wrong with our society—an homage, if you will, to all the inane, banal platitudes that we readily accept and thrust unthinkingly upon our children. Giannoulas further notes that he is not the only satirist to take shots at Barney. Saturday Night Live, Jay Leno, and a movie starring Tom Arnold have all engaged in parodies at the ungainly dinosaur's expense.

Perhaps the most insightful criticism regarding Barney is that his shows do not assist children in learning to deal with negative feelings and emotions. [Critics charge that] Barney offers our children a one-dimensional world where everyone must be happy and everything must be resolved right away. Giannoulas claims that, through careful use of parody, he sought to highlight the differences between Barney and the Chicken. Giannoulas was not merely profiting from the spectacle of a Barney look-alike making an appearance in his show. Instead, he was engaged in a sophisticated critique of society's acceptance of this ubiquitous and insipid creature.

Lyons ultimately filed a suit against Giannoulas and TFC, alleging trademark infringement, false association, unfair competition, and trademark dilution under the Lanham Act, copyright infringement, and other claims. The district court granted the defendants' motion for summary judgment. In addition, the district court awarded attorneys' fees to the defendants based on provisions in the Copyright Act. Lyons has filed a timely appeal with respect to the Lanham Act claims, the Copyright Act claims, and the award of attorneys' fees.

A trademark is a word, name, symbol or device adopted and used by a manufacturer to identify the source of goods. To establish a trademark violation, Lyons must establish that Giannoulas has used in commerce a mark confusingly similar to Lyons's. The district court held that there was no likelihood of consumer confusion. In reaching this decision, the district court relied on its finding that the Chicken's performance was clearly meant to be a parody.

Lyons makes two arguments with respect to its trademark confusion claim. First, Lyons argues that Giannoulas's use of Barney was not intended as a parody. Because Lyons continues to contest this issue on appeal, we first address whether there are any genuine issues of material fact regarding whether Giannoulas was engaged in parodying Barney. Lyons's second argument is that the district court accorded too much weight to its finding that Giannoulas's use was a parody.

In general, a parody is defined as an artistic work that imitates the characteristic style of an author or a work for comic effect or ridicule. Giannoulas claims that his use of a Barney look-alike clearly qualifies as a parody. He used the minimum necessary to evoke Barney—while he used a character dressed like Barney that danced like Barney, he did not make any other references to the mythical world in which Barney resides. He did not, for instance, incorporate any of Barney's other "friends" into his act, have the character imitate Barney's voice, or perform any of Barney's songs. According to Giannoulas, Barney was clearly the butt of a joke and he referenced the Barney character only to the extent necessary to conjure up the character's image in his audience's mind.

Lyons argues that the conduct was not a parody but simply the use of Barney. To support this claim, Lyons points to two kinds of proffered evidence. First, Lyons notes that Giannoulas himself admits that he did not have a definite plan when he incorporated Barney into the act. Lyons argues that this creates an issue of fact regarding whether Giannoulas really intended to parody Barney or simply intended to profit from incorporating the Barney character into his act. This argument is meritless. Clearly, in the context in which Giannoulas intended to insert a reference to the Barney character, the humor came from the incongruous nature of such an appearance, not from an attempt to benefit from Barney's goodwill. This point is clearly established by the fact that the Chicken's actions toward Barney seem to have always been antagonistic. Although the performance may have evolved into a far more sophisticated form of commentary, even at its inception, it was clearly meant as a parody.

The second argument made by Lyons is that the audience could not have understood the performance to be a parody. Lyons assumes that the target audience here is children and that children would clearly believe that the caricature actually was Barney. Although Lyons is correct that the intended audience is an important factor in determining whether a performance qualifies as a parody, Lyons presented no credible evidence that a significant portion of the audience at evening sporting events are children. Even if young children—like the two-year-old who had such a traumatic reaction to the down-trodden Barney—are in attendance, we would expect them to be supervised by parents who could explain the nature of the parody. We therefore agree with the district court that Giannoulas's use of the caricature clearly qualifies as a parody.

In order to understand Giannoulas's second argument, we must first review our own precedent with respect to consumer confusion under the Lanham Act. Our case law has set out a long list of non-exclusive, non-dispositive factors to consider when determining whether a use can result in confusion. These factors are referred to as the "digits of confusion." In determining whether a likelihood of confusion exists, this court considers the following non-exhaustive list of factors: (1) the type of trademark allegedly infringed, (2) the similarity between the two marks, (3) the similarity of the products or services, (4) the identity of the retail outlets and purchasers, (5) the identity of the advertising media used, (6) the defendant's intent, and (7) any evidence of actual confusion.

The district court relied on its finding that the conduct was a parody when considering each of the remaining factors or digits. The crux of Lyons's argument is that, when considering whether conduct is likely to cause consumer confusion, even if there is overwhelming evidence that the conduct is a parody, the other digits of confusion must still be considered separately, without reference to whether the conduct is a parody. If, after conducting this analysis, there are factors that support the plaintiff's claim, he argues that the plaintiff should be permitted to proceed to trial. We find this analysis absolutely absurd. Such an approach would all but require a trial for any trademark suit where the conduct was a parody. A brief consideration of only one of the digits of confusion makes this point clear. The first digit, that is, the type of trademark allegedly infringed, questions whether the trademark is so distinctive that a consumer encountering the defendant's mark would be likely to assume that the source of a product or service is the owner of the trademark. Thus, under the traditional analysis, the stronger the trademark, the more likely that this factor would weigh in favor of the plaintiff. However, as the district court correctly noted in this case, when a consumer encounters the use of a trademark in a setting that is clearly a parody, the strength of the mark may actually make it easier for the consumer to realize that the use is a parody. Therefore, a strong mark is not as relevant a factor when the use is that of parody. It seems reasonable to us to expect that most comedians will seek to satirize images or figures who will be widely recognized by their audiences. It therefore seems unlikely that comedians will target trademarks that do not have significant strength. If the district court were not able to consider the relevance that parody plays in this analysis, the district court would almost always have to conclude that this digit of confusion weighed in favor of the plaintiff. Such a result would effectively tie the district court's hands unnecessarily and prevent the district court from applying common sense.

We conclude that the district court did not err in considering the other digits of confusion in the light of its finding that the Chicken's performance is a parody. For the foregoing reasons, the ruling of the district court is affirmed.

## Points for Discussion

1. Theoretically, the main reason for having trademark law is to protect the general public's desire for a degree of predictability and consistency in products and services. If any dingy hotel could call itself the Hyatt,

travelers would have no way of knowing how to find acceptable accommodations. Does this interest in protecting the consumer have any relevance at all to trademark parody situations such as this one involving Barney the dinosaur?

2. How far should the trademark parodist's rights extend? Should a cartoonist be able to depict Charles Schulz's *Peanuts* characters in a host of depraved situations (e.g., drug abuse, violent sexual practices)? Would it make a difference whether the depictions were a one-time-only event—such as in a painting—or if the parodist created a whole new daily comic strip using Charlie Brown and the others' faces without permission?

# 7

# *Access to Information*

The U.S. Supreme Court has occasionally remarked that the First Amendment provides at least some measure of protection for the process of news gathering. Still, it is clear that the First Amendment deals mostly with the media's right to report information they already know and does not create a right to *learn* that information in the first place. The legislative branch has filled much of the vacuum, however, through federal and state laws governing access to publicly held information, and creating a presumption that official meetings of government agencies will be conducted in public view.

The first case in this chapter, *Saxbe v. Washington Post,* is one of several Supreme Court decisions from the 1970s putting the press on notice that they are granted no special rights of access to sensitive government property (here, a jail) beyond those granted to the general public. Then, we see how the Hawaii Supreme Court, in *Borreca v. Fasi,* admitted that public officials have no obligation to hold press conferences, all the while admonishing them that they may not discriminate against "unfriendly" media at whatever press conferences they choose to hold.

The federal Freedom of Information Act (FOIA) is the impetus for hundreds of court cases annually. In many of these cases, courts are called on to determine whether one of the statute's exemptions from the presumption of disclosure is implicated by the specific information sought by a requestor. *Kurzon v. Department of Health and Human Services* is one such case. It involves FOIA's exemption 6, which covers "personnel, medical, and similar" files that, if disclosed, would violate someone's privacy. But what does it mean to be "similar," and how much privacy do persons discussed in such files have a right to expect?

Finally, we examine a case from the Texas Supreme Court—*Acker v. Texas Water Commission*—that interprets that state's Open Meetings Act, warning public officials that even the most casual exchange of views in the most informal of settings might constitute a "meeting."

**126**

# Saxbe v. Washington Post

## 417 U.S. 843 (1974)

*Justice Stewart delivered the opinion of the Court.*

In March 1972, the respondents requested permission from the petitioners, the officials responsible for administering federal prisons, to conduct several interviews with specific inmates in the prisons at Lewisburg, Pennsylvania, and Danbury, Connecticut. The petitioners denied permission for such interviews on the authority of Policy Statement 1220.1A, prohibiting any personal interviews between newsmen and individually designated federal prison inmates. [Respondents contend] that the prohibition of all press interviews with prison inmates abridges the protection that the First Amendment accords the news gathering activity of a free press.

The District Court agreed with this contention and held that the Policy Statement, insofar as it totally prohibited all press interviews at the institutions involved, violated the First Amendment. The Court of Appeals affirmed, holding that press interviews with prison inmates could not be totally prohibited as the Policy Statement purported to do, but may "be denied only where it is the judgment of the administrator directly concerned, based on either the demonstrated behavior of the inmate, or special conditions existing at the institution at the time the interview is requested, or both, that the interview presents a serious risk of administrative or disciplinary problems."

The policies of the Federal Bureau of Prisons regarding visitations to prison inmates accord liberal visitation privileges to inmates' families, their attorneys, and religious counsel. Even friends of inmates are allowed to visit, although their privileges appear to be somewhat more limited. Other than members of these limited groups with personal and professional ties to the inmates, members of the general public are not permitted under the Bureau's policy to enter the prisons and interview consenting inmates. This policy is applied with an even hand to all prospective visitors, including newsmen, who, like other members of the public, may enter the prisons to visit friends or family members. But, again like members of the general public, they may not enter the prison and insist on visiting an inmate with whom they have no such relationship.

Except for the limitation in Policy Statement 1220.1A on face-to-face press–inmate interviews, members of the press are accorded substantial access to the federal prisons in order to observe and report the conditions they find there. Indeed, journalists are given access to the prisons and to prison inmates that in significant respects exceeds that afforded to members of the general public. For example, Policy Statement 1220.1A permits press representatives to tour the prisons and to photograph any prison facilities. During such tours a newsman is permitted to conduct brief interviews with any inmates he might encounter. In addition, newsmen and inmates are permitted virtually unlimited written correspondence with each other. Outgoing correspondence from inmates to press representatives is neither censored nor inspected. Incoming mail from press representatives is inspected only for contraband or statements inciting illegal action. Moreover, prison officials are available to the press and are required by Policy Statement 1220.1A to "give all possible assistance" to press representatives "in providing background and a specific report" concerning any inmate complaints.

The respondents have also conceded in their brief that Policy Statement 1220.1A "has been interpreted by the Bureau to permit a newsman to interview a randomly selected group of inmates." As a result, the reporter respondent in this case was permitted to interview a randomly selected group of inmates at the Lewisburg prison. Finally, in light of the constant turnover in the prison population, it is clear that there is always a large group of recently released prisoners who are available to both the press and the general public as a source of information about conditions in the federal prisons.

Thus, it is clear that Policy Statement 1220.1A is not part of any attempt by the Federal Bureau of Prisons to conceal from the public the conditions prevailing in federal prisons. This limitation on prearranged press interviews with individually designated inmates was motivated by disciplinary and administrative considerations. The interest of the press is often concentrated on a relatively small number of inmates who, as a result, become virtual "public figures" within the prison society and gain a disproportionate degree of notoriety and influence among their fellow inmates. As a result those inmates who are conspicuously publicized tend to become the source of substantial disciplinary problems that can engulf a large portion of the population at a prison.

It is unnecessary to engage in any delicate balancing of such penal considerations against the legitimate demands of the First Amendment. For it is apparent that the sole limitation imposed on news gathering by Policy Statement 1220.1A is no more than a particularized application of the general rule that nobody may enter the prison and designate an inmate whom he would like to visit, unless the prospective visitor is a lawyer, clergyman, relative, or friend of that inmate. This limitation on visitations is justified by the truism that prisons are institutions where public access is generally limited. In this regard, the Bureau of Prisons visitation policy does not place the press in any less advantageous position than the public generally. Indeed, the total access to federal prisons and prison inmates that the Bureau of Prisons accords to the press far surpasses that available to other members of the public.

Newsmen have no constitutional right of access to prisons or their inmates beyond that afforded the general public. The proposition that the

Constitution imposes upon government the affirmative duty to make available to journalists sources of information not available to members of the public generally finds no support in the words of the Constitution or in any decision of this Court. Thus, since Policy Statement 1220.1A does not deny the press access to sources of information available to members of the general public, we hold that it does not abridge the freedom that the First Amendment guarantees. Accordingly, the judgment of the Court of Appeals is reversed and the case is remanded to the District Court for further proceedings consistent with this opinion. It is so ordered.

## Points for Discussion

1. Is there a danger that the Bureau of Prisons policy will prevent those interviews most likely to be of public interest? Suppose, for example, that a specific inmate complains of a guard's act of brutality or that the press wishes to confirm reports that a particular inmate of some notoriety is being given special treatment.

2. Justice Stewart emphasizes the many alternative means by which reporters can gather information about the penal system without having to conduct targeted interviews. Do you think that those alternatives are satisfactory? Why or why not, and under what circumstances?

## ◼ *Borreca v. Fasi*

### 369 F. Supp. 906 (D. Haw. 1974)

*Judge King:*

The Honolulu Star-Bulletin is Hawaii's leading newspaper of general circulation. Richard Borreca started working for the Honolulu Star-Bulletin as a news reporter in 1970. For the past two years, his assignment has been Honolulu's city hall, which includes attending the mayor's news conferences. During 1973, Mayor Fasi concluded that Borreca was irresponsible, inaccurate, biased, and malicious in reporting on the mayor and the city administration. This conclusion was based on the news stories written by Borreca. Mayor Fasi expressed his dislike for Borreca personally and stated that he would not talk to Borreca "until Hell freezes over." He declared Borreca *persona non grata* at city hall and instructed his staff, and specifically his administrative assistant James Lee Loomis, to keep Borreca out of the mayor's office.

Loomis, on behalf of the mayor and as part of his usual duties, announced general news conferences in the mayor's office for November 2 and 22 and December 13 and 19, 1973. A general news conference was defined by Loomis as a conference where all media generally are informed of the mayor's intention to hold a news conference and all are free to attend. Loomis testified as to notice of these conferences that: "Customarily I will have my people notify the two city desks of the two dailies [the afternoon Honolulu Star-Bulletin and the morning The Honolulu Advertiser], call the three television stations [KGMB-TV, KHON-TV, and KITV], one or two radio stations that we know directly would usually care, and we notify the two wire services [AP and UPI]. They in turn put out the word of the news conferences to their subscribers which would include anybody."

The usual format at these news conferences was that a prepared release would be handed out and explained to the attending representatives of the news media who would ask questions mostly confined to the subject matter of the release. Borreca presented himself at the mayor's office on November 2, 1973, as the Honolulu Star-Bulletin's representative at the news conference. Loomis informed Borreca that Borreca would not be allowed to attend; [he] was in fact blocked and denied entry and no one from the Honolulu Star-Bulletin was in attendance at this conference.

Borreca again presented himself at the mayor's office on November 22, 1973, as the Honolulu Star-Bulletin's representative at that news conference. It is a fair inference from the evidence that Borreca expected to be excluded and purposely sought a confrontation with Loomis, which confrontation occurred and the verbal parts of which Borreca recorded on a portable tape recorder, transcribed, and wrote up for the next day's afternoon newspaper.

Borreca was in fact excluded from this news conference and the two December news conferences and no one from the Honolulu Star-Bulletin was in attendance at these conferences. Mayor Fasi informed the Honolulu Star-Bulletin that any other reporter from that newspaper would be welcome, but the newspaper declined to change Borreca's assignment or to send another representative to the mayor's news conferences.

It is clear from the evidence that the mayor's objections to Borreca are based solely on what appeared in the Honolulu Star-Bulletin as Borreca's city hall news stories. No other ground for objection has been given, although Loomis mentioned "other acts" by Borreca. These "other acts" turned out to be Loomis' observation that Borreca seldom took notes thereby increasing the probability of inaccurate reporting, and the statements (mentioned above) attributed to Borreca indicating bias and malice against Mayor Fasi. For purposes of this motion for a preliminary injunction only and without prejudice to his right to contest the negative statements made about him by the mayor and Loomis, Borreca offers no rebuttal evidence regarding the accuracy of his reporting or his attitude toward the mayor.

Freedom of the press as guaranteed by the First Amendment is safeguarded by the due process clause of the Fourteenth Amendment against invasions by state action. First Amendment freedom of the press includes a limited right of reasonable access to news. This right of access includes a right of access to the public galleries, the press rooms, and the press conferences dealing with government. The limitations that may be placed by state action on this right of access are determined by a balancing process in which the importance of the news gathering activity and the degree and type of the restraint sought to be imposed are balanced against the state interest to be served. Where First Amendment rights are involved, the asserted state interest must be compelling and the proposed state action must be the least restrictive means available for the asserted governmental end.

Mayor Fasi argues that his ostracism of Borreca and ultimatum to the Honolulu Star-Bulletin are not invasions of freedom of the press or do not involve state action. With respect to the first point, the mayor argues that the Honolulu Star-Bulletin is not prevented from having a representative at a news conference as anyone other than Borreca would be admitted, Borreca is not denied access to news as he may obtain a copy of each news release and of any other written material, and the right of access to news does not include a requirement that Mayor Fasi respond to Borreca's questioning.

One would have to be naive to believe that an individual reporter is solely responsible for the manner in which that reporter's news stories appear in print. Thus Mayor Fasi's objections to Borreca's performance as a reporter can equally be taken as objections to the Honolulu Star-Bulletin's approach to city hall news. Requiring a newspaper's reporter to pass a subjective compatibility-accuracy test as a condition precedent to the right of that reporter to gather news is no different in kind from requiring a newspaper to submit its proposed news stories for editing as a condition precedent to the right of that newspaper to have a reporter cover the news. Each is a form of censorship.

News conferences are not held solely or even primarily for the benefit of the news media. Structured news conferences on limited topics covered by redistributed news releases serve the purpose of the person holding the conference as much if not more than of the news media. Manipulation of the news is a highly developed technique, utilizing staff news specialists, self-serving handouts, programmed appearances, and positive and negative reinforcement in dealing with reporters and news media. Hand-picking those in attendance intensifies the manipulation. In some respects, therefore, these events are less newsworthy than a freer give and take between interviewers and interviewee. To say, however, that attendance at such a news conference is not a legitimate news gathering activity is absurd.

As a general proposition, the mayor is quite correct in his position that he is not required to respond in any way to any question put to him by any representative of any news media. Whether repeated selective discriminatory unreasonable refusal to respond to all questions by an individual reporter would form the basis of an action for damages under 42 U.S.C. § 1983 is not before the court at this time. Certainly no mandatory injunction requiring the mayor to answer questions would be granted, if for no other reason than its unenforceability.

With respect to the mayor's second point, he argues that his news conferences are private affairs held in his private office at his discretion. The mayor is too modest. As the chief executive of the City and County of Honolulu, his statements on municipal and county operations and concerns are embryonic executive directives. They are public communications put forth by him in his official capacity. If he chooses to hold a general news conference in his inner office, for that purpose and to that extent his inner office becomes a public gathering place. When he uses public buildings and public employees to call and hold general news conferences on public matters he is operating in the public and not the private sector of his activities. His oral order to his staff to exclude Borreca from his office is an executive directive by him in the exercise of his authority as mayor which authority he derives from the constitution and laws of the State of Hawaii. The actions of his staff members in excluding Borreca are actions by public employees in their official capacities taken pursuant to the mayor's directive.

A free press is not necessarily an angelic press. Newspapers take sides, especially in political contests. Newspaper reporters are not always accurate and objective. They are subject to criticism, and the right of a governmental official to criticize is within First Amendment guarantees. But when criticism transforms into an attempt to use the powers of governmental office to intimidate or to discipline the press or one of its members because of what appears in print, a compelling governmental interest that cannot be served by less restrictive means must be shown for such use to meet Constitutional standards. No compelling governmental interest has been shown or even claimed here.

The mayor suggests that there is no requirement that he hold any news conferences, and that he may select individual representatives of the news media with whom to meet in situations other than general news conferences. The mayor is no doubt right again, as a general proposition. On the other hand, it is not necessary to the decision of the pending aspect of the motion for a preliminary injunction to discuss, and I therefore express no opinion, on the possible application to these situations of the equal protection clause of the Fourteenth Amendment, or of the possible implications of de facto discrimination against individual news gatherers or against selected segments of the news media.

Plaintiffs have demonstrated a probability of success on the merits of their action insofar as Mayor Fasi is concerned. With respect to Defendant James Lee Loomis, injunctive relief against him is unnecessary as he would be covered by the general injunctive language including Defendant Fasi and anyone acting on his behalf or pursuant to his directions.

Plaintiffs are entitled to a preliminary injunction enjoining Defendant Frank F. Fasi from preventing, or from instructing or advising any person to prevent, Plaintiff Richard Borreca from attending any press conference on the same basis and to the same extent that other news reporters attend press conferences.

## Points for Discussion

1. Judge King says that "freedom of the press includes a limited right of reasonable access to news." But who or what is "the press"? Would a white supremacist group that happened to publish a newsletter be able to send its "reporter" to the mayor's press conferences?

2. Suppose that the room in which the mayor conducted press conferences is too small to accommodate all the media representatives who wish to attend. Might Fasi then be able to prevent Borreca (and others) from attending? What kinds of "objective" criteria might Fasi be forced to use in determining which media outlets would and would not be admitted?

## Kurzon v. Department of Health and Human Services

**649 F.2d 65 (1st Cir. 1981)**

*Judge Coffin:*

Appellant brought this action in the district court under the Freedom of Information Act, to compel disclosure of names and addresses of unsuccessful applicants for research grants from the National Cancer Institute. To support its withholding of this information, the government relied on the authority of exemption 6, which removes from the FOIA's mandatory disclosure requirement "personnel and medical files and similar files the disclosure of which would constitute a clearly unwarranted invasion of personal privacy." The district court determined that disclosure, while not significantly advancing the public interest, could substantially injure the professional reputations of the applicants, and entered summary judgment for the government.

Appellant, a physician and former clinical researcher, allegedly wanted to test his theory that the peer review method by which the National Institutes of Health (NIH) evaluate grant applications is biased against unorthodox proposals. He intended to interest a university group in studying rejected projects to determine if innovative research proposals had been fairly evaluated by the peer review system. The district court did not address the question whether the requested information constituted a medical, personnel or similar file, but proceeded directly to balance the privacy interest of the unfunded applicants against the public interest to be served by disclosure. The district court found appellant's proffered justification for disclosure seriously deficient in several respects. The court noted that appellant had failed to present "any direct or probative data" to support his thesis, that his approach was "rather vague and unpromising" and that his suggestion of an ombudsman to be an advocate for innovative research proposals amounted to a "review of the reviewers." An ombudsman would be incompatible, in the district court's view, with the "scholarly and thoughtful reflection" needed for review of grant proposals. Even assuming that appellant's proposal had merit, the district court doubted that a survey of disappointed applicants, who "would naturally be inclined to possess subjective and possibly unreliable estimations of the worth of their ideas," would be helpful in designing ways to improve the peer review method.

The court noted that NIH had conducted its own study of the peer review system and that appellant had failed to contribute to that study, despite an invitation to do so. Finally, the district court found that appellant could obtain the requested information at reasonable cost through alternative means by soliciting names and addresses in scientific publications. Based on these perceived deficiencies in appellant's methodology and proposals for reform, the district court concluded that granting appellant's information request would advance the public interest only slightly.

The district court next evaluated the privacy interest at stake. While recognizing that the FOIA policy in favor of disclosure would prevail against a minor invasion of privacy, the court concluded that disclosure of the requested information "would be a serious unwarranted invasion of privacy and might reflect opinions about the competence of the applicant or his professional qualifications." The district court reasoned that although a project having high scientific interest could be passed over for reasons unrelated to its merit, rejection might nevertheless convey a sense of failure and permit the inference that the true reason for rejection was lack of merit. Balancing this threat to privacy against the public interest in disclosure, the district court decided that disclosure of the "sensitive personal information" sought by appellant would be clearly unwarranted.

To determine if exemption 6 was properly invoked, we must inquire whether the names and addresses of unsuccessful grant applicants are sufficiently similar to medical and personnel files to fall within the scope of exemption 6 and, if so, whether disclosure would cause a clearly unwarranted invasion of personal privacy. In cases where the lack of similarity proves dispositive, addressing that issue first avoids the difficulties inherent in attempting to balance meaningfully widely disparate interests.

One such difficulty is illustrated by the district court's scrutiny of appellant's particular plans for making use of the information he requested. The tendency thus to define the relevant public interest narrowly in order to permit a more concrete comparison of public and private interests is understandable, but out of place in this context. By considering not only the probable efficacy of appellant's proposed survey but also the worth of his specific suggestions for reform, the district court failed to observe the distinction between the importance of the subject matter of the request and the prospects of the requester as standard-bearer for the public interest. The several exhibits submitted in support of appellant's motion for summary judgment demonstrated that the peer review method, and particularly its possible stultifying effect on innovative research, were matters of serious and continuing concern within the scientific community. The existence of an NIH study examining the very criticism raised by appellant, though perhaps rendering his efforts redundant, confirms rather than diminishes the importance of appellant's concern.

Had the district court viewed the public interest through a wider lens, it would have accorded greater weight to that interest. Because the court also deemed the harm threatened by disclosure to be substantial, suggesting a close question on balancing interests, it would have done well to consider first the privacy interest at stake, beginning with the question whether the names and addresses requested constituted a "similar file." The common denominator of files covered by exemption 6 has been described as the extent to which they contain "intimate details" of a "highly personal" nature. While exemption 6 was intended to shield against a variety of embarrassing disclosures, the test is not merely whether the information is in some sense personal but whether it is "of the same magnitude as highly personal or as intimate in nature as that at stake in personnel and medical records." Our consideration of the degree and nature of harm to grant applicants threatened by disclosure leads us to conclude that the information sought in this case is not sufficiently personal or private to satisfy the "similar file" requirement. The degree of intrusion is limited, in the first instance, by the slight informational content of the requested material. The only information sought is a list of names and business addresses, we may assume coupled with the knowledge that these applicants' proposals were not funded. Rejection, moreover, is not so rare an occurrence as to stigmatize the unfunded applicant. The record shows that approximately twice as many applications are rejected as are not.

The evidence of stigma, apart from this statistic, is equally frail. Although the affiants assembled by the government were unanimous in their view that a negative inference "could be drawn" from the fact of rejection, none identified who might be likely to draw such an unwarranted inference. All were agreed, on the other hand, that in fact no such inference should be drawn because of the many possible reasons, unrelated to merit, for rejection. We think the upshot of these statements is that those in a position to influence a researcher's career, his or her superiors and peers, are likely to share the more sophisticated view of the government's affiants that rejection of a grant proposal is not a reliable indicator of merit.

Additionally, we are not persuaded that the nature of the privacy interest threatened, taken in conjunction with the degree of potential harm, warrants the protection of exemption 6. The adverse effect of a rejection of a grant proposal, if it exists at all, is limited to the professional rather than personal qualities of the applicant, to the possible negative reflection on an applicant's performance in "grantsmanship" (the professional competition among research scientists for grants). It obviously is not a reference to more serious "professional" deficiencies such as unethical behavior. While protection of professional reputation, even in this strict sense, is not beyond the purview of exemption 6, it is not at its core.

Finally, federal grant applicants cannot reasonably expect that their efforts to secure government funds, especially in a field so much in the public eye as cancer research, will remain purely private matters. There is an obvious public element to the process and the results, as recognized in the NIH practice of releasing both the applications and identities of funded grant applicants. Nor, evidently, was a promise of anonymity necessary to attract applicants. There was no such promise, either express or implied, as to applicant identities. Though we need not decide here what effect an affirmative, specific promise of confidentiality might have if one were given, the lack of such a representation does not aid the government's position in this case. Those cases that have held the "similar file" requirement satisfied have generally described far greater invasions of privacy than that threatened here.

For the foregoing reasons the judgment of the district court is reversed.


## Points for Discussion

1. For an unsuccessful grant applicant's identity to be revealed should not be seen as a privacy invasion, Judge Coffin argues, at least in part because this particular funding competition had a 67 percent or so rejection rate ("The record shows that approximately twice as many applications are rejected as are not"). Suppose, however, that virtually all applicants had been funded. Would or should that alter the FOIA analysis?

2. Judge Coffin also suggests that there is no true issue of privacy at work here because, at most, a rejected application for funding reflects negatively on a researcher's "grantsmanship," not on his or her personal qualities. Suppose, however, that Kurzon sought transcripts of any discussions by National Cancer Institute review panels in which charges had been made about an applicant's integrity. Perhaps, for example, a

reviewer claims that an applicant has "fudged" data in previous studies or has lent his name to too many publications in which he has really had very minimal input. Would or should that alter the FOIA analysis?

# Acker v. Texas Water Commission

**790 S.W.2d 299 (Tex. 1990)**

*Justice Doggett:*

The vital issue in this case is whether the decision making of a state agency in a contested administrative case should be done openly or secretly. We believe the law requires openness.

Charles M. Acker received a favorable recommendation from the hearings examiner at the Texas Water Commission on a requested permit for a wastewater treatment plant. Thereafter, during a recess of a public hearing conducted by the three member Commission, Commissioners Hopkins and Roming were allegedly overheard conversing about this application in a restroom. This purported discussion concerned Acker's costs in complying with a city subdivision ordinance. When the public meeting reconvened, Commissioners Hopkins and Houchins voted to deny the application, and Commissioner Roming voted to grant it. Claiming a violation of the Texas Open Meetings Act, Acker brought suit seeking to set aside this order. The trial court granted Acker summary judgment based upon this asserted violation, but was reversed by the court of appeals on grounds that section 17 of the Texas Administrative Procedure and Texas Register Act [TAPTRA] allows private communications between agency members. We affirm the judgment, although not the reasoning, of the court of appeals and remand to the trial court for further proceedings.

The Open Meetings Act, enacted in 1967, [provides that] executive and legislative decisions of our governmental officials as well as the underlying reasoning must be discussed openly before the public rather than secretly behind closed doors. In order to effect this policy, this statute requires that "every regular, special, or called meeting or session of every governmental body shall be open to the public." A "meeting" includes any deliberation involving a "quorum" or majority of the members of a governing body at which they act on or discuss any public business or policy over which they have control. Any verbal exchange between a majority of the members concerning any issue within their jurisdiction constitutes a "deliberation." When a majority of a public decision making body is considering a pending issue, there can be no "informal" discussion. There is either formal consideration of a matter in compliance with the Open Meetings Act or an illegal meeting. Our citizens are entitled to more than a result. They are entitled not only to know what government decides but to observe how and why every decision is reached. The explicit command of the statute is for openness at every stage of the deliberations.

The court of appeals created a gaping hole in the Open Meetings Act through the meaning accorded to the subsequent enactment of section 17 of TAPTRA. That court held that TAPTRA authorizes a quorum of a state commission without any prior notice to meet and deliberate privately about any aspect of a pending contested proceeding. This holding effectively eviscerates the Open Meetings Act for application to the executive branch of our government. In administrative review of contested issues from a to z—from alcoholic beverages to zoos—secrecy would suddenly be authorized. This serious circumvention of open government is not warranted under the rules of statutory construction. A statute is presumed to have been enacted by the legislature with complete knowledge of the existing law and with reference to it. TAPTRA was enacted in 1975 to "afford minimum standards of uniform practice and procedure for state agencies." A subsequent amendment to section 17 of TAPTRA provided that "an agency member may communicate ex parte with other members of the agency." Without attempting to reconcile the Open Meetings Act with this provision, the court of appeals considered the latter impliedly to have repealed the former for purposes of all administrative agency consideration of contested cases.

Such statutory repeals by implication are not favored. A legislative enactment covering a subject dealt with by an older law, but not repealing that law, should be harmonized whenever possible with its predecessor in such a manner as to give effect to both. Accordingly, section 17 of TAPTRA can be harmonized with the Open Meetings Act by allowing a state commission's members to confer ex parte, but only when less than a quorum is present. Such coordinating preserves both TAPTRA and the objective of the Open Meetings Act to forbid ex parte deliberations.

Since the two statutes in question can be harmonized in a manner not compelling implicit revocation of the Open Meetings Act, we now consider whether the Commission violated the Act as a matter of law. In the review of a summary judgment, the movant has the burden of showing that there is no genuine issue of material fact and that it is entitled to judgment as a matter of law. Evidence favorable to the non-movant will be taken as true when deciding whether a material fact issue exists. All reasonable inferences must be indulged in favor of the non-movant and any doubts resolved in its favor.

The trial court's finding of an improper, closed meeting by two of the three members of the Commission is supported by the affidavit of Andrew M. Taylor who overheard the Roming/Hopkins conversation. As one of Acker's attorneys in the proceedings before the Commission, Taylor was an interested witness. His relationship with Acker, however, is not enough to defeat the motion.

Both Commissioners Roming and Hopkins testified by affidavit that they had no recollection of any conversation outside the hearing, and that considering their past behavior and habit at the Texas Water Commission, the occurrence of such a conversation was highly unlikely. The habit or custom of a person doing a particular act is relevant in determining his conduct on the occasion in question. These affidavits are sufficient to controvert the summary judgment evidence of Taylor, thereby raising a fact question and defeating Acker's motion.

We hold that a meeting between a majority of the Commissioners to discuss among themselves contested issues outside a public hearing violates section 2 of the Open Meetings Act. We further hold that in this case the Commissioners' affidavits raised a material fact issue precluding summary judgment. We affirm the judgment, although not the reasoning, of the court of appeals and remand this case to the trial court for further proceedings consistent with this opinion.

## Points for Discussion

1. The Texas Open Meetings Act defines a "deliberation" as "any verbal exchange between a majority of the members concerning any issue within their jurisdiction." Would there have been a violation of the law had Commissioners Hopkins and Roming's men's room conversation consisted of no more than, "That Acker sure is an ugly SOB, don't you think?" and, "Yup. And his mother dresses him funny, too!"?

2. The court reconciles the Open Meetings Act with TAPTRA by permitting nonpublic, *ex parte* meetings to take place as long as a quorum is not present. At least this way, any such nonpublic meetings will not result in a final decision. What happens, though, in the case of a commission consisting only of three members? Two is a quorum, but two is also the minimum number of participants in a discussion. Can members of such a commission therefore never have a nonpublic discussion?

# 8 *Reporting on the Judiciary*

There is a certain tension between the First Amendment's free speech and free press guarantees and the Sixth Amendment, which promises criminal defendants that their juries will be impartial. Might not certain kinds of media coverage, especially of sensational crimes, make it difficult to find jurors who can render a judgment solely on the evidence to be presented to them in the courtroom? The cases in this chapter offer a glimpse into how courts have addressed this difficult question.

We begin with *Sheppard v. Maxwell,* a 1966 U.S. Supreme Court case dealing with the trial of Dr. Sam Sheppard for the murder of his wife. You may recognize this case as the basis for the TV series and motion picture *The Fugitive.* In the course of overturning Sheppard's conviction, the Supreme Court tells trial judges that they need to do a better job of keeping the press (and trial participants) in line.

In *Nebraska Press Association v. Stuart,* the Supreme Court tells trial judges under what circumstances they may impose a "gag order," prohibiting the media from publishing certain categories of information about a pending criminal investigation or an ongoing trial.

In addition to their name—*Press-Enterprise Company v. Superior Court*—the next two cases have in common the question as to when trial judges will be permitted to close the courtroom to the press and public. The first case deals with the closure of a *voir dire* (jury selection) hearing, while the second involves an elaborate "preliminary hearing" as conducted in California.

Finally, in *United States v. McVeigh,* we see how the judge in the Oklahoma City bombing case dealt with a media request for information concerning how much tax money was being spent to help provide Timothy McVeigh with an adequate defense team. Judge Leonard Matsch had to consider not only what the public has a right to know, but when they need to know it.

# ◼ *Sheppard v. Maxwell*

384 U.S. 333 (1966)

*Justice Clark delivered the opinion of the Court.*

This federal habeas corpus application involves the question whether Sheppard was deprived of a fair trial in his state conviction for the second-degree murder of his wife because of the trial judge's failure to protect Sheppard sufficiently from the massive, pervasive and prejudicial publicity that attended his prosecution. Marilyn Sheppard, petitioner's pregnant wife, was bludgeoned to death in the upstairs bedroom of their lakeshore home in Bay Village, Ohio, a suburb of Cleveland.

Sheppard was not granted a change of venue to a locale away from where the publicity originated; nor was his jury sequestered. The Sheppard jurors were subjected to newspaper, radio and television coverage of the trial while not taking part in the proceedings. They were allowed to go their separate ways outside of the courtroom, without adequate directions not to read or listen to anything concerning the case. Moreover, the jurors were thrust into the role of celebrities by the judge's failure to insulate them from reporters and photographers. The numerous pictures of the jurors, with their addresses, which appeared in the newspapers before and during the trial itself exposed them to expressions of opinion from both cranks and friends. The fact that anonymous letters had been received by prospective jurors should have made the judge aware that this publicity seriously threatened the jurors' privacy.

Sheppard stood indicted for the murder of his wife; the State was demanding the death penalty. For months the virulent publicity about Sheppard and the murder had made the case notorious. Charges and countercharges were aired in the news media besides those for which Sheppard was called to trial. In addition, only three months before trial, Sheppard was examined for more than five hours without counsel during a three-day inquest which ended in a public brawl. The inquest was televised live from a high school gymnasium seating hundreds of people. Furthermore, the trial began two weeks before a hotly contested election at which both Chief Prosecutor Mahon and Judge Blythin were candidates for judgeships.

While we cannot say that Sheppard was denied due process by the judge's refusal to take precautions against the influence of pretrial publicity alone, the court's later rulings must be considered against the setting in which the trial was held. In light of this background, we believe that the arrangements made by the judge with the news media caused Sheppard to be deprived of that judicial serenity and calm to which he was entitled. The fact is that bedlam reigned at the courthouse during the trial and newsmen took over practically the entire courtroom, hounding most of the participants in the trial, especially Sheppard. At a temporary table within a few feet of the jury box and counsel table sat some 20 reporters staring at Sheppard and taking notes. The erection of a press table for reporters inside the bar is unprecedented. The bar of the court is reserved for counsel, providing them a safe place in which to keep papers and exhibits, and to confer privately with client and co-counsel. It is designed to protect the witness and the jury from any distractions, intrusions or influences, and to permit bench discussions of the judge's rulings away from the hearing of the public and the jury. Having assigned almost all of the available seats in the courtroom to the news media the judge lost his ability to supervise that environment. The movement of the reporters in and out of the courtroom caused frequent confusion and disruption of the trial. And the record reveals constant commotion within the bar. Moreover, the judge gave the throng of newsmen gathered in the corridors of the courthouse absolute free rein. Participants in the trial, including the jury, were forced to run a gauntlet of reporters and photographers each time they entered or left the courtroom. The total lack of consideration for the privacy of the jury was demonstrated by the assignment to a broadcasting station of space next to the jury room on the floor above the courtroom, as well as the fact that jurors were allowed to make telephone calls during their five-day deliberation.

There can be no question about the nature of the publicity which surrounded Sheppard's trial. As the trial progressed, the newspapers summarized and interpreted the evidence, devoting particular attention to the material that incriminated Sheppard, and often drew unwarranted inferences from testimony. Nor is there doubt that this deluge of publicity reached at least some of the jury. Despite the extent and nature of the publicity to which the jury was exposed during trial, the judge refused defense counsel's other requests that the jurors be asked whether they had read or heard specific prejudicial comment about the case. In these circumstances, we can assume that some of this material reached members of the jury.

The court's fundamental error is compounded by the holding that it lacked power to control the publicity about the trial. From the very inception of the proceedings the judge announced that neither he nor anyone else could restrict prejudicial news accounts. And he reiterated this view on numerous occasions. Since he viewed the news media as his target, the judge never considered other means that are often utilized to reduce the appearance of prejudicial material and to protect the jury from outside influence. We conclude that these procedures would have been sufficient to guarantee Sheppard a fair trial and so do not consider what sanctions might be available against a recalcitrant press nor the charges of bias now made against the state trial judge.

The carnival atmosphere at trial could easily have been avoided since the courtroom and courthouse premises are subject to the control of the court. The judge should have adopted stricter rules governing the use of the courtroom by newsmen, as Sheppard's counsel requested. The number of reporters in the courtroom itself could have been limited at the first sign that their presence would disrupt the trial. They certainly should not have been placed inside the bar. Furthermore, the judge should have more closely regulated the conduct of newsmen in the courtroom. For instance, the judge belatedly asked them not to handle and photograph trial exhibits lying on the counsel table during recesses.

Secondly, the court should have insulated the witnesses. All of the newspapers and radio stations apparently interviewed prospective witnesses at will, and in many instances disclosed their testimony. Although the witnesses were barred from the courtroom during the trial the full verbatim testimony was available to them in the press. This completely nullified the judge's imposition of the rule.

Thirdly, the court should have made some effort to control the release of leads, information, and gossip to the press by police officers, witnesses, and the counsel for both sides. Much of the information thus disclosed was inaccurate, leading to groundless rumors and confusion. Defense counsel immediately brought to the court's attention the tremendous amount of publicity in the Cleveland press that "misrepresented entirely the testimony" in the case. Under such circumstances, the judge should have at least warned the newspapers to check the accuracy of their accounts. And it is obvious that the judge should have further sought to alleviate this problem by imposing control over the statements made to the news media by counsel, witnesses, and especially the Coroner and police officers. The prosecution repeatedly made evidence available to the news media which was never offered in the trial. Much of the "evidence" disseminated in this fashion was clearly inadmissible. The exclusion of such evidence in court is rendered meaningless when news media make it available to the public. The trial court might well have proscribed extrajudicial statements by any lawyer, party, witness, or court official which divulged prejudicial matters, such as the refusal of Sheppard to submit to interrogation or take any lie detector tests; any statement made by Sheppard to officials; the identity of prospective witnesses or their probable testimony; any belief in guilt or innocence; or like statements concerning the merits of the case. The court could also have requested the appropriate city and county officials to promulgate a regulation with respect to dissemination of information about the case by their employees. In addition reporters who wrote or broadcast prejudicial stories could have been warned as to the impropriety of publishing material not introduced in the proceedings.

Due process requires that the accused receive a trial by an impartial jury free from outside influences. Given the pervasiveness of modern communications and the difficulty of effacing prejudicial publicity from the minds of the jurors, the trial courts must take strong measures to ensure that the balance is never weighed against the accused. Of course, there is nothing that proscribes the press from reporting events that transpire in the courtroom. But where there is a reasonable likelihood that prejudicial news prior to trial will prevent a fair trial, the judge should continue the case until the threat abates, or transfer it to another county not so permeated with publicity. In addition, sequestration of the jury was something the judge should have raised *sua ponte* with counsel. If publicity during the proceedings threatens the fairness of the trial, a new trial should be ordered.

Since the state trial judge did not fulfill his duty to protect Sheppard from the inherently prejudicial publicity which saturated the community and to control disruptive influences in the courtroom, the case is remanded to the District Court with instructions to order that Sheppard be released from custody unless the State puts him to its charges again within a reasonable time. It is so ordered.

## Points for Discussion

1. Justice Clark makes much of the fact that jurors "were subjected to newspaper, radio and television coverage of the trial." That cannot constitute an argument, however, for *always* taking the extreme step of sequestering juries (putting them up at a hotel, cutting off virtually all contact with the outside world during the trial and their deliberations). In what circumstances do you think it is appropriate to sequester a jury?

2. The trial judge is criticized for permitting police officers, witnesses, and attorneys to provide "information" and "gossip" to the press. Clearly Justice Clark thinks the trial judge should have imposed some kind of a gag order on these media sources. What should be the outer limits of such gag orders? Would it seem a bit silly, for example, for a prosecutor to be prohibited from telling the press that he thinks the defendant is guilty? Why *else* would he be prosecuting the case?

## ◼ *Nebraska Press Association v. Stuart*

**427 U.S. 539 (1976)**

*Chief Justice Burger delivered the opinion of the Court.*

On the evening of October 18, 1975, local police found the six members of the Henry Kellie family murdered in their home in Sutherland, Neb., a town of about 850 people. Police released the description of a suspect, Erwin Charles Simants, to the reporters who had hastened to the scene of the crime. Simants was arrested and arraigned in Lincoln County Court the following morning, ending a tense night for this small rural community.

The crime immediately attracted widespread news coverage, by local, regional, and national newspapers, radio, and television stations. Three days after the crime, the County Attorney and Simants' attorney joined in asking the County Court to enter a restrictive order, because of the reasonable likelihood of prejudicial news. The County Court granted the prosecutor's motion for a restrictive order; [as later modified by the Nebraska Supreme Court, it] prohibited reporting of three matters: (a) the existence and nature of any confessions or admissions made by the defendant to law enforcement officers, (b) any confessions or admissions made to any third parties, except members of the press, and (c) other facts "strongly implicative" of the accused. The court noted that Nebraska statutes required the District Court to try Simants within six months of his arrest, and that a change of venue could move the trial only to adjoining counties, which had been subject to essentially the same publicity as Lincoln County. The order at issue in this case expired by its own terms when the jury was impaneled. There were no restraints on publication once the jury was selected, and there are now no restrictions on what may be spoken or written about the Simants case.

The problems presented by this case are almost as old as the Republic. Neither in the Constitution nor in contemporaneous writings do we find that the conflict between these two important rights was anticipated, yet it is inconceivable that the authors of the Constitution were unaware of the potential conflicts between the right to an unbiased jury and the guarantee of freedom of the press. The speed of communication and the pervasiveness of the modern news media have exacerbated these problems, however, as numerous appeals demonstrate. The excesses of press and radio and lack of responsibility of those in authority in the Bruno Hauptmann case and others led to efforts to develop voluntary guidelines for courts, lawyers, press, and broadcasters. The effort was renewed in 1965 when the American Bar Association embarked on a project to develop standards for all aspects of criminal justice, including guidelines to accommodate the right to a fair trial and the rights of a free press. Other groups have undertaken similar studies. In the wake of these efforts, the cooperation between bar associations and members of the press led to the adoption of voluntary guidelines like Nebraska's.

In practice, of course, even the most ideal guidelines are subjected to powerful strains when a case such as Simants' arises, with reporters from many parts of the country on the scene. Reporters from distant places are unlikely to consider themselves bound by local standards. They report to editors outside the area covered by the guidelines, and their editors are likely to be guided only by their own standards. To contemplate how a state court can control acts of a newspaper or broadcaster outside its jurisdiction, even though the newspapers and broadcasts reach the very community from which jurors are to be selected, suggests something of the practical difficulties of managing such guidelines.

The Sixth Amendment guarantees "trial, by an impartial jury . . . " in federal criminal prosecutions; the Due Process Clause of the Fourteenth Amendment guarantees the same right in state criminal prosecutions. In the overwhelming majority of criminal trials, pre-trial publicity presents few unmanageable threats to this important right. But when the case is a "sensational" one tensions develop between the right of the accused to trial by an impartial jury and the rights guaranteed others by the First Amendment.

Pre-trial publicity—even pervasive, adverse publicity—does not inevitably lead to an unfair trial. The capacity of the jury eventually impaneled to decide the case fairly is influenced by the tone and extent of the publicity, which is in part, and often in large part, shaped by what attorneys, police, and other officials do to precipitate news coverage. The trial judge has a major responsibility. What the judge says about a case, in or out of the courtroom, is likely to appear in newspapers and broadcasts. More important, the measures a judge takes or fails to take to mitigate the effects of pre-trial publicity may well determine whether the defendant receives a trial consistent with the requirements of due process.

The costs of failure to afford a fair trial are high. In the most extreme cases, the risk of injustice [is] avoided when convictions were reversed. But a reversal means that justice has been delayed for both the defendant and the State; in some cases, because of lapse of time retrial is impossible or further prosecution is gravely handicapped. Moreover, in borderline cases in which the conviction is not reversed, there is some possibility of an injustice unredressed.

The state trial judge in the case before us acted responsibly, out of a legitimate concern, in an effort to protect the defendant's right to a fair trial. What we must decide is not simply whether the Nebraska courts erred in seeing the possibility of real danger to the defendant's rights, but whether in the circumstances of this case the means employed were foreclosed by another provision of the Constitution.

None of our decided cases on prior restraint [of speech] involved restrictive orders entered to protect a defendant's right to a fair and impartial jury. Prior restraints on speech and publication are the most serious and the least tolerable infringement on First Amendment rights. The damage can be particularly great when the prior restraint falls upon the communication of news and commentary on current events. The protection against prior restraint should have particular force as applied to reporting of criminal proceedings, whether the crime in question is a single isolated act or a pattern of criminal conduct. The press does not simply publish information about trials but guards against the miscarriage of justice by subjecting the police, prosecutors, and judicial processes to extensive public scrutiny and criticism. The extraordinary protections afforded by the First Amendment carry with them something in the nature of a fiduciary duty to exercise the protected rights responsibly—a duty widely acknowledged but not always observed by editors and publishers. It is not asking too much to suggest that those who exercise First Amendment rights in newspapers or broadcasting enterprises direct some effort to protect the rights of an accused to a fair trial by unbiased jurors.

Of course, the order at issue does not prohibit but only postpones publication. Some news can be delayed and most commentary can even more readily be delayed without serious injury, and there often is a self-imposed delay when responsible editors call for verification of information. But such delays are normally slight and they are self-imposed. Delays imposed by governmental authority are a different matter.

The authors of the Bill of Rights did not undertake to assign priorities as between First Amendment and Sixth Amendment rights, ranking one as superior to the other. In this case, the petitioners would have us declare the right of an accused subordinate to their right to publish in all circumstances. But if the authors of these guarantees, fully aware of the potential conflicts between them, were unwilling or unable to resolve the issue by assigning to one priority over the other, it is not for us to rewrite the Constitution by undertaking what they declined to do. It is unnecessary, after nearly two centuries, to establish a priority applicable in all circumstances.

The Nebraska courts in this case enjoined the publication of certain kinds of information about the Simants case. Our review of the pre-trial record persuades us that the trial judge was justified in concluding that there would be intense and pervasive pre-trial publicity concerning this case. He could also reasonably conclude, based on common human experience, that publicity might impair the defendant's right to a fair trial. His conclusion as to the impact of such publicity on prospective jurors was of necessity speculative, dealing as he was with factors unknown and unknowable.

We find little in the record [to help us determine] whether measures short of an order restraining all publication would have insured the defendant a fair trial. [Such measures include] change of trial venue to a place less exposed to the intense publicity that seemed imminent in Lincoln County; postponement of the trial to allow public attention to subside; searching questioning of prospective jurors, to screen out those with fixed opinions as to guilt or innocence; and the use of emphatic and clear instructions on the sworn duty of each juror to decide the issues only on evidence presented in open court. Sequestration of jurors is, of course, always available. Although that measure insulates jurors only after they are sworn, it also enhances the likelihood of dissipating the impact of pre-trial publicity and emphasizes the elements of the jurors' oaths.

We have examined this record to determine the probable efficacy of the measures short of prior restraint on the press and speech. There is no finding that alternative measures would not have protected Simants' rights, and the Nebraska Supreme Court did no more than imply that such measures might not be adequate. Moreover, the record is lacking in evidence to support such a finding.

We must also assess the probable efficacy of prior restraint on publication as a workable method of protecting Simants' right to a fair trial, and we cannot ignore the reality of the problems of managing and enforcing pre-trial restraining orders. Finally, we note that the events disclosed by the record took place in a community of 850 people. It is reasonable to assume that, without any news accounts being printed or broadcast, rumors would travel swiftly by word of mouth. One can only speculate on the accuracy of such reports, given the generative propensities of rumors; they could well be more damaging than reasonably accurate news accounts. But plainly a whole community cannot be restrained from discussing a subject intimately affecting life within it. Given these practical problems, it is far from clear that prior restraint on publication would have protected Simants' rights.

The record demonstrates, as the Nebraska courts held, that there was indeed a risk that pre-trial news accounts, true or false, would have some adverse impact on the attitudes of those who might be called as jurors. But on the record now before us it is not clear that further publicity, unchecked, would so distort the views of potential jurors that 12 could not be found who would, under proper instructions, fulfill their sworn duty to render a just verdict exclusively on the evidence presented in open court.

Of necessity our holding is confined to the record before us. However difficult it may be, we need not rule out the possibility of showing the kind of threat to fair trial rights that would possess the requisite degree of certainty to justify restraint. Our analysis ends as it began, with a confrontation between prior restraint imposed to protect one vital constitutional guarantee and the explicit command of another that the freedom to speak and publish shall not be abridged. We reaffirm that the guarantees of freedom of expression are not an absolute prohibition under all circumstances, but the barriers to prior restraint remain high and the presumption against its use continues intact. We hold that, with respect to the order entered in this case prohibiting reporting or commentary on judicial proceedings held in public, the barriers have not been overcome; to the extent that this order restrained publication of such material, it is clearly invalid. To the extent that it prohibited publication based on information gained from other sources, we conclude that the heavy burden imposed as a condition to securing a prior restraint was not met and the judgment of the Nebraska Supreme Court is therefore reversed.

## Points for Discussion

**1.** Chief Justice Burger admits that trial judges can only speculate about the likely impact of prejudicial pretrial publicity on potential jurors. Yet he insists that trial judges demonstrate "findings" that remedies less restrictive on First Amendment values than imposing a gag order on the press would not succeed in remedying any such effect. How might trial judges go about gathering such elusive data?

**2.** Trial judges very rarely impose gag orders; they do so only in the most "sensational" cases. But does not media coverage of sensational trials often carry important life lessons? The "preppy murder" case from New York City in the 1980s, for example—where the accused claimed that he killed his victim accidentally, during "rough" but consensual sex—served as a clarion call for more effective parenting, especially among the wealthy classes from which both victim and accused came. Can you think of other such "sensational" crime stories that prompted you to do some deep thinking about your own life?

## ■ *Press-Enterprise Company v. Superior Court* (I)

### 464 U.S. 501 (1984)

*Chief Justice Burger delivered the opinion of the Court.*

Albert Greenwood Brown, Jr., was tried and convicted of the rape and murder of a teenage girl, and sentenced to death in California Superior Court. Before the voir dire examination of prospective jurors began, petitioner, Press-Enterprise Co., moved that the voir dire be open to the public and the press. Petitioner contended that the public had an absolute right to attend the trial, and asserted that the trial commenced with the voir dire proceedings. The State opposed petitioner's motion, arguing that if the press were present, juror responses would lack the candor necessary to assure a fair trial. The trial judge agreed; the voir dire consumed six weeks and all but approximately three days was closed to the public.

After the jury was empaneled, petitioner moved the trial court to release a complete transcript of the voir dire proceedings. Counsel for Brown argued that release of the transcript would violate the jurors' right of privacy. The prosecutor agreed, adding that the prospective jurors had answered questions under an implied promise of confidentiality. The court denied petitioner's motion. After Brown had been convicted and sentenced to death, petitioner again applied for release of the transcript. In denying this application, the judge stated: "The jurors were questioned in private relating to past experiences, and some of the jurors had some special experiences in sensitive areas that do not appear to be appropriate for public discussion." The California Supreme Court denied petitioner's request for a hearing.

The process of juror selection is itself a matter of importance, not simply to the adversaries but to the criminal justice system. A review of the historical evidence reveals that, since the development of trial by jury, the process of selection of jurors has presumptively been a public process with exceptions only for good cause shown. The roots of open trials reach back to the days before the Norman Conquest when cases in England were brought before "moots," a town meeting kind of body such as the local court of the hundred or the county court. Attendance was virtually compulsory on the part of the freemen of the community, who represented the "patria," or the "country," in rendering judgment. The public aspect thus was almost a necessary incident of jury trials, since the presence of a jury already insured the presence of a large part of the public.

As the jury system evolved in the years after the Norman Conquest, and the jury came to be but a small segment representing the community, the obligation of all freemen to attend criminal trials was relaxed; however, the public character of the proceedings, including jury selection, remained unchanged.

The presumptive openness of the jury selection process in England, not surprisingly, carried over into proceedings in colonial America. Public jury selection was the common practice in America when the Constitution was adopted.

For present purposes, how we allocate the "right" to openness as between the accused and the public, or whether we view it as a component inherent in the system benefitting both, is not crucial. No right ranks higher than the right of the accused to a fair trial. But the primacy of the accused's right is difficult to separate from the right of everyone in the community to attend the voir dire which promotes fairness.

The open trial thus plays as important a role in the administration of justice today as it did for centuries before our separation from England. The value of openness lies in the fact that people not actually attending trials can have confidence that standards of fairness are being observed; the sure knowledge that anyone is free to attend gives assurance that established procedures are being followed and that deviations will become known. Openness thus enhances both the basic fairness of the criminal trial and the appearance of fairness so essential to public confidence in the system. This openness has what is sometimes described as a "community therapeutic value." Criminal acts, especially violent crimes, often provoke public concern, even outrage and hostility; this in turn generates a community urge to retaliate and desire to have justice done. Whether this is viewed as retribution or otherwise is irrelevant. When the public is aware that the law is being enforced and the criminal justice system is functioning, an outlet is provided for these understandable reactions and emotions. Proceedings held in secret would deny this outlet and frustrate the broad public interest; by contrast, public proceedings vindicate the concerns of the victims and the community in knowing that offenders are being brought to account for their criminal conduct by jurors fairly and openly selected.

The presumption of openness may be overcome only by an overriding interest based on findings that closure is essential to preserve higher values and is narrowly tailored to serve that interest. The interest is to be articulated along with findings specific enough that a reviewing court can determine whether the closure order was properly entered. We now turn to whether the presumption of openness has been rebutted in this case.

Although three days of voir dire in this case were open to the public, six weeks of the proceedings were closed, and media requests for the transcript were denied. The Superior Court asserted two interests in support of its closure order and orders denying a transcript: the right of the defendant to a fair trial, and the right to privacy of the prospective jurors. Of course the right of an accused to fundamental fairness in the jury selection process is a compelling interest. But the California court's conclusion that Sixth Amendment and privacy interests were sufficient to warrant prolonged closure was unsupported by findings showing that an open proceeding in fact threatened those interests; hence it is not possible to conclude that closure was warranted. Even with findings adequate to support closure, the trial court's orders denying access to voir dire testimony failed to consider whether alternatives were available to protect the interests of the prospective jurors that the trial court's orders sought to guard. Absent consideration of alternatives to closure, the trial court could not constitutionally close the voir dire.

The jury selection process may, in some circumstances, give rise to a compelling interest of a prospective juror when interrogation touches on deeply personal matters that person has legitimate reasons for keeping out of the public domain. The trial involved testimony concerning an alleged rape of a teenage girl. Some questions may have been appropriate to prospective jurors that would give rise to legitimate privacy interests of those persons. For example, a prospective juror might privately inform the judge that she, or a member of her family, had been raped but had declined to seek prosecution because of the embarrassment and emotional trauma from the very disclosure of the episode. The privacy interests of such a prospective juror must be balanced against the historic values we have discussed and the need for openness of the process. To preserve fairness and at the same time protect legitimate privacy, a trial judge must at all times maintain control of the process of jury selection and should inform the array of prospective jurors, once the general nature of sensitive questions is made known to them, that those individuals believing public questioning will prove damaging because of embarrassment, may properly request an opportunity to present the problem to the judge in camera but with counsel present and on the record.

By requiring the prospective juror to make an affirmative request, the trial judge can ensure that there is in fact a valid basis for a belief that disclosure infringes a significant interest in privacy. This process will minimize the risk of unnecessary closure. The exercise of sound discretion by the court may lead to excusing such a person from jury service. When limited closure is ordered, the constitutional values sought to be protected by holding open proceedings may be satisfied later by making a transcript of the closed proceedings available within a reasonable time, if the judge determines that disclosure can be accomplished while safeguarding the juror's valid privacy interests. Even then a valid privacy right may rise to a level that part of the transcript should be sealed, or the name of a juror withheld, to protect the person from embarrassment.

The judge at this trial closed an incredible six weeks of voir dire without considering alternatives to closure. Later the court declined to release a transcript of the voir dire even while stating that "most of the information" in the transcript was "dull and boring." Those parts of the transcript reasonably entitled to privacy could have been sealed without such a sweeping order; a trial judge should explain why the material is entitled to privacy.

Assuming that some jurors had protectible privacy interests in some of their answers, the trial judge provided no explanation as to why his broad order denying access to information at the voir dire was not limited to information that was actually sensitive and deserving of privacy protection. Nor did he consider whether he could disclose the substance of the sensitive answers while preserving the anonymity of the jurors involved. Thus not only was there a failure to articulate findings with the requisite specificity but there was also a failure to consider alternatives to closure and to total suppression of the transcript. The trial judge should seal only such parts of the transcript as necessary to preserve the anonymity of the individuals sought to be protected.

The judgment of the Court of Appeal is vacated, and the case is remanded for proceedings not inconsistent with this opinion. It is so ordered.

## *Points for Discussion*

1. Chief Justice Burger emphasizes that the juror selection process has traditionally been considered a public event and that this openness serves important societal functions. Does that mean that prospective jurors must expect that everything they say in the courtroom can be made public?

2. There is an unavoidable tension between jurors' argued privacy rights and the right of the accused to be judged by impartial peers. In a murder case such as this one, involving both rape and race (the defendant was black, the victim white), the kinds of questions most likely to be "sensitive" from the jurors' perspective (Are you a rape victim? What kinds of racially prejudiced attitudes do you harbor?) are precisely the ones that the defendant will want to have answered. How should this tension be resolved?

## Press-Enterprise Company v. Superior Court (II)

### 478 U.S. 1 (1986)

*Chief Justice Burger delivered the opinion of the Court.*

We granted certiorari to decide whether petitioner has a First Amendment right of access to the transcript of a preliminary hearing growing out of a criminal prosecution. On December 23, 1981, the State of California charged Robert Diaz with murder, alleging that Diaz, a nurse, murdered 12 patients by administering massive doses of the heart drug lidocaine. The preliminary hearing on the complaint commenced on July 6, 1982. Diaz moved to exclude the public from the proceedings under Cal. Penal Code Ann. §868, which requires such proceedings to be open unless "exclusion of the public is necessary in order to protect the defendant's right to a fair and impartial trial." The Magistrate granted the unopposed motion, finding that closure was necessary because the case had attracted national publicity.

The preliminary hearing continued for 41 days. At the conclusion of the hearing, petitioner Press-Enterprise Company asked that the transcript of the proceedings be released. The Magistrate refused and sealed the record. On January 21, 1983, the State moved in Superior Court to have the transcript of the preliminary hearing released to the public; petitioner later joined in support of the motion. Diaz opposed the motion, contending that release of the transcript would result in prejudicial pretrial publicity. The Superior Court found that there was "a reasonable likelihood that release of all or any part of the transcripts might prejudice defendant's right to a fair and impartial trial." Diaz waived his right to a jury trial and the Superior Court released the transcript.

In this Court, petitioner challenges the Superior Court's original refusal to release the transcript of the preliminary hearing. The specific relief petitioner seeks has already been granted—the transcript of the preliminary hearing was released after Diaz waived his right to a jury trial. However, this controversy is capable of repetition, yet evading review. It can reasonably be assumed that petitioner will be subjected to a similar closure order and, because criminal proceedings are typically of short duration, such an order will likely evade review.

The California Supreme Court decided that [preliminary hearings may be closed] upon finding a reasonable likelihood of substantial prejudice which would impinge upon the right to a fair trial. It is difficult to disagree in the abstract with that court's analysis balancing the defendant's right to a fair trial against the public right of access. It is also important to remember that these interests are not necessarily inconsistent. Plainly, the defendant has a right to a fair trial but one of the important means of assuring a fair trial is that the process be open to neutral observers. The right to an open public trial is a shared right of the accused and the public, the common concern being the assurance of fairness.

The right asserted here is that of the public under the First Amendment. The California Supreme Court concluded that the First Amendment was not implicated because the proceeding was not a criminal trial, but a preliminary hearing. However, the First Amendment question cannot be resolved solely on the label we give the event, i.e., "trial" or otherwise, particularly where the preliminary hearing functions much like a full-scale trial.

In cases dealing with the claim of a First Amendment right of access to criminal proceedings, our decisions have emphasized two complementary considerations. First, we have considered whether the place and process have historically been open to the press and general public. The public trial, one of the essential qualities of a court of justice in England, was recognized early on in the Colonies. Second, the Court has traditionally considered whether public access plays a significant positive role in the functioning of the particular process in question. Although many governmental processes operate best under public scrutiny, it takes little imagination to recognize that there are some kinds of government operations that would be totally frustrated if conducted openly. A classic example is our grand jury system. Other proceedings plainly require public access.

The considerations that led the Court to [find a] First Amendment right of access to criminal trials and the selection of jurors lead us to conclude that the right of access applies to preliminary hearings as conducted in California.

First, there has been a tradition of accessibility to preliminary hearings of the type conducted in California. Although grand jury proceedings have traditionally been closed to the public and the accused, preliminary hearings conducted before neutral and detached magistrates have been open to the public. Long ago in the celebrated trial of Aaron Burr for treason, for example, with Chief Justice Marshall sitting as trial judge, the probable-cause hearing was held in the Hall of the House of Delegates in Virginia, the courtroom being too small to accommodate the crush of interested citizens.

From Burr until the present day, the near uniform practice of state and federal courts has been to conduct preliminary hearings in open court.

The second question is whether public access to preliminary hearings as they are conducted in California plays a particularly significant positive role in the actual functioning of the process. Public access to criminal trials and the selection of jurors is essential to the proper functioning of the criminal justice system. California preliminary hearings are sufficiently like a trial to justify the same conclusion. In California, to bring a felon to trial, the prosecutor has a choice of securing a grand jury indictment or a finding of probable cause following a preliminary hearing. Even when the accused has been indicted by a grand jury, however, he has an absolute right to an elaborate preliminary hearing before a neutral magistrate. The accused has the right to personally appear at the hearing, to be represented by counsel, to cross-examine hostile witnesses, to present exculpatory evidence, and to exclude illegally obtained evidence. If the magistrate determines that probable cause exists, the accused is bound over for trial; such a finding leads to a guilty plea in the majority of cases.

It is true that unlike a criminal trial, the California preliminary hearing cannot result in the conviction of the accused and the adjudication is before a magistrate or other judicial officer without a jury. But these features, standing alone, do not make public access any less essential to the proper functioning of the proceedings in the overall criminal justice process. Because of its extensive scope, the preliminary hearing is often the final and most important step in the criminal proceeding. Similarly, the absence of a jury, long recognized as an inestimable safeguard against the corrupt or overzealous prosecutor and against the compliant, biased, or eccentric judge, makes the importance of public access to a preliminary hearing even more significant.

Denying the transcript of a 41-day preliminary hearing would frustrate what we have characterized as the community therapeutic value of openness. Criminal acts, especially certain violent crimes, provoke public concern, outrage, and hostility. When the public is aware that the law is being enforced and the criminal justice system is functioning, an outlet is provided for these understandable reactions and emotions. We therefore conclude that the qualified First Amendment right of access to criminal proceedings applies to preliminary hearings as they are conducted in California.

Since a qualified First Amendment right of access attaches to preliminary hearings in California, the proceedings cannot be closed unless specific, on the record findings are made demonstrating that closure is essential to preserve higher values and is narrowly tailored to serve that interest. If the interest asserted is the right of the accused to a fair trial, the preliminary hearing shall be closed only if specific findings are made demonstrating that, first, there is a substantial probability that the defendant's right to a fair trial will be prejudiced by publicity that closure would prevent and, second, reasonable alternatives to closure cannot adequately protect the defendant's fair trial rights.

The California Supreme Court, interpreting its access statute, concluded that "the magistrate shall close the preliminary hearing upon finding a reasonable likelihood of substantial prejudice." As the court itself acknowledged, the "reasonable likelihood" test places a lesser burden on the defendant than the "substantial probability" test which we hold is called for by the First Amendment. Moreover, that court failed to consider whether alternatives short of complete closure would have protected the interests of the accused. The standard applied by the California Supreme Court failed to consider the First Amendment right of access to criminal proceedings. Accordingly, the judgment of the California Supreme Court is reversed.

## Points for Discussion

1. At this preliminary hearing, defendant Diaz called no witnesses. As such, the thousands of pages of transcripts necessarily contained a rather one-sided picture of the accused. Should this fact properly be considered by a magistrate trying to determine whether to close a hearing and whether and when to release the transcripts to the press?

2. Chief Justice Burger notes that the preliminary hearing often is the only trial in that a ruling to bind the defendant over for trial often leads to a plea bargain. To the extent that this counts as an argument for openness, might it not also suggest that grand jury proceedings—which have traditionally been conducted in secrecy—should be open, because they, too, often are the "only" trial a defendant will see?

## ■ *United States v. McVeigh*

### 918 F. Supp. 1452 (W.D. Okla. 1996)

*Judge Matsch:*

[Numerous media companies] have filed motions asking that documents filed in this case under seal be unsealed where appropriate, that the clerk be directed to provide public access to a complete copy of the docket sheets and that procedures be established for consideration of future requests that documents be sealed or proceedings be closed to the public. These motions were accepted for filing in this case even though the movants are not parties to the proceeding. The government and each of the defendants have filed responses to these motions and oral arguments were heard.

The motions raise important questions under the First, Fifth and Sixth Amendments to the United States Constitution.

Every criminal prosecution in a federal court begins with some investigation by one or more law enforcement agencies of government to develop an evidentiary base for the necessary showing of probable cause. The documents generated during the investigation and the conduct of the investigators are largely shielded from public view.

The media motions to open sealed documents will be determined by the answers to these questions: Does the matter involve activity within the tradition of free public access to information concerning criminal prosecutions? Will public access play a significant positive role in the activity and in the functioning of the process? Is there a substantial probability that some recognized interest of higher value than public access to information will be prejudiced or affected adversely by the disclosure? Does the need for protection of that interest override the qualified First Amendment right of access? Is the closure by the court essential to protect that interest, considering all reasonable alternatives? This same analysis will also be used in considering any future motions to seal.

The present focus of attention is on documents generated in activities not directly related to the process of adjudication. Accordingly, they are not within the strong presumption of open access to proceedings in court. Historically, some types of court documents have been kept secret for important policy reasons. They include pre-sentence reports, search warrants and supporting affidavits. The majority of the documents under seal in the clerk's office are applications and orders for payment of interim fees and support services for defense attorneys. The court has provided funding for an extensive factual investigation, including extensive travel for interviews of persons who may have relevant information. Authority to retain experts for consultation in a wide ranging variety of disciplines has been granted. The defendants' lawyers have vigorously pursued their duty to investigate.

Media counsel have shown their sensitivity to the secrecy required for the defense investigation and trial preparation by restricting their requests to the amounts paid out to the attorneys and others providing services to the defense. There is no tradition of public access to that information while the investigation and preparation for trial are in progress. To the contrary, the requests must be submitted ex parte and in camera to keep privileged information from the prosecution. Disclosures to the public would, of course, become known to government counsel.

There is no doubt that the cost of the legal defense paid for from public funds for each of the defendants in this case will become public information at some time. The question is when. Media counsel argue that the public is interested in the amount spent for the defense during the course of the case because the funds are public and the taxpayers may question both the reasonableness and the appropriateness of the expenditures. The legitimacy of those interests is unquestioned. Yet, there are important interests to be protected before the entry of final judgments in this case.

The movants concede that disclosing the services performed and the reason for them would inappropriately reveal the defendants' investigations and strategies. All of the reasons supporting grand jury secrecy are equally applicable to the pre-trial preparation of the defense of capital charges. This includes the protection of people from public speculation about their possible involvement in the criminal conduct at issue. That is particularly important in this case given the horrendous destruction of life and property from the bombing of a building housing government agencies, the widespread publicity and the prolixity of punditry about the identity and motivation of possible perpetrators.

An additional interest is the protection of appointed counsel from vilification and accusations of improper motivations in the conduct of their responsibilities in the representation of these defendants. Because of the inhibitions imposed upon them by their professional responsibilities, these lawyers are unable to respond to such accusations or to make public explanations of their conduct. Moreover, any "robust debate" about expenditures for the defense of the accused at this stage would be counterproductive to the process of adjudication by diverting counsel from proceeding with the task of preparing for trial. The interests adversely affected by disclosure now are the effectiveness of defense counsel and fairness of the trial process.

Revealing only the amounts of interim payments is not a reasonable alternative to full disclosure. It would distort the public perception about the fairness of the process because the expenditures, out of context, would emphasize costs without any information about benefits obtained. Public access to these cost figures would be detrimental, not helpful, to the functioning of the court at this stage of the proceeding.

Accordingly, this court finds and concludes that the request for the amounts of expenditures made for defense services before trial must be denied for the protection of the interests identified in this opinion. [These data] shall remain sealed until the entry of final judgments as to both defendants.

## Points for Discussion

1. Do you agree with Judge Matsch that whatever interest the public had in learning how many of its tax dollars were being spent on the defense of the Oklahoma City bombers could wait to be satisfied until the end of the trials?

2. Judge Matsch focuses here on the needs of the defense—understandably so in that the Sixth Amendment tells us about rights enjoyed by the *ac-*

*cused* to a fair trial. Suppose that the media sought information that the defense might not have minded being revealed, such as to check on the credibility of rumors that McVeigh had been tortured by law enforcement officers during his interrogation. Should the constitutional analysis be different then?

# 9

# *Protecting News Sources*

Read the first few paragraphs of the front-page stories in a newspaper known for investigative journalism, and you will see how, for better or worse, American journalists rely frequently on confidential sources. Whistle-blowers are afraid of losing their jobs, political dissidents are afraid of violent reprisals. Scores of journalists over the years have gone to jail rather than reveal the identity of their sources.

In this chapter, we look at cases in which the government wants a reporter to reveal information. Our first case is the landmark *Branzburg v. Hayes,* in which the Supreme Court tells us that reporters enjoy no special constitutional immunity from the obligation to testify when called in front of a grand jury. Interestingly, although reporter Paul Branzburg lost, the test his attorneys put before the court—that a reporter could be compelled to testify only if there is strong reason to believe he or she is the only logical source of information needed by the government—has since been accepted and applied by lower courts in a variety of situations.

Our next case, *Zurcher v. Stanford Daily,* tells law enforcement agencies that they may not only subpoena reporters for relevant information, but may also conduct a search of the newsroom itself (presuming they first obtain a valid search warrant). So outraged was the press by this decision that Congress was persuaded to pass the Privacy Protection Act of 1980, which greatly limits the circumstances in which newsrooms can be searched.

*Gonzales v. NBC* serves as a reminder that civil litigants may sometimes be able to use the court system to compel disclosure of relevant information from news media outlets that are not themselves parties to the original litigation. In this particular case, both the plaintiff and the defendant persuaded a federal court that the NBC network was in possession of data crucial to their legal claims.

Finally, we look at *Cohen v. Cowles Media Company,* wherein the media did not valiantly try to protect a source, but rather violated their promise not to publish the source's name. The Supreme Court reasons in much the same way it did in the earlier *Branzburg* case, concluding that the media enjoy no special immunity from liability for breaking promises.

# ■ *Branzburg v. Hayes*

## 408 U.S. 665 (1972)

*Justice White wrote the opinion of the Court.*

The issue in these cases is whether requiring newsmen to appear and testify before state or federal grand juries abridges the freedom of speech and press guaranteed by the First Amendment. We hold that it does not.

Petitioner [Paul] Branzburg [is] a staff reporter for the *Courier-Journal,* a daily newspaper published in Louisville, Kentucky. On November 15, 1969, the *Courier-Journal* carried a story under petitioner's by-line describing in detail his observations of two young residents of Jefferson County synthesizing hashish from marijuana. The article stated that petitioner had promised not to reveal the identity of the two hashish makers. Petitioner was shortly subpoenaed by the Jefferson County grand jury; he appeared, but refused to identify the individuals he had seen possessing marijuana or the persons he had seen making hashish from marijuana. A state trial court judge ordered petitioner to answer these questions and rejected his contention that the Kentucky reporters' privilege statute, the First Amendment of the United States Constitution, or §§1, 2, and 8 of the Kentucky Constitution authorized his refusal to answer. The Kentucky Court of Appeals construed [the reporters' privilege statute] as affording a newsman the privilege of refusing to divulge the identity of an informant who supplied him with information, but held that the statute did not permit a reporter to refuse to testify about events he had observed personally, including the identities of those persons he had observed.

Although he does not claim an absolute privilege against official interrogation in all circumstances, [Branzburg] asserts that the reporter should not be forced either to appear or to testify before a grand jury or at trial until and unless sufficient grounds are shown for believing that the reporter possesses information relevant to a crime the grand jury is investigating, that the information the reporter has is unavailable from other sources, and that the need for the information is sufficiently compelling to override the claimed invasion of First Amendment interests occasioned by the disclosure. The heart of the claim is that the burden on news gathering resulting from compelling reporters to disclose confidential information outweighs any public interest in obtaining the information.

We do not question the significance of free speech, press, or assembly to the country's welfare. Nor is it suggested that news gathering does not qualify for First Amendment protection; without some protection for seeking out the news, freedom of the press could be eviscerated. But this case involves no prior restraint or restriction on what the press may publish, and no express or implied command that the press publish what it prefers to withhold. The use of confidential sources by the press is not forbidden or restricted; reporters remain free to seek news from any source by means within the law. The sole issue before us is the obligation of reporters to respond to grand jury subpoenas as other citizens do and to answer questions relevant to an investigation into the commission of crime. Citizens generally are not constitutionally immune from grand jury subpoenas; and neither the First Amendment nor any other constitutional provision protects the average citizen from disclosing to a grand jury information that he has received in confidence. The claim is, however, that reporters are exempt from these obligations because if forced to respond to subpoenas and identify their sources or disclose other confidences, their informants will refuse or be reluctant to furnish newsworthy information in the future. This asserted burden on news gathering is said to make compelled testimony from newsmen constitutionally suspect and to require a privileged position for them.

It is clear that the First Amendment does not invalidate every incidental burdening of the press that may result from the enforcement of civil or criminal statutes of general applicability. Otherwise valid laws serving substantial public interests may be enforced against the press as against others, despite the possible burden that may be imposed.

The prevailing constitutional view of the newsman's privilege is very much rooted in the ancient role of the grand jury that has the dual function of determining if there is probable cause to believe that a crime has been committed and of protecting citizens against unfounded criminal prosecutions. Grand jury proceedings are constitutionally mandated for the institution of federal criminal prosecutions for capital or other serious crimes, and its constitutional prerogatives are rooted in long centuries of Anglo-American history. The Fifth Amendment provides that "no person shall be held to answer for a capital, or otherwise infamous crime, unless on a presentment or indictment of a Grand Jury." The adoption of the grand jury in our Constitution as the sole method for preferring charges in serious criminal cases shows the high place it held as an instrument of justice. The grand jury is similarly guaranteed by many state constitutions and plays an important role in fair and effective law enforcement in the overwhelming majority of the States. Because its task is to inquire into the existence of possible criminal conduct and to return only well-founded indictments, its investigative powers are necessarily broad. The grand jury's authority to subpoena witnesses is not only historic, but essential to its task.

A number of States have provided newsmen a statutory privilege of varying breadth, but the majority have not done so, and none has been provided by federal statute. Until now the only testimonial privilege for unofficial witnesses that is rooted in the Federal Constitution is the Fifth Amendment privilege against compelled self-incrimination. We are asked to create another by interpreting the First Amendment to grant newsmen a testimonial privilege that other citizens do not enjoy. This we decline to do. We perceive no basis for holding that the public interest in law enforcement and in ensuring effective grand jury proceedings is insufficient to override the consequential, but uncertain, burden on news gathering that is said to result from insisting that reporters, like other citizens, respond to relevant questions put to them in the course of a valid grand jury investigation or criminal trial.

We cannot seriously entertain the notion that the First Amendment protects a newsman's agreement to conceal the criminal conduct of his source, or evidence thereof, on the theory that it is better to write about crime than to do something about it.

The argument that the flow of news will be diminished by compelling reporters to aid the grand jury in a criminal investigation is not irrational, nor are the records before us silent on the matter. But we remain unclear how often and to what extent informers are actually deterred from furnishing information when newsmen are forced to testify before a grand jury.

Reliance by the press on confidential informants does not mean that all such sources will in fact dry up because of the later possible appearance of the newsman before a grand jury. The reporter may never be called and if he objects to testifying, the prosecution may not insist. Also, the relationship of many informants to the press is a symbiotic one which is unlikely to be greatly inhibited by the threat of subpoena: quite often, such informants are members of a minority political or cultural group that relies heavily on the media to propagate its views, publicize its aims, and magnify its exposure to the public.

It is obvious that agreements to conceal information relevant to commission of crime have very little to recommend them from the standpoint of public policy. Concealment of crime and agreements to do so are not looked upon with favor. Such conduct deserves no encomium, and we decline now to afford it First Amendment protection by denigrating the duty of a citizen, whether reporter or informer, to respond to a grand jury subpoena and answer relevant questions put to him.

From the beginning of our country the press has operated without constitutional protection for press informants, and the press has flourished. The existing constitutional rules have not been a serious obstacle to either the development or retention of confidential news sources by the press.

We do not deal [here] with a governmental institution that has abused its proper function, as a legislative committee does when it exposes for the sake of exposure. Nothing in the record indicates that these grand juries were probing at will and without relation to existing need. Nor did the grand juries attempt to invade protected First Amendment rights by forcing wholesale disclosure of names and organizational affiliations for a purpose that was not germane to the determination of whether crime has been committed.

The administration of a constitutional newsman's privilege would present practical and conceptual difficulties of a high order. Sooner or later, it would be necessary to define those categories of newsmen who qualified for the privilege, a questionable procedure in light of the traditional doctrine that liberty of the press is the right of the lonely pamphleteer who uses carbon paper or a mimeograph just as much as of the large metropolitan publisher who utilizes the latest photo composition methods. The informative function asserted by representatives of the organized press in the present cases is also performed by lecturers, political pollsters, novelists, academic researchers, and dramatists. Almost any author may quite accurately assert that he is contributing to the flow of information to the public, that he relies on confidential sources of information, and that these sources will be silenced if he is forced to make disclosures before a grand jury.

At the federal level, Congress has freedom to determine whether a statutory newsman's privilege is necessary and desirable and to fashion standards and rules as narrow or broad as deemed necessary to deal with the evil discerned and, equally important, to refashion those rules as experience from time to time may dictate. There is also merit in leaving state legislatures free, within First Amendment limits, to fashion their own standards in light of the conditions and problems with respect to the relations between law enforcement officials and press in their own areas. It goes without saying, of course, that we are powerless to bar state courts from responding in their own way and construing their own constitutions so as to recognize a newsman's privilege, either qualified or absolute.

In addition, there is much force in the pragmatic view that the press has at its disposal powerful mechanisms of communication and is far from helpless to protect itself from harassment or substantial harm.

Finally, as we have earlier indicated, news gathering is not without its First Amendment protections, and grand jury investigations if instituted or conducted other than in good faith, would pose wholly different issues for resolution under the First Amendment. Official harassment of the press undertaken not for purposes of law enforcement but to disrupt a reporter's relationship with his news sources would have no justification. Grand juries are subject to judicial control and subpoenas to motions to quash. We do not expect courts will forget that grand juries must operate within the limits of the First Amendment as well as the Fifth.

We turn, therefore, to the disposition of the case before us. Petitioner refused to answer questions that directly related to criminal conduct that he had observed and written about. Petitioner saw the commission of the statutory felonies of unlawful possession of marijuana and the unlawful conversion of it into hashish. If what petitioner wrote was true, he had direct information to provide the grand jury concerning the commission of serious crimes.

## Points for Discussion

1. Branzburg's informants were clearly engaged in criminal acts; thus, it is equally clear why they wanted to stay anonymous. What other categories of noncriminal informants does the Court recognize, and what motivations would such informants have for seeking anonymity from reporters?

2. Justice White refuses to create a reporter's privilege in part because he is unclear as to how one might go about defining who is and is not a reporter. Pretend you are a state legislator drafting a reporter's privilege statute. How will you define "reporter" in your state's law?

## ■ *Zurcher v. Stanford Daily*

**436 U.S. 547 (1978)**

*Justice White delivered the opinion of the Court.*

Late in the day on Friday, April 9, 1971, officers of the Palo Alto Police Department and of the Santa Clara County Sheriff's Department responded to a call from the director of the Stanford University Hospital requesting the removal of a large group of demonstrators who had seized the hospital's administrative offices and occupied them since the previous afternoon. After several futile efforts to persuade the demonstrators to leave peacefully, more drastic measures were employed. The demonstrators had barricaded the doors at both ends of a hall adjacent to the administrative offices. The police chose to force their way in at the west end of the corridor. As they did so, a group of demonstrators emerged through the doors at the east end and, armed with sticks and clubs, attacked the group of nine police officers stationed there. One officer was knocked to the floor and struck repeatedly on the head; another suffered a broken shoulder. All nine were injured. There were no police photographers at the east doors, and most bystanders and reporters were on the west side. The officers themselves were able to identify only two of their assailants, but one of them did see at least one person photographing the assault at the east doors.

On Sunday, April 11, a special edition of the Stanford Daily (Daily), a student newspaper published at Stanford University, carried articles and photographs devoted to the hospital protest and the violent clash between demonstrators and police. The photographs carried the byline of a Daily staff member and indicated that he had been at the east end of the hospital hallway where he could have photographed the assault on the nine officers. The next day, the Santa Clara County District Attorney's Office secured a warrant from the Municipal Court for an immediate search of the Daily's offices for negatives, film, and pictures showing the events and occurrences at the hospital on the evening of April 9. The warrant affidavit contained no allegation or indication that members of the Daily staff were in any way involved in unlawful acts at the hospital.

The search pursuant to the warrant was conducted later that day by four police officers and took place in the presence of some members of the Daily staff. The Daily's photographic laboratories, filing cabinets, desks, and wastepaper baskets were searched. Locked drawers and rooms were not opened. The officers apparently had opportunity to read notes and correspondence during the search. The search revealed only the photographs that had already been published on April 11, and no materials were removed from the Daily's office.

A month later the Daily and various members of its staff, respondents here, brought a civil action in the United States District Court for the Northern District of California seeking declaratory and injunctive relief. The complaint alleged that the search of the Daily's office had deprived respondents under color of state law of rights secured to them by the First, Fourth, and Fourteenth Amendments of the United States Constitution. The District Court denied the request for an injunction but, on respondents' motion for summary judgment, granted declaratory relief. The Court of Appeals affirmed. We reverse.

Under existing law, valid warrants may be issued to search any property, whether or not occupied by a third party, at which there is probable cause to believe that fruits, instrumentalities, or evidence of a crime will be found. Nothing on the face of the Amendment suggests that a third-party search warrant should not normally issue. The Warrant Clause speaks of search warrants issued on "probable cause" and "particularly describing the place to be searched, and the persons or things to be seized." In situations where the State does not seek to seize "persons" but only those "things" which there is probable cause to believe are located on the place to be searched, there is no apparent basis in the language of the Amendment for also imposing the requirements for a valid arrest—probable cause to believe that the third party is implicated in the crime. The critical element in a reasonable search is not that the owner of the property is suspected of crime but that there is reasonable cause to believe that the specific "things" to be searched for and seized are located on the property to which entry is sought.

The District Court held, and respondents assert here, that whatever may be true of third-party searches generally, where the third party is a newspaper, there are additional factors derived from the First Amendment that justify a nearly per se rule forbidding the search warrant and permitting only the subpoena duces tecum. The general submission is that searches of newspaper offices for evidence of crime reasonably believed to be on the premises will seriously threaten the ability of the press to gather, analyze, and disseminate news. This is said to be true for several reasons: First, searches will be physically disruptive to such an extent that timely publication will be impeded. Second, confidential sources of information will dry up, and the press will also lose opportunities to cover various events because of fears of the participants that press files will be readily available to the authorities. Third, reporters will be deterred from recording and preserving their recollections for future use if such information is subject to seizure. Fourth, the processing of news and its dissemination will be chilled by the prospects that searches will disclose internal editorial deliberations. Fifth, the press will resort to self-censorship to conceal its possession of information of potential interest to the police.

It is true that the struggle from which the Fourth Amendment emerged is largely a history of conflict between the Crown and the press, and that in issuing warrants and determining the reasonableness of a search, state and federal magistrates should be aware that unrestricted power of search and seizure could also be an instrument for stifling liberty of expression. Where the materials sought to be seized may be protected by the First Amendment, the requirements of the Fourth Amendment must be applied with scrupulous exactitude. Where presumptively protected materials are sought to be seized, the warrant requirement should be administered to leave as little as possible to the discretion or whim of the officer in the field.

Similarly, where seizure is sought of allegedly obscene materials, the judgment of the arresting officer alone is insufficient to justify issuance of a search warrant or a seizure without a warrant incident to arrest. Neither the Fourth Amendment nor the cases requiring consideration of First Amendment values in issuing search warrants, however, call for imposing the regime ordered by the District Court. Aware of the long struggle between Crown and press and desiring to curb unjustified official intrusions, the Framers took the enormously important step of subjecting searches to the test of reasonableness and to the general rule requiring search warrants issued by neutral magistrates. They nevertheless did not forbid warrants where the press was involved, did not require special showings that subpoenas would be impractical, and did not insist that the owner of the place to be searched, if connected with the press, must be shown to be implicated in the offense being investigated. Further, the prior cases do no more than insist that the courts apply the warrant requirements with particular exactitude when First Amendment interests would be endangered by the search. As we see it, no more than this is required where the warrant requested is for the seizure of criminal evidence reasonably believed to be on the premises occupied by a newspaper. Properly administered, the preconditions for a warrant—probable cause, specificity with respect to the place to be searched and the things to be seized, and overall reasonableness—should afford sufficient protection against the harms that are assertedly threatened by warrants for searching newspaper offices.

There is no reason to believe, for example, that magistrates cannot guard against searches of the type, scope, and intrusiveness that would actually interfere with the timely publication of a newspaper. Nor, if the requirements of specificity and reasonableness are properly applied, policed, and observed, will there be any occasion or opportunity for officers to rummage at large in newspaper files or to intrude into or to deter normal editorial and publication decisions. The warrant issued in this case authorized nothing of this sort. Nor are we convinced that confidential sources will disappear and that the press will suppress news because of fears of warranted searches. Whatever incremental effect there may be in this regard if search warrants, as well as subpoenas, are permissible in proper circumstances, it does not make a constitutional difference in our judgment.

The fact is that respondents and amici have pointed to only a very few instances in the entire United States since 1971 involving the issuance of warrants for searching newspaper premises. This reality hardly suggests abuse; and if abuse occurs, there will be time enough to deal with it. Furthermore, the press is not only an important, critical, and valuable asset to society, but it is not easily intimidated—nor should it be.

Respondents also insist that the press should be afforded opportunity to litigate the State's entitlement to the material it seeks before it is turned over or seized and that whereas the search warrant procedure is defective in this respect, resort to the subpoena would solve the problem. But presumptively protected materials are not necessarily immune from seizure under warrant for use at a criminal trial. A neutral magistrate carrying out his responsibilities under the Fourth Amendment has ample tools at his disposal to confine warrants to search within reasonable limits. We note finally that if the evidence sought by warrant is sufficiently connected with the crime to satisfy the probable-cause requirement, it will very likely be sufficiently relevant to justify a subpoena and to withstand a motion to quash.

We accordingly reject the reasons given by the District Court and adopted by the Court of Appeals for holding the search for photographs at the Stanford Daily to have been unreasonable within the meaning of the Fourth Amendment and in violation of the First Amendment. Nor has anything else presented here persuaded us that the Amendments forbade this search. It follows that the judgment of the Court of Appeals is reversed. So ordered.

## Points for Discussion

1. In *Branzburg v. Hayes,* the Supreme Court told reporters that they were not exempt from citizens' obligation to testify when called before a grand jury, but that they might not have to reveal the identity of their confidential sources. Is a newsroom search, as compared with a subpoena to reveal documents, more likely to result in the revealing of confidential sources? Why or why not?

**2.** Justice Stewart, in his dissenting opinion in the *Zurcher* case, wrote the following:

> Perhaps as a matter of abstract policy a newspaper office should receive no more protection from unannounced police searches than, say, the office of a doctor or the office of a bank. But we are here to uphold a Constitution. And our Constitution does not explicitly protect the practice of medicine or the business of banking from all abridgment by government. It does explicitly protect the freedom of the press.

Do you agree with him that the First Amendment's explicit mention of "the press" argues for a separate constitutional standard for newsroom searches? Why or why not?

## Gonzales v. NBC

**194 F.3d 29 (2d Cir. 1998)**

*Judge Leval:*

In May, 1996, Albert Gonzales and Mary Gonzales commenced a civil rights action [alleging] that defendant Darrell Pierce, a Louisiana Deputy Sheriff, pulled the Gonzaleses over on Interstate 10 on November 28, 1995, without any probable cause or reasonable suspicion, and detained them by reason of their Hispanic origin. Plaintiffs further allege that it was Deputy Pierce's practice to stop travelers without probable cause or reasonable suspicion in order to extort valuable property from them, and to detain and question "minority citizens, including Hispanics," longer than similarly situated Caucasians. The complaint seeks compensatory and punitive damages as well as injunctive relief.

On January 3, 1997, NBC aired a segment on its "Dateline" television program reporting on what it described as pervasive abuses by law enforcement officers in Louisiana who conduct unwarranted stops of motorists, particularly of out-of-state travelers. According to the report, these stops often lead to harassment and seizure of property. The report included a videotaped stop of one of its employees, Pat Weiland, by Deputy Pierce. Weiland, a Dateline producer and a cameraman, rented a car, equipped it with hidden cameras, and traveled incognito on Louisiana roadways to investigate allegations of malfeasance by Louisiana highway patrolmen. In May, 1996, six months after the Gonzaleses were pulled over, Deputy Pierce stopped Weiland, claiming Weiland had been slowing down and speeding up. The Dateline report asserted that the car had in fact been on cruise control below the posted speed limit. The report also maintained that footage recorded by hidden cameras demonstrated that no traffic laws had been violated, and that the car had been stopped without probable cause. The actual video images broadcast in the report, however, showed only a few brief clips of the car in motion, as well as footage of Deputy Pierce pulling over the vehicle and examining the currency compartment of a passenger's wallet.

In August, 1997, the Gonzaleses served NBC with a subpoena seeking the original, unedited camera footage of Deputy Pierce's stop of Weiland, as well as deposition testimony from NBC representatives about the events recorded on the videotape. Approximately one month later, Deputy Pierce served NBC with a similar subpoena. NBC objected to both subpoenas in part on the grounds that they sought materials protected from disclosure by the qualified privilege for journalists.

The district court granted in relevant part the motions to compel NBC's compliance with the subpoenas. The court first noted that the parties had agreed that the scope of any applicable privilege is governed by federal law because the underlying case asserted a federal claim. Quoting from Second Circuit precedent, the court then explained that "to protect the important interests of reporters and the public in preserving the confidentiality of journalists' sources, disclosure may be ordered only upon a clear and specific showing that the information is: (1) highly material and relevant, (2) necessary or critical to the maintenance of the claim, and (3) not obtainable from other available sources." The district court also posited that the reporters' privilege applies to both confidential and non-confidential sources.

The court then held that the three requirements for overcoming the qualified privilege were met in this case: The Gonzaleses had made a showing that the tapes were "highly material and relevant," because their claims against Deputy Pierce alleged a pattern and practice of illegal stops, and each additional instance of proof they could marshal was therefore significant. The Gonzaleses had established that the tapes were "necessary or critical to the maintenance of their claim," because they were seeking punitive damages and injunctive relief, which they could obtain only by demonstrating a pattern and practice of conduct. Finally, as to the third requirement, the court held that the Gonzaleses had shown that the evidence in the tapes was "not obtainable from other available sources."

The court then found that Deputy Pierce's need for the tapes was equally compelling. In main, the court reasoned that if the tapes were to establish that Deputy Pierce had probable cause to stop the Dateline car, "they would provide unique evidence of both his proper behavior and his veracity." The court also opined that the tapes were "critical to [Deputy Pierce's] defense against the punitive damages and injunctive relief claims, especially in light of Sheriff Edwards' stated intentions to terminate Deputy Pierce if the tapes reveal that he acted improperly." Finally, the court expressed the view that "compelling production of the tapes is further supported by the fact that no confidential information is at issue here."

Accordingly, the district court ordered NBC to comply with the part of the subpoenas requiring production of the out takes. After NBC failed to comply, the court entered an additional order holding NBC in contempt. NBC appealed. As noted above, on our initial review, we affirmed on the ground that the qualified privilege for press materials does not apply to matter received from nonconfidential sources. On NBC's motion for rehearing, we have reconsidered our disposition.

If the parties to any lawsuit were free to subpoena the press at will, it would likely become standard operating procedure for those litigating against an entity that had been the subject of press attention to sift through press files in search of information supporting their claims. The resulting wholesale exposure of press files to litigant scrutiny would burden the press with heavy costs of subpoena compliance, and could otherwise impair its ability to perform its duties—particularly if potential sources were deterred from speaking to the press, or insisted on remaining anonymous, because of the likelihood that they would be sucked into litigation. Incentives would also arise for press entities to clean out files containing potentially valuable information lest they incur substantial costs in the event of future subpoenas. And permitting litigants unrestricted, court-enforced access to journalistic resources would risk the symbolic harm of making journalists appear to be an investigative arm of the judicial system, the government, or private parties.

For these reasons, we reaffirm that the qualified privilege for journalists applies to nonconfidential, as well as to confidential, information. However, it is important to recognize that, where the protection of confidential sources is not involved, the nature of the press interest protected by the privilege is narrower. Accordingly, we now hold that, while nonconfidential press materials are protected by a qualified privilege, the showing needed to overcome the privilege is less demanding than the showing required where confidential materials are sought. Where a civil litigant seeks nonconfidential materials from a nonparty press entity, the litigant is entitled to the requested discovery notwithstanding a valid assertion of the journalists' privilege if he can show that the materials at issue are of likely relevance to a significant issue in the case, and are not reasonably obtainable from other available sources.

The district court held that both the Gonzaleses and Deputy Pierce had made a showing sufficient to overcome NBC's assertion of the journalists' privilege with respect to the Dateline out takes. Because the out takes were not materials obtained by NBC in confidence, we need only determine whether the parties to the Louisiana Action have established that the out takes are of likely relevance to a significant issue in the case, and contain information not reasonably obtainable from other available sources. We answer both questions affirmatively.

The out takes are clearly relevant to a significant issue in the case. The District Court reasonably found they may assist the trier of fact in assessing whether Deputy Pierce had probable cause to stop the NBC vehicle and might help determine whether he engaged in a pattern or practice of stopping vehicles without probable cause, as the Plaintiffs allege. We are also persuaded that the out takes contain information that is not reasonably obtainable from other available sources, because they can provide unimpeachably objective evidence of Deputy Pierce's conduct. We agree with the district court that in this instance a deposition is not an adequate substitute for the information that may be obtained from the videotapes.

We conclude that (i) NBC's videotapes are protected by a qualified journalists' privilege applicable to nonconfidential press materials; (ii) the privilege applicable to nonconfidential press information is overcome on a showing that the materials sought are of likely relevance to a significant issue in the case and are not reasonably obtainable through other available sources; and (iii) the parties to the Louisiana Action, who subpoenaed the tapes, have satisfied the test to overcome NBC's privilege. The orders of the district court granting the motions to compel production of the out takes, and holding NBC in contempt, are hereby AFFIRMED.

## Points for Discussion

1. TV news magazine programs such as *Dateline* often get story ideas from reading about ongoing lawsuits. If you were the producer of such a program, would the *Gonzales* decision make you less likely to do a story that might create footage of interest to the litigants?

2. The *Gonzales* court tells us that the news media's claims are less weighty when litigants seek information that is not "confidential" (such as the identity of a source promised anonymity). But remember the press interests identified by the court. One such interest was to avoid the "symbolic harm of making journalists appear to be an investigative arm of the judicial system, the government, or private parties." Is the likelihood of such harm at all dependent on whether the information sought is "confidential"?

## ■ *Cohen v. Cowles Media Company*

### 501 U.S. 663 (1991)

*Justice White delivered the opinion of the Court.*

The question before us is whether the First Amendment prohibits a plaintiff from recovering damages, under state promissory estoppel law, for a newspaper's breach of a promise of confidentiality given to the plaintiff in exchange for information. We hold that it does not.

During the closing days of the 1982 Minnesota gubernatorial race, Dan Cohen, an active Republican associated with Wheelock Whitney's Independent-Republican gubernatorial campaign, approached reporters from the St. Paul Pioneer Press Dispatch (Pioneer Press) and the Minneapolis Star and Tribune (Star Tribune) and offered to provide documents relating to a candidate in the upcoming election. Cohen made clear to the reporters that he would provide the information only if he was given a promise of confidentiality. Reporters from both papers promised to keep Cohen's identity anonymous and Cohen turned over copies of two public court records concerning Marlene Johnson, the Democratic-Farmer-Labor candidate for Lieutenant Governor. The first record indicated that Johnson had been charged in 1969 with three counts of unlawful assembly, and the second that she had been convicted in 1970 of petit theft. Both newspapers interviewed Johnson for her explanation and one reporter tracked down the person who had found the records for Cohen. As it turned out, the unlawful assembly charges arose out of Johnson's participation in a protest of an alleged failure to hire minority workers on municipal construction projects, and the charges were eventually dismissed. The petit theft conviction was for leaving a store without paying for $6 worth of sewing materials. The incident apparently occurred at a time during which Johnson was emotionally distraught, and the conviction was later vacated.

After consultation and debate, the editorial staffs of the two newspapers independently decided to publish Cohen's name as part of their stories concerning Johnson. In their stories, both papers identified Cohen as the source of the court records, indicated his connection to the Whitney campaign, and included denials by Whitney campaign officials of any role in the matter. The same day the stories appeared, Cohen was fired by his employer.

Cohen sued respondents, the publishers of the Pioneer Press and Star Tribune, in Minnesota state court, alleging fraudulent misrepresentation and breach of contract. The trial court rejected respondents' argument that the First Amendment barred Cohen's lawsuit. A jury returned a verdict in Cohen's favor, awarding him $200,000 in compensatory damages and $500,000 in punitive damages. The Minnesota Court of Appeals, in a split decision, reversed the award of punitive damages after concluding that Cohen had failed to establish a fraud claim, the only claim which would support such an award. However, the court upheld the finding of liability for breach of contract and the $200,000 compensatory damages award. A divided Minnesota Supreme Court reversed the compensatory damages award.

The initial question we face is whether a private cause of action for promissory estoppel involves "state action" within the meaning of the Fourteenth Amendment such that the protections of the First Amendment are triggered. For if it does not, then the First Amendment has no bearing on this case.

Our cases teach that the application of state rules of law in state courts in a manner alleged to restrict First Amendment freedoms constitutes "state action" under the Fourteenth Amendment. In this case, the Minnesota Supreme Court held that if Cohen could recover at all it would be on the theory of promissory estoppel, a state-law doctrine which, in the absence of a contract, creates obligations never explicitly assumed by the parties. These legal obligations would be enforced through the official power of the Minnesota courts. Under our cases, that is enough to constitute "state action" for purposes of the Fourteenth Amendment.

Generally applicable laws do not offend the First Amendment simply because their enforcement against the press has incidental effects on its ability to gather and report the news. Truthful information sought to be published must have been lawfully acquired. The press may not with impunity break and enter an office or dwelling to gather news. Neither does the First Amendment relieve a newspaper reporter of the obligation shared by all citizens to respond to a grand jury subpoena and answer questions relevant to a criminal investigation, even though the reporter might be required to reveal a confidential source. The press, like others interested in publishing, may not publish copyrighted material without obeying the copyright laws. Similarly, the media must obey the National Labor Relations Act and the Fair Labor Standards Act, may not restrain trade in violation of the antitrust laws, and must pay non-discriminatory taxes. Accordingly, enforcement of such general laws against the press is not subject to stricter scrutiny than would be applied to enforcement against other persons or organizations. There can be little doubt that the Minnesota doctrine of promissory estoppel is a law of general applicability. It does not target or single out the press. Rather, insofar as we are advised, the doctrine is generally applicable to the daily transactions of all the citizens of Minnesota. The First Amendment does not forbid its application to the press. Minnesota law simply requires those making promises to keep them. The parties themselves, as in this case, determine the scope of their legal obligations, and any restrictions that may be placed on the publication of truthful information are self-imposed. Also, it is not at all clear that respondents obtained Cohen's name "lawfully" in this case, at least for purposes of publishing it. Respondents obtained Cohen's name only by making a promise that they did not honor.

Nor is Cohen attempting to use a promissory estoppel cause of action to avoid the strict requirements for establishing a libel or defamation claim. As the Minnesota Supreme Court observed here, "Cohen could not sue for defamation because the information disclosed [his name] was true." Cohen is not seeking damages for injury to his reputation or his state of mind. He sought damages in excess of $50,000 for breach of a promise that caused him to lose his job and lowered his earning capacity.

Respondents and amici argue that permitting Cohen to maintain a cause of action for promissory estoppel will inhibit truthful reporting because news organizations will have legal incentives not to disclose a confidential source's identity even when that person's identity is itself newsworthy. But if this is the case, it is no more than the incidental, and constitutionally insignificant, consequence of applying to the press a generally applicable law that requires those who make certain kinds of promises to keep them.

Although we conclude that the First Amendment does not confer on the press a constitutional right to disregard promises that would otherwise be enforced under state law, we reject Cohen's request that in reversing the Minnesota Supreme Court's judgment we reinstate the jury verdict awarding him $200,000 in compensatory damages. The Minnesota Supreme Court's incorrect conclusion that the First Amendment barred Cohen's claim may well have truncated its consideration of whether a promissory estoppel claim had otherwise been established under Minnesota law and whether Cohen's jury verdict could be upheld on a promissory estoppel basis. Or perhaps the State Constitution may be construed to shield the press from a promissory estoppel cause of action such as this one. These are matters for the Minnesota Supreme Court to address and resolve in the first instance on remand. Accordingly, the judgment of the Minnesota Supreme Court is reversed, and the case is remanded for further proceedings not inconsistent with this opinion.

So ordered.

## *Points for Discussion*

1. If Cohen wanted the damaging information about Johnson to be printed without implicating himself or the Whitney campaign, why did he not just mail it anonymously to reporters? As it turns out, some evidence at trial suggested a reason. Cohen knew that the reporters' next step would be to make a visit themselves to the county clerk's office, where they would not only be able to examine the Johnson court records but would also see the list of persons who had recently had access to the records, including one person with known connections to the Whitney campaign. Does knowing this part of the story affect your belief about the wisdom of the Supreme Court's decision?

2. The doctrine of promissory estoppel does not seem to be limited to promises of confidentiality. What might happen, for example, if a source thought she was "promised" that an article flowing from an interview with her would paint her in a favorable light? Should she later conclude that the reporter's portrayal of her was less than flattering, should she have a right to sue?

# 10

# Regulation of Advertising

For most of this country's history, it was assumed that advertising is beyond the scope of the First Amendment. Not until 1976 did the U.S. Supreme Court bring purely commercial messages within the First Amendment umbrella. The first case in this chapter, *Virginia State Board of Pharmacy v. Virginia Citizens Consumer Council,* was the vehicle the Court used to effect this change.

The *Virginia Pharmacy* case, however, only said that advertising should enjoy some First Amendment protection; it did not say how much. The latter issue was addressed by the Court four years later in *Central Hudson Gas & Electric v. Public Service Commission of New York,* our second case.

*Rubin v. Coors Brewing Company,* from 1995, is an example of the Court applying the *Central Hudson* test to a specific factual situation, here involving a federal regulation prohibiting beer distributors from listing on their product labels the percent of alcohol in each bottle.

Our last case, *Ragin v. New York Times,* is a federal appellate decision on a fairly controversial issue (at least in the sense that federal courts in other jurisdictions have ruled differently). The question posed by the case is whether and at what point a pattern of real estate display ads that depict disproportionately white faces becomes part of the act of illegal housing discrimination.

## ■ *Virginia State Board of Pharmacy v. Virginia Citizens Consumer Council*

### 425 U.S. 748 (1976)

*Justice Blackmun delivered the opinion of the Court.*

The plaintiff-appellees in this case attack, as violative of the First and Fourteenth Amendments, that portion of §54-524.35 of Va. Code Ann. (1974), which provides that a pharmacist licensed in Virginia is guilty of unprofessional conduct if he "publishes, advertises or promotes, directly or indirectly, in any manner whatsoever, any amount, price, fee, premium, discount, rebate or credit terms for any drugs which may be dispensed only by prescription."

The plaintiffs are an individual Virginia resident who suffers from diseases that require her to take prescription drugs on a daily basis, and two nonprofit organizations. Their claim is that the First Amendment entitles the user of prescription drugs to receive information that pharmacists wish to communicate to them through advertising and other promotional means, concerning the prices of such drugs.

Certainly that information may be of value. Drug prices in Virginia, for both prescription and nonprescription items, strikingly vary from outlet to outlet even within the same locality. The phenomenon of widely varying drug prices is apparently national in scope.

The question first arises whether, even assuming that First Amendment protection attaches to the flow of drug price information, it is a protection enjoyed by the appellees as recipients of the information, and not solely, if at all, by the advertisers themselves who seek to disseminate that information. Freedom of speech presupposes a willing speaker. But where a speaker exists, as is the case here, the protection afforded is to the communication, to its source and to its recipients both.

The appellants contend that the advertisement of prescription drug prices is outside the protection of the First Amendment because it is "commercial speech." There can be no question that in past decisions the Court has given some indication that commercial speech is unprotected.

Last Term, in *Bigelow v. Virginia,* 421 U.S. 809 (1975), the notion of unprotected "commercial speech" all but passed from the scene. We reversed a conviction for violation of a Virginia statute that made the circulation of any publication to encourage or promote the processing of an abortion in Virginia a misdemeanor. The defendant had published in his newspaper the availability of abortions in New York. The advertisement in question, in addition to announcing that abortions were legal in New York, offered the services of a referral agency in that State. We rejected the contention that the publication was unprotected because it was commercial. Some fragment of hope for the continuing validity of a "commercial speech" exception arguably might have persisted because of the subject matter of the advertisement in *Bigelow.* We noted that in announcing the availability of legal abortions in New York, the advertisement "did more than simply propose a commercial transaction. It contained factual material of clear 'public interest.' "

Here, in contrast, the question whether there is a First Amendment exception for "commercial speech" is squarely before us. Our pharmacist does not wish to editorialize on any subject, cultural, philosophical, or political. He does not wish to report any particularly newsworthy fact, or to make generalized observations even about commercial matters. The "idea" he wishes to communicate is simply this: "I will sell you the X prescription drug at the Y price." Our question, then, is whether this communication is wholly outside the protection of the First Amendment. Our answer is that it is not.

Those whom the suppression of prescription drug price information hits the hardest are the poor, the sick, and particularly the aged. A disproportionate amount of their income tends to be spent on prescription drugs; yet they are the least able to learn, by shopping from pharmacist to pharmacist, where their scarce dollars are best spent. When drug prices vary as strikingly as they do, information as to who is charging what becomes more than a convenience. It could mean the alleviation of physical pain or the enjoyment of basic necessities.

Society also may have a strong interest in the free flow of commercial information. Advertising, however tasteless and excessive it sometimes may seem, is nonetheless dissemination of information as to who is producing and selling what product, for what reason, and at what price. So long as we preserve a predominantly free enterprise economy, the allocation of our resources in large measure will be made through numerous private economic decisions. It is a matter of public interest that those decisions, in the aggregate, be intelligent and well informed. To this end, the free flow of commercial information is indispensable. And if it is indispensable to the proper allocation of resources in a free enterprise system, it is also indispensable to the formation of intelligent opinions as to how that system ought to be regulated or altered. Therefore, even if the First Amendment were thought to be primarily an instrument to enlighten public decision making in a democracy, we could not say that the free flow of information does not serve that goal.

Justifications for the advertising ban have to do principally with maintaining a high degree of professionalism on the part of licensed pharmacists. It is claimed that the aggressive price competition that will result from unlimited advertising will make it impossible for the pharmacist to supply professional services in the compounding, handling, and dispensing of prescription drugs. Such services are time consuming and expensive; if competitors who economize by eliminating them are permitted to advertise their resulting lower prices, the more painstaking and conscientious pharmacist will be forced either to follow suit or to go out of business.

The strength of these proffered justifications is greatly undermined by the fact that high professional standards, to a substantial extent, are guaranteed by the close regulation to which pharmacists in Virginia are subject. Surely, any pharmacist guilty of professional dereliction that actually endangers his customer will promptly lose his license.

On close inspection it is seen that the State's protectiveness of its citizens rests in large measure on the advantages of their being kept in ignorance. The advertising ban does not directly affect professional standards one way or the other. It affects them only through the reactions it is assumed people will have to the free flow of drug price information. There is no claim that the advertising ban in any way prevents the cutting of corners by the pharmacist who is so inclined. That pharmacist is likely to cut corners in any event. The only effect the advertising ban has on him is to insulate him from price competition and to open the way for him to make a substantial, and perhaps even excessive, profit in addition to providing an inferior service. The more painstaking pharmacist is also protected but, again, it is a protection based in large part on public ignorance.

It appears to be feared that if the pharmacist who wishes to provide low cost, and assertedly low quality, services is permitted to advertise, he will be taken up on his offer by too many unwitting customers. They will choose the low-cost, low-quality service and drive the "professional" pharmacist out of business. They will respond only to costly and excessive advertising, and end up paying the price. They will go from one pharmacist to another, following the discount, and destroy the pharmacist-customer relationship. They will lose respect for the profession because it advertises. All this is not in their best interests, and all this can be avoided if they are not permitted to know who is charging what.

There is, of course, an alternative to this highly paternalistic approach. That alternative is to assume that this information is not in itself harmful, that people will perceive their own best interests if only they are well enough informed, and that the best means to that end is to open the channels of communication rather than to close them. If they are truly open, nothing prevents the "professional" pharmacist from marketing his own assertedly superior product, and contrasting it with that of the low-cost, high-volume prescription drug retailer. But the choice among these alternative approaches is not ours to make or the Virginia General Assembly's. It is precisely this kind of choice, between the dangers of suppressing information, and the dangers of its misuse if it is freely available, that the First Amendment makes for us. Virginia is free to require whatever professional standards it wishes of its pharmacists; it may subsidize them or protect them from competition in other ways. But it may not do so by keeping the public in ignorance of the entirely lawful terms that competing pharmacists are offering. In this sense, the justifications Virginia has offered for suppressing the flow of prescription drug price information, far from persuading us that the flow is not protected by the First Amendment, have reinforced our view that it is. We so hold.

## Points for Discussion

1. Justice Blackmun's opinion makes clear that this ruling is the first time the Court will hold that purely commercial advertising is entitled to First Amendment protection. Yet he also argues that advertising is an important means of fostering "enlighten[ed] public decision making in a democracy." Does he thus equate commercial speech with political speech and in fact suggest that smart shopping is, somehow, patriotic?

2. Most Americans have stronger opinions about which fast-food chain (if any) they prefer than which political candidate. Indeed, most Americans cannot even recognize their own representatives in Congress. Should these realities count as reasons for viewing commercial speech as at least as valuable as political speech?

# ■ *Central Hudson Gas & Electric v. Public Service Commission of New York*

### 447 U.S. 557 (1980)

*Justice Powell delivered the opinion of the Court.*

This case presents the question whether a regulation of the Public Service Commission of the State of New York violates the First and Fourteenth Amendments because it completely bans promotional advertising by an electrical utility.

In December 1973, the [Public Service] Commission ordered electric utilities in New York State to cease all advertising that "promotes the use of electricity." The order was based on the Commission's finding that "the interconnected utility system in New York State does not have sufficient fuel stocks or sources of supply to continue furnishing all customer demands for the 1973–1974 winter." Three years later, when the fuel shortage had eased, the Commission requested comments from the public on its proposal to continue the ban on promotional advertising. Central Hudson Gas & Electric Corp., the appellant in this case, opposed the ban on First Amendment grounds. After reviewing the public comments, the Commission extended the prohibition in a Policy Statement issued on February 25, 1977.

The Policy Statement divided advertising expenses into two broad categories: promotional—advertising intended to stimulate the purchase of utility services—and institutional and informational, a broad category inclusive of all advertising not clearly intended to promote sales. The Commission declared all promotional advertising contrary to the national policy of conserving energy. It acknowledged that the ban is not a perfect vehicle for conserving energy. For example, the Commission's order prohibits promotional advertising to develop consumption during periods when demand for electricity is low. By limiting growth in "off-peak" consumption, the ban limits the "beneficial side effects" of such growth in terms of more efficient use of existing powerplants. And since oil dealers are not under the Commission's jurisdiction and thus remain free to advertise, it was recognized that the ban can achieve only "piecemeal conservationism." Still, the Commission adopted the restriction because it was deemed likely to result in some dampening of unnecessary growth in energy consumption.

The Commission's order explicitly permitted "informational" advertising designed to encourage "shifts of consumption" from peak demand times to periods of low electricity demand. Informational advertising would not seek to increase aggregate consumption, but would invite a leveling of demand throughout any given 24-hour period.

Appellant challenged the order in state court, arguing that the Commission had restrained commercial speech in violation of the First and Fourteenth Amendments. The Commission's order was upheld by the trial court and at the intermediate appellate level. The New York Court of Appeals affirmed. We noted probable jurisdiction, and now reverse.

The Commission's order restricts only commercial speech, that is, expression related solely to the economic interests of the speaker and its audience. In applying the First Amendment to this area, we have rejected the highly paternalistic view that government has complete power to suppress or regulate commercial speech. Even when advertising communicates only an incomplete version of the relevant facts, the First Amendment presumes that some accurate information is better than no information at all. Nevertheless, our decisions have recognized the commonsense distinction between speech proposing a commercial transaction, which occurs in an area traditionally subject to government regulation, and other varieties of speech. The Constitution therefore accords a lesser protection to commercial speech than to other constitutionally guaranteed expression. The protection available for particular commercial expression turns on the nature both of the expression and of the governmental interests served by its regulation.

The First Amendment's concern for commercial speech is based on the informational function of advertising. Consequently, there can be no constitutional objection to the suppression of commercial messages that do not accurately inform the public about lawful activity. The government may ban forms of communication more likely to deceive the public than to inform it, or commercial speech related to illegal activity.

If the communication is neither misleading nor related to unlawful activity, the government's power is more circumscribed. The State must assert a substantial interest to be achieved by restrictions on commercial speech. Moreover, the regulatory technique must be in proportion to that interest. The limitation on expression must be designed carefully to achieve the State's goal. Compliance with this requirement may be measured by two criteria. First, the restriction must directly advance the state interest involved; the regulation may not be sustained if it provides only ineffective or remote support for the government's purpose. Second, if the governmental interest could be served as well by a more limited restriction on commercial speech, the excessive restrictions cannot survive.

In commercial speech cases, then, a four-part analysis has developed. At the outset, we must determine whether the expression is protected by the First Amendment. For commercial speech to come within that provision, it at least must concern lawful activity and not be misleading. Next, we ask whether the asserted governmental interest is substantial. If both inquiries yield positive answers, we must determine whether the regulation directly advances the governmental interest asserted, and whether it is not more extensive than is necessary to serve that interest.

We now apply this four-step analysis for commercial speech to the Commission's arguments in support of its ban on promotional advertising. The Commission does not claim that the expression at issue either is inaccurate or relates to unlawful activity.

The Commission offers two state interests as justifications for the ban on promotional advertising. The first concerns energy conservation. Any increase in demand for electricity—during peak or off-peak periods—means greater consumption of energy. The Commission argues that the State's interest in conserving energy is sufficient to support suppression of advertising designed to increase consumption of electricity. In view of our country's dependence on energy resources beyond our control, no one can doubt the importance of energy conservation. Plainly, therefore, the state interest asserted is substantial.

The Commission also argues that promotional advertising will aggravate inequities caused by the failure to base the utilities' rates on marginal cost. The utilities argued to the Commission that if they could promote the use of electricity in periods of low demand, they would improve their utilization of generating capacity. The Commission responded that promotion of off-peak consumption also would increase consumption during peak periods. If peak demand were to rise, the absence of marginal cost rates would mean that the rates charged for the additional power would not reflect the true costs of expanding production. Instead, the extra costs would be borne by all consumers through higher overall rates. Without promotional advertising, the Commission stated, this inequitable turn of events would be less likely to occur. The choice among rate structures involves difficult and important questions of economic supply and distributional fairness. The State's concern that rates be fair and efficient represents a clear and substantial governmental interest.

Next, we focus on the relationship between the State's interests and the advertising ban. Under this criterion, the Commission's laudable concern over the equity and efficiency of appellant's rates does not provide a constitutionally adequate reason for restricting protected speech. The link between the advertising prohibition and appellant's rate structure is, at most, tenuous. The impact of promotional advertising on the equity of appellant's rates is highly speculative. Advertising to increase off-peak usage would have to increase peak usage, while other factors that directly affect the fairness and efficiency of appellant's rates remained constant. Such conditional and remote eventualities simply cannot justify silencing appellant's promotional advertising.

In contrast, the State's interest in energy conservation is directly advanced by the Commission order at issue here. There is an immediate connection between advertising and demand for electricity. Central Hudson would not contest the advertising ban unless it believed that promotion would increase its sales. Thus, we find a direct link between the state interest in conservation and the Commission's order.

We come finally to the critical inquiry in this case: whether the Commission's complete suppression of speech ordinarily protected by the First Amendment is no more extensive than necessary to further the State's interest in energy conservation. The Commission's order reaches all promotional advertising, regardless of the impact of the touted service on overall energy use. But the energy conservation rationale, as important as it is, cannot justify suppressing information about electric devices or services that would cause no net increase in total energy use. In addition, no showing has been made that a more limited restriction on the content of promotional advertising would not serve adequately the State's interests.

Appellant insists that but for the ban, it would advertise products and services that use energy efficiently. These include the "heat pump," which both parties acknowledge to be a major improvement in electric heating, and the use of electric heat as a "backup" to solar and other heat sources. Although the Commission has questioned the efficiency of electric heating before this Court, neither the Commission's Policy Statement nor its order denying rehearing made findings on this issue. In the absence of authoritative findings to the contrary, we must credit as within the realm of possibility the claim that electric heat can be an efficient alternative in some circumstances.

The Commission's order prevents appellant from promoting electric services that would reduce energy use by diverting demand from less efficient sources, or that would consume roughly the same amount of energy as do alternative sources. In neither situation would the utility's advertising endanger conservation or mislead the public. To the extent that the Commission's order suppresses speech that in no way impairs the State's interest in energy conservation, the Commission's order violates the First and Fourteenth Amendments and must be invalidated.

The Commission also has not demonstrated that its interest in conservation cannot be protected adequately by more limited regulation of appellant's commercial expression. To further its policy of conservation, the Commission could attempt to restrict the format and content of Central Hudson's advertising. It might, for example, require that the advertisements include information about the relative efficiency and expense of the offered service, both under current conditions and for the foreseeable future. In the absence of a showing that more limited speech regulation would be ineffective, we cannot approve the complete suppression of Central Hudson's advertising.

Our decision today in no way disparages the national interest in energy conservation. We accept without reservation the argument that conservation, as well as the development of alternative energy sources, is an imperative national goal. Administrative bodies empowered to regulate electric utilities have the authority—and indeed the duty—to take appropriate action to further this goal. When, however, such action involves the suppression of speech, the First and Fourteenth Amendments require that the restriction be no more extensive than is necessary to serve the state interest. In this case, the record before us fails to show that the total ban on promotional advertising meets this requirement.

Accordingly, the judgment of the New York Court of Appeals is reversed.

## Points for Discussion

1. Commercial speech is defined by the Court here as "expression related solely to the economic interests of the speaker and its audience." Would not a labor leader's call for a strike fit that definition? Or a political candidate's promises of tax reforms? How, then, can we distinguish commercial speech from political speech?

2. Justice Powell accepts as common sense the assumption that advertising for a product or service will tend to increase demand for it. Thus, if the state wishes to decrease consumption of that product or service, the *Central Hudson* test would seem to penalize *effective* advertising. Is this a proper function of the First Amendment, or should the public be protected only from false, misleading advertising?

## ■ *Rubin v. Coors Brewing Company*

### 514 U.S. 476 (1995)

*Justice Thomas delivered the opinion of the Court.*

Respondent brews beer. In 1987, respondent applied to the Bureau of Alcohol, Tobacco and Firearms (BATF), an agency of the Department of the Treasury, for approval of proposed labels and advertisements that disclosed the alcohol content of its beer. BATF rejected the application on the ground that the Federal Alcohol Administration Act [FAAA] prohibited disclosure of the alcohol content of beer on labels or in advertising. Respondent then filed suit in the District Court for the District of Colorado. The Government took the position that the ban was necessary to suppress the threat of "strength wars" among brewers, who, without the regulation, would seek to compete in the marketplace based on the potency of their beer.

The District Court upheld the ban on the disclosure of alcohol content in advertising but invalidated the ban as it applied to labels. Although the Government asked the Tenth Circuit to review the invalidation of the labeling ban, respondent did not appeal the court's decision sustaining the advertising ban. The Court of Appeals affirmed the District Court. We conclude that the ban infringes respondent's freedom of speech, and we therefore affirm.

Soon after the ratification of the Twenty-first Amendment, which repealed the Eighteenth Amendment and ended the Nation's experiment with Prohibition, Congress enacted the FAAA. The statute establishes national rules governing the distribution, production, and importation of alcohol and established a Federal Alcohol Administration to implement these rules. Section 5(e)(2) of the Act prohibits any producer, importer, wholesaler, or bottler of alcoholic beverages from selling, shipping, or delivering in interstate or foreign commerce any malt beverages, distilled spirits, or wines in bottles "unless such products are labeled [to] provide the consumer with adequate information as to the . . . alcoholic content thereof (except that statements of, or statements likely to be considered as statements of, alcoholic content of malt beverages are prohibited unless required by State law and except that, in case of wines, statements of alcoholic content shall be required only for wines containing more than 14 per cent of alcohol by volume)."

The Act defines " 'malt beverage[s]' " in such a way as to include all beers and ales. Implementing regulations promulgated by BATF prohibit the disclosure of alcohol content on beer labels. In addition to prohibiting numerical indications of alcohol content, the labeling regulations proscribe descriptive terms that suggest high content, such as "strong," "full strength," "extra strength," "high test," "high proof," "pre-war strength," and "full old-time alcoholic strength." The prohibitions do not preclude labels from identifying a beer as "low alcohol," "reduced alcohol," "non-alcoholic," or "alcohol-free." By statute and by regulation, the labeling ban must give way if state law requires disclosure of alcohol content.

Both parties agree that the information on beer labels constitutes commercial speech. We now apply *Central Hudson* test to §205(e)(2). Respondent seeks to disclose only truthful, verifiable, and nonmisleading factual information about alcohol content on its beer labels. Thus, our analysis focuses on the substantiality of the interest behind §205(e)(2) and on whether the labeling ban bears an acceptable fit with the Government's goal.

The Government identifies two interests it considers sufficiently "substantial" to justify the labeling ban. First, the Government contends that it advances Congress' goal of curbing "strength wars" by beer brewers who might seek to compete for customers on the basis of alcohol content. Respondent counters that Congress actually intended the FAAA to achieve the far different purpose of preventing brewers from making inaccurate claims concerning alcohol content. According to respondent, when Congress passed the FAAA in 1935, brewers did not have the technology to produce beer with alcohol levels within predictable tolerances—a skill that modern beer producers now possess. Further, respondent argues that the true policy guiding federal alcohol regulation is not aimed at suppressing strength wars. If such were the goal, the Government would not pursue the opposite policy with respect to wines and distilled spirits. Although §205(e)(2) requires BATF to promulgate regulations barring the disclosure of alcohol content on beer labels, it also orders BATF to require the disclosure of alcohol content on the labels of wines and spirits.

Rather than suppressing the free flow of factual information in the wine and spirits markets, the Government seeks to control competition on the basis of strength by monitoring distillers' promotions and marketing. Respondent quite correctly notes that the general thrust of federal alcohol policy appears to favor greater disclosure of information, rather than less. Respondent offers a plausible reading of the purpose behind §205(e)(2), but the prevention of misleading statements of alcohol content need not be the exclusive government interest served. The Government here has a significant interest in protecting the health, safety, and welfare of its citizens by preventing brewers from competing on the basis of alcohol strength, which could lead to greater alcoholism and its attendant social costs.

The Government attempts to bolster its position by arguing that the labeling ban not only curbs strength wars, but also facilitates state efforts to regulate alcohol under the Twenty-first Amendment. [The FAAA] prohibits disclosure of alcohol content only in States that do not affirmatively require brewers to provide that information. In the Government's view, this saves States that might wish to ban such labels the trouble of enacting their own legislation, and it discourages beer drinkers from crossing state lines to buy beer they believe is stronger.

We conclude that the Government's interest in preserving state authority is not sufficiently substantial to meet the requirements of *Central Hudson.* Even if the Federal Government possessed the broad authority to facilitate state powers, in this case the Government has offered nothing that suggests that States are in need of federal assistance. States clearly possess ample authority to ban the disclosure of alcohol content—subject, of course, to the same First Amendment restrictions that apply to the Federal Government.

The remaining *Central Hudson* factors require that a valid restriction on commercial speech directly advance the governmental interest and be no more extensive than necessary to serve that interest. The Government attempts to meet its burden by pointing to current developments in the consumer market. It claims that beer producers are already competing and advertising on the basis of alcohol strength in the "malt liquor" segment of the beer market. The Government attempts to show that this competition threatens to spread to the rest of the market by directing our attention to respondent's motives in bringing this litigation. Respondent allegedly suffers from consumer misperceptions that its beers contain less alcohol than other brands. According to the Government, once respondent gains relief from §205(e)(2), it will use its labels to overcome this handicap.

Under the Government's theory, §205(e)(2) suppresses the threat of such competition by preventing consumers from choosing beers on the basis of alcohol content. It is assuredly a matter of common sense that a restriction on the advertising of a product characteristic will decrease the extent to which consumers select a product on the basis of that trait. In addition to common sense, the Government urges us to turn to history as a guide. According to the Government, at the time Congress enacted the FAAA, the use of labels displaying alcohol content had helped produce a strength war. Section 205(e)(2) allegedly relieved competitive pressures to market beer on the basis of alcohol content, resulting over the long term in beers with lower alcohol levels.

We conclude that §205(e)(2) cannot directly and materially advance its asserted interest because of the overall irrationality of the Government's regulatory scheme. While the laws governing labeling prohibit the disclosure of alcohol content unless required by state law, federal regulations apply a contrary policy to beer advertising. These restrictions prohibit statements of alcohol content in advertising, but, unlike §205(e)(2), they apply only in States that affirmatively prohibit such advertisements. As only 18 States at best prohibit disclosure of content in advertisements, brewers remain free to disclose alcohol content in advertisements, but not on labels, in much of the country. The failure to prohibit the disclosure of alcohol content in advertising, which would seem to constitute a more influential weapon in any strength war than labels, makes no rational sense if the Government's true aim is to suppress strength wars.

Other provisions of the FAAA and its regulations similarly undermine §205(e)(2)'s efforts to prevent strength wars. While §205(e)(2) bans the disclosure of alcohol content on beer labels, it allows the exact opposite in the case of wines and spirits. Thus, distilled spirits may contain statements of alcohol content, and such disclosures are required for wines with more than 14 percent alcohol. If combating strength wars were the goal, we would assume that Congress would regulate disclosure of alcohol content for the strongest beverages as well as for the weakest ones. Further, the Government permits brewers to signal high alcohol content through use of the term "malt liquor." Although the Secretary has proscribed the use of various colorful terms suggesting high alcohol levels, manufacturers still can distinguish a class of stronger malt beverages by identifying them as malt liquors. One would think that if the Government sought to suppress strength wars by prohibiting numerical disclosures of alcohol content, it also would preclude brewers from indicating higher alcohol beverages by using descriptive terms.

While we are mindful that respondent only appealed the constitutionality of §205(e)(2), these exemptions and inconsistencies bring into question the purpose of the labeling ban. To be sure, the Government's interest in combating strength wars remains a valid goal. But the irrationality of this unique and puzzling regulatory framework ensures that the labeling ban will fail to achieve that end. There is little chance that §205(e)(2) can directly and materially advance its aim, while other provisions of the same Act directly undermine and counteract its effects.

Nor do we think that respondent's litigating positions can be used against it as proof that the Government's regulation is necessary. That respondent wishes to disseminate factual information concerning alcohol content does not demonstrate that it intends to compete on the basis of alcohol content. Brewers may have many different reasons—only one of which might be a desire to wage a strength war—why they wish to disclose the potency of their beverages.

Respondent suggests several alternatives [to the labeling ban], such as directly limiting the alcohol content of beers, prohibiting marketing efforts emphasizing high alcohol strength (which is apparently the policy in some other western nations), or limiting the labeling ban only to malt liquors, which is the segment of the market that allegedly is threatened with a strength war. We agree that the availability of these options, all of which could advance the Government's asserted interest in a manner less intrusive to respondent's First Amendment rights, indicates that §205(e)(2) is more extensive than necessary.

In sum, although the Government may have a substantial interest in suppressing strength wars in the beer market, the FAAA's countervailing provisions prevent §205(e)(2) from furthering that purpose in a direct and material fashion. The FAAA's defects are further highlighted by the availability of alternatives that would prove less intrusive to the First Amendment's protections for commercial speech. Because we find that §205(e)(2) fails the *Central Hudson* test, we affirm the decision of the court below.

## *Points for Discussion*

1. Justice Thomas's opinion tells us that, even if common sense suggests that a governmental regulation furthers a legitimate state's interest, it can be thrown out if the larger context of other, competing regulations calls into question the government's logic. What might be some implications of this stance? For example, can a beach town's laws against commercial highway billboards be thrown out because, if the town were *really* serious about protecting the aesthetics of its environment, it would have also banned the use of "fly-by" advertisements by airplanes with streamers?

2. Suppose that a nonprofit consumer magazine were to publish on its cover that "Coors beer has 4.73 percent alcohol by volume." This statement would likely not be considered "commercial speech." Why, then, does the identical message become commercial when Coors itself disseminates it? Does the identity (and commercial motivation?) of the speaker make the difference? If so, why is it that we consider neither a book review nor a publisher's insertion of excerpts from that review on a book's dust jacket commercial speech?

## ■ *Ragin v. New York Times*

### 923 F.2d 995 (2d Cir. 1991)

*Judge Winter:*

The Times is the publisher of the *New York Times*, a nationally known newspaper. The individual plaintiffs are black persons who have been looking for housing in the New York metropolitan area. Plaintiff Open Housing Center, Inc., is a not-for-profit New York corporation, one of the primary goals of which is to eliminate racially discriminatory housing practices. On January 12, 1989, plaintiffs commenced this action under the Fair Housing Act, the Civil Rights Act of 1866, the Civil Rights Act of 1870, and the Thirteenth Amendment. Plaintiffs sought a declaratory judgment, injunctive relief, and compensatory and punitive damages. The complaint alleges:

> During the twenty year period since the Act was passed, advertisements appeared in the Sunday Times featuring thousands of human models of whom virtually none were black. While many of the white human models depict representative or potential home owners or renters, the few blacks represented are usually depicted as building maintenance employees, doormen, entertainers, sports figures, small children or cartoon characters. The Times has continued to publish numerous advertisements that picture all-white models in advertisements for realty located in predominantly white buildings, developments, communities or neighborhoods. It has also published a few advertisements that picture all black models in advertisements for realty located in predominantly black buildings, developments, communities or neighborhoods.
>     The use of human models in advertising personalizes the advertisements and encourages consumers to identify themselves in a positive way with the models and housing featured. In real estate advertisements, human models often represent actual or potential purchasers or renters, or the type of potential purchasers or renters that

the real estate owner has targeted as desirable occupants. Therefore, the repeated and continued depiction of white human models and the virtual absence of any black human models indicates a preference on the basis of race.

Section 3604(c) states in pertinent part that it is unlawful "to publish any advertisement, with respect to the sale or rental of a dwelling that indicates any preference based on race." Beginning our analysis with the statutory language, the first critical word is the verb "indicates." Giving that word its common meaning, we read the statute to be violated if an ad for housing suggests to an ordinary reader that a particular race is preferred or dis-preferred for the housing in question. The second critical word is the noun "preference." The Times asks us to read that word to preclude liability for a publisher where the ad in question is not facially discriminatory and the publisher has no other evidence of a discriminatory intent. We share that general view but with important qualifications.

The Times's conception of what kinds of ads might be deemed by a trier of fact as facially suggesting to an ordinary reader a racial preference is intolerably narrow. At oral argument, suggested as examples of such a facial message were real estate advertisements depicting burning crosses or swastikas. We do not limit the statute—not to say trivialize it—by construing it to outlaw only the most provocative and offensive expressions of racism or statements indicating an outright refusal to sell or rent to persons of a particular race. Congress used broad language in Section 3604(c), and there is no cogent reason to narrow the meaning of that language. Ordinary readers may reasonably infer a racial message from advertisements that are more subtle than the hypothetical swastika or burning cross, and we read the word "preference" to describe any ad that would discourage an ordinary reader of a particular race from answering it.

Moreover, the statute prohibits all ads that indicate a racial preference to an ordinary reader whatever the advertiser's intent. To be sure, the intent of the creator of an ad may be relevant to a factual determination of the message conveyed, but the touchstone is nevertheless the message. If, for example, an advertiser seeking to reach a group of largely white consumers were to create advertisements that discouraged potential black consumers from responding, the statute would bar the ads, whether or not the creator of the ad had a subjective racial intent.

Keeping these general, and fairly obvious, propositions in mind, we turn to the allegations of the complaint. A threshold question is whether Section 3604(c) reaches the use of models as a medium for the expression of a racial preference. We hold that it does. Congress prohibited all expressions of racial preferences in housing advertisements and did not limit the prohibition to racial messages conveyed through certain means. Neither the text of the statute nor its legislative history suggests that Congress intended to exempt from its proscriptions subtle methods of indicating racial preferences.

The next question is whether and in what circumstances the use of models may convey an illegal racial message. We begin with another proposition that seems to us fairly obvious: namely, that a trier of fact could find that in this age of mass communication and sophisticated modes of persuasion, advertisers target as potential consumers groups with certain racial as well as other characteristics. In some circumstances, such targeting conveys a racial preference, or so a trier might find. We live in a race-conscious society, and real estate advertisers seeking the attention of groups that are largely white may see greater profit in appealing to white consumers in a manner that consciously or unconsciously discourages non-whites. They may do so out of simple inertia or because of the fear that the use of black models will deter more white consumers than it attracts black consumers. In any event, a trier plausibly may conclude that in some circumstances ads with models of a particular race and not others will be read by the ordinary reader as indicating a racial preference.

The Times does not deny that advertisers target groups but rather vigorously presses the claim that if Section 3604(c) is applied to the Times, the specter of racially conscious decisions and of racial quotas in advertising will become a reality. We need not enter the public debate over the existence or merits of racial quotas in fields other than advertising, or look to the scope of Supreme Court decisions that permit race-conscious decisions. We do believe, however, that the Times's concerns are overblown. The quota controversy principally concerns selection of persons for competitive opportunities, such as employment or admission to college. These are circumstances in which opinions differ whether individual skills or purely academic qualifications should govern and whether a race-conscious decision is itself an act of racial discrimination. The use of models in advertising, however, involves wholly different considerations. Advertising is a make-up-your-own world in which one builds an image from scratch, selecting those portrayals that will attract targeted consumers and discarding those that will put them off. Locale, setting, actions portrayed, weather, height, weight, gender, hair color, dress, race and numerous other factors are varied as needed to convey the message intended. A soft-drink manufacturer seeking to envelop its product in an aura of good will and harmony may portray a group of persons of widely varying nationalities and races singing a cheerful tune on a mountaintop. A chain of fast-food retailers may use models of the principal races found in urban areas where its stores are located. Similarly, a housing complex may decide that the use of models of one race alone will maximize the number of potential consumers who respond, even though it may also discourage consumers of other races.

In advertising, a conscious racial decision regarding models thus seems almost inevitable. All the statute requires is that in this make-up-your-own world the creator of an ad not make choices among models that create a suggestion of a racial preference. The deliberate inclusion of a black model where necessary to avoid such a message seems to us a far cry from the alleged practices that are at the core of the debate over quotas. If race-conscious decisions are inevitable in the make-up-your-own world of advertising, a statutory interpretation that may lead to some race-conscious decision-making to avoid indicating a racial preference is hardly a danger to be averted at all costs.

Moreover, the Times's argument would prevent a trier of fact from scrutinizing the selection of models and inferring from that selection and from the surrounding circumstances a race-conscious decision. The creator of an ad may testify, "Gosh, I didn't notice until this trial that all the models for tenants were white and the model for a custodian was black." However, a trier may justifiably disbelieve such an assertion in light of all the circumstances, much as triers of fact are allowed to draw inferences of racial intent in other contexts, or may consider such an assertion an inadvertent or unconscious expression of racism.

Given this scope for fact-finding, the present complaint cannot be dismissed for failure to state a claim for relief.

The Times argues that Section 3604(c) is void for vagueness. Even if we indulge in the assumption that the vagueness doctrine applies to civil actions, we believe the ordinary reader standard provides constitutionally adequate notice of the prohibited conduct. The Times's argument seems based on an unstated premise either that the selection of models in advertising is entirely random or that publishers of major newspapers lack the sophistication to notice racial messages that are apparent to others. The premise regarding the random selection of models is baseless, and we have more confidence in the perspicacity of publishers than do the Times's lawyers. Of course, close questions will arise, as they do in every area of the law, but we cannot say in the context of a facial challenge to the statute that the ordinary reader is a hopelessly vague legal standard.

The Times also claims that the district court's interpretation of Section 3604(c) violates the First Amendment. We disagree. Judge Haight held that real estate advertisements that indicate a racial preference "further an illegal commercial activity: racial discrimination in the sale or rental of real estate." From this premise he concluded that such advertisements are constitutionally unprotected. The Times contends that, because the activity being advertised is the rental or sale of realty, a legal activity, the advertisements are entitled to protection as lawful commercial speech.

The Supreme Court has made clear that the Constitution accords a lesser protection to commercial speech than to other constitutionally guaranteed expression. It is the informational content of advertising that gives rise to its First Amendment protection. The Fair Housing Act prohibits discrimination in the sale or rental of housing, as well as ads that indicate a racial preference. The complaint alleges that the ads in question discourage black people from pursuing housing opportunities by conveying a racial message. The Times's publication of real estate advertisements that indicate a racial preference is, therefore, not protected commercial speech.

The Times contends that the press cannot be compelled to act as an enforcer of otherwise desirable laws and that such an obligation imposes unconstitutional special burdens on the press, and that the press is ill-equipped to conduct the monitoring of advertisements that Section 3604(c) requires. The Times thus admits that it presently reviews advertising submissions to avoid publishing ads that do not meet its "Standards of Advertising Acceptability." Given that this extensive monitoring—for purposes that are both numerous and often quite vague—is routinely performed, it strains credulity beyond the breaking point to assert that monitoring ads for racial messages imposes an unconstitutional burden.

Accordingly, the judgment of the district court is affirmed.

## Points for Discussion

1. The *Central Hudson* test tells us that advertising that is either deceptive or is publicizing an illegal product or service can be regulated or forbidden altogether without running afoul of the First Amendment. If the pattern of advertising described in the *Ragin* case is part of the act of illegal housing discrimination, should that not be the end of the inquiry? Why did the Court bother to consider how much of a burden the prohibition of such advertising would place on the newspaper?

2. If you were a *New York Times* editor, how would you implement the Court's decision? Would you review the pattern of faces in real estate ads on a weekly or monthly basis? Would you tell each individual advertiser that every ad they submit that includes human faces must depict a variety of such faces, of different races? Might you simply forbid the use of human faces altogether?

# 11

# *Sexually Oriented Speech*

This chapter looks at a category of speech—graphic sexual content—that the U.S. Supreme Court says is protected only marginally, if at all, by the First Amendment. Four cases are included here.

*Miller v. California* is the landmark 1973 ruling providing the definition of obscenity still used by the Court. Two key components of that definition are that otherwise prohibitable works may be protected if they boast "serious literary, artistic, political, or scientific value" (often called the SLAPS test) and that the scope of prohibited works can vary from community to community.

Although the Court has said that truly obscene works are exceptions to the general principle that the government may not proscribe speech on the basis of its content, *Stanley v. Georgia* creates an exception to that exception. Unlike Miller, who was a commercial purveyor of pornography, Stanley was convicted of reading obscene materials in the privacy of his own home. This difference was of constitutional import, the Court determined.

And if *Stanley* counts as an exception to an exception, the next case—*Osborne v. Ohio*—must count as a third-order exception. In this 1990 decision, the Court rules that states may criminalize the mere possession of child pornography. Child pornography is a form of sexual expression that need not be obscene, but that does depict juveniles in lewd sexual ways. Even private consumption of such materials in the home can properly be reached by the law, the Court says, not only because of the special evils associated with child pornography, but also because the state's interests are different from and greater than those it has in trying to regulate or prohibit more "mainstream" obscenity.

Finally, we examine the Seventh Circuit Court of Appeals decision in *American Booksellers Association v. Hudnut,* rejecting the attempt by the city of Indianapolis to treat pornography as a civil rights issue, one that demeans not only the performers who produce it, but also women who are sexually assaulted by men who unquestioningly accept the demeaning image of women found in much pornography.

194

# ■ *Miller v. California*

**413 U.S. 15 (1973)**

*Chief Justice Burger delivered the opinion of the Court.*

Appellant conducted a mass mailing campaign to advertise the sale of illustrated books, euphemistically called "adult" material. After a jury trial, he was convicted of violating California Penal Code §311.2 (a), a misdemeanor, by knowingly distributing obscene matter. Appellant's conviction was specifically based on his conduct in causing five unsolicited advertising brochures to be sent through the mail in an envelope addressed to a restaurant in Newport Beach, California. The envelope was opened by the manager of the restaurant and his mother. They had not requested the brochures; they complained to the police. The brochures primarily consist of pictures and drawings very explicitly depicting men and women in groups of two or more engaging in a variety of sexual activities, with genitals often prominently displayed.

This Court has recognized that the States have a legitimate interest in prohibiting dissemination or exhibition of obscene material when the mode of dissemination carries with it a significant danger of offending the sensibilities of unwilling recipients or of exposure to juveniles. It is in this context that we are called on to define the standards which must be used to identify obscene material that a State may regulate without infringing on the First Amendment as applicable to the States through the Fourteenth Amendment.

We acknowledge the inherent dangers of undertaking to regulate any form of expression. State statutes designed to regulate obscene materials must be carefully limited. As a result, we now confine the permissible scope of such regulation to works which depict or describe sexual conduct. That conduct must be specifically defined by the applicable state law, as written or authoritatively construed. The basic guidelines for the trier of fact must be: (a) whether the average person, applying contemporary community standards would find that the work, taken as a whole, appeals to the prurient interest; (b) whether the work depicts or describes, in a patently offensive way, sexual conduct specifically defined by the applicable state law; and (c) whether the work, taken as a whole, lacks serious literary, artistic, political, or scientific value.

We emphasize that it is not our function to propose regulatory schemes for the States. That must await their concrete legislative efforts. It is possible, however, to give a few plain examples. State statutes [might legitimately cover] patently offensive representations or descriptions of ultimate sexual acts, normal or perverted, actual or simulated; and/or patently offensive representations or descriptions of masturbation, excretory functions, and lewd exhibition of the genitals.

Sex and nudity may not be exploited without limit by films or pictures exhibited or sold in places of public accommodation any more than live sex and nudity can be exhibited or sold without limit in such public places. At a minimum, prurient, patently offensive depiction or description of sexual conduct must have serious literary, artistic, political, or scientific value to merit First Amendment protection. For example, medical books for the education of physicians and related personnel necessarily use graphic illustrations and descriptions of human anatomy. In resolving the inevitably sensitive questions of fact and law, we must continue to rely on the jury system, accompanied by the safeguards that judges, rules of evidence, presumption of innocence, and other protective features provide, as we do with rape, murder, and a host of other offenses against society and its individual members.

Under the holdings announced today, no one will be subject to prosecution for the sale or exposure of obscene materials unless these materials depict or describe patently offensive "hard core" sexual conduct specifically defined by the regulating state law, as written or construed. We are satisfied that these specific prerequisites will provide fair notice to a dealer in such materials that his public and commercial activities may bring prosecution. If the inability to define regulated materials with ultimate, god-like precision altogether removes the power of the States or the Congress to regulate, then "hard core" pornography may be exposed without limit to the juvenile, the passerby, and the consenting adult alike.

Under a National Constitution, fundamental First Amendment limitations on the powers of the States do not vary from community to community, but this does not mean that there are, or should or can be, fixed, uniform national standards of precisely what appeals to the prurient interest or is patently offensive. These are essentially questions of fact, and our Nation is simply too big and too diverse for this Court to reasonably expect that such standards could be articulated for all 50 States in a single formulation, even assuming the prerequisite consensus exists. When triers of fact are asked to decide whether "the average person, applying contemporary community standards" would consider certain materials "prurient," it would be unrealistic to require that the answer be based on some abstract formulation. The adversary system, with lay jurors as the usual ultimate fact finders in criminal prosecutions, has historically permitted triers of fact to draw on the standards of their community, guided always by limiting instructions on the law. To require a State to structure obscenity proceedings around evidence of a national "community standard" would be an exercise in futility. It is neither realistic nor constitutionally sound to read the First Amendment as requiring that the people of Maine or Mississippi accept public depiction of conduct found tolerable in Las Vegas, or New York City.

The primary concern with requiring a jury to apply the standard of "the average person, applying contemporary community standards" is to be certain that, so far as material is not aimed at a deviant group, it will be judged by its impact on an average person, rather than a particularly susceptible or sensitive person—or indeed a totally insensitive one. We hold that the requirement that the jury evaluate the materials with reference to "contemporary standards of the State of California" [as was done in this case] serves this protective purpose and is constitutionally adequate.

In our view, to equate the free and robust exchange of ideas and political debate with commercial exploitation of obscene material demeans the grand conception of the First Amendment and its high purposes in the historic struggle for freedom. The First Amendment protects works which, taken as a whole, have serious literary, artistic, political, or scientific value, regardless of whether the government or a majority of the people approve of the ideas these works represent. There is no evidence, empirical or historical, that the stern 19th century American censorship of public distribution and display of material relating to sex in any way limited or affected expression of serious literary, artistic, political, or scientific ideas. On the contrary, it is beyond any question that the era following Thomas Jefferson to Theodore Roosevelt was an extraordinarily vigorous period, not just in economics and politics, but in belles lettres and in the outlying fields of social and political philosophies. We do not see the harsh hand of censorship of ideas—good or bad, sound or unsound—and "repression" of political liberty lurking in every state regulation of commercial exploitation of human interest in sex. One can concede that the "sexual revolution" of recent years may have had useful byproducts in striking layers of prudery from a subject long irrationally kept from needed ventilation. But it does not follow that no regulation of patently offensive "hard core" materials is needed or permissible; civilized people do not allow unregulated access to heroin because it is a derivative of medicinal morphine.

The judgment of the Appellate Department of the Superior Court, Orange County, California, is vacated and the case remanded to that court for further proceedings not inconsistent with the First Amendment standards established by this opinion. Vacated and remanded.

> *Editor's Note:* "Vacating" the lower court judgment in this way is not at all the same thing as "overturning" the judgment would have been. Indeed, because the definition of obscenity offered by Chief Justice Burger gives states more freedom to prosecute than the one used at Miller's trial, Burger is really inviting the California courts to uphold the initial conviction.

## Points for Discussion

1. The majority says, without fanfare, that sexual messages may be prohibited "when the mode of dissemination carries with it a significant danger of offending the sensibilities of unwilling recipients or of exposure to juveniles." But why single out *sexual* messages for this treatment? Might a Jew be equally offended by the local church marquee's claim that "Jesus is the *only* way?" Isn't the prolife demonstrator's

shouting that "abortion is murder" designed, at least in part, to offend the sensibilities of abortion clinics' approaching clients?

2. Suppose that you are a juror in an obscenity case and also that you are not especially offended by the materials you are called on to judge. Yet you are not supposed to apply your own feelings. Rather, you are asked to call to mind the "average person" in your community. How would you figure out what such a person's reaction would be to this material? Would the average person find the work appeals to the "prurient interest" or was "patently offensive"? How would you guess?

## ■ *Stanley v. Georgia*

### 394 U.S. 557 (1969)

*Justice Marshall delivered the opinion of the Court.*

An investigation of appellant's alleged bookmaking activities led to the issuance of a search warrant for appellant's home. Federal and state agents found very little evidence of bookmaking activity, but while looking through a desk drawer in an upstairs bedroom, one of the federal agents, accompanied by a state officer, found three reels of eight-millimeter film. Using a projector and screen found in an upstairs living room, they viewed the films. The state officer concluded that they were obscene and seized them. Appellant was charged with possession of obscene matter and placed under arrest. He was tried before a jury and convicted. The Supreme Court of Georgia affirmed.

Appellant argues that the Georgia obscenity statute, insofar as it punishes mere private possession of obscene matter, violates the First Amendment, as made applicable to the States by the Fourteenth Amendment. For reasons set forth below, we agree that the mere private possession of obscene matter cannot constitutionally be made a crime. Georgia contends that since obscenity is not within the area of constitutionally protected speech or press, the States are free, subject to the limits of other provisions of the Constitution, to deal with it any way deemed necessary, just as they may deal with possession of other things thought to be detrimental to the welfare of their citizens. If the State can protect the body of a citizen, may it not, argues Georgia, protect his mind?

It is true that [our previous decisions] declare, seemingly without qualification, that obscenity is not protected by the First Amendment. However, [no] decision of this Court dealt with the precise problem involved in the present case—private possession of obscene materials. [The earlier cases] dealt with the power of the State and Federal Governments to prohibit or regulate certain public actions taken or intended to be taken with respect to obscene matter, [such as] sale or distribution of obscene materials or possession with intent to sell or distribute, [or] sale of obscene material to children.

It is now well established that the Constitution protects the right to receive information and ideas. This right to receive information and ideas, regardless of their social worth, is fundamental to our free society. Moreover, in the context of this case—a prosecution for mere possession of printed or filmed matter in the privacy of a person's own home—that right takes on an added dimension. For also fundamental is the right to be free, except in very limited circumstances, from unwanted governmental intrusions into one's privacy.

These are the rights that appellant is asserting in the case before us. He is asserting the right to read or observe what he pleases—the right to satisfy his intellectual and emotional needs in the privacy of his own home. He is asserting the right to be free from state inquiry into the contents of his library. Georgia contends that appellant does not have these rights, that there are certain types of materials that the individual may not read or even possess. Georgia justifies this assertion by arguing that the films in the present case are obscene. But we think that mere categorization of these films as "obscene" is insufficient justification for such a drastic invasion of personal liberties guaranteed by the First and Fourteenth Amendments. Whatever may be the justifications for other statutes regulating obscenity, we do not think they reach into the privacy of one's own home. If the First Amendment means anything, it means that a State has no business telling a man, sitting alone in his own house, what books he may read or what films he may watch. Our whole constitutional heritage rebels at the thought of giving government the power to control men's minds. And yet, in the face of these traditional notions of individual liberty, Georgia asserts the right to protect the individual's mind from the effects of obscenity. We are not certain that this argument amounts to anything more than the assertion that the State has the right to control the moral content of a person's thoughts. To some, this may be a noble purpose, but it is wholly inconsistent with the philosophy of the First Amendment.

Nor is it relevant that obscene materials in general, or the particular films before the Court, are arguably devoid of any ideological content. The line between the transmission of ideas and mere entertainment is much too elusive for this Court to draw, if indeed such a line can be drawn at all. Whatever the power of the state to control public dissemination of ideas inimical to the public morality, it cannot constitutionally premise legislation on the desirability of controlling a person's private thoughts.

Perhaps recognizing this, Georgia asserts that exposure to obscene materials may lead to deviant sexual behavior or crimes of sexual violence. There appears to be little empirical basis for that assertion. But more important, if the State is only concerned about printed or filmed materials inducing antisocial conduct, we believe that in the context of private consumption of ideas and information we should adhere to the view that among free men, the deterrents ordinarily to be applied to prevent crime are education and punishment for violations of the law. Given the present state of knowledge, the State may no more prohibit mere possession of obscene matter on the ground that it may lead to antisocial conduct than it may prohibit possession of chemistry books on the ground that they may lead to the manufacture of homemade spirits.

There is always the danger that obscene material might fall into the hands of children, or that it might intrude upon the sensibilities or privacy of the general public. No such dangers are present in this case.

Finally, we are faced with the argument that prohibition of possession of obscene materials is a necessary incident to statutory schemes prohibiting distribution. That argument is based on alleged difficulties of proving an intent to distribute or in producing evidence of actual distribution. We are not convinced that such difficulties exist, but even if they did we do not think that they would justify infringement of the individual's right to read or observe what he pleases. Because that right is so fundamental to our scheme of individual liberty, its restriction may not be justified by the need to ease the administration of otherwise valid criminal laws.

We hold that the First and Fourteenth Amendments prohibit making mere private possession of obscene material a crime. The States retain broad power to regulate obscenity; that power simply does not extend to mere possession by the individual in the privacy of his own home. Accordingly, the judgment of the court below is reversed and the case is remanded for proceedings not inconsistent with this opinion.

## *Points for Discussion*

1. In other decisions, the Court upheld laws making it illegal to send obscene works through the mails, or through such interstate public transport as airplanes or trains, or to import them from another country. Such rulings led Justice Douglas to comment that he could not understand "how the right to possession enunciated in *Stanley* has any meaning when States are allowed to outlaw the commercial transactions which give rise to such possession." How would you answer Justice Douglas?

2. The Court says here that "the line between the transmission of ideas and mere entertainment" is an elusive one, suggesting that works are more likely to be protected by the First Amendment to the extent that they contain "ideas." Yet isn't that which upsets many people most about some kinds of pornography precisely the "ideas" they convey? Many pornographic films, after all, depict women enjoying being penetrated by force in every available orifice. Do not such depictions convey "ideas" about women and about relationships between the sexes generally?

# Osborne v. Ohio

### 495 U.S. 103 (1990)

*Justice White delivered the opinion of the Court.*

In order to combat child pornography, Ohio enacted Rev. Code Ann. §2907.323(A)(3) (Supp. 1989), which provides in pertinent part:

(A) No person shall do any of the following:
(3) Possess or view any material or performance that shows a minor who is not the person's child or ward in a state of nudity, unless one of the following applies:
(a) The material or performance is sold, disseminated, displayed, possessed, controlled, brought or caused to be brought into this state, or presented for a bona fide artistic, medical, scientific, educational, religious, governmental, judicial, or other proper purpose, by or to a physician, psychologist, sociologist, scientist, teacher, person pursuing bona fide studies or research, librarian, clergyman, prosecutor, judge, or other person having a proper interest in the material or performance.
(b) The person knows that the parents, guardian, or custodian has consented in writing to the photographing or use of the minor in a state of nudity and to the manner in which the material or performance is used or transferred.

Petitioner, Clyde Osborne, was convicted of violating this statute and sentenced to six months in prison, after the Columbus, Ohio, police, pursuant to a valid search, found four photographs in Osborne's home. Each photograph depicts a nude male adolescent posed in a sexually explicit position. The Ohio Supreme Court affirmed Osborne's conviction. The court first rejected Osborne's contention that the First Amendment prohibits the States from proscribing the private possession of child pornography. Next, the Court found that §2907.323(A)(3) is not unconstitutionally overbroad. In so doing, the Court, read §2907.323(A)(3) as only applying to depictions of nudity involving a lewd exhibition or graphic focus on a minor's genitals. The Court also found that scienter [i.e., that the defendant was aware of the sexually graphic nature of the photos] is an essential element of a §2907.323(A)(3) offense. Osborne objected that the trial judge had not insisted that the government prove lewd exhibition and scienter as elements of his crime. The Ohio Supreme Court rejected these contentions because Osborne had failed to object to the jury instructions given at his trial and the court did not believe that the failures of proof amounted to plain error.

The threshold question in this case is whether Ohio may constitutionally proscribe the possession and viewing of child pornography or whether, as Osborne argues, our decision in *Stanley v. Georgia,* 394 U.S. 557 (1969), compels the contrary result. In *Stanley,* we struck down a Georgia law outlawing the private possession of obscene material. We recognized that the statute impinged upon Stanley's right to receive information in the privacy of his home, and we found Georgia's justifications for its law inadequate.

*Stanley* should not be read too broadly. [It] was a narrow holding and, since the decision in that case, the value of permitting child pornography has been characterized [by this Court] as "exceedingly modest, if not *de minimis.*" But assuming, for the sake of argument, that Osborne has a First Amendment interest in viewing and possessing child pornography, we nonetheless find this case distinct from *Stanley* because the interests underlying child pornography prohibitions far exceed the interests justifying the Georgia law at issue in *Stanley.* In *Stanley,* Georgia primarily sought to proscribe the private possession of obscenity because it was concerned that obscenity would poison the minds of its viewers. We responded that "whatever the power of the state to control public dissemination of ideas inimical to the public morality, it cannot constitutionally premise legislation on the desirability of controlling a person's private thoughts." The difference here is obvious: The State does not rely on a paternalistic interest in regulating Osborne's mind. Rather, Ohio has enacted §2907.323(A)(3) in order to protect the victims of child pornography; it hopes to destroy a market for the exploitative use of children.

The use of children as subjects of pornographic materials is harmful to the physiological, emotional, and mental health of the child. It is also surely reasonable for the State to conclude that it will decrease the production of child pornography if it penalizes those who possess and view the product, thereby decreasing demand. The advertising and selling of child pornography provide an economic motive for and are thus an integral part of the production of such materials, an activity illegal throughout the Nation. It rarely has been suggested that the constitutional freedom for speech and press extends its immunity to speech or writing used as an integral part of conduct in violation of a valid criminal statute.

Osborne contends that the State should use other measures, besides penalizing possession, to dry up the child pornography market. Osborne points out that in *Stanley* we rejected Georgia's argument that its prohibition on obscenity possession was a necessary incident to its proscription on obscenity distribution. This holding, however, must be viewed in light of the weak interests asserted by the State in that case. *Stanley* itself emphasized that we did not "mean to express any opinion on statutes making criminal possession of other types of printed, filmed, or recorded materials," [that] "in such cases, compelling reasons may exist for overriding the right of the individual to possess those materials."

Given the importance of the State's interest in protecting the victims of child pornography, we cannot fault Ohio for attempting to stamp out this vice at all levels in the distribution chain. Much of the child pornography market [is] underground; as a result, it is difficult, if not impossible, to solve the child pornography problem by only attacking production and distribution.

Other interests also support the Ohio law. First, the materials produced by child pornographers permanently record the victim's abuse. The pornography's continued existence causes the child victims continuing harm by haunting the children in years to come. The State's ban on possession and viewing encourages the possessors of these materials to destroy them. Second, encouraging the destruction of these materials is also desirable because evidence suggests that pedophiles use child pornography to seduce other children into sexual activity. Given the gravity of the State's interests in this context, we find that Ohio may constitutionally proscribe the possession and viewing of child pornography.

Osborne next argues that even if the State may constitutionally ban the possession of child pornography, his conviction is invalid because §2907.323(A)(3) is unconstitutionally overbroad in that it criminalizes an intolerable range of constitutionally protected conduct. The Ohio statute, on its face, purports to prohibit the possession of "nude" photographs of minors. We have stated that depictions of nudity, without more, constitute protected expression. Relying on this observation, Osborne argues that the statute as written is substantially overbroad. We are skeptical of this claim because, in light of the statute's exemptions and "proper purposes" provisions, the statute may not be substantially overbroad. However that may be, Osborne's overbreadth challenge, in any event, fails because the statute, as construed by the Ohio Supreme Court on Osborne's direct appeal, plainly survives overbreadth scrutiny. Under the Ohio Supreme Court reading, the statute prohibits "the possession or viewing of material or performance of a minor who is in a state of nudity, where such nudity constitutes a lewd exhibition or involves a graphic focus on the genitals, and where the person depicted is neither the child nor the ward of the person charged." By limiting the statute's operation in this manner, the Ohio Supreme Court avoided penalizing persons for viewing or possessing innocuous photographs of naked children. We have upheld similar language against overbreadth challenges in the past.

The Ohio Supreme Court also concluded that the State had to establish scienter in order to prove a violation of §2907.323(A)(3). Osborne contends that it was impermissible for the Ohio Supreme Court to apply its construction of §2907.323(A)(3) to him—i.e., to rely on the narrowed construction of the statute when evaluating his overbreadth claim. Our cases, however, have long held that a statute as construed may be applied to conduct occurring prior to the construction, provided such application affords fair warning to the defendant. Osborne had notice that his conduct was proscribed. It is obvious from the face of §2907.323(A)(3) that the goal of the statute is to eradicate child pornography. The provision criminalizes the viewing and possessing of material depicting children in a state of nudity for other than "proper purposes." The provision appears in the "Sex Offenses" chapter of the Ohio Code. That Osborne's photographs of adolescent boys in sexually explicit situations constitute child pornography hardly needs elaboration. Therefore, although §2907.323(A)(3) as written may have been imprecise at its fringes, someone in Osborne's position would not be surprised to learn that his possession of the four photographs at issue in this case constituted a crime.

Osborne contends that a court may not construe the statute to avoid overbreadth problems and then apply the statute, as construed, to past conduct. The implication of this argument is that if a statute is overbroad as written, then the statute is void and incurable. As a result, when reviewing a conviction under a potentially overbroad statute, a court must either affirm or strike down the statute on its face, but the court may not, as the Ohio Supreme court did in this case, narrow the statute, affirm on the basis of the narrowing construction, and leave the statute in full force. We disagree.

If we accepted this proposition, it would require a radical reworking of our law. Courts routinely construe statutes so as to avoid the statutes' potentially overbroad reach, apply the statute in that case, and leave the statute in place.

Osborne contends that when courts construe statutes so as to eliminate overbreadth, convictions of those found guilty of unprotected conduct covered by the statute must be reversed and any further convictions for prior reprehensible conduct are barred. Furthermore, because he contends that overbroad laws implicating First Amendment interests are nullities and incapable of valid application from the outset, this would mean that judicial construction could not save the statute even as applied to subsequent conduct unprotected by the First Amendment. The overbreadth doctrine, as we have recognized, is indeed strong medicine, and requiring that statutes be facially invalidated whenever overbreadth is perceived would very likely invite reconsideration or redefinition of the doctrine in a way that would not serve First Amendment interests.

*Editor's Note:* Although Osborne's First Amendment claims were rejected, the Supreme Court overturns his conviction, finding that the jury had not been properly instructed as to all the elements of the Ohio obscenity statute.

## Points for Discussion

1. The Ohio statute provided an exception for images gathered for "a bona fide . . . educational . . . or other proper purpose, by or to a . . . person pursuing bona fide studies or research." One of the state's major inter-

ests in prohibiting child pornography, however, is to protect the child victims' privacy: the material's "continued existence causes the child victims continuing harm by haunting the children in years to come." From the child victim's perspective, what difference does it make if the images of their abuse are in the hands of a researcher—a reporter?—or a bus driver? Does the exception ignore the state's interest?

2. Do the statute's exemptions also suffer from a degree of vagueness? Would a sex manual, for example, qualify as an "educational" purpose? What about photos created for a "proper" use (such as a medical textbook), but that become favored images among participants in an online chat room catering to pedophiles?

## ■ *American Booksellers Association v. Hudnut*

**771 F.2d 323 (7th Cir. 1985)**

*Judge Easterbrook:*

Indianapolis enacted an ordinance defining "pornography" as a practice that discriminates against women. Pornography is to be redressed through the administrative and judicial methods used for other discrimination. The City's definition of pornography is considerably different from obscenity, which the Supreme Court has held is not protected by the First Amendment.

To be obscene under *Miller v. California,* a publication must, taken as a whole, appeal to the prurient interest, must contain patently offensive depictions or descriptions of specified sexual conduct, and on the whole have no serious literary, artistic, political, or scientific value. Offensiveness must be assessed under the standards of the community. Both offensiveness and an appeal to something other than "normal, healthy sexual desires" are essential elements of obscenity.

Pornography under the ordinance is "the graphic sexually explicit subordination of women, whether in pictures or in words, that also includes one or more of the following:

(1) Women are presented as sexual objects who enjoy pain or humiliation;
(2) Women are presented as sexual objects who experience sexual pleasure in being raped;
(3) Women are presented as sexual objects tied up or cut up or mutilated or bruised or physically hurt, or as dismembered or truncated or fragmented or severed into body parts;

(4) Women are presented as being penetrated by objects or animals;

(5) Women are presented in scenarios of degradation, injury, abasement, torture, shown as filthy or inferior, bleeding, bruised, or hurt in a context that makes these conditions sexual; or

(6) Women are presented as sexual objects for domination, conquest, violation, exploitation, possession, or use, or through postures or positions of servility or submission or display."

The statute provides that the "use of men, children, or transsexuals in the place of women in paragraphs (1) through (6) above shall also constitute pornography under this section." The ordinance as passed in April 1984 defined "sexually explicit" to mean actual or simulated intercourse or the uncovered exhibition of the genitals, buttocks or anus. An amendment in June 1984 deleted this provision, leaving the term undefined.

The Indianapolis ordinance does not refer to the prurient interest, to offensiveness, or to the standards of the community. It demands attention to particular depictions, not to the work judged as a whole. It is irrelevant under the ordinance whether the work has literary, artistic, political, or scientific value. The City and many amici point to these omissions as virtues. They maintain that pornography influences attitudes, and the statute is a way to alter the socialization of men and women rather than to vindicate community standards of offensiveness. And as one of the principal drafters of the ordinance has asserted, "if a woman is subjected, why should it matter that the work has other value?"

Civil rights groups and feminists have entered this case as amici on both sides. Those supporting the ordinance say that it will play an important role in reducing the tendency of men to view women as sexual objects, a tendency that leads to both unacceptable attitudes and discrimination in the workplace and violence away from it. Those opposing the ordinance point out that much radical feminist literature is explicit and depicts women in ways forbidden by the ordinance and that the ordinance would reopen old battles. It is unclear how Indianapolis would treat works from James Joyce's *Ulysses* to Homer's *Iliad;* both depict women as submissive objects for conquest and domination.

We do not try to balance the arguments for and against an ordinance such as this. The ordinance discriminates on the ground of the content of the speech. Speech treating women in the approved way—in sexual encounters premised on equality—is lawful no matter how sexually explicit. Speech treating women in the disapproved way—as submissive in matters sexual or as enjoying humiliation—is unlawful no matter how significant the literary, artistic, or political qualities of the work taken as a whole. The state may not ordain preferred viewpoints in this way. The Constitution forbids the state to declare one perspective right and silence opponents.

The ordinance contains four prohibitions. People may not "traffic" in pornography, "coerce" others into performing in pornographic works, or "force" pornography on anyone. Anyone injured by someone who has seen or read pornography has a right of action against the maker or seller.

Trafficking is defined [in the statute] as the "production, sale, exhibition, or distribution of pornography." The offense excludes exhibition in a public or educational library, but a "special display" in a library may be sex discrimination. [Later the law says that] the trafficking paragraph "shall not be construed to make isolated passages or isolated parts actionable."

"Coercion into pornographic performance" is defined as "coercing, intimidating or fraudulently inducing any person . . . into performing for pornography . . . ."

"Forcing pornography on a person" [is defined as] the "forcing of pornography on any woman, man, child, or transsexual in any place of employment, in education, in a home, or in any public place." The statute does not define forcing, but one of its authors states that the definition reaches pornography shown to medical students as part of their education or given to language students for translation.

[Also prohibited is] the "assault, physical attack, or injury of any woman, man, child, or transsexual in a way that is directly caused by specific pornography."

For purposes of all four offenses, it is generally "not a defense that the respondent did not know or intend that the materials were pornography." But the ordinance provides that damages are unavailable in trafficking cases unless the complainant proves "that the respondent knew or had reason to know that the materials were pornography." It is a complete defense to a trafficking case that all of the materials in question were pornography only by virtue of category (6) of the definition of pornography. In cases of assault caused by pornography, those who seek damages from "a seller, exhibitor or distributor" must show that the defendant knew or had reason to know of the material's status as pornography. By implication, those who seek damages from an author need not show this.

A woman aggrieved by trafficking in pornography may file a complaint "as a woman acting against the subordination of women" with the office of equal opportunity. A man, child, or transsexual also may protest trafficking "but must prove injury in the same way that a woman is injured."

The office investigates and within 30 days makes a recommendation to a panel of the equal opportunity advisory board. The panel then decides whether there is reasonable cause to proceed and may refer the dispute to a conciliation conference or to a complaint adjudication committee for a hearing. The committee uses the same procedures ordinarily associated with civil rights litigation. It may make findings and enter orders, including both orders to cease and desist and orders to restore complainant's losses. Either party may appeal the committee's decision to the board, which reviews the record before the committee and may modify its decision.

Under Indiana law an administrative decision takes effect when rendered, unless a court issues a stay. The board's decisions are subject to review in the ordinary course. When the board finds that a person has engaged in trafficking or that a seller, exhibitor, or distributor is responsible for an assault, it must initiate judicial review of its own decision, and the statute prohibits injunctive relief in these cases in advance of the court's final decision.

The district court held the ordinance unconstitutional. The court concluded that the ordinance regulates speech rather than the conduct involved in making pornography. The regulation of speech could be justified, the court thought, only by a compelling interest in reducing sex discrimination, an interest Indianapolis had not established. The ordinance is also vague and overbroad, the court believed, and establishes a prior restraint of speech.

Collectively the plaintiffs (or their members, whose interests they represent) make, sell, or read just about every kind of material that could be affected by the ordinance, from hard-core films to W.B. Yeats's poem "Leda and the Swan" (from the myth of Zeus in the form of a swan impregnating an apparently subordinate Leda), to the collected works of James Joyce, D.H. Lawrence, and John Cleland.

Under the First Amendment the government must leave to the people the evaluation of ideas. Bald or subtle, an idea is as powerful as the audience allows it to be. A belief may be pernicious—the beliefs of Nazis led to the death of millions, those of the Klan to the repression of millions. A pernicious belief may prevail. Totalitarian governments today rule much of the planet, practicing suppression of billions and spreading dogma that may enslave others. One of the things that separates our society from theirs is our absolute right to propagate opinions that the government finds wrong or even hateful.

The ideas of the Klan may be propagated. Communists may speak freely and run for office. The Nazi Party may march through a city with a large Jewish population. People may criticize the President by misrepresenting his positions, and they have a right to post their misrepresentations on public property. People may seek to repeal laws guaranteeing equal opportunity in employment or to revoke the constitutional amendments granting the vote to blacks and women. They may do this because above all else, the First Amendment means that government has no power to restrict expression because of its message or its ideas.

Under the ordinance graphic sexually explicit speech is "pornography" or not depending on the perspective the author adopts. Speech that "subordinates" women and also, for example, presents women as enjoying pain, humiliation, or rape, or even simply presents women in "positions of servility or submission or display" is forbidden, no matter how great the literary or political value of the work taken as a whole. Speech that portrays women in positions of equality is lawful, no matter how graphic the sexual content. This is thought control. It establishes an "approved" view of women, of how they may react to sexual encounters, of how the sexes may relate to each other. Those who espouse the approved view may use sexual images; those who do not, may not.

Indianapolis justifies the ordinance on the ground that pornography affects thoughts. Men who see women depicted as subordinate are more likely to treat them so. Pornography is an aspect of dominance. It does not persuade people so much as change them. It works by socializing, by establishing the expected and the permissible. In this view pornography is not an idea; pornography is the injury.

There is much to this perspective. Beliefs are also facts. People often act in accordance with the images and patterns they find around them. People raised in a religion tend to accept the tenets of that religion, often without independent examination. People taught from birth that black people are fit only for slavery rarely rebelled against that creed; beliefs coupled with the self-interest of the masters established a social structure that inflicted great harm while enduring for centuries. Words and images act at the level of the subconscious before they persuade at the level of the conscious. Even the truth has little chance unless a statement fits within the framework of beliefs that may never have been subjected to rational study.

Therefore we accept the premises of this legislation. Depictions of subordination tend to perpetuate subordination. The subordinate status of women in turn leads to affront and lower pay at work, insult and injury at home, battery and rape on the streets. In the language of the legislature, "pornography is central in creating and maintaining sex as a basis of discrimination. Pornography is a systematic practice of exploitation and subordination based on sex which differentially harms women. The bigotry and contempt it produces, with the acts of aggression it fosters, harm women's opportunities for equality and rights of all kinds."

Yet this simply demonstrates the power of pornography as speech. All of these unhappy effects depend on mental intermediation. Pornography affects how people see the world, their fellows, and social relations. If pornography is what pornography does, so is other speech. Hitler's orations affected how some Germans saw Jews. Communism is a world view, not simply a Manifesto by Marx and Engels or a set of speeches. Efforts to suppress communist speech in the United States were based on the belief that the public acceptability of such ideas would increase the likelihood of totalitarian government. Religions affect socialization in the most pervasive way. A religion can dominate an entire approach to life, governing much more than the relation between the sexes. Many people believe that the existence of television, apart from the content of specific programs, leads to intellectual laziness, to a penchant for violence, to many other ills. The Alien and Sedition Acts passed during the administration of John Adams rested on a sincerely held belief that disrespect for the government leads to social collapse and revolution—a belief with support in the history of many nations. Most governments of the world act on this empirical regularity, suppressing critical speech. In the United States, however, the strength of the support for this belief is irrelevant. Seditious libel is protected speech unless the danger is not only grave but also imminent.

Racial bigotry, anti-semitism, violence on television, reporters' biases—these and many more influence the culture and shape our socialization. None is directly answerable by more speech, unless that speech too finds its place in the popular culture. Yet all is protected as speech, however insidious. Any other answer leaves the government in control of all of the institutions of culture, the great censor and director of which thoughts are good for us.

Sexual responses often are unthinking responses, and the association of sexual arousal with the subordination of women therefore may have a substantial effect. But almost all cultural stimuli provoke unconscious responses. Religious ceremonies condition their participants. Teachers convey messages by selecting what not to cover; the implicit message about what is off limits or unthinkable may be more powerful than the messages for which they present rational argument. Television scripts contain unarticulated assumptions. People may be conditioned in subtle ways. If the fact that speech plays a role in a process of conditioning were enough to permit governmental regulation, that would be the end of freedom of speech.

It is possible to interpret the claim that the pornography is the harm in a different way. Indianapolis emphasizes the injury that models in pornographic films and pictures may suffer. The record contains materials depicting sexual torture, penetration of women by red-hot irons and the like. These concerns have nothing to do with written materials subject to the statute, and physical injury can occur with or without the "subordination" of women. A state may make injury in the course of producing a film unlawful independent of the viewpoint expressed in the film.

[But] the image of pain is not necessarily pain. In *Body Double,* a suspense film directed by Brian DePalma, a woman who has disrobed and presented a sexually explicit display is murdered by an intruder with a drill. The drill runs through the woman's body. The film is sexually explicit and a murder occurs—yet no one believes that the actress suffered pain or died. In *Barbarella* a character played by Jane Fonda is at times displayed in sexually explicit ways and at times shown "bleeding, bruised, [and] hurt in a context that makes these conditions sexual"—and again no one believes that Fonda was actually tortured to make the film. In *Carnal Knowledge* a woman grovels to please the sexual whims of a character played by Jack Nicholson; no one believes that there was a real sexual submission, and the Supreme Court held the film protected by the First Amendment. And this works both ways. The description of women's sexual domination of men in *Lysistrata* was not real dominance. Depictions may affect slavery, war, or sexual roles, but a book about slavery is not itself slavery, or a book about death by poison a murder.

Much of Indianapolis's argument rests on the belief that when speech is "unanswerable," and the metaphor that there is a "marketplace of ideas" does not apply, the First Amendment does not apply either. The metaphor is honored; Milton's *Aeropagitica* and John Stewart Mill's *On Liberty* defend freedom of speech on the ground that the truth will prevail, and many of the most important cases under the First Amendment recite this position. The Framers undoubtedly believed it. As a general matter it is true. But the Constitution does not make the dominance of truth a necessary condition of freedom of speech. To say that it does would be to confuse an outcome of free speech with a necessary condition for the application of the amendment.

A power to limit speech on the ground that truth has not yet prevailed and is not likely to prevail implies the power to declare truth. At some point the government must be able to say (as Indianapolis has said): "We know what the truth is, yet a free exchange of speech has not driven out falsity, so that we must now prohibit falsity." If the government may declare the truth, why wait for the failure of speech? Under the First Amendment, however, there is no such thing as a false idea, so the government may not restrict speech on the ground that in a free exchange truth is not yet dominant.

At any time, some speech is ahead in the game; the more numerous speakers prevail. Supporters of minority candidates may be forever "excluded" from the political process because their candidates never win, because few people believe their positions. This does not mean that freedom of speech has failed.

We come, finally, to the argument that pornography is "low value" speech, that it is enough like obscenity that Indianapolis may prohibit it. Some cases hold that speech far removed from politics and other subjects at the core of the Farmers' concerns may be subjected to special regulation. These cases do not sustain statutes that select among viewpoints, however.

Indianapolis seeks to prohibit certain speech because it believes this speech influences social relations and politics on a grand scale, that it controls attitudes at home and in the legislature. This precludes a characterization of the speech as low value. True, pornography and obscenity have sex in common. But Indianapolis left out of its definition any reference to literary, artistic, political, or scientific value. The ordinance applies to graphic sexually explicit subordination in works great and small. The Court sometimes balances the value of speech against the costs of its restriction, but it does this by category of speech and not by the content of particular works.

Indianapolis has created an approved point of view and so [the precedents it cites are not applicable].

The definition of "pornography" is unconstitutional. No construction or excision of particular terms could save it. The offense of trafficking in pornography necessarily falls with the definition.

The offense of coercion to engage in a pornographic performance has elements that might be constitutional. Without question a state may prohibit fraud, trickery, or the use of force to induce people to perform—in pornographic films or in any other films. Such a statute may be written without regard to the viewpoint depicted in the work. We suppose that if someone forced a prominent political figure, at gunpoint, to endorse a candidate for office, a state could forbid the commercial sale of the film containing that coerced endorsement. The same principle allows a court to enjoin the publication of stolen trade secrets and award damages for the publication of copyrighted matter without permission. But the Indianapolis ordinance, unlike our hypothetical statute, is not neutral with respect to viewpoint. The ban on distribution of works containing coerced performances is limited to pornography; coercion is irrelevant if the work is not pornography, and we have held the definition of pornography to be defective root and branch. A legislature might replace "pornography" with "any film containing explicit sex" or some similar expression, but rewriting is work for the legislature, [not the courts].

The offense of forcing pornography on unwilling recipients is harder to assess. Many kinds of forcing (such as giving texts to students for translation) may themselves be protected speech. A state may permit people to insulate themselves from categories of speech—such as sexually explicit mailings—but the government must leave the decision about what items are forbidden in the hands of the potentially offended recipients. Exposure to sex is not something the government may prevent. We therefore could not save the offense of "forcing" by redefining "pornography" as all sexually-offensive speech or some related category. The statute needs a definition of "forcing" that removes the government from the role of censor.

The section creating remedies for injuries and assaults attributable to pornography also is salvageable in principle, although not by us. The First Amendment does not prohibit redress of all injuries caused by speech. Injury to reputation is redressed through the law of libel, which is constitutional subject to strict limitations. A state may not penalize speech that does not cause immediate injury. The law of libel has the potential to muzzle the press. A law awarding damages for assaults caused by speech also has the power to muzzle the press, and again courts would place careful limits on the scope of the right. Certainly no damages could be awarded unless the harm flowed directly from the speech and there was an element of intent on the part of the speaker.

Much speech is dangerous. Chemists whose work might help someone build a bomb, political theorists whose papers might start political movements that lead to riots, speakers whose ideas attract violent protesters, all these and more leave loss in their wake. Unless the remedy is very closely confined, it could be more dangerous to speech than all the libel judgments in history. The constitutional requirements for a valid recovery for assault caused by speech might turn out to be too rigorous for any plaintiff to meet. But the Indianapolis ordinance requires the complainant to show that the attack was "directly caused by specific pornography," and it is not beyond the realm of possibility that a state court could construe this limitation in a way that would make the statute constitutional. We are not authorized to prevent the state from trying.

Again, however, the assault statute is tied to "pornography," and we cannot find a sensible way to repair the defect without seizing power that belongs elsewhere. Indianapolis might choose to have no ordinance if it cannot be limited to viewpoint-specific harms, or it might choose to extend the scope to all speech, just as the law of libel applies to all speech. An attempt to repair this ordinance would be nothing but a blind guess.

No amount of struggle with particular words and phrases in this ordinance can leave anything in effect. The district court came to the same conclusion. Its judgment is therefore affirmed.

## *Points for Discussion*

1. The city of Indianapolis believes, and the court admits, that even nonobscene sexual depictions may cause harm. Can you think of any way that the city—or social activists—could help protect women from the harms of pornography without running into First Amendment barriers?

2. Imagine you are an antipornography activist who wants to produce a documentary film exposing the evils of the commercial sex trade. In what ways might the Indianapolis ordinance create legal problems for you (especially if you felt the need to include highly graphic and exploitative images in your film)?

# 12 *Broadcast, Cable, and Satellite TV Regulation*

In this chapter, we look at cases involving laws and regulations that would be clearly unconstitutional if applied to the print media. The system of communication law in the United States, however, has long embraced the notion that the electromagnetic spectrum, the "airwaves," belong to the public. Thus, those who are granted a license to broadcast TV or radio programming using those airwaves must do so in the public interest. The Federal Communications Commission (FCC) was created in 1934 to promulgate and enforce broadcast regulations.

We begin with *Red Lion Broadcasting v. FCC,* where the Court upheld the Personal Attack and Political Editorializing rules, both of which make highly detailed demands on broadcast licensees. The rules were struck down in 2000. Next we look at *Becker v. FCC,* in which a political candidate insisted, much to the dismay of a local broadcaster, on including highly graphic visuals of aborted fetuses in his TV campaign advertisements. *FCC v. Pacifica Foundation* dealt with a New York radio station that was sanctioned by the Commission for playing a comedy routine by George Carlin called "Filthy Words." Next, we examine *Turner Broadcasting System v. FCC*, a case that deals with the complicated relationship between over-the-air broadcasters and local cable TV franchises. Regulations affecting the latter industry, the Court says, will be subjected by the Court to a level of scrutiny somewhere between the strictness it uses when adjudicating laws affecting print media and the more lax standard used with respect to broadcast regulations.

Finally, we examine *Time Warner Entertainment v. FCC,* decided in early 2001. The case is unique among those excerpted in this book in that it has almost nothing to say about the actual content of messages. Rather, it focuses on questions of ownership rules: how many U.S. households receiving some kind of cable or satellite system may any single cable company reach, and how many channels on a given cable system may be owned by the cable company itself. *Time Warner* may be a harbinger of things to come; for the next few decades we are likely to see an increase in communication law cases involving struggles among competing companies and industries for the right to reach U.S. households.

# ▉ *Red Lion Broadcasting v. FCC*

## 395 U.S. 367 (1969)

*Justice White delivered the opinion of the Court.*

The Federal Communications Commission has for many years imposed on radio and television broadcasters the requirement that discussion of public issues be presented on broadcast stations, and that each side of those issues must be given fair coverage. This is known as the fairness doctrine, which originated very early in the history of broadcasting and has maintained its present outlines for some time. Two aspects of the fairness doctrine, relating to personal attacks in the context of controversial public issues and to political editorializing, were codified more precisely in the form of FCC regulations in 1967.

> *Editor's Note:* The main features of the Fairness Doctrine were rescinded in the 1980s; moreover, the Personal Attack and Political Editorializing rules at issue here were struck down in 2000. The *Red Lion* decision is still a landmark of communication law, however, and no Court majority has ever repudiated the reasons offered here for treating broadcast and print media differently.

The Red Lion Broadcasting Company is licensed to operate a Pennsylvania radio station, WGCB. On November 27, 1964, WGCB carried a 15-minute broadcast by the Reverend Billy James Hargis as part of a "Christian Crusade" series. A book by Fred J. Cook entitled "Goldwater—Extremist on the Right" was discussed by Hargis, who said that Cook had been fired by a newspaper for making false charges against city officials; that Cook had then worked for a Communist-affiliated publication; that he had defended Alger Hiss and attacked J. Edgar Hoover and the Central Intelligence Agency; and that he had now written a "book to smear and destroy Barry Goldwater." When Cook heard of the broadcast he concluded that he had been personally attacked and demanded free reply time, which the station refused. After an exchange of letters among Cook, Red Lion, and the FCC, the FCC declared that the Hargis broadcast constituted a personal attack on Cook; that Red Lion had failed to meet its obligation under the fairness doctrine, to send a tape, transcript, or summary of the broadcast to Cook and offer him reply time; and that the station must provide reply time whether or not Cook would pay for it. On review in the Court of Appeals for the District of Columbia Circuit, the FCC's position was upheld as constitutional and otherwise proper.

The history of the emergence of the fairness doctrine and of the related legislation shows that the Commission's action in the Red Lion case did not exceed its authority, and that in adopting the new regulations the

Commission was implementing congressional policy rather than embarking on a frolic of its own.

Before 1927, the allocation of frequencies was left entirely to the private sector, and the result was chaos. It quickly became apparent that broadcast frequencies constituted a scarce resource whose use could be regulated and rationalized only by the Government. Without government control, the medium would be of little use because of the cacophony of competing voices, none of which could be clearly and predictably heard. Consequently, the Federal Radio Commission [FRC] was established. Very shortly thereafter the Commission expressed its view that the "public interest requires ample play for the free and fair competition of opposing views, and the commission believes that the principle applies to all discussions of issues of importance to the public."

This doctrine was applied through denial of license renewals or construction permits, both by the FRC, and its successor FCC. There is a twofold duty laid down by the FCC's decisions. The broadcaster must give adequate coverage to public issues, and coverage must be fair in that it accurately reflects the opposing views. This must be done at the broadcaster's own expense if sponsorship is unavailable.

Moreover, the duty must be met by programming obtained at the licensee's own initiative if available from no other source. The Federal Radio Commission had imposed these two basic duties on broadcasters since the outset, and in particular respects the personal attack rules and regulations at issue here have spelled them out in greater detail. When a personal attack has been made on a figure involved in a public issue, [Commission rules] require that the individual attacked himself be offered an opportunity to respond. Likewise, where one candidate is endorsed in a political editorial, the other candidates must themselves be offered reply time to use personally or through a spokesman.

The broadcaster does not have the option of presenting the attacked party's side himself or choosing a third party to represent that side. The simple fact that the attacked men or unendorsed candidates may respond themselves or through agents is not a critical distinction, and indeed, it is not unreasonable for the FCC to conclude that the objective of adequate presentation of all sides may best be served by allowing those most closely affected to make the response, rather than leaving the response in the hands of the station which has attacked their candidacies, endorsed their opponents, or carried a personal attack upon them.

The statutory authority of the FCC to promulgate these regulations derives from the mandate to the "Commission from time to time, as public convenience, interest, or necessity requires" to promulgate "such rules and regulations and prescribe such restrictions and conditions . . . as may be necessary to carry out the provisions of this chapter . . . " 47 U.S.C. §303 and §303(r).

In 1959 the Congress amended the statutory requirement of §315 that equal time be accorded each political candidate to except certain appearances on news programs, but added that this constituted no exception "from the obligation imposed upon them under this Act to operate in the public interest and to afford reasonable opportunity for the discussion of conflicting views on issues of public importance." This language makes it very plain that Congress, in 1959, announced that the phrase "public interest," which had been in the Act since 1927, imposed a duty on broadcasters to discuss both sides of controversial public issues. In other words, the amendment vindicated the FCC's general view that the fairness doctrine inhered in the public interest standard. When the Congress ratified the FCC's implication of a fairness doctrine in 1959 it did not, of course, approve every past decision or pronouncement by the Commission on this subject, or give it a completely free hand for the future. The statutory authority does not go so far. But we cannot say that when a station publishes personal attacks or endorses political candidates, it is a misconstruction of the public interest standard to require the station to offer time for a response rather than to leave the response entirely within the control of the station which has attacked either the candidacies or the men who wish to reply in their own defense. When a broadcaster grants time to a political candidate, Congress itself requires that equal time be offered to his opponents. It would exceed our competence to hold that the Commission is unauthorized by the statute to employ a similar device where personal attacks or political editorials are broadcast by a radio or television station. In light of the fact that the "public interest" in broadcasting clearly encompasses the presentation of vigorous debate of controversial issues of importance and concern to the public.

The broadcasters challenge the fairness doctrine and its specific manifestations in the personal attack and political editorial rules on conventional First Amendment grounds, alleging that the rules abridge their freedom of speech and press. Their contention is that the First Amendment protects their desire to use their allotted frequencies continuously to broadcast whatever they choose, and to exclude whomever they choose from ever using that frequency.

Although broadcasting is clearly a medium affected by a First Amendment interest, differences in the characteristics of new media justify differences in the First Amendment standards applied to them. For example, the ability of new technology to produce sounds more raucous than those of the human voice justifies restrictions on the sound level, and on the hours and places of use, of sound trucks so long as the restrictions are reasonable and applied without discrimination.

Just as the Government may limit the use of sound-amplifying equipment potentially so noisy that it drowns out civilized private speech, so may the Government limit the use of broadcast equipment. The right of free speech of a broadcaster, the user of a sound truck, or any other individual does not embrace a right to snuff out the free speech of others.

When two people converse face to face, both should not speak at once if either is to be clearly understood. But the range of the human voice is so limited that there could be meaningful communications if half the people in the United States were talking and the other half listening. Just as clearly, half the people might publish and the other half read. But the reach of radio signals is incomparably greater than the range of the human voice and the problem of interference is a massive reality. The lack of know-how and equipment may keep many from the air, but only a tiny fraction of those with resources and intelligence can hope to communicate by radio at the same time if intelligible communication is to be had, even if the entire radio spectrum is utilized in the present state of commercially acceptable technology.

Where there are substantially more individuals who want to broadcast than there are frequencies to allocate, it is idle to posit an unabridgeable First Amendment right to broadcast comparable to the right of every individual to speak, write, or publish. If 100 persons want broadcast licenses but there are only 10 frequencies to allocate, all of them may have the same "right" to a license; but if there is to be any effective communication by radio, only a few can be licensed and the rest must be barred from the airwaves. It would be strange if the First Amendment, aimed at protecting and furthering communications, prevented the Government from making radio communication possible by requiring licenses to broadcast and by limiting the number of licenses so as not to overcrowd the spectrum. Congress unquestionably has the power to grant and deny licenses and to eliminate existing stations. No one has a First Amendment right to a license or to monopolize a radio frequency; to deny a station license because the public interest requires it is not a denial of free speech. By the same token, as far as the First Amendment is concerned those who are licensed stand no better than those to whom licenses are refused. A license permits broadcasting, but the licensee has no constitutional right to be the one who holds the license or to monopolize a radio frequency to the exclusion of his fellow citizens. There is nothing in the First Amendment which prevents the Government from requiring a licensee to share his frequency with others and to conduct himself as a proxy or fiduciary with obligations to present those views and voices which are representative of his community and which would otherwise, by necessity, be barred from the airwaves.

This is not to say that the First Amendment is irrelevant to public broadcasting. On the contrary, it has a major role to play as the Congress itself recognized in §326, which forbids FCC interference with "the right of free speech by means of radio communication." Because of the scarcity of radio frequencies, the Government is permitted to put restraints on licensees in favor of others whose views should be expressed on this unique medium. But the people as a whole retain their interest in free speech by radio and their collective right to have the medium function consistently with the ends and purposes of the First Amendment. It is the right of the viewers and listeners, not the right of the broadcasters, which is paramount. It is the purpose of the First Amendment to preserve an uninhibited marketplace of ideas in which truth will ultimately prevail, rather than to countenance monopolization of that market, whether it be by the Government itself or a private licensee. It is the right of the public to receive suitable access to social, political, esthetic, moral, and other ideas and experiences which is crucial here. That right may not constitutionally be abridged either by Congress or by the FCC.

Rather than confer frequency monopolies on a relatively small number of licensees, in a Nation of 200,000,000, the Government could surely have decreed that each frequency should be shared among all or some of those who wish to use it, each being assigned a portion of the broadcast day or the broadcast week. The ruling and regulations at issue here do not go quite so far. They assert that under specified circumstances, a licensee must offer to make available a reasonable amount of broadcast time to those who have a view different from that which has already been expressed on his station. The expression of a political endorsement, or of a personal attack while dealing with a controversial public issue, simply triggers this time sharing.

Nor can we say that it is inconsistent with the First Amendment goal of producing an informed public capable of conducting its own affairs to require a broadcaster to permit answers to personal attacks occurring in the course of discussing controversial issues, or to require that the political opponents of those endorsed by the station be given a chance to communicate with the public. Otherwise, station owners and a few networks would have unfettered power to make time available only to the highest bidders, to communicate only their own views on public issues, people and candidates, and to permit on the air only those with whom they agreed. There is no sanctuary in the First Amendment for unlimited private censorship operating in a medium not open to all.

It is strenuously argued, however, that if political editorials or personal attacks will trigger an obligation in broadcasters to afford the opportunity for expression to speakers who need not pay for time and whose views are unpalatable to the licensees, then broadcasters will be irresistibly forced to self-censorship and their coverage of controversial public issues will be eliminated or at least rendered wholly ineffective. Such a result would indeed be a serious matter, for should licensees actually eliminate their coverage of controversial issues, the purposes of the doctrine would be stifled.

At this point, however, as the Federal Communications Commission has indicated, that possibility is at best speculative. The communications industry, and in particular the networks, have taken pains to present controversial issues in the past, and even now they do not assert that they intend to abandon their efforts in this regard. It would be better if the FCC's encouragement were never necessary to induce the broadcasters to meet their responsibility. And if experience with the administration of these doctrines indicates that they have the net effect of reducing rather than enhancing the volume and quality of coverage, there will be time enough to reconsider the constitutional implications. The fairness doctrine in the past has had no such overall effect.

That this will occur now seems unlikely, however, since if present licensees should suddenly prove timorous, the Commission is not powerless to insist that they give adequate and fair attention to public issues. It does not violate the First Amendment to treat licensees given the privilege of using scarce radio frequencies as proxies for the entire community, obligated to give suitable time and attention to matters of great public concern. To condition the granting or renewal of licenses on a willingness to present representative community views on controversial issues is consistent with the ends and purposes of those constitutional provisions forbidding the abridgment of freedom of speech and freedom of the press. Congress need not stand idly by and permit those with licenses to ignore the problems which beset the people or to exclude from the airways anything but their own views of fundamental questions.

We need not and do not now ratify every past and future decision by the FCC with regard to programming. There is no question here of the Commission's refusal to permit the broadcaster to carry a particular program or to publish his own views; of a discriminatory refusal to require the licensee to broadcast certain views which have been denied access to the airwaves; of government censorship of a particular program; or of the official government view dominating public broadcasting. Such questions would raise more serious First Amendment issues. But we do hold that the Congress and the Commission do not violate the First Amendment when they require a radio or television station to give reply time to answer personal attacks and political editorials.

It is argued that even if at one time the lack of available frequencies for all who wished to use them justified the Government's choice of those who would best serve the public interest by acting as proxy for those who would present differing views, or by giving the latter access directly to broadcast facilities, this condition no longer prevails so that continuing control is not justified. To this there are several answers.

Scarcity is not entirely a thing of the past. Advances in technology, such as microwave transmission, have led to more efficient utilization of the frequency spectrum, but uses for that spectrum have also grown apace. Portions of the spectrum must be reserved for vital uses unconnected with human communication, such as radio-navigational aids used by aircraft and vessels. Conflicts have even emerged between such vital functions as defense preparedness and experimentation in methods of averting midair collisions through radio warning devices. "Land mobile services" such as police, ambulance, fire department, public utility, and other communications systems have been occupying an increasingly crowded portion of the frequency spectrum and there are, apart from licensed amateur radio operators' equipment, 5,000,000 transmitters operated on the "citizens' band" which is also increasingly congested. Among the various uses for radio frequency space, including marine, aviation, amateur, military, and common carrier users, there are easily enough claimants to permit use of the whole with an even smaller allocation to broadcast radio and television uses than now exists.

Comparative hearings between competing applicants for broadcast spectrum space are by no means a thing of the past. The radio spectrum has become so congested that at times it has been necessary to suspend new applications. The very high frequency television spectrum is, in the country's major markets, almost entirely occupied, although space reserved for ultra high frequency television transmission, which is a relatively recent development as a commercially viable alternative, has not yet been completely filled.

The rapidity with which technological advances succeed one another to create more efficient use of spectrum space on the one hand, and to create new uses for that space by ever growing numbers of people on the other, makes it unwise to speculate on the future allocation of that space. It is enough to say that the resource is one of considerable and growing importance whose scarcity impelled its regulation by an agency authorized by Congress. Nothing in this record, or in our own researches, convinces us that the resource is no longer one for which there are more immediate and potential uses than can be accommodated, and for which wise planning is essential. This does not mean, of course, that every possible wavelength must be occupied at every hour by some vital use in order to sustain the congressional judgment. The substantial capital investment required for many uses, in addition to the potentiality for confusion and interference inherent in any scheme for continuous kaleidoscopic reallocation of all available space may make this unfeasible.

Even where there are gaps in spectrum utilization, the fact remains that existing broadcasters have often attained their present position because of their initial government selection in competition with others before new technological advances opened new opportunities for further uses. Long experience in broadcasting, confirmed habits of listeners and viewers, network affiliation, and other advantages in program procurement give existing broadcasters a substantial advantage over new entrants, even where new entry is technologically possible. These advantages are the fruit of a preferred position conferred by the Government. Some present possibility for new entry by competing stations is not enough, in itself, to render unconstitutional the Government's effort to assure that a broadcaster's programming ranges widely enough to serve the public interest.

In view of the scarcity of broadcast frequencies, the Government's role in allocating those frequencies, and the legitimate claims of those unable without governmental assistance to gain access to those frequencies for expression of their views, we hold the regulations and ruling at issue here are both authorized by statute and constitutional. The judgment of the Court of Appeals in Red Lion is affirmed.

## Points for Discussion

1. The First Amendment would not be offended, Justice White says, had Congress created a broadcast industry very different from the one we have now. For example, station "owners" could have been treated as common carriers, akin to phone companies, which must let anyone who can pay the requisite fees to use their facilities. Can you imagine the United States ever moving to such a system? Why or why not?

2. The *Red Lion* decision is predicated on the "spectrum scarcity" rationale—that more people want broadcast licenses than can be granted them—for accepting more regulation on broadcast media than on print media. Justice White admits, however, that this rationale is in turn dependent on "the present state of commercially acceptable technology." What do you suppose he means by this, and how have changes in technology between 1969 and today affected the spectrum scarcity rationale?

## ▇ *Becker v. FCC*

**95 F.3d 75 (D.C. Cir. 1996)**

*Judge Buckley:*

These consolidated cases arise from the efforts of a candidate for federal office to air political advertisements portraying images of aborted fetuses during time periods of his selection. The candidate, Daniel Becker, seeks review of a Federal Communications Commission order permitting a broadcast licensee to restrict the broadcast of campaign advertisements that may be "harmful to children" to times of the day when children are less likely to be in the viewing audience. [He claims] that the ruling violates sections 312(a)(7) and 315(a) of the Communications Act of 1934. We agree.

[Section 312] of the Communications Act requires broadcasters to provide candidates for federal office with "reasonable access" to the broadcast media; [Section 315] guarantees all candidates for elective office equal opportunities in the use of the broadcast media, and it deprives licensees of the power of censorship over the material a candidate may wish to broadcast.

The 1992 election season witnessed the advent of political advertisements depicting the aftermath of abortions. In that year, Daniel Becker was a qualified candidate for election to the United States House of Representatives from Georgia's Ninth Congressional District. At 7:58 P.M. on July 19, Station WAGA-TV, which was then licensed to Gillett Communications of Atlanta, Inc., aired, at Mr. Becker's request, a campaign advertisement that included photographs of aborted fetuses. WAGA-TV received numerous complaints from viewers who saw the advertisement.

Anticipating that Mr. Becker would wish to broadcast similar materials later in the campaign, Gillett filed a petition with the Commission requesting a declaratory ruling on the following question: Whether a licensee may channel a use by a legally-qualified federal candidate to a safe harbor when children are not generally present in the audience if the licensee determines in good faith that the proposed use is indecent or otherwise unsuitable for children.

After viewing a tape of Mr. Becker's July 1992 advertisement, the FCC's Mass Media Bureau found that the advertisement was not indecent. It also concluded that "[the requested 'safe harbor'] would violate Section 312(a)(7) of the Act, because channeling material that is not indecent would deprive federal candidates of their rights to determine how best to conduct their campaigns."

In October 1992, Mr. Becker again sought to purchase air time from WAGA-TV. WAGA-TV refused to air the program at the time requested, claiming that the advertisement would violate the indecency provision of 18 U.S.C. §1464. It stated that it would carry the program only within the safe harbor hours of midnight to 6:00 A.M. Becker filed a complaint with the FCC on October 27, 1992.

On November 22, 1994, the FCC issued the Memorandum Opinion and Order that is the subject of this appeal, [concluding] (1) that Mr. Becker's initial advertisement was not indecent; (2) that there was evidence in the record "indicating that the graphic political advertisements at issue can be psychologically damaging to children"; (3) that "nothing in 312(a)(7) precludes a broadcaster's exercise of some discretion with respect to placement of political advertisements so as to protect children"; and (4) that channeling would not violate the no-censorship provision of section 315(a).

Section 312(a)(7) provides that a station's license may be revoked "for willful or repeated failure to allow reasonable access to or to permit purchase of reasonable amounts of time for the use of a broadcasting station by a legally qualified candidate for Federal elective office on behalf of his candidacy." [The Commission's guidelines require] that commercial broadcasters "make program time available during prime time and other time periods unless unusual circumstances exist that render it reasonable to deny access." Prime time constitutes that part of the day in which the audience is likely to be the largest; the FCC has identified the hours of 7–11 P.M. as comprising prime time in the Eastern and Pacific time zones, and the hours of 6–10 P.M. in the Central and Mountain time zones.

We believe that, by permitting a licensee to channel political advertisements that it believes may harm children, the [Commission] frustrates Congress's primary purpose in enacting section 312(a)(7); namely, to ensure candidates access to the time periods with the greatest audience potential. It is not possible, on the one hand, to channel a political advertisement to a time when there is little risk that large numbers of children may be in the audience, and, on the other, to assure the candidate of as broad an audience potential as is consistent with his right of reasonable access. We are faced, then, with competing interests—the licensee's desire to spare children the sight of images that are not indecent but may nevertheless prove harmful, and the interest of a political candidate in exercising his statutory right of access to the time periods with the greatest audience potential. The Commission has made it clear that when these two interests are in conflict, the licensee is free to decide in favor of the children.

While it is possible to visualize accommodations at the margin in which a political message is broadcast during school hours or the late, late evening when significantly fewer children are watching television, any such accommodation is apt to deprive a candidate of particular categories of adult viewers whom he may be especially anxious to reach. We can surmise, for example, that early shift factory workers whom a candidate wishes to reach are not apt to stay up beyond their normal bedtimes just to see his political advertisements. Thus, the ruling creates a situation where a candidate's ability to reach his target audience may be limited and his personal campaign strategies ignored.

In many instances it will be impossible to separate the message from the image, when the point of the political advertisement is to call attention to the perceived horrors of a particular issue. Indeed, this was the apparent purpose of many of the candidates who ran abortion advertisements similar to Mr. Becker's. And the political uses of television for shock effect is not limited to abortion. Other subjects that could easily lead to shocking and graphic visual treatment include the death penalty, gun control, rape, euthanasia and animal rights.

Section 315(a) contains the Act's "equal opportunity" and "no censorship" provisions. The case law interpreting section 315(a) has uniformly barred licensees from exercising any power of censorship over the content of political broadcasts. [The Commission maintains that its current ruling does not] grant licensees the ability to delete political statements, [but] simply recognizes that a licensee may, consistent with its public interest obligations, channel political advertisements containing graphic abortion imagery to times when the likelihood that children will be in the audience is diminished. This added measure of licensee discretion, [the Commission argues], does not constitute "censorship" as that term is used in the Communications Act. The FCC further argues that, in any event, the competing public interest in protecting the welfare of children outweighs "the minimal intrusion on a candidate's unfettered ability to present his message at the particular time preferred by the candidate."

The Supreme Court has stated that the term censorship, as commonly understood, connotes any examination of thought or expression in order to prevent publication of "objectionable" material. We find no clear expression of legislative intent, nor any other convincing reason to indicate Congress meant to give "censorship" a narrower meaning in §315. The basic purpose of section 315(a) is to permit the full and unrestricted discussion of political issues by legally qualified candidates. The section reflects Congress's deep hostility to censorship either by the Commission or by a licensee. Not only does the power to channel confer on a licensee the power to discriminate between candidates, it can force one of them to back away from what he considers to be the most effective way of presenting his position on a controversial issue lest he be deprived of the audience he is most anxious to reach. This self-censorship must surely frustrate the full and unrestricted discussion of political issues envisioned by Congress.

We believe that a licensee's right to channel political advertisements will inevitably interfere with a candidate's freedom of expression by requiring him to choose between what he wishes to say and the audience he wishes to address. Finally, section 315(a) not only prohibits censorship, it also requires that candidates be given "equal opportunities" to use a broadcaster's facilities. To satisfy this requirement, a broadcaster must make available periods of approximately equal audience potential to competing candidates to the extent that this is possible. The FCC claims that the Declaratory Ruling does not involve the equal opportunity provision because there was no equal opportunity request before it. Because the equal opportunity requirements "forbid any kind of discrimination by a station between competing candidates," however, channeling clearly implicates the equal opportunity provision of section 315(a).

This is so because if a station channels one candidate's message but allows his opponent to broadcast his messages in prime time, the first candidate will have been denied the equal opportunity guaranteed by this section. On the other hand, if the station relegates the opponent's advertisements to the broadcasting Siberia to which the first candidate was assigned, it would be violating the opponent's right of reasonable access under section 312(a)(7). We agree with petitioners that these provisions may not be read to create such a tension.

We conclude from the above that permitting the content-based channeling of political advertisements thwarts the objectives of both section 312(a)(7) and section 315(a) by restricting candidates' ability to fully and completely inform the voters, and by inhibiting the full and unrestricted discussion of political issues by legally qualified candidates. Therefore, we grant the petitions for review and vacate the ruling.

So ordered.

## Points for Discussion

1. Suppose that a political candidate wanted his TV ads to consist of hardcore pornography, the kind of material that would normally be illegal to broadcast or even print. Such a situation almost emerged when *Hustler* publisher Larry Flynt flirted with the idea of running for office. Should stations be permitted to refuse to run such advertising?

2. If you were a political consultant, how would you advise your clients to balance their own desire to reach, and grab the attention of, as many potential voters as possible, while not offending those same voters? When do you think attention-getting devices cross the line and become counterproductively offensive?

## ▪ FCC v. Pacifica Foundation

### 438 U.S. 726 (1978)

*Justice Stevens delivered the opinion of the Court.*

This case requires that we decide whether the Federal Communications Commission has any power to regulate a radio broadcast that is indecent but not obscene. A satiric humorist named George Carlin recorded a 12-minute monologue entitled "Filthy Words" before a live audience in a California theater. He began by referring to his thoughts about "the words you couldn't say on the public, ah, airwaves, um, the ones you definitely wouldn't say, ever." He proceeded to list those words and repeat them over and over again in a variety of colloquialisms.

At about 2 o'clock in the afternoon on Tuesday, October 30, 1973, a New York radio station, owned by respondent Pacifica Foundation, broadcast the Filthy Words monologue. A few weeks later a man, who stated that he had heard the broadcast while driving with his young son, wrote a letter complaining to the Commission. He stated that, although he could perhaps understand the "record's being sold for private use, I certainly cannot understand the broadcast of same over the air that, supposedly, you control." The complaint was forwarded to the station for comment. In its response, Pacifica explained that the monologue had been played during a program about contemporary society's attitude toward language and that, immediately before its broadcast, listeners had been advised that it included "sensitive language which might be regarded as offensive to some." Pacifica characterized George Carlin as "a significant social satirist" who examines "the language of ordinary people." Pacifica stated that it was not aware of any other complaints about the broadcast.

On February 21, 1975, the Commission issued a declaratory order granting the complaint and holding that Pacifica "could have been the subject of administrative sanctions." The Commission did not impose formal sanctions, but it did state that the order would be "associated with the station's license file, and in the event that subsequent complaints are received, the Commission will then decide whether it should utilize any of the available sanctions it has been granted by Congress."

In its memorandum opinion the Commission stated that it intended to clarify the standards which will be utilized in considering the growing number of complaints about indecent speech on the airwaves. Advancing several reasons for treating broadcast speech differently from other forms of expression, the Commission found a power to regulate indecent broadcasting in two statutes: 18 U.S.C. §1464, which forbids the use of "any obscene, indecent, or profane language by means of radio communications," and 47 U.S.C. §303(g), which requires the Commission to "encourage the larger and more effective use of radio in the public interest."

The Commission characterized the language used in the Carlin monologue as "patently offensive," though not necessarily obscene: "The concept of indecent is intimately connected with the exposure of children to language that describes, in terms patently offensive as measured by contemporary community standards for the broadcast medium, sexual or excretory activities and organs, at times of the day when there is a reasonable risk that children may be in the audience." Thus, the Commission suggested, if an offensive broadcast had literary, artistic, political, or scientific value, and were preceded by warnings, it might not be indecent in the late evening, but would be so during the day, when children are in the audience.

Applying these considerations to the language used in the monologue as broadcast by respondent, the Commission concluded that certain words depicted sexual and excretory activities in a patently offensive manner, and noted that they "were broadcast at a time when children were undoubtedly in the audience (i. e., in the early afternoon)." In summary, the Commission stated: "We therefore hold that the language as broadcast was indecent."

After the order issued, the Commission was asked to clarify its opinion by ruling that the broadcast of indecent words as part of a live newscast would not be prohibited. The Commission issued another opinion in which it pointed out that it "never intended to place an absolute prohibition on the broadcast of this type of language, but rather sought to channel it to times of day when children most likely would not be exposed to it."

The relevant statutory questions are whether the Commission's action is forbidden "censorship" within the meaning of 47 U.S.C. §326 and whether speech that concededly is not obscene may be restricted as "indecent" under the authority of 18 U.S.C. §1464. The questions are not unrelated, for the two statutory provisions have a common origin. Nevertheless, we analyze them separately.

Section 29 of the Radio Act of 1927 provided: "Nothing in this Act shall be understood or construed to give the licensing authority the power of censorship over the radio communications or signals transmitted by any radio station." The prohibition against censorship unequivocally denies the Commission any power to edit proposed broadcasts in advance and to excise material considered inappropriate for the airwaves. The prohibition, however, has never been construed to deny the Commission the power to review the content of completed broadcasts in the performance of its regulatory duties. Entirely apart from the fact that the subsequent review of program content is not the sort of censorship at which the statute was directed, its history makes it perfectly clear that it was not intended to limit the Commission's power to regulate the broadcast of obscene, indecent, or profane language. A single section of the 1927 Act is the source of both the anticensorship provision and the Commission's authority to impose sanctions for the broadcast of indecent or obscene language. Quite plainly, Congress intended to give meaning to both provisions. Respect for that intent requires that the censorship language be read as inapplicable to the prohibition on broadcasting obscene, indecent, or profane language. We conclude, therefore, that §326 does not limit the Commission's authority to impose sanctions on licensees who engage in obscene, indecent, or profane broadcasting.

The only other statutory question presented by this case is whether the afternoon broadcast of the "Filthy Words" monologue was indecent within the meaning of §1464. The Commission identified several words that referred to excretory or sexual activities or organs, stated that the repetitive, deliberate use of those words in an afternoon broadcast when children are in the audience was patently offensive, and held that the broadcast was indecent. Pacifica takes issue with the Commission's definition of indecency, but does not dispute the Commission's preliminary determination that each of the components of its definition was present. Specifically, Pacifica does not quarrel with the conclusion that this afternoon broadcast was patently offensive. Pacifica's claim that the broadcast was not indecent within the meaning of the statute rests entirely on the absence of prurient appeal. The plain language of the statute does not support Pacifica's argument. The words "obscene, indecent, or profane" are written in the disjunctive, implying that each has a separate meaning. Prurient appeal is an element of the obscene, but the normal definition of "indecent" merely refers to nonconformance with accepted standards of morality.

*Editor's Note:* The next three paragraphs come from a section of Justice Stevens's opinion joined by only two other justices; it is thus not majority doctrine.

Pacifica argues that, inasmuch as the recording is not obscene, the Constitution forbids any abridgment of the right to broadcast it on the radio. When the issue is narrowed to the facts of this case, the question is whether the First Amendment denies government any power to restrict the public broadcast of indecent language in any circumstances. For if the government has any such power, this was an appropriate occasion for its exercise.

The words of the Carlin monologue are unquestionably "speech" within the meaning of the First Amendment. It is equally clear that the Commission's objections to the broadcast were based in part on its content. The question in this case is whether a broadcast of patently offensive words dealing with sex and excretion may be regulated because of its content. Obscene materials have been denied the protection of the First Amendment because their content is so offensive to contemporary moral standards. But the fact that society may find speech offensive is not a sufficient reason for suppressing it. Indeed, if it is the speaker's opinion that gives offense, that consequence is a reason for according it constitutional protection. For it is a central tenet of the First Amendment that the government must remain neutral in the marketplace of ideas. If there were any reason to believe that the Commission's characterization of the Carlin monologue as offensive could be traced to its political content—or even to the fact that it satirized contemporary attitudes about four-letter words—First Amendment protection might be required. But that is simply not this case. These words offend for the same reasons that obscenity offends. Such utterances are no essential part of any exposition of ideas, and are of such slight social value as a step to truth that any benefit that may be derived from them is clearly outweighed by the social interest in order and morality.

Although these words ordinarily lack literary, political, or scientific value, they are not entirely outside the protection of the First Amendment. Some uses of even the most offensive words are unquestionably protected. Indeed, we may assume, [for argument's sake], that this monologue would be protected in other contexts. Nonetheless, the constitutional protection accorded to a communication containing such patently offensive sexual and excretory language need not be the same in every context. It is a characteristic of speech such as this that both its capacity to offend and its social value vary with the circumstances. Words that are commonplace in one setting are shocking in another.

We have long recognized that each medium of expression presents special First Amendment problems. And of all forms of communication, it is broadcasting that has received the most limited First Amendment protection. Thus, although other speakers cannot be licensed except under laws that carefully define and narrow official discretion, a broadcaster may be deprived of his license and his forum if the Commission decides that such an action would serve the public interest, convenience, and necessity. Similarly, although the First Amendment protects newspaper publishers from being required to print the replies of those whom they criticize, it affords no such protection to broadcasters; on the contrary, they must give free time to the victims of their criticism.

The reasons for these distinctions are complex, but two have relevance to the present case. First, the broadcast media have established a uniquely pervasive presence in the lives of all Americans. Patently offensive, indecent material presented over the airwaves confronts the citizen, not only in public, but also in the privacy of the home, where the individual's right to be left alone plainly outweighs the First Amendment rights of an intruder. Because the broadcast audience is constantly tuning in and out, prior warnings cannot completely protect the listener or viewer from unexpected program content. To say that one may avoid further offense by turning off the radio when he hears indecent language is like saying that the remedy for an assault is to run away after the first blow. One may hang up on an indecent phone call, but that option does not give the caller a constitutional immunity or avoid a harm that has already taken place.

Second, broadcasting is uniquely accessible to children, even those too young to read. Pacifica's broadcast could have enlarged a child's vocabulary in an instant. Other forms of offensive expression may be withheld from the young without restricting the expression at its source. Bookstores and motion picture theaters, for example, may be prohibited from making indecent material available to children. [Similarly], the government's interest in the well-being of its youth and in supporting parents' claim to authority in their own household [can justify] the regulation of otherwise protected expression.

It is appropriate, in conclusion, to emphasize the narrowness of our holding. This case does not involve a two-way radio conversation between a cab driver and a dispatcher, or a telecast of an Elizabethan comedy. We have not decided that an occasional expletive in either setting would justify any sanction or, indeed, that this broadcast would justify a criminal prosecution. The Commission's decision rested entirely on a nuisance rationale under which context is all-important. The concept requires consideration of a host of variables. The time of day was emphasized by the Commission. The content of the program in which the language is used will also affect the composition of the audience, and differences between radio, television, and perhaps closed-circuit transmissions, may also be relevant. As Mr. Justice Sutherland wrote, a "nuisance may be merely a right thing in the wrong place,—like a pig in the parlor instead of the barnyard." We simply hold that when the Commission finds that a pig has entered the parlor, the exercise of its regulatory power does not depend on proof that the pig is obscene.

The judgment of the Court of Appeals is reversed.

## Points for Discussion

1. In his dissenting opinion, Justice Brennan charges the Court with usurping parental authority in the name of protecting children. "Some parents may actually find Mr. Carlin's unabashed attitude towards the seven 'dirty words' healthy, and deem it desirable to expose their children to the manner in which Mr. Carlin defuses the taboo surrounding the words." How would you answer Brennan?

2. Currently, the FCC permits the broadcast of admittedly indecent (but not obscene) programming between 10 P.M. and 6 A.M. Do you think that is a reasonable compromise? Why or why not? Do you think any of the more popular "shock jock" programs on radio are indecent?

# ■ *Turner Broadcasting System v. FCC*

## 520 U.S. 180 (1997)

*Justice Kennedy delivered the opinion of the Court.*

Sections 4 and 5 of the Cable Television Consumer Protection and Competition Act of 1992 require cable television systems to dedicate some of their channels to local broadcast television stations. Earlier in this case, we held the so-called "must-carry" provisions to be content-neutral restrictions on speech, subject to intermediate First Amendment scrutiny. A plurality of the Court considered the record as then developed insufficient. The case now presents the two questions left open during the first appeal: First, whether the record as it now stands supports Congress' predictive judgment that the must-carry provisions further important governmental interests; and second, whether the provisions do not burden substantially more speech than necessary to further those interests. We answer both questions in the affirmative, and conclude the must-carry provisions are consistent with the First Amendment.

Soon after Congress enacted the Cable Television Consumer Protection and Competition Act of 1992, appellants brought suit against the United States and the Federal Communications Commission, challenging the constitutionality of the must-carry provisions under the First Amendment.

A content-neutral regulation will be sustained under the First Amendment if it advances important governmental interests unrelated to the suppression of free speech and does not burden substantially more speech than necessary to further those interests. Must-carry was designed to serve three interrelated interests: (1) preserving the benefits of free, over-the-air local broadcast television, (2) promoting the widespread dissemination of information from a multiplicity of sources, and (3) promoting fair competition in the market for television programming. Each of those is an important governmental interest. Forty percent of American households continue to rely on over-the-air signals for television programming. Despite the growing importance of cable television and alternative technologies, broadcasting is demonstrably a principal source of information and entertainment for a great part of the Nation's population. We have identified a corresponding governmental purpose of the highest order in ensuring public access to a multiplicity of information sources. And it is undisputed the Government has an interest in eliminating restraints on fair competition, even when the individuals or entities subject to particular regulations are engaged in expressive activity protected by the First Amendment.

The Government downplays the importance of showing a risk to the broadcast industry as a whole and suggests the loss of even a few broadcast stations is a matter of critical importance. Taking the opposite approach, appellants argue Congress' interest in preserving broadcasting is not implicated unless it is shown the industry as a whole would fail without must-carry, and suggest Congress' legitimate interest extends only as far as preserving a minimum amount of television broadcast service.

These alternative formulations are inconsistent with Congress' stated interests in enacting must-carry. The congressional findings do not reflect concern that, absent must-carry, "a few voices" would be lost from the television marketplace. In explicit factual findings, Congress expressed clear concern that the "marked shift in market share from broadcast television to cable television services," resulting from increasing market penetration by cable services, as well as the expanding horizontal concentration and vertical integration of cable operators, combined to give cable systems the incentive and ability to delete, reposition, or decline carriage to local broadcasters in an attempt to favor affiliated cable programmers. Congress predicted that "absent the reimposition of [must-carry], additional local broadcast signals will be deleted, repositioned, or not carried," with the end result that "the economic viability of free local broadcast television and its ability to originate quality local programming will be seriously jeopardized." At the same time, Congress was under no illusion that there would be a complete disappearance of broadcast television nationwide in the absence of must-carry. Congress recognized broadcast programming (and network programming in particular) "remains the most popular programming on cable systems." Indeed, reflecting the popularity and strength of some broadcasters, Congress included in the Cable Act a provision permitting broadcasters to charge cable systems for carriage of the broadcasters' signals. Congress was concerned not that broadcast television would disappear in its entirety without must-carry, but that without it, "significant numbers of broadcast stations will be refused carriage on cable systems," and those "broadcast stations denied carriage will either deteriorate to a substantial degree or fail altogether."

Nor do the congressional findings support appellants' suggestion that legitimate legislative goals would be satisfied by the preservation of a rump broadcasting industry providing a minimum of broadcast service to Americans without cable. It has long been a basic tenet of national communications policy that the widest possible dissemination of information from diverse and antagonistic sources is essential to the welfare of the public. Consistent with this objective, the Cable Act's findings reflect a concern that congressional action was necessary to prevent a reduction in the number of media voices available to consumers. Congress found must-carry necessary to serve the goals of the original Communications Act of 1934 of "providing a fair, efficient, and equitable distribution of broadcast services." Although Congress set no definite number of broadcast stations sufficient for these purposes, the Cable Act's requirement that all cable operators with more than 12 channels set aside one-third of their channel capacity for local broadcasters, refutes the notion that Congress contemplated preserving only a bare minimum of stations. To the extent the appellants question the substantiality of the Government's interest in preserving something more than a minimum number of stations in each community, their position is meritless.

Broadcast television is an important source of information to many Americans. Though it is but one of many means for communication, by tradition and use for decades now it has been an essential part of the national discourse on subjects across the whole broad spectrum of speech, thought, and expression. Congress has an independent interest in preserving a multiplicity of broadcasters to ensure that all households have access to information and entertainment on an equal footing with those who subscribe to cable.

[We now] consider whether the must-carry provisions were designed to address a real harm, and whether those provisions will alleviate it in a material way. We turn first to the harm or risk which prompted Congress to act. The Government's assertion that the economic health of local broadcasting is in genuine jeopardy and in need of the protections afforded by must-carry rests on two component propositions: First, significant numbers of broadcast stations will be refused carriage on cable systems absent must-carry. Second, the broadcast stations denied carriage will either deteriorate to a substantial degree or fail altogether. In reviewing the constitutionality of a statute, courts must accord substantial deference to the predictive judgments of Congress. This principle has special significance in cases, like this one, involving congressional judgments concerning regulatory schemes of inherent complexity and assessments about the likely interaction of industries undergoing rapid economic and technological change.

We have no difficulty in finding a substantial basis to support Congress' conclusion that a real threat justified enactment of the must-carry provisions. There was specific support for its conclusion that cable operators had considerable and growing market power over local video programming markets. Cable served at least 60 percent of American households in 1992, and evidence indicated cable market penetration was projected to grow beyond 70 percent. As Congress noted, cable operators possess a local monopoly over cable households. Only one percent of communities are served by more than one cable system. Cable operators thus exercise control over most (if not all) of the television programming that is channeled into the subscriber's home and can thus silence the voice of competing speakers with a mere flick of the switch.

Evidence indicated the structure of the cable industry would give cable operators increasing ability and incentive to drop local broadcast stations from their systems, or reposition them to a less-viewed channel. Horizontal concentration was increasing as a small number of multiple system operators (MSO's) acquired large numbers of cable systems nationwide. The trend was accelerating, giving the MSO's increasing market power. In 1985, the 10 largest MSO's controlled cable systems serving slightly less than 42 percent of all cable subscribers; by 1989, the figure was nearly 54 percent. Vertical integration in the industry also was increasing. As Congress was aware, many MSO's owned or had affiliation agreements with cable programmers. Evidence indicated that before 1984 cable operators had equity interests in 38 percent of cable programming networks. In the late 1980's, 64 percent of new cable programmers were held in vertical ownership. Congress concluded that vertical integration gives cable operators the incentive and ability to favor their affiliated programming services. Extensive testimony indicated that cable operators would have an incentive to drop local broadcasters and to favor affiliated programmers. After hearing years of testimony, and reviewing volumes of documentary evidence and studies offered by both sides, Congress concluded that the cable industry posed a threat to broadcast television.

In addition, evidence before Congress indicated that cable systems would have incentives to drop local broadcasters in favor of other programmers less likely to compete with them for audience and advertisers. Independent local broadcasters tend to be the closest substitutes for cable programs, because their programming tends to be similar, and because both primarily target the same type of advertiser: those interested in cheaper (and more frequent) ad spots than are typically available on network affiliates. The ability of broadcast stations to compete for advertising is greatly increased by cable carriage, which increases viewership substantially. With expanded viewership, broadcast presents a more competitive medium for television advertising. Empirical studies indicate that cable-carried broadcasters so enhance competition for advertising that even modest increases in the numbers of broadcast stations carried on cable are correlated with significant decreases in advertising revenue to cable systems. Empirical evidence also indicates that demand for premium cable services (such as pay-per-view) is reduced when a cable system carries more independent broadcasters.

Cable systems also have more systemic reasons for seeking to disadvantage broadcast stations: Simply stated, cable has little interest in assisting, through carriage, a competing medium of communication. The incentive to subscribe to cable is lower in markets with many over-the-air viewing options. Evidence adduced on remand indicated cable systems have little incentive to carry, and a significant incentive to drop, broadcast stations that will only be strengthened by access to the 60 percent of the television market that cable typically controls. Congress could therefore reasonably conclude that cable systems would drop broadcasters in favor of programmers—even unaffiliated ones—less likely to compete with them for audience and advertisers.

It was more than a theoretical possibility in 1992 that cable operators would take actions adverse to local broadcasters; indeed, significant numbers of broadcasters had already been dropped. The record before Congress contained extensive anecdotal evidence about scores of adverse carriage decisions against broadcast stations. [One study] indicated that in 1988, 280 out of 912 responding broadcast stations had been dropped or denied carriage in 1,533 instances. Even assuming that every station dropped or denied coverage responded to the survey, it would indicate that nearly a quarter (21 percent) of the approximately 1,356 broadcast stations then in existence had been denied carriage. The same study reported 869 of 4,303 reporting cable systems had denied carriage to 704 broadcast stations in 1,820 instances, and 279 of those stations had qualified for carriage under the prior must-carry rules. A contemporaneous study of public television stations indicated that in the vast majority of cases, dropped stations were not restored to the cable service.

Substantial evidence demonstrated that absent must-carry the already serious problem of noncarriage would grow worse. The record included anecdotal evidence showing the cable industry was acting with restraint in dropping broadcast stations in an effort to discourage reregulation. There was also substantial evidence that advertising revenue would be of increasing importance to cable operators as subscribership growth began to flatten, providing a steady, increasing incentive to deny carriage to local broadcasters in an effort to capture their advertising revenue.

The harm Congress feared was that stations dropped or denied carriage would be at a serious risk of financial difficulty, and would deteriorate to a substantial degree or fail altogether. Congress had before it substantial evidence to support its conclusion. Considerable evidence, consisting of statements compiled from dozens of broadcasters who testified before Congress and the FCC, confirmed that broadcast stations had fallen into bankruptcy, curtailed their broadcast operations, and suffered serious reductions in operating revenues as a result of adverse carriage decisions by cable systems. Congress thus had ample basis to conclude that attaining cable carriage would be of increasing importance to ensuring a station's viability. We hold Congress could conclude from the substantial body of evidence before it that absent legislative action, the free local off-air broadcast system is endangered.

To be sure, the record also contains evidence to support a contrary conclusion. Appellants (and the dissent in the District Court) make much of the fact that the number of broadcast stations and their advertising revenue continued to grow during the period without must-carry, albeit at a diminished rate. Evidence indicated that only 31 broadcast stations actually went dark during the period without must-carry (one of which failed after a tornado destroyed its transmitter), and during the same period some 263 new stations signed on the air. New evidence appellants produced indicates the average cable system voluntarily carried local broadcast stations accounting for about 97 percent of television ratings in noncable households. Appellants, as well as the dissent in the District Court, contend that in light of such evidence, it is clear the must-carry law is not necessary to assure the economic viability of the broadcast system as a whole. This assertion misapprehends the relevant inquiry. The question is not whether Congress, as an objective matter, was correct to determine must-carry is necessary to prevent a substantial number of broadcast stations from losing cable carriage and suffering significant financial hardship. Rather, the question is whether the legislative conclusion was reasonable and supported by substantial evidence in the record.

Content-neutral regulations do not pose the same inherent dangers to free expression that content-based regulations do, and thus are subject to a less rigorous analysis, which affords the Government latitude in designing a regulatory solution. Under intermediate scrutiny, the Government may employ the means of its choosing so long as the regulation promotes a substantial governmental interest that would be achieved less effectively absent the regulation, and does not burden substantially more speech than is necessary to further that interest. The must-carry provisions have the potential to interfere with protected speech in two ways. First, the provisions restrain cable operators' editorial discretion in creating programming packages by reducing the number of channels over which they exercise unfettered control. Second, the rules render it more difficult for cable programmers to compete for carriage on the limited channels remaining. Appellants say the burden of must-carry is great, but the evidence indicates the actual effects are modest. Significant evidence indicates the vast majority of cable operators have not been affected in a significant manner by must-carry. Cable operators have been able to satisfy their must-carry obligations 87 percent of the time using previously unused channel capacity; 94.5 percent of the 11,628 cable systems nationwide have not had to drop any programming in order to fulfill their must-carry obligations; the remaining 5.5 percent have had to drop an average of only 1.22 services from their programming; and cable operators nationwide carry 99.8 percent of the programming they carried before enactment of must-carry. Appellees note that only 1.18 percent of the approximately 500,000 cable channels nationwide is devoted to channels added because of must-carry; weighted for subscribership, the figure is 2.4 percent. Appellees contend the burdens of must-carry will soon diminish as cable channel capacity increases, as is occurring nationwide.

We do not understand appellants to dispute in any fundamental way the accuracy of those figures, only their significance. They note national averages fail to account for greater crowding on certain (especially urban) cable systems, and contend that half of all cable systems, serving two-thirds of all cable subscribers, have no available capacity. Appellants argue that the rate of growth in cable programming outstrips cable operators' creation of new channel space, that the rate of cable growth is lower than claimed, and that must-carry infringes First Amendment rights now irrespective of future growth. Finally, they say that regardless of the percentage of channels occupied, must-carry still represents thousands of real and individual infringements of speech. While the parties' evidence is susceptible of varying interpretations, a few definite conclusions can be drawn about the burdens of must-carry. It is undisputed that broadcast stations gained carriage on 5,880 channels as a result of must-carry. While broadcast stations occupy another 30,006 cable channels nationwide, this carriage does not represent a significant First Amendment harm to either system operators or cable programmers because those stations were carried voluntarily before 1992, and even appellants represent that the vast majority of those channels would continue to be carried in the absence of any legal obligation to do so.

The 5,880 channels occupied by added broadcasters represent the actual burden of the regulatory scheme. Appellants concede most of those stations would be dropped in the absence of must-carry, so the figure approximates the benefits of must-carry as well. Because the burden imposed by must-carry is congruent to the benefits it affords, we conclude must-carry is narrowly tailored to preserve a multiplicity of broadcast stations for the 40 percent of American households without cable. Congress took steps to confine the breadth and burden of the regulatory scheme. For example, the more popular stations (which appellants concede would be carried anyway) will likely opt to be paid for cable carriage under the "retransmission consent" provision of the Cable Act; those stations will nonetheless be counted towards systems' must-carry obligations. Congress exempted systems of 12 or fewer channels, and limited the must-carry obligation of larger systems to one-third of capacity; allowed cable operators discretion in choosing which competing and qualified signals would be carried; and permitted operators to carry public stations on unused public, educational, and governmental channels in some circumstances. Appellants say the must-carry provisions are overbroad because they require carriage in some instances when the Government's interests are not implicated: the must-carry rules prohibit a cable system operator from dropping a broadcaster even if the operator has no anticompetitive motives, and even if the broadcaster that would have to be dropped would survive without cable access. We are not persuaded that either possibility is so prevalent that must-carry is substantially overbroad. Cable systems serving 70 percent of subscribers are vertically integrated with cable programmers, so anticompetitive motives may be implicated in a majority of systems' decisions not to carry broadcasters. Some broadcasters will opt for must-carry although they would not suffer serious financial harm in its absence. Broadcasters with stronger finances tend, however, to be popular ones that ordinarily seek payment from cable systems for transmission, so their reliance on must-carry should be minimal. It appears, for example, that no more than a few hundred of the 500,000 cable channels nationwide are occupied by network affiliates opting for must-carry, a number insufficient to render must-carry substantially broader than necessary to achieve the government's interest. Even on the doubtful assumption that a narrower but still practicable must-carry rule could be drafted to exclude all instances in which the Government's interests are not implicated, our cases establish that content-neutral regulations are not invalid simply because there is some imaginable alternative that might be less burdensome on speech.

Appellants urge [in lieu of must-carry rules] the use of input selector or "A/B" switches, which, in combination with antennas, would permit viewers to switch between cable and broadcast input, allowing cable subscribers to watch broadcast programs not carried on cable. Congress examined the use of A/B switches as an alternative. The data showed that: many households lacked adequate antennas to receive broadcast signals; A/B switches suffered from technical flaws; viewers might be required to reset channel settings repeatedly in order to view both UHF and cable channels; and installation and use of the switch with other common video equipment (such as videocassette recorders) could be cumbersome or impossible.

Appellants [alternatively] suggest a system of subsidies for financially weak stations. Appellants have not proposed any particular subsidy scheme, so it is difficult to determine whether this option presents a feasible means of achieving the Government's interests, let alone one preferable to must-carry under the First Amendment. To begin with, a system of subsidies would serve a very different purpose than must-carry. Must-carry is intended not to guarantee the financial health of all broadcasters, but to ensure a base number of broadcasters survive to provide service to noncable households. Must-carry is simpler to administer and less likely to involve the Government in making content-based determinations about programming. The must-carry rules distinguish between categories of speakers based solely on the technology used to communicate.

Appellants also suggest a system of antitrust enforcement or an administrative complaint procedure to protect broadcasters from cable operators' anticompetitive conduct. Congress could conclude, however, that the considerable expense and delay inherent in antitrust litigation, and the great disparities in wealth and sophistication between the average independent broadcast station and average cable system operator, would make these remedies inadequate substitutes for guaranteed carriage.

Judgments about how competing economic interests are to be reconciled in the complex and fast-changing field of television are for Congress to make. Appellants' challenges to must-carry reflect little more than disagreement over the level of protection broadcast stations are to be afforded and how protection is to be attained. We cannot displace Congress' judgment respecting content-neutral regulations with our own, so long as its policy is grounded on reasonable factual findings supported by evidence that is substantial for a legislative determination. Those requirements were met in this case, and in these circumstances the First Amendment requires nothing more. The judgment of the District Court is affirmed. It is so ordered.

## Points for Discussion

**1.** Justice Kennedy's opinion is rather complex, requiring the reader to follow his evaluation of Congress' analysis of the economics of the cable industry. Can you, in your own words, explain the differences between "horizontal" and "vertical" concentration of ownership?

**2.** Congress and the Supreme Court seem to agree that the main reason for must-carry rules is to ensure the survival of free, over-the-air TV stations—so that one need not be able to afford to pay a monthly cable bill in order to have television service. If this is indeed the basis for the rules, why not restrict their application to broadcast stations that can demonstrate likely financial hardship if not carried by their local cable system?

## ■ *Time Warner Entertainment v. FCC*

**240 F. 3d 1126 (D.C. Cir. 2001)**

*Judge Williams:*

Section 11(c) of the Cable Television Consumer Protection and Competition Act of 1992 directs the Federal Communications Commission to set two types of limits on cable operators. The first type is horizontal, limits on the number of cable subscribers a person is authorized to reach through cable systems. The second type is vertical, limiting the number of channels on a cable system that can be occupied by a video programmer in which a cable operator has an attributable interest.

The horizontal rule imposes a 30% limit on the number of subscribers that may be served by a multiple cable system operator ("MSO"). Both the numerator and denominator of this fraction include only current subscribers to multichannel video program distributor ("MVPD") services. Subscribers include not only users of traditional cable services but also subscribers to non-cable MVPD services such as Direct Broadcast Satellite ("DBS"), a rapidly growing segment of the MVPD market.

In an express effort to encourage competition through new provision of cable, the Commission excluded from any MSO's numerator all new subscribers signed up by virtue of "overbuilding," the industry's term for cable laid in competition with a pre-existing cable operator. [Thus] the rule's main bite is on firms obtaining subscribers through merger or acquisition.

The vertical limit is currently set at 40% of channel capacity, reserving 60% for programming by non-affiliated firms. Channels assigned to broadcast stations, leased access, and for public, educational, or governmental uses are included in the calculation of channel capacity. Capacity over 75 channels is not subject to the limit, so a cable operator is never required to reserve more than 45 channels for others (.60 × 75 = 45).

As cable operators, Time Warner and AT&T exercise editorial discretion in selecting the programming they will make available to their subscribers, and are entitled to the protection of the speech and press provisions of the First Amendment. The horizontal limit interferes with petitioners' speech rights by restricting the number of viewers to whom they can speak. The vertical limit restricts their ability to exercise their editorial control over a portion of the content they transmit.

Constitutional authority to impose some limit is not authority to impose any limit imaginable. [In this kind of case] we apply intermediate scrutiny. A governmental regulation subject to intermediate scrutiny will be upheld if it advances important governmental interests unrelated to the suppression of free speech and does not burden substantially more speech than necessary to further those interests. The interests asserted in support of the horizontal and vertical limits are the promotion of diversity in ideas and speech and the preservation of competition. [We believe that] Congress has drawn reasonable inferences, based upon substantial evidence, that increases in the concentration of cable operators threatened diversity and competition in the cable industry. But the FCC must still justify the limits that it has chosen as not burdening substantially more speech than necessary. In addition, in demonstrating that the recited harms are real, not merely conjectural, the FCC must show a record that validates the regulations, not just the abstract statutory authority.

The FCC asserts that a 30% horizontal limit satisfies its statutory obligation to ensure that no single cable operator or group of cable operators can unfairly impede the flow of video programming from the video programmer to the consumer. It interpreted this statutory language as a directive to prohibit large MSOs—either by the action of a single MSO or the coincidental or collusive actions of several MSOs—from precluding the entry into the market of a new cable programmer. In setting the limit at 30%, it assumed there was a serious risk of collusion. But while collusion is a form of anti-competitive behavior that implicates an important government interest, the FCC has not presented substantial evidence that such collusion has in fact occurred or is likely to occur; so its assumptions are mere conjecture.

The FCC alternatively relies on its supposed grant of authority to regulate the non-collusive actions of large MSOs. Congress may indeed have the power to regulate the coincidental but independent actions of cable operators solely in the interest of diversity, but where an administrative interpretation of a statute invokes the outer limits of Congress' power, we expect a clear indication that Congress intended that result. The 1992 Cable Act, as we shall see, instead expresses the contrary intention.

The FCC determines that the average cable network needs to reach 15 million subscribers to be economically viable. This is 18.56% of the roughly 80 million MVPD subscribers, and the FCC rounds it up to 20% of such subscribers. The FCC then divines that the average cable programmer will succeed in reaching only about 50% of the subscribers linked to cable companies that agree to carry its programming, because of channel capacity, programming tastes of particular cable operators, or other factors. The average programmer therefore requires an open field of 40% of the market to be viable (.20/.50 = .40).

Finally, to support the 30% limit that it says is necessary to assure this minimum, the Commission reasons as follows: With a 30% limit, a programmer has an open field of 40% of the market even if the two largest cable companies deny carriage, acting individually or collusively. A 50% rule is inadequate because, if a duopoly were to result, the probability of tacit collusion is higher with 2 competitors than 3 competitors. Even if collusion were not to occur, independent rejections by two MSOs could doom a new programmer, thwarting congressional intent as the Commission saw it. A 40% limit is insufficient for the same reason: two MSOs, representing a total of 80% of the market, might decline to carry the new network and leave only 20% open, which by hypothesis is not enough (because of the 50% success rate). Although the Commission doesn't spell out the intellectual process, it is necessarily defining the requisite "open field" as the residue of the market after a programmer is turned down either (1) by one cable company acting alone, or (2) by a set of companies acting either (a) collusively or (b) independently but nonetheless in some way that, because of the combined effect of their choices, threatens fulfillment of the statutory purposes. We address the FCC's authority to regulate each of these scenarios in turn.

The Commission is on solid ground in asserting authority to be sure that no single company could be in a position single-handedly to deal a programmer a death blow. Statutory authority flows plainly from the instruction that the Commission's regulations "ensure that no cable operator or group of cable operators can unfairly impede, either because of the size of any individual operator or because of joint actions of operators of sufficient size, the flow of video programming from the video programmer to the consumer."

Constitutional authority is equally plain. As the Supreme Court [has] said, "We have identified a corresponding governmental purpose of the highest order in ensuring public access to a multiplicity of information sources. If this interest in diversity is to mean anything in this context, the government must be able to ensure that a programmer have at least two conduits through which it can reach the number of viewers needed for viability—independent of concerns over anticompetitive conduct."

Assuming the validity of the premises supporting the FCC's conclusion that a 40% open field is necessary (a question that we need not answer here), the statute's express concern for the act of "any individual operator" would justify a horizontal limit of 60%. To reach the 30% limit, the FCC's action necessarily involves one or the other of two additional propositions: Either there is a material risk of collusive denial of carriage by two or more companies, or the statute authorizes the Commission to protect programmers against the risk of completely independent rejections by two or more companies leaving less than 40% of the MVPD audience potentially accessible. Neither proposition is sound.

First, we consider whether there is record support for inferring a non-conjectural risk of collusive rejection. Either Congress or the Commission could supply that record. Congress appears to have made no judgment regarding collusion. The statute plainly alludes to the possibility of collusion when it authorizes regulations to protect against "joint actions by a group of operators of sufficient size." But this phrase, while granting the Commission authority to take action in the event that it finds collusion extant or likely, is not itself a congressional finding of actual or probable collusion.

The Commission never explains why the vertical integration of MSOs gives them mutual incentive to reach carriage decisions beneficial to each other, what may be the firms' incentives to buy from one another, or what the probabilities are that firms would engage in reciprocal buying (presumably to reduce each other's average programming costs). Further, even if one accepts the proposition that an MSO could benefit from sharing the services of specific programmers, programming is not more attractive for this purpose merely because it originates with another MSO's affiliate rather than with an independent. The only justification that the FCC offers in support of its collusion hypothesis is the economic commonplace that, all other things being equal, collusion is less likely when there are more firms. This observation will always be true, although marginally less so for each additional firm; but by itself it lends no insight into the question of what the appropriate horizontal limit is. The FCC [must] do more than simply posit the existence of the disease sought to be cured. It [must] draw reasonable inferences based on substantial evidence. The FCC has put forth no evidence at all that indicates the prospects for collusion.

Congress required that in setting the horizontal limit, the FCC take particular account of the market structure, including the nature and market power of the local franchise. Petitioners assert that the Commission's failure to take adequate account of the competitive pressures brought by the availability and increasing success of DBS make the horizontal limit arbitrary and capricious. Although DBS accounts for only 15.4% of current MVPD households, the annual increase in its total subscribership is almost three times that of cable (nearly three million additional subscribers over the period June 1999 to June 2000, as against one million for cable). To the extent petitioners argue that the horizontal limit must fail because market share does not equal market power, they misconstrue the statutory command. The Commission is not required to design a limit that falls solely on firms possessing market power. The provision is directed to the Commission's intellectual process, and requires it, in evaluating the harms posed by concentration and in setting the subscriber limit, to assess the determinants of market power in the cable industry and to draw a connection between market power and the limit set.

The Commission has [not] satisfied this obligation. Having failed to identify a non-conjectural harm, the Commission could not possibly have addressed the connection between the harm and market power. But the assessment of a real risk of anti-competitive behavior—collusive or not—is itself dependent on an understanding of market power, and the Commission's statements ignore the true relevance of competition. If an MVPD refuses to offer new programming, customers with access to an alternative MVPD may switch. The FCC shows no reason why this logic does not apply to the cable industry. It seems clear that in revisiting the horizontal rules the Commission will have to take account of the impact of DBS on that market power.

There remains the Commission's alternative ground—that programming choices made unilaterally by multiple cable companies might reduce a programmer's open field below the 40% benchmark. The only support the Commission offered for regulation based on this possibility was the idea that every additional chance for a programmer to secure access would enhance diversity.

The 30% limit, [the Commission argues], serves the salutary purpose of ensuring that there will be at least 4 MSOs in the marketplace. The rule thus maximizes the potential number of MSOs that will purchase programming. With more MSOs making purchasing decisions, this increases the likelihood that the MSOs will make different programming choices and a greater variety of media voices will therefore be available to the public.

Petitioners challenge the FCC's authority to regulate for this purpose on both constitutional and statutory grounds. Everything else being equal, [petitioners allow], each additional voice may be said to enhance diversity. But at some point, surely, the marginal value of such an increment in diversity would not qualify as an important governmental interest. Is moving from 100 possible combinations to 101 important? It is not clear to us how a court could determine the point where gaining such an increment is no longer important.

We need not face that issue, however, because we conclude that Congress has not given the Commission authority to impose, solely on the basis of the diversity precept, a limit that does more than guarantee a programmer two possible outlets (each of them a market adequate for viability).

We begin with the statutory language. The relevant section requires the FCC to [protect consumers from "unfair"] impediments to the flow of programming. The word "unfair" is of course extremely vague. Certainly, the action of several firms that is "joint," in the sense of collusive, may often entail unfairness of a conventional sort. The statute goes further, plainly treating exercise of editorial discretion by a single cable operator as unfair simply because that operator is the only game in town. But we cannot see how the word unfair could plausibly apply to the legitimate, independent editorial choices of multiple MSOs. A broad interpretation is plausible only for actions that impinge at least to some degree on the interest in competition that lay at the heart of Congress's concern. The Commission's reading of the clause effectively opens the door to illimitable restrictions in the name of diversity. The fact that Congress's interest in anti-competitive behavior may have been animated by an interest in preserving diversity doesn't give the FCC carte blanche to [h]obble cable operators in the name of the latter value alone.

On the record before us, we conclude that the 30% horizontal limit is in excess of statutory authority. While a 60% limit might be appropriate as necessary to ensure that programmers had an adequate open field even in the face of rejection by the largest company, the present record supports no more. In addition, the statute allows the Commission to act prophylactically against the risk of unfair conduct by cable operators that might unduly impede the flow of programming, either by the joint actions of two or more companies or the independent action of a single company of sufficient size. But the Commission has pointed to nothing in the record supporting a non-conjectural risk of anticompetitive behavior, either by collusion or other means. Accordingly, we reverse and remand with respect to the 30% rule.

The FCC presents its 40% vertical limit as advancing the same interests invoked in support of its statutory authority to adopt the rule: diversity in programming and fair competition. As with the horizontal rules the FCC must defend the rules themselves under intermediate scrutiny and justify its chosen limit as not burdening substantially more speech than necessary. Far from satisfying this test, the FCC seems to have plucked the 40% limit out of thin air. The FCC relies almost exclusively on the congressional findings that vertical integration in the cable industry could make it difficult for non-cable affiliated programmers to secure carriage on vertically integrated cables systems and that vertically integrated program suppliers have the incentive and the ability to favor their affiliated cable operators and program distributors.

We recognize that in drawing a numerical line an agency will ultimately indulge in some inescapable residue of arbitrariness; even if 40% is a highly justifiable pick, no one could expect the Commission to show why it was materially better than 39% or 41%. But the agency must at least reveal a rational connection between the facts found and the choice made. Here the FCC must also meet First Amendment intermediate scrutiny. Yet it appears to provide nothing but the conclusion that "we believe that a 40% limit is appropriate to balance the goals." What are the conditions that make 50% too high and 30% too low? How great is the risk presented by current market conditions? These questions are left unanswered by the Commission's discussion.

The FCC argued before us that no MSO has yet complained that the 40% vertical limit has required it to alter programming. This is no answer at all, as it says nothing about plans that the rule may have scuttled. Petitioners responded that their subsidiaries frequently must juggle their channel lineups to stay within the cap.

Given the [Commission's] pursuit of diversity, one might expect some inquiry into whether innovative independent originators of programming find greater success selling to affiliated or to unaffiliated programming firms, but there is none.

Petitioners [also] attack the Commission's refusal to exclude from the vertical limit cable operators that are subject to effective competition. The FCC makes two arguments to justify its refusal to exempt MVPDs that are subject to effective competition. First, it says that the definition of competition provided by [Congress] was not adopted for this specific purpose but rather for relief from rate regulation. If the criteria [in the statute] are unsuitable, the Commission can consider concepts of effective competition that it finds more apt for these purposes.

Second, the FCC comments that if a competing MVPD favored its own affiliated programmers, the presence of competition would have no tendency to create room for independent programmers. But this theory seems contradicted by the Commission's own observation that no vertically integrated MPVD has complained of reaching the 40% limit. Vertically integrated MVPDs evidently use loads of independent programming. Further, although cable operators continue to expand their interests in programmers, the proportion of vertically integrated channels continued to decline for each of the last two years. Even if competing MSOs filled all of their channels with affiliates' products (as unlikely as that seems), the Commission nowhere explains why, in the pursuit of diversity, the independence of competing vertically integrated MVPDs is inferior to the independence of unaffiliated programmers. In any event, the Commission's point here does not respond to the intuition that competition spurs a firm's search for the best price-quality trade-off.

We find that the FCC has failed to justify its vertical limit as not burdening substantially more speech than necessary. Accordingly, we reverse and remand to the FCC for further consideration.

We reverse and remand the horizontal and vertical limits, including the refusal to exempt cable operators subject to effective competition from the vertical limits, for further proceedings.

## Points for Discussion

1. One of the challenges facing the FCC is to determine the relationship between media ownership and diversity of "voices" enjoyed by viewers. From your own perspective, which do you think would give you more variety: a single cable or satellite provider offering 100 channels, or three competing services offering a combined total of 60 channels?

2. The court concludes here that the Commission's vertical limits—the limits on the ratio of channels offered on a cable or satellite service provider's system in which the provider may own a financial interest— infringe on the providers' "editorial control." Do you believe that cable and satellite systems choose which channels to offer on their systems based on judgments about competing channels's editorial content? If such decisions are based instead on straightforward market considerations (i.e., which channels customers are most likely to want and be willing to pay for), how should that fact affect the First Amendment analysis?

# 13 *The Internet*

In this final chapter, we take a first stab at the emerging area of communication law as applied to cyberspace. The cases here were carefully selected so as to provide examples of how different judges have perceived the Internet. Is it just one more new medium of communication, such as cable television? Or, does it represent a revolutionary change in the communication landscape? Readers are encouraged to focus especially on those portions of these decisions where judges struggle to make sense of this new medium by analogizing it to other, more familiar means of communication.

We begin with *Reno v. ACLU,* the Supreme Court's first foray into Internet law, striking down key elements of the Communications Decency Act, itself a portion of the Telecommunications Act of 1996. Following close on the heels of the *Reno* decision was a district court decision from Virginia—*Mainstream Loudoun v. Board of Trustees of the Loudoun County Library*—which concerned what steps public librarians may take to shield children from X-rated Web sites.

Next we examine *Tasini v. New York Times.* This case concerns the narrow and perhaps not earthshaking question of whether freelance writers, in the absence of a contractual clause one way or the other, sign away their right to determine whether their newspaper articles will appear at a later date in a computer database such as NEXIS. For our purposes, the decision's importance lies in the court's understanding of the mechanics of such full-text databases. The decision excerpted here is from the Second Circuit Court of Appeals. The case, however, was heard by the U.S. Supreme Court in March 2001, with a decision expected by July.

Our next case is *Brookfield Communications Inc. v. West Coast Entertainment,* a trademark infringement suit that forced the Ninth Circuit Court of Appeals to develop a rather sophisticated understanding of not only Internet domain names, but also how hidden codes such as metatags interact with Internet search engines.

Finally we look at *A&M Records v. Napster,* part of the complex legal and economic struggle between the major record labels and the upstart Internet company that enables users to engage in millions of "peer to peer" exchanges of music files.

# ▓ *Reno v. ACLU*

## 521 U.S. 844 (1997)

*Justice Stevens delivered the opinion of the Court.*

At issue is the constitutionality of two statutory provisions enacted to protect minors from "indecent" and "patently offensive" communications on the Internet. Notwithstanding the legitimacy and importance of the congressional goal of protecting children from harmful materials, we agree with the three-judge District Court that the statute abridges the freedom of speech protected by the First Amendment.

The Internet is an international network of interconnected computers, a unique and wholly new medium of worldwide human communication. About 40 million people used the Internet [by 1996], a number that is expected to mushroom to 200 million by 1999.

Anyone with access to the Internet may take advantage of a wide variety of communication and information retrieval methods. These methods are constantly evolving and difficult to categorize precisely. But, as presently constituted, those most relevant to this case are e-mail, listservs ("mail exploders"), newsgroups, chat rooms, and the World Wide Web. All of these methods can be used to transmit text; most can transmit sound, pictures, and moving video images.

Navigating the Web is relatively straightforward. A user may either type the address of a known page or enter one or more keywords into a commercial search engine in an effort to locate sites on a subject of interest. A particular Web page may contain the information sought by the "surfer," or, through its links, it may be an avenue to other documents located anywhere on the Internet. Users generally explore a given Web page, or move to another, by clicking a computer mouse on one of the page's icons or links. Access to most Web pages is freely available, but some allow access only to those who have purchased the right from a commercial provider. The Web is thus comparable, from the readers' viewpoint, to both a vast library including millions of readily available and indexed publications and a sprawling mall offering goods and services.

From the publishers' point of view, it constitutes a vast platform from which to address and hear from a world-wide audience of millions of readers, viewers, researchers, and buyers. Any person or organization with a computer connected to the Internet can "publish" information. Publishers include government agencies, educational institutions, commercial entities, advocacy groups, and individuals. Publishers may either make their material available to the entire pool of Internet users, or confine access to a selected group, such as those willing to pay for the privilege.

Sexually explicit material on the Internet includes text, pictures, and chat and extends from the modestly titillating to the hardest-core. These files are created, named, and posted in the same manner as material that is not sexually explicit, and may be accessed either deliberately or unintentionally during the course of an imprecise search. Once a provider posts its content on the Internet, it cannot prevent that content from entering any community.

Though such material is widely available, users seldom encounter such content accidentally. A document's title or a description of the document will usually appear before the document itself, and in many cases the user will receive detailed information about a site's content before he or she need take the step to access the document. Almost all sexually explicit images are preceded by warnings as to the content. For that reason, the odds are slim that a user would enter a sexually explicit site by accident. Unlike communications received by radio or television, the receipt of information on the Internet requires a series of affirmative steps more deliberate and directed than merely turning a dial. A child requires some sophistication and some ability to read to retrieve material and thereby to use the Internet unattended.

Systems have been developed to help parents control the material that may be available on a home computer with Internet access. A system may either limit a computer's access to an approved list of sources that have been identified as containing no adult material, it may block designated inappropriate sites, or it may attempt to block messages containing identifiable objectionable features. Although parental control software currently can screen for certain suggestive words or for known sexually explicit sites, it cannot now screen for sexually explicit images. Nevertheless, the evidence indicates that a reasonably effective method by which parents can prevent their children from accessing sexually explicit and other material which parents may believe is inappropriate for their children will soon be available.

The problem of age verification differs for different uses of the Internet. The District Court categorically determined that there is no effective way to determine the identity or the age of a user who is accessing material through e-mail, [listservs], newsgroups, or chat rooms. The Government offered no evidence that there was a reliable way to screen recipients and participants in such fora for age. Moreover, even if it were technologically feasible to block minors' access to newsgroups and chat rooms containing discussions of art, politics, or other subjects that potentially elicit "indecent" or "patently offensive" contributions, it would not be possible to block their access to that material and still allow them access to the remaining content, even if the overwhelming majority of that content was not indecent.

Technology exists by which an operator of a Web site may condition access on the verification of requested information such as a credit card number or an adult password. Credit card verification is only feasible, however, either in connection with a commercial transaction in which the card is used, or by payment to a verification agency. Using credit card possession as a surrogate for proof of age would impose costs on non-commercial Web sites that would require many of them to shut down.

Commercial pornographic sites that charge their users for access have assigned them passwords as a method of age verification. The record does not contain any evidence concerning the reliability of these technologies. Even if passwords are effective for commercial purveyors of indecent material, the District Court found that an adult password requirement would impose significant burdens on noncommercial sites, both because they would discourage users from accessing their sites and because the cost of creating and maintaining such screening systems would be beyond their reach.

The Telecommunications Act of 1996 was an unusually important legislative enactment. Title V—known as the "Communications Decency Act of 1996" (CDA)—[includes] the two statutory provisions challenged in this case. The first prohibits the knowing transmission of obscene or indecent messages to any recipient under 18 years of age. The second provision prohibits the knowing sending or displaying of "patently offensive messages" in a manner that is available to a person under 18 years of age.

The breadth of these prohibitions is qualified by two affirmative defenses. One covers those who take "good faith, reasonable, effective, and appropriate actions" to restrict access by minors to the prohibited communications. The other covers those who restrict access to covered material by requiring certain designated forms of age proof, such as a verified credit card or an adult identification number or code.

Immediately after the President signed the statute, 20 plaintiffs challenged the constitutionality of [the CDA]. A three-judge District Court was convened, [which] entered a preliminary injunction against enforcement of both of the challenged provisions.

The judgment of the District Court enjoins the Government from enforcing the prohibitions in CDA insofar as they relate to indecent communications, but expressly preserves the Government's right to investigate and prosecute the obscenity or child pornography activities. The Government argues that the District Court erred in holding that the CDA violated both the First Amendment because it is overbroad and the Fifth Amendment because it is vague. While we discuss the vagueness of the CDA because of its relevance to the First Amendment overbreadth inquiry, we conclude that the judgment should be affirmed without reaching the Fifth Amendment issue.

In arguing for reversal, the Government contends that the CDA is plainly constitutional under three of our prior decisions: *Ginsberg v. New York*, 390 U.S. 629 (1968); *FCC v. Pacifica Foundation*, 438 U.S. 726 (1978); and *Renton v. Playtime Theatres, Inc.*, 475 U.S. 41 (1986). A close look at these cases, however, raises—rather than relieves—doubts concerning the constitutionality of the CDA.

In *Ginsberg,* we upheld the constitutionality of a New York statute that prohibited selling to minors under 17 years of age material that was considered obscene as to them even if not obscene as to adults. In four important respects, the statute upheld in *Ginsberg* was narrower than the CDA. First, we noted in *Ginsberg* that the prohibition against sales to minors does not bar parents who so desire from purchasing the magazines for their children. Under the CDA, by contrast, neither the parents' consent—nor even their participation—in the communication would avoid the application of the statute. Second, the New York statute applied only to commercial transactions, whereas the CDA contains no such limitation. Third, the New York statute cabined its definition of material that is harmful to minors with the requirement that it be "utterly without redeeming social importance for minors." The CDA fails to provide us with any definition of the term "indecent" and, importantly, omits any requirement that "patently offensive" material lack serious literary, artistic, political, or scientific value. Fourth, the New York statute defined a minor as a person under the age of 17, whereas the CDA, in applying to all those under 18 years, includes an additional year of those nearest majority.

In *Pacifica,* we upheld a declaratory order of the Federal Communications Commission, holding that the broadcast of a recording of a 12-minute monologue entitled "Filthy Words" that had previously been delivered to a live audience could have been the subject of administrative sanctions. The Commission had found that the repetitive use of certain words referring to excretory or sexual activities or organs in an afternoon broadcast when children are in the audience was patently offensive and concluded that the monologue was indecent "as broadcast." The Court concluded that the ease with which children may obtain access to broadcasts justified special treatment of indecent broadcasting.

There are significant differences between the order upheld in *Pacifica* and the CDA. First, the order in *Pacifica,* issued by an agency that had been regulating radio stations for decades, targeted a specific broadcast that represented a rather dramatic departure from traditional program content in order to designate when—rather than whether—it would be permissible to air such a program in that particular medium. The CDA's broad categorical prohibitions are not limited to particular times and are not dependent on any evaluation by an agency familiar with the unique characteristics of the Internet. Second, unlike the CDA, the Commission's declaratory order was not punitive; we expressly refused to decide whether the indecent broadcast would justify a criminal prosecution. Finally, the Commission's order applied to a medium which as a matter of history had received the most limited First Amendment protection, in large part because warnings could not adequately protect the listener from unexpected program content. The Internet, however, has no comparable history. Moreover, the District Court found that the risk of encountering indecent material by accident is remote because a series of affirmative steps is required to access specific material.

In *Renton,* we upheld a zoning ordinance that kept adult movie theatres out of residential neighborhoods. The ordinance was aimed not at the content of the films shown in the theaters, but rather at the "secondary effects"—such as crime and deteriorating property values—that these theaters fostered. According to the Government, the CDA is constitutional because it constitutes a sort of "cyberzoning" on the Internet. But the CDA applies broadly to the entire universe of cyberspace. And the purpose of the CDA is to protect children from the primary effects of "indecent" and "patently offensive" speech, rather than any "secondary" effect of such speech. Thus, the CDA is a content-based blanket restriction on speech, and, as such, cannot be properly analyzed as a form of time, place, and manner regulation. Listeners' reaction to speech is not a content-neutral basis for regulation.

These precedents, then, surely do not require us to uphold the CDA and are fully consistent with the application of the most stringent review of its provisions. [They] provide no basis for qualifying the level of First Amendment scrutiny that should be applied to this medium.

Regardless of whether the CDA is so vague that it violates the Fifth Amendment, the many ambiguities concerning the scope of its coverage render it problematic for purposes of the First Amendment. Could a speaker confidently assume that a serious discussion about birth control practices, homosexuality, the First Amendment issues raised by [George Carlin's "Filthy Words"], or the consequences of prison rape would not violate the CDA? This uncertainty undermines the likelihood that the CDA has been carefully tailored to the congressional goal of protecting minors from potentially harmful materials.

The vagueness of the CDA is a matter of special concern for two reasons. First, the CDA is a content-based regulation of speech. The vagueness of such a regulation raises special First Amendment concerns because of its obvious chilling effect on free speech. Second, the CDA is a criminal statute. In addition to the opprobrium and stigma of a criminal conviction, the CDA threatens violators with penalties including up to two years in prison for each act of violation. The severity of criminal sanctions may well cause speakers to remain silent rather than communicate even arguably unlawful words, ideas, and images. As a practical matter, this increased deterrent effect, coupled with the risk of discriminatory enforcement of vague regulations, poses great First Amendment concerns.

We are persuaded that the CDA lacks the precision that the First Amendment requires when a statute regulates the content of speech. In order to deny minors access to potentially harmful speech, the CDA effectively suppresses a large amount of speech that adults have a constitutional right to receive and to address to one another. That burden on adult speech is unacceptable if less restrictive alternatives would be at least as effective in achieving the legitimate purpose that the statute was enacted to serve. The District Court found that despite its limitations, currently available user-based software suggests that a reasonably effective method by which parents can prevent their children from accessing sexually explicit and other material which parents may believe is inappropriate for their children will soon be widely available.

The breadth of the CDA's coverage is wholly unprecedented, not limited to commercial speech or commercial entities. Its open-ended prohibitions embrace all nonprofit entities and individuals posting indecent messages or displaying them on their own computers in the presence of minors. The general, undefined terms "indecent" and "patently offensive" cover large amounts of nonpornographic material with serious educational or other value. Moreover, the "community standards" criterion as applied to the Internet means that any communication available to a nation-wide audience will be judged by the standards of the community most likely to be offended by the message. The regulated subject matter may extend to discussions about prison rape or safe sexual practices, artistic images that include nude subjects, and arguably the card catalogue of the Carnegie Library. Under the CDA, a parent allowing her 17-year-old to use the family computer to obtain information on the Internet that she, in her parental judgment, deems appropriate could face a lengthy prison term. Similarly, a parent who sent his 17-year-old college freshman information on birth control via e-mail could be incarcerated even though neither he, his child, nor anyone in their home community, found the material indecent or patently offensive, if the college town's community thought otherwise.

The breadth of this content-based restriction of speech imposes an especially heavy burden on the Government to explain why a less restrictive provision would not be as effective as the CDA. It has not done so. The arguments in this Court have referred to possible alternatives such as requiring that indecent material be "tagged" in a way that facilitates parental control of material coming into their homes, making exceptions for messages with artistic or educational value, providing some tolerance for parental choice, and regulating some portions of the Internet—such as commercial web sites—differently than others, such as chat rooms. Particularly in the light of the absence of any detailed findings by the Congress, or even hearings addressing the special problems of the CDA, we are persuaded that the CDA is not narrowly tailored if that requirement has any meaning at all.

Relying on the "good faith, reasonable, effective, and appropriate actions" provision, the Government suggests that "tagging" provides a defense that saves the constitutionality of the Act. The suggestion assumes that transmitters may encode their indecent communications in a way that would indicate their contents, thus permitting recipients to block their reception with appropriate software. It is the requirement that the good faith action must be "effective" that makes this defense illusory. The Government recognizes that its proposed screening software does not currently exist. Even if it did, there is no way to know whether a potential recipient will actually block the encoded material.

We agree with the District Court's conclusion that the CDA places an unacceptably heavy burden on protected speech, and that the defenses do not constitute the sort of narrow tailoring that will save an otherwise patently invalid unconstitutional provision.

The Government asserts that—in addition to its interest in protecting children—its "equally significant" interest in fostering the growth of the Internet provides an independent basis for upholding the constitutionality of the CDA. The Government apparently assumes that the unregulated availability of "indecent" and "patently offensive" material on the Internet is driving countless citizens away from the medium because of the risk of exposing themselves or their children to harmful material. We find this argument singularly unpersuasive. The dramatic expansion of this new marketplace of ideas contradicts the factual basis of this contention. The record demonstrates that the growth of the Internet has been and continues to be phenomenal. As a matter of constitutional tradition, in the absence of evidence to the contrary, we presume that governmental regulation of the content of speech is more likely to interfere with the free exchange of ideas than to encourage it. The interest in encouraging freedom of expression in a democratic society outweighs any theoretical but unproven benefit of censorship.

For the foregoing reasons, the judgment of the district court is affirmed. It is so ordered.

## Points for Discussion

1. Much of Justice Stevens's ultimate decision seems to rest on his belief, based on the lower court's findings, that "the odds are slim that [an Internet] user would enter a sexually explicit site by accident." Does this assertion jibe with your own experience in surfing the Web?

2. Justice Steven's invoking of the hypothetical parent of a seventeen-year-old college student might make you wonder why the same concern did not persuade the Court in the earlier *Pacifica* decision (see Chapter 12) that the rights of parents who *want* their mature kids to be able to listen to George Carlin's routines on the radio should be respected. Are you satisfied with the way Stevens distinguishes *Pacifica* from the *Reno* case? Why or why not?

# ■ *Mainstream Loudoun v. Board of Trustees of the Loudoun County Library*

## 2 F. Supp. 2d 783 (E.D. Va. 1998)

*Judge Brinkema:*

The plaintiffs in this case are an association, Mainstream Loudoun, and ten individual plaintiffs, all of whom are both members of Mainstream Loudoun and adult patrons of Loudoun County public libraries. Defendants are the Board of Trustees of the Loudoun County Public Library. The Loudoun County public library system has six branches and provides patrons with access to the Internet and the World Wide Web. Library Board members are appointed by County officials and are not elected.

On October 20, 1997, the Library Board voted to adopt a "Policy on Internet Sexual Harassment," which requires that site-blocking software be installed on all library computers so as to: a. block child pornography and obscene material (hard core pornography); and b. block material deemed Harmful to Juveniles under applicable Virginia statutes and legal precedents (soft core pornography). To implement the Policy, the Library Board chose "X-Stop," a commercial software product intended to limit access to sites deemed to violate the Policy.

Plaintiffs allege that the Policy impermissibly blocks their access to protected speech such as the Quaker Home Page, the Zero Population Growth website, and the site for the American Association of University Women–Maryland. They also claim that there are no clear criteria for blocking decisions and that defendants maintain an unblocking policy that unconstitutionally chills plaintiffs' receipt of constitutionally protected materials. Plaintiffs allege that the Policy imposes an unconstitutional restriction on their right to access protected speech on the Internet, and seek declaratory and injunctive relief, as well as costs and attorneys' fees.

Defendants claim that they are immune from suit under section 509 of the Telecommunications Act of 1996, [which provides that] "no provider or user of an interactive computer service shall be held liable on account of any action voluntarily taken in good faith to restrict access to or availability of material that the provider or user considers to be obscene, lewd, lascivious, filthy, excessively violent, harassing, or otherwise objectionable, whether or not such material is constitutionally protected." Although defendants' interpretation of [the CDA] is facially attractive, it is not supported by that section's legislative history or relevant case law. [The relevant section] was enacted to minimize state regulation of Internet speech by encouraging private content providers to self-regulate against offensive material; [it] was not enacted to insulate government regulation of Internet speech from judicial review.

Defendants concede that the Policy prohibits access to speech on the basis of its content. Thus, the central question before this Court is whether a public library may, without violating the First Amendment, enforce content-based restrictions on access to Internet speech. No cases directly address this issue. However, the parties agree that the most analogous authority on this issue is *Board of Education v. Pico,* 457 U.S. 853 (1982), in which the Supreme Court reviewed the decision of a local board of education to remove certain books from a high school library based on the board's belief that the books were "anti-American, anti-Christian, anti-Semitic, and just plain filthy." The Second Circuit had reversed the district court's grant of summary judgment to the school board on plaintiff's First Amendment claim. A sharply-divided Court voted to affirm the Court of Appeal's decision to remand the case for a determination of the school board's motives. However, the Court did not render a majority opinion. Justice Brennan, joined by three Justices, wrote what is commonly referred to as the "plurality" opinion. Justice Brennan held that the First Amendment necessarily limits the government's right to remove materials on the basis of their content from a high school library. Justice Brennan reasoned that the right to receive information is inherent in the right to speak and that "the State may not, consistently with the spirit of the First Amendment, contract the spectrum of available knowledge." Justice Brennan explained that this principle was particularly important given the special role of the school's library as a locus for free and independent inquiry. At the same time, Justice Brennan recognized that public high schools play a crucial inculcative role in "the preparation of individuals for participation as citizens" and are therefore entitled to great discretion "to establish and apply their curriculum in such a way as to transmit community values." Accordingly, Justice Brennan held that the school board members could not remove books "simply because they dislike the ideas contained [in them]," but that the board might remove books for reasons of educational suitability, for example pervasive vulgarity.

In a concurring opinion, Justice Blackmun focused not on the right to receive information recognized by the plurality, but on the school board's discrimination against disfavored ideas. Justice Blackmun explicitly recognized that Pico's facts invoked two significant, competing interests: the inculcative mission of public high schools and the First Amendment's core proscription against content-based regulation of speech. Justice Blackmun noted that the State must normally demonstrate a compelling reason for content-based regulation, but that a more limited form of protection should apply in the context of public high schools. Balancing the two principles above, Justice Blackmun agreed with the plurality that the school board could not remove books based on mere disapproval of their content but could limit its collection for reasons of educational suitability or budgetary constraint.

Defendants contend that the *Pico* plurality opinion has no application to this case because it addressed only decisions to remove materials from libraries and specifically declined to address library decisions to acquire materials. Defendants liken the Internet to a vast Interlibrary Loan system, and contend that restricting Internet access to selected materials is merely a decision not to acquire such materials rather than a decision to remove them from a library's collection. As such, defendants argue, the instant case is outside the scope of the *Pico* plurality.

We conclude that defendants have misconstrued the nature of the Internet. By purchasing Internet access, each Loudoun library has made all Internet publications instantly accessible to its patrons. Unlike an Interlibrary loan or outright book purchase, no appreciable expenditure of library time or resources is required to make a particular Internet publication available to a library patron. In contrast, a library must actually expend resources to restrict Internet access to a publication that is otherwise immediately available. In effect, by purchasing one such publication, the library has purchased them all. The Internet therefore more closely resembles a collection of encyclopedias from which defendants have laboriously redacted portions deemed unfit for library patrons. As such, the Library Board's action is more appropriately characterized as a removal decision. We therefore conclude that the principles discussed in the *Pico* plurality are relevant and apply to the Library Board's decision to promulgate and enforce the Policy.

Defendants argue that any limitation on their discretion to remove materials would force them to act as an unwilling conduit of information, [and] that they [should be] entitled to unfettered discretion in deciding what materials to make available to library patrons. Adopting defendants' position, however, would require this Court to ignore the *Pico* plurality's decision to remand the case. Moreover, all of the *Pico* Justices, including the dissenters, recognized that any discretion accorded to school libraries was uniquely tied to the public school's role as educator. Of [special] significance to our case is Justice Rehnquist's observation that high school libraries must be treated differently from public libraries: "Unlike university or public libraries, elementary and secondary school libraries are not designed for free-wheeling inquiry." Indeed, Chief Justice Burger and Justice Rehnquist justified giving public schools broad discretion to remove books in part by noting that such materials remained available in public libraries. Accordingly, neither the dissent nor the plurality of *Pico* can be said to support defendants' argument that public libraries enjoy unfettered discretion to remove materials from their collections.

To the extent that *Pico* applies to this case, we conclude that it stands for the proposition that the First Amendment applies to, and limits, the discretion of a public library to place content-based restrictions on access to constitutionally protected materials within its collection. Furthermore, the factors which justified giving high school libraries broad discretion to remove materials in *Pico* are not present in this case. The plaintiffs in this case are adults rather than children. Children, whose minds and values are still developing, have traditionally been afforded less First Amendment protection, particularly within the context of public high schools. In contrast, adults are deemed to have acquired the maturity needed to participate fully in a democratic society, and their right to speak and receive speech is entitled to full First Amendment protection.

More importantly, the tension Justice Blackmun recognized between the inculcative role of high schools and the First Amendment's prohibition on content-based regulation of speech does not exist here. Public libraries lack the inculcative mission that is the guiding purpose of public high schools. Instead, public libraries are places of freewheeling and independent inquiry. Adult library patrons are presumed to have acquired already the fundamental values needed to act as citizens, and have come to the library to pursue their personal intellectual interests rather than the curriculum of a high school classroom. As such, no curricular motive justifies a public library's decision to restrict access to Internet materials on the basis of their content.

Finally, the unique advantages of Internet speech eliminate any resource-related rationale libraries might otherwise have for engaging in content-based discrimination. The Supreme Court has analogized the Internet to a vast library including millions of readily available and indexed publications, the content of which is as diverse as human thought. Unlike more traditional libraries, however, there is no marginal cost associated with acquiring Internet publications. Instead, all, or nearly all, Internet publications are jointly available for a single price. Indeed, it costs a library more to restrict the content of its collection by means of blocking software than it does for the library to offer unrestricted access to all Internet publications. Nor do Internet publications, which exist only in "cyberspace," take up shelf space or require physical maintenance of any kind. Accordingly, considerations of cost or physical resources cannot justify a public library's decision to restrict access to Internet materials.

In sum, there is no basis for qualifying the level of First Amendment scrutiny that must be applied to a public library's decision to restrict access to Internet publications. We are therefore left with the First Amendment's central tenet that content-based restrictions on speech must be justified by a compelling governmental interest and must be narrowly tailored to achieve that end. Accordingly, we hold that the Library Board may not adopt and enforce content-based restrictions on access to protected Internet speech absent a compelling state interest and means narrowly drawn to achieve that end.

This holding does not obligate defendants to act as unwilling conduits of information, because the Library Board need not provide access to the Internet at all. Having chosen to provide access, however, the Library Board may not thereafter selectively restrict certain categories of Internet speech because it disfavors their content. Having determined that a public library must satisfy strict scrutiny before it may engage in content-based regulation of protected speech, we now consider the speech regulated by the Policy. The Policy prohibits access to three types of speech: obscenity, child pornography, and materials deemed "harmful to juveniles." Obscenity and child pornography are not entitled to the protections of the First Amendment, and the government may legitimately restrict access to such materials. Indeed, transmitting obscenity and child pornography, whether via the Internet or other means, is already illegal under federal law for both adults and juveniles. In the instant case, however, plaintiffs allege that the X-Stop filtering software chosen by defendants restricts many publications which are not obscene or pornographic, including materials unrelated to sex altogether, such as the Quaker's website. Moreover, plaintiffs allege that X-Stop fails to block access to pornographic materials arguably covered by the Policy. Most importantly, plaintiffs allege that the decision as to which materials to block is made by a California corporation based on secret criteria not disclosed even to defendants, criteria which may or may not bear any relation to legal definitions of obscenity or child pornography. As such, plaintiffs argue that the means called for by the Policy are not narrowly tailored to any legitimate interest defendants may have in regulating obscenity and child pornography.

The Policy also prohibits access to materials which are "deemed Harmful to Juveniles under applicable Virginia statutes and legal precedents." This appears to be a reference to Virginia Code §18.2-390, which defines materials "Harmful to Juveniles" to include sexual content that: "(a) predominately appeals to the prurient, shameful or morbid interest of juveniles, (b) is patently offensive to prevailing standards in the adult community as a whole with respect to what is suitable material for juveniles, and (c) is, when taken as a whole, lacking in serious literary, artistic, political or scientific value for juveniles."

Plaintiffs allege that the Policy improperly limits adult Internet speech to what is fit for children. As plaintiffs point out, even when government regulation of content is undertaken for a legitimate purpose, whether it be to prevent the communication of obscene speech or materials harmful to children, the means it uses must be a reasonable response to the threat which will alleviate the harm in a direct and material way. Plaintiffs have adequately alleged a lack of such reasonable means here. As such, plaintiffs have stated a valid First Amendment claim which may go forward.

Defendants contend that, even if the First Amendment limits the Library Board's discretion to remove materials, the unblocking procedure ensures the constitutionality of the Policy because it allows library staff to make certain that only constitutionally unprotected materials are blocked. Under the unblocking policy, library patrons who have been denied access to a site may submit a written request which must include their name, telephone number, and a detailed explanation of why they desire access to the blocked site. The library staff then decides whether the request should be granted.

Plaintiffs argue that the unblocking procedure constitutes an unconstitutional burden on the right of library patrons to access protected speech. The unblocking policy forces adult patrons to petition the Government for access to otherwise protected speech, for example speech "Harmful to Juveniles." Indeed, the Loudoun County unblocking policy appears [especially] chilling because it grants library staff standardless discretion to refuse access to protected speech. As such, defendants' alleged unblocking procedure does not in any way undercut plaintiffs' First Amendment claim.

This Court holds that several material factual issues remain which mandate against summary judgment at this time. These include, but are not limited to, defendants' justification for the Policy, the Internet sites blocked by X-Stop, and the degree of defendants' knowledge of and control over the sites X-Stop blocks. Accordingly, defendants' Motion for Summary Judgment will be DENIED.

### Points for Discussion

1. Imagine a not-too-distant future world in which virtually all research is done on the Internet, where books, newspapers, and magazines as we know them cease to exist except online. To the extent that access to all such information sources is free (paid for by advertisers), will librarians have any gatekeeping role to play? If not, would that be a change for the better or for the worse?

2. Suppose that instead of using the blocking software on all its computers, the Loudoun Country library system installed it only on computers earmarked for juvenile users. Would such a compromise be constitutional? Should parents be able to override the library's default decision and insist that their children of whatever age be granted unfettered access to the Internet?

## ■ *Tasini v. New York Times*

**206 F.3d 161 (2d Cir. 1999)**

*Judge Winter:*

Six freelance writers appeal from a grant of summary judgment dismissing their complaint [alleging] that appellees had infringed appellants' various copyrights by putting individual articles previously published in periodicals on electronic databases available to the public. On cross motions for summary judgment, the United States District Court for the Southern District of New York held that appellees' use of the articles was protected by the "privilege" afforded to publishers of "collective works" under Section 201(c) of the Copyright Act of 1976. We reverse and remand with instructions to enter judgment for appellants.

Appellants are freelance writers who write articles for publication in periodicals. Their complaint alleged that certain articles were original works written for first publication by one of the appellee publishers between 1990 and 1993. None of the articles was written at a time when its Author was employed by the particular periodical; nor was any such article written pursuant to a work-for-hire contract. The Authors registered a copyright in each of the articles.

The appellee newspaper and magazine publishers are periodical publishers who regularly create "collective works" that contain articles by freelance authors as well as works created for-hire or by employees. With respect to the freelance articles pertinent to this appeal, the Publishers' general practice was to negotiate due-dates, word counts, subject matter and price; no express transfer of rights under the Author's copyright was sought.

Appellee Mead Data Central Corp. owns and operates the NEXIS electronic database. NEXIS is a massive database that includes the full texts of articles appearing in literally hundreds of newspapers and periodicals spanning many years. Mead has entered into licensing agreements with each of the Publishers. Pursuant to these agreements, the Publishers provide Mead with much of the content of their periodicals, in digital form, for inclusion in NEXIS. Subscribers to NEXIS are able to access an almost infinite combination of articles from one or more publishers by using the database's advanced search engine. The articles may be retrieved individually or, for example, together with others on like topics. Such retrieval makes the article available without any material from the rest of the periodical in which it first appeared.

We briefly describe the process by which an issue of a periodical is made available to Mead for inclusion in NEXIS. First, an individual issue of the paper is stripped, electronically, into separate files representing individual articles. In the process, a substantial portion of what appears in that particular issue of the periodical is not made part of a file transmitted to Mead, including, among other things, formatting decisions, pictures, maps and tables, and obituaries. Moreover, although the individual articles are "tagged" with data indicating the section and page on which the article initially appeared, certain information relating to the initial page layout is lost, such as placement above or below the fold in the case of *The New York Times*. After Mead further codes the individual files, the pieces are incorporated into the NEXIS database.

The gist of the Authors' claim is that the copyright each owns in his or her individual articles was infringed when the Publishers provided them to the electronic databases. Appellees do not dispute that the Authors own the copyright in their individual works. Rather, they argue that the Publishers own the copyright in the "collective works" that they produce and are afforded the privilege, under Section 201(c) of the Act, of "reproducing and distributing" the individual works in "any revision of that collective work." The crux of the dispute is, therefore, whether one or more of the pertinent electronic databases may be considered a "revision" of the individual periodical issues from which the articles were taken. The district court held that making the articles available on the databases constitutes a revision of the individual periodicals and that appellees' licensing arrangements were protected under Section 201(c). It therefore granted appellees' motion for summary judgment.

In support of their claim, the Authors [argue that] Section 201(c) protects only the Publishers' initial inclusion of individually copyrighted works in their collective works and does not permit the inclusion of individually copyrighted works in electronic databases. The district court [disagreed]. We hold that Section 201(c) does not permit the Publishers to license individually copyrighted works for inclusion in electronic databases.

Section 201 of the Act provides, that as to contributions to collective works, the "copyright in each separate contribution . . . is distinct from copyright in the collective work as a whole, and vests initially in the author of the contribution." Correspondingly, Section 103, which governs copyright in compilations and derivative works, provides in pertinent part that "the copyright in a compilation or derivative work extends only to the material contributed by the author of such work, as distinguished from the preexisting material employed in the work, and does not imply any exclusive right in the preexisting material." Section 101 states that "the term 'compilation' includes collective works." It further defines "collective work" as "a work, such as a periodical issue, anthology, or encyclopedia, in which a number of contributions, constituting separate and independent works in themselves, are assembled into a collective whole."

Publishers of collective works are not permitted to include individually copyrighted articles without receiving a license or other express transfer of rights from the author. However, Section 201(c) creates a presumptive privilege to authors of collective works. Section 201(c) creates a presumption that when the author of an article gives the publisher the author's permission to include the article in a collective work, as here, the author also gives a non-assignable, non-exclusive privilege to use the article as identified in the statute. It provides in pertinent part that: "In the absence of an express transfer of the copyright or of any rights under it, the owner of copyright in the collective work is presumed to have acquired only the privilege of reproducing and distributing the contribution as part of that particular collective work, any revision of that collective work, and any later collective work in the same series."

Under this statutory framework, the author of an individual contribution to a collective work owns the copyright to that contribution, absent an express agreement setting other terms. Moreover, the presumptive privilege granted to a collective-work author to use individually copyrighted contributions is limited to the reproduction and distribution of the individual contribution as part of "(i) that particular [i.e., the original] collective work; (ii) any revision of that collective work; and (iii) any later collective work in the same series."

We begin, as we must, with the language of the statute. The most natural reading of the "revision" of "that collective work" clause is that Section 201(c) protects only later editions of a particular issue of a periodical, such as the final edition of a newspaper. Because later editions are not identical to earlier editions, use of the individual contributions in the later editions might not be protected under the preceding clause. In this regard, we note that the statutory definition of "collective work" lists as examples "a periodical issue, anthology, or encyclopedia." The use of these particular kinds of collective works as examples supports our reading of the revision clause. Issues of periodicals, as noted, are often updated by revised editions. The House Report on the Act noted that the "revision" clause in Section 201(c) was not intended to permit the inclusion of previously published freelance contributions "in a new anthology or an entirely different magazine or other collective work," i.e., in later collective works not in the same series.

Moreover, if the contents of an electronic database are merely a revision of a particular collective work, e.g., the August 16, 1999 edition of *The New York Times,* then the third clause of Section 201(c)—permitting the reproduction and distribution of an individually copyrighted work as part of "a later collective work in the same series"—would be superfluous. An electronic database can contain hundreds or thousands of editions of hundreds or thousands of periodicals, including newspapers, magazines, anthologies, and encyclopedias. To view the contents of databases as revisions would eliminate any need for a privilege for "a later collective work in the same series."

The permitted uses set forth in Section 201(c) are an exception to the general rule that copyright vests initially in the author of the individual contribution. Reading "revision of that collective work" as broadly as appellees suggest would cause the exception to swallow the rule. Under Publishers' theory of Section 201(c), the question of whether an electronic database infringes upon an individual author's article would essentially turn upon whether the rest of the articles from the particular edition in which the individual article was published could also be retrieved individually. However, Section 201(c) would not permit a Publisher to sell a hard copy of an Author's article directly to the public even if the Publisher also offered for individual sale all of the other articles from the particular edition. We see nothing in the revision provision that would allow the Publishers to achieve the same goal indirectly through NEXIS.

In light of this discussion, there is no feature peculiar to the databases at issue in this appeal that would cause us to view them as revisions. NEXIS is a database comprising thousands or millions of individually retrievable articles taken from hundreds or thousands of periodicals. It can hardly be deemed a revision of each edition of every periodical that it contains. Moreover, NEXIS does almost nothing to preserve the copyrightable aspects of the Publishers' collective works, as distinguished from the preexisting material employed in the work. The aspects of a collective work that make it an original work of authorship are the selection, coordination, and arrangement of the preexisting materials. However, in placing an edition of a periodical such as the August 16, 1999 *New York Times,* in NEXIS, some of the paper's content, and perhaps most of its arrangement are lost. Even if a NEXIS user so desired, he or she would have a hard time recapturing much of the material contributed by the author of such collective work. In this context, it is significant that neither the Publishers nor NEXIS evince any intent to compel, or even to permit, an end user to retrieve an individual work only in connection with other works from the edition in which it ran. Quite the contrary, *The New York Times* actually forbids NEXIS from producing "facsimile reproductions" of particular editions. What the end user can easily access, of course, are the preexisting materials that belong to the individual author.

We emphasize that the only issue we address is whether, in the absence of a transfer of copyright or any rights thereunder, collective-work authors may re-license individual works in which they own no rights. Because there has by definition been no express transfer of rights in such cases, our decision turns entirely on the default allocation and presumption of rights provided by the Act. Publishers and authors are free to contract around the statutory framework. Indeed, both the Publishers and Mead were aware of the fact that Section 201(c) might not protect their licensing agreements, and [the *Times*] has already instituted a policy of expressly contracting for electronic re-licensing rights.

We therefore reverse and remand with instructions to enter judgment for appellants.

## *Points for Discussion*

1. In using NEXIS, you might purposely limit your search to one especially prestigious media outlet, such as the *New York Times.* This eliminates the need to sift through hundreds of irrelevant or redundant "hits." Such a strategy seems to be a computer-enhanced version of reading through a big stack of previous issues of that one newspaper. One might argue that such a search uses the original issue in which the article appeared (with no need even to rely on the "revision" clause). How would you assess such an argument?

2. Suppose that the *Times* did permit Mead to include more features of each day's newspaper layout into its database (photos, different size and style fonts, etc). How might that affect the copyright issue?

# ■ *Brookfield Communications Inc. v. West Coast Entertainment*

## 174 F.3d 1036 (9th Cir. 1999)

*Judge O'Scannlain:*

We must venture into cyberspace to determine whether federal trademark and unfair competition laws prohibit a video rental store chain from using an entertainment-industry information provider's trademark in the domain name of its web site and in its web site's metatags. Brookfield Communications, Inc. appeals the district court's denial of its motion for a preliminary injunction prohibiting West Coast Entertainment Corporation from using in commerce terms confusingly similar to Brookfield's trademark, "MovieBuff." Brookfield gathers and sells information about the entertainment industry. Founded in 1987 for the purpose of creating and marketing software and services for professionals in the entertainment industry, Brookfield initially offered software applications featuring information such as recent film submissions, industry credits, professional contacts, and future projects. These offerings targeted major Hollywood film studios, independent production companies, agents, actors, directors, and producers.

Brookfield expanded into the broader consumer market with computer software featuring a searchable database containing entertainment-industry related information marketed under the MovieBuff mark around December 1993. Brookfield's MovieBuff software now targets smaller companies and individual consumers who are not interested in purchasing Brookfield's professional level alternative, *The Studio System,* and includes comprehensive, searchable, entertainment-industry databases and related software applications containing information such as movie credits, box office receipts, films in development, film release schedules, entertainment news, and listings of executives, agents, actors, and directors. This MovieBuff software comes in three versions—(1) the MovieBuff Pro Bundle, (2) the MovieBuff Pro, and (3) MovieBuff—and is sold through various retail stores, such as Borders, Virgin Megastores, and Nobody Beats the Wiz.

Sometime in 1996, Brookfield attempted to register the World Wide Web domain name "moviebuff.com" with Network Solutions, Inc., but was informed that the requested domain name had already been registered by West Coast. Brookfield subsequently registered "brookfieldcomm.com" in May 1996 and "moviebuffonline.com" in September 1996. Sometime in 1996 or 1997, Brookfield began using its web sites to sell its MovieBuff computer software and to offer an Internet-based searchable database marketed under the MovieBuff mark. Brookfield sells its MovieBuff computer software through its "brookfieldcomm.com" and "moviebuffonline.com" web sites and offers subscribers online access to the MovieBuff database itself at its "inhollywood.com" web site.

On August 19, 1997, Brookfield applied to the Patent and Trademark Office for federal registration of MovieBuff as a mark to designate both goods and services. Both federal trademark registrations issued on September 29, 1998. Brookfield had previously obtained a California state trademark registration for the mark MovieBuff in 1994. In October 1998, Brookfield learned that West Coast—one of the nation's largest video rental store chains with over 500 stores—intended to launch a web site at "moviebuff.com" containing a searchable entertainment database similar to MovieBuff. West Coast had registered "moviebuff.com" with Network Solutions on February 6, 1996 and claims that it chose the domain name because the term Movie Buff is part of its service mark, "The Movie Buff's Movie Store," on which a federal registration issued in 1991. West Coast notes further that, since at least 1988, it has also used various phrases including the term Movie Buff to promote goods and services available at its video stores in Massachusetts, including "The Movie Buff's Gift Guide" and "A Movie Buff's Top Ten."

On November 10, Brookfield delivered to West Coast a cease-and-desist letter alleging that West Coast's planned use of the "moviebuff.com" would violate Brookfield's trademark rights. The next day, West Coast issued a press release announcing the imminent launch of its web site full of "movie reviews, Hollywood news and gossip, provocative commentary, and coverage of the independent film scene and films in production." Brookfield fired back immediately with a visit to the United States District Court for the Central District of California, and this lawsuit was born. On November 27, West Coast filed an opposition brief in which it argued first that Brookfield could not prevent West Coast from using "moviebuff.com" in commerce because West Coast was the senior user. West Coast claimed that it was the first user of MovieBuff because it had used its federally registered trademark, "The Movie Buff's Movie Store" since 1986 in advertisements, promotions, and letterhead in connection with retail services featuring videocassettes and video game cartridges. Alternatively, West Coast claimed seniority on the basis that it had garnered common-law rights in the domain name by using "moviebuff.com" before Brookfield began offering its MovieBuff Internet-based searchable database on the Web. In addition to asserting seniority, West Coast contended that its planned use of "moviebuff.com" would not cause a likelihood of confusion with Brookfield's trademark "MovieBuff" and thus would not violate the Lanham Act.

The district court concluded that West Coast was the senior user of the mark "MovieBuff" for both of the reasons asserted by West Coast. The court also determined that Brookfield had not established a likelihood of confusion.

To resolve the legal issues before us, we must first understand the basics of the Internet and the World Wide Web. The Internet is a global network of interconnected computers which allows individuals and organizations around the world to communicate and to share information with one another. The Web, a collection of information resources contained in documents located on individual computers around the world, is the most widely used and fastest-growing part of the Internet except perhaps for electronic mail. Prevalent on the Web are multimedia web pages—computer data files written in Hypertext Markup Language—which contain information such as text, pictures, sounds, audio and video recordings, and links to other web pages. Each web page has a corresponding domain address, which is an identifier somewhat analogous to a telephone number or street address. Domain names consist of a second-level domain—simply a term or series of terms (e.g., westcoastvideo)—followed by a top-level domain. Commercial entities generally use the ".com" top-level domain. To obtain a domain name, an individual or entity files an application with Network Solutions listing the domain name the applicant wants. Because each web page must have an unique domain name, Network Solution checks to see whether the requested domain name has already been assigned to someone else. If so, the applicant must choose a different domain name. Other than requiring an applicant to make certain representations, Network Solutions does not make an independent determination about a registrant's right to use a particular domain name.

Using a Web browser, a cyber "surfer" may navigate the Web—searching for, communicating with, and retrieving information from various web sites. A specific web site is most easily located by using its domain name. Upon entering a domain name into the web browser, the corresponding web site will quickly appear on the computer screen. Sometimes, however, a Web surfer will not know the domain name of the site he is looking for, whereupon he has two principal options: trying to guess the domain name or seeking the assistance of an Internet search engine.

Oftentimes, an Internet user will begin by hazarding a guess at the domain name, especially if there is an obvious domain name to try. Web users often assume, as a rule of thumb, that the domain name of a particular company will be the company name followed by ".com." Sometimes, a trademark is better known than the company itself, in which case a Web surfer may assume that the domain address will be "'trademark'.com," [as in] "usatoday.com." Guessing domain names, however, is not a risk-free activity. One looking for the latest information on Panavision, International, L.P., would sensibly try "panavision.com." Until recently, that Web surfer would have instead found a web site owned by Dennis Toeppen featuring photographs of the City of Pana, Illinois. Having registered several domain names that logically would have corresponded to the web sites of major companies such as Panavision, Delta Airlines, Neiman Marcus, and Lufthansa, Toeppen sought to sell "panavision.com" to Panavision, which gives one a taste of some of the trademark issues that have arisen in cyberspace.

A Web surfer's second option when he does not know the domain name is to utilize an Internet search engine, such as Yahoo, Altavista, or Lycos. When a keyword is entered, the search engine processes it through a self-created index of web sites to generate a (sometimes long) list relating to the entered keyword. Each search engine uses its own algorithm to arrange indexed materials in sequence, so the list of web sites that any particular set of keywords will bring up may differ depending on the search engine used. Search engines look for keywords in places such as domain names, actual text on the web page, and metatags. Metatags are HTML code intended to describe the contents of the web site. There are different types of metatags, but those of principal concern to us are the "description" and "keyword" metatags. The description metatags are intended to describe the web site; the keyword metatags, at least in theory, contain keywords relating to the contents of the web site. The more often a term appears in the metatags and in the text of the web page, the more likely it is that the web page will be "hit" in a search for that keyword and the higher on the list of hits the web page will appear.

With this basic understanding of the Internet and the Web, we may now analyze the legal issues before us.

We review the district court's denial of preliminary injunctive relief for an abuse of discretion. Under this standard, reversal is appropriate only if the district court based its decision on clearly erroneous findings of fact or erroneous legal principles. A plaintiff is entitled to a preliminary injunction in a trademark case when he demonstrates either (1) a combination of probable success on the merits and the possibility of irreparable injury or (2) the existence of serious questions going to the merits and that the balance of hardships tips sharply in his favor. Brookfield must establish that West Coast is using a mark confusingly similar to a valid, protectible trademark of Brookfield's. The district court denied Brookfield's motion for preliminary injunctive relief because it concluded that Brookfield had failed to establish that it was the senior user of the "MovieBuff" mark or that West Coast's use of the "moviebuff.com" domain name created a likelihood of confusion.

To resolve whether West Coast's use of "moviebuff.com" constitutes trademark infringement or unfair competition, we must first determine whether Brookfield has a valid, protectible trademark interest in the "MovieBuff" mark. Brookfield's registration of the mark on the Principal Register in the Patent and Trademark Office constitutes prima facie evidence of the validity of the registered mark and of Brookfield's exclusive right to use the mark on the goods and services specified in the registration. Nevertheless, West Coast can rebut this presumption by showing that it used the mark in commerce first, since a fundamental tenet of trademark law is that ownership of an inherently distinctive mark such as "MovieBuff" is governed by priority of use.

It is uncontested that Brookfield began selling "MovieBuff" software in 1993 and that West Coast did not use "moviebuff.com" until 1996. According to West Coast, however, the fact that it has used "The Movie Buff's Movie Store" as a trademark since 1986 makes it the first user for purposes of trademark priority. In the alternative, West Coast claims priority on the basis that it used "moviebuff.com" in commerce before Brookfield began offering its "MovieBuff" searchable database on the Internet. We analyze these contentions in turn.

Conceding that the first time that it actually used "moviebuff.com" was in 1996, West Coast argues that its earlier use of "The Movie Buff's Movie Store" constitutes use of "moviebuff.com." West Coast has not provided any Ninth Circuit precedent approving of this theory, but neither has Brookfield pointed us to any case law rejecting it. We are not without guidance, however, as our sister circuits have explicitly recognized the ability of a trademark owner to claim priority in a mark based on the first use date of a similar, but technically distinct, mark—but only in the exceptionally narrow instance where the previously used mark is the legal equivalent of the mark in question or indistinguishable therefrom such that consumers consider both as the same mark. This constructive use theory is known as "tacking," as the trademark holder essentially seeks to tack his first use date in the earlier mark onto the subsequent mark.

We agree that tacking should be allowed if two marks are so similar that consumers generally would regard them as essentially the same. Where such is the case, the new mark serves the same identificatory function as the old mark. Giving the trademark owner the same rights in the new mark as he has in the old helps to protect source-identifying trademarks from appropriation by competitors and thus furthers the trademark law's objective of reducing the costs that customers incur in shopping and making purchasing decisions. Without tacking, a trademark owner's priority in his mark would be reduced each time he made the slightest alteration to the mark, which would discourage him from altering the mark in response to changing consumer preferences, evolving aesthetic developments, or new advertising and marketing styles.

The standard for tacking, however, is exceedingly strict. [One court ruled], for example, that priority in *Clothes That Work. For the Work You Do* could not be tacked onto *Clothes That Work*. [Another] held that "DCI" and "dci" were too dissimilar to support tacking.

The present case is clear cut: "The Movie Buff's Movie Store" and "moviebuff.com" are very different, in that the latter contains three fewer words, drops the possessive, omits a space, and adds ".com" to the end. Because West Coast failed to make the slightest showing that consumers view these terms as identical, we must conclude that West Coast cannot tack its priority in "The Movie Buff's Movie Store" onto "moviebuff.com." Since tacking does not apply, we must therefore conclude that Brookfield is the senior user because it marketed "MovieBuff" products well before West Coast began using "moviebuff.com" in commerce.

West Coast argues that we are mixing apples and oranges when we compare its first use date of "moviebuff.com" with the first sale date of "MovieBuff" software. West Coast reminds us that Brookfield uses the "MovieBuff" mark with both computer software and the provision of an Internet database; according to West Coast, its use of "moviebuff.com" can cause confusion only with respect to the latter. West Coast asserts that we should accordingly determine seniority by comparing West Coast's first use date of "moviebuff.com" not with when Brookfield first sold software, but with when it first offered its database online.

Brookfield first used "MovieBuff" on its Internet-based products and services in August 1997, so West Coast can prevail only if it establishes first use earlier than that. In the literal sense of the word, West Coast "used" the term "moviebuff.com" when it registered that domain address in February 1996. Registration with Network Solutions, however, does not in itself constitute "use" for purposes of acquiring trademark priority. The Lanham Act grants trademark protection only to marks that are used to identify and to distinguish goods or services in commerce—which typically occurs when a mark is used in conjunction with the actual sale of goods or services. The purpose of a trademark is to help consumers identify the source, but a mark cannot serve a source-identifying function if the public has never seen the mark and thus is not meritorious of trademark protection until it is used in public in a manner that creates an association among consumers between the mark and the mark's owner.

The district court, while recognizing that mere registration of a domain name was not sufficient to constitute commercial use for purposes of the Lanham Act, nevertheless held that registration of a domain name with the intent to use it commercially was sufficient to convey trademark rights. This analysis, however, contradicts both the express statutory language and the case law which firmly establishes that trademark rights are not conveyed through mere intent to use a mark commercially.

West Coast no longer disputes that its use—for purposes of the Lanham Act—of "moviebuff.com" did not commence until after February 1996. It instead relies on the alternate argument that its rights vested when it began using "moviebuff.com" in e-mail correspondence with lawyers and customers sometime in mid-1996. West Coast's argument is not without support in our case law—we have indeed held that trademark rights can vest even before any goods or services are actually sold if the totality of one's prior actions, taken together, can establish a right to use the trademark. However, West Coast must establish that its e-mail correspondence constituted use in a way sufficiently public to identify or distinguish the marked goods in an appropriate segment of the public mind as those of the adopter of the mark. West Coast fails to meet this standard. Its purported use is akin to putting one's mark on a business office door sign, letterheads, architectural drawings, or on a prototype displayed to a potential buyer, [all] of which have been held to be insufficient to establish trademark rights. Although widespread publicity of a company's mark may be sufficient to create an association among the public between the mark and West Coast, mere use in limited e-mail correspondence with lawyers and a few customers is not.

For the foregoing reasons, we conclude that the district court erred in concluding that Brookfield failed to establish a likelihood of success on its claim of being the senior user. Establishing seniority, however, is only half the battle. Brookfield must also show that the public is likely to be somehow confused about the source or sponsorship of West Coast's "moviebuff.com" web site—and somehow to associate that site with Brookfield.

We begin by comparing the allegedly infringing mark to the federally registered mark. The district court found West Coast's domain name "moviebuff.com" to be quite different than Brookfield's domain name "moviebuffonline.com." Comparison of domain names, however, is irrelevant as a matter of law, since the Lanham Act requires that the allegedly infringing mark be compared with the claimant's *trademark,* which here is "MovieBuff," not "moviebuffonline.com." Properly framed, it is readily apparent that West Coast's allegedly infringing mark is essentially identical to Brookfield's mark "MovieBuff." In terms of appearance, there are differences in capitalization and the addition of ".com" in West Coast's complete domain name, but these differences are inconsequential in light of the fact that Web addresses are not caps-sensitive and that the ".com" top-level domain signifies the site's commercial nature.

Looks aren't everything, so we consider the similarity of sound and meaning. The two marks are pronounced the same way, except that one would say "dot com" at the end of West Coast's mark. Because many companies use domain names comprised of ".com" as the top-level domain with their corporate name or trademark as the second-level domain, the addition of ".com" is of diminished importance in distinguishing the mark. The irrelevance of the ".com" becomes further apparent once we consider similarity in meaning. The domain name is more than a mere address: like trademarks, second-level domain names communicate information as to source. Many Web users are likely to associate "moviebuff.com" with the trademark "MovieBuff," thinking that it is operated by the company that makes "MovieBuff" products and services. As "MovieBuff" and "moviebuff.com" are, for all intents and purposes, identical in terms of sight, sound, and meaning, we conclude that the similarity factor weighs heavily in favor of Brookfield.

The similarity of marks alone does not necessarily lead to consumer confusion. Accordingly, we must proceed to consider the relatedness of the products and services offered. Related goods are generally more likely than unrelated goods to confuse the public as to the producers of the goods. In light of the virtual identity of marks, if they were used with identical products or services likelihood of confusion would follow as a matter of course.

The district court classified West Coast and Brookfield as non-competitors largely on the basis that Brookfield is primarily an information provider while West Coast primarily rents and sells videotapes. It noted that West Coast's web site is used more by the somewhat curious video consumer who wants general movie information, while entertainment industry professionals, aspiring entertainment executives and professionals, and highly focused moviegoers are more likely to need or to want the more detailed information provided by "MovieBuff." This analysis, however, overemphasizes differences in principal lines of business. Instead, the focus is on whether the consuming public is likely somehow to associate West Coast's products with Brookfield. Here, both companies offer products and services relating to the entertainment industry generally, and their principal lines of business both relate to movies specifically. Thus, Brookfield and West Coast are not properly characterized as non-competitors.

Not only are they not non-competitors, the competitive proximity of their products is actually quite high. Just as Brookfield's "MovieBuff" is a searchable database with detailed information on films, West Coast's web site features a similar searchable database, which Brookfield points out is licensed from a direct competitor of Brookfield. Undeniably then, the products are used for similar purposes. The two companies compete for the patronage of an overlapping audience. The use of similar marks to offer similar products accordingly weighs heavily in favor of likelihood of confusion.

In addition to the relatedness of products, West Coast and Brookfield both utilize the Web as a marketing and advertising facility, a factor that courts have consistently recognized as exacerbating the likelihood of confusion. Both companies, apparently recognizing the rapidly growing importance of Web commerce, are maneuvering to attract customers via the Web. Not only do they compete for the patronage of an overlapping audience on the Web, both "MovieBuff" and "moviebuff.com" are utilized in conjunction with Web-based products.

Given the virtual identity of "moviebuff.com" and "MovieBuff," the relatedness of the products and services accompanied by those marks, and the companies' simultaneous use of the Web as a marketing and advertising tool, many forms of consumer confusion are likely to result. People surfing the Web for information on "MovieBuff" may confuse "MovieBuff" with the searchable entertainment database at "moviebuff.com" and simply assume that they have reached Brookfield's web site. In the Internet context, in particular, entering a web site takes little effort—usually one click from a linked site or a search engine's list; thus, Web surfers are more likely to be confused as to the ownership of a web site than traditional patrons of a brick-and-mortar store would be of a store's ownership. Alternatively, they may incorrectly believe that West Coast licensed "MovieBuff" from Brookfield, or that Brookfield otherwise sponsored West Coast's database. Other consumers may simply believe that West Coast bought out Brookfield or that they are related companies.

Yet other forms of confusion are likely to ensue. Consumers may wrongly assume that the "MovieBuff" database they were searching for is no longer offered, having been replaced by West Coast's entertainment database, and thus simply use the services at West Coast's web site. And even where people realize, immediately upon accessing "moviebuff.com," that they have reached a site operated by West Coast and wholly unrelated to Brookfield, West Coast will still have gained a customer by appropriating the goodwill that Brookfield has developed in its "MovieBuff" mark. A consumer who was originally looking for Brookfield's products or services may be perfectly content with West Coast's database (especially as it is offered free of charge); but he reached West Coast's site because of its use of Brookfield's mark as its second-level domain name, which is a misappropriation of Brookfield's goodwill by West Coast.

Likelihood of confusion is determined on the basis of a "reasonably prudent consumer." What is expected of this reasonably prudent consumer depends on the circumstances. We expect him to be more discerning—and less easily confused—when he is purchasing expensive items, and when the products being sold are marketed primarily to expert buyers. On the other hand, when dealing with inexpensive products, customers are likely to exercise less care, thus making confusion more likely.

The complexity in this case arises because we must consider both entertainment professionals, who probably will take the time and effort to find the specific product they want, and movie devotees, who will be more easily confused as to the source of the database offered at West Coast's web site. In addition, West Coast's site is likely to be visited by many casual movie watchers. The entertainment professional, movie devotee, and casual watcher are likely to exercise high, little, and very little care, respectively. Who is the reasonably prudent consumer? We need not, however, decide this question now because the purchaser confusion factor, even considered in the light most favorable to West Coast, is not sufficient to overcome the likelihood of confusion strongly established by the other factors we have analyzed.

In light of the foregoing analysis, we conclude that Brookfield has demonstrated a likelihood of success on its claim that West Coast's use of "moviebuff.com" violates the Lanham Act. We are fully aware that although the question of whether confusion is likely a factual determination woven into the law, we nevertheless must review only for clear error the district court's conclusion that the evidence of likelihood of confusion in this case was slim. Here, however, we are left with the definite and firm conviction that a mistake has been made.

So far we have considered only West Coast's use of the domain name "moviebuff.com." Because Brookfield requested that we also preliminarily enjoin West Coast from using marks confusingly similar to "MovieBuff" in metatags and buried code, we must also decide whether West Coast can, consistently with the trademark and unfair competition laws, use "MovieBuff" or "moviebuff.com" in its HTML code. At first glance, our resolution of the infringement issues in the domain name context would appear to dictate a similar conclusion of likelihood of confusion with respect to West Coast's use of "moviebuff.com" in its metatags. We are, after all, dealing with the same marks, the same products and services, the same consumers, etc. Disposing of the issue so readily, however, would ignore the fact that the likelihood of confusion in the domain name context resulted largely from the associational confusion between West Coast's domain name "moviebuff.com" and Brookfield's trademark "MovieBuff." The question in the metatags context is quite different. Here, we must determine whether West Coast can use "MovieBuff" or "moviebuff.com" in the metatags of its web site at "westcoastvideo.com" or at any other domain address other than "moviebuff.com" (which we have determined that West Coast may not use).

Although entering "MovieBuff" into a search engine is likely to bring up a list including "westcoastvideo.com" if West Coast has included that term in its metatags, the resulting confusion is not as great as where West Coast uses the "moviebuff.com" domain name. First, when the user inputs "MovieBuff" into an Internet search engine, the list produced by the search engine is likely to include both West Coast's and Brookfield's web sites. Thus, in scanning such list, the Web user will often be able to find the particular web site he is seeking. Moreover, even if the Web user chooses the web site belonging to West Coast, he will see that the domain name of the web site he selected is "westcoastvideo.com." Since there is no confusion resulting from the domain address, and since West Coast's initial web page prominently displays its own name, it is difficult to say that a consumer is likely to be confused about whose site he has reached or to think that Brookfield somehow sponsors West Coast's web site.

Nevertheless, West Coast's use of "moviebuff.com" in metatags will still result in what is known as initial interest confusion. Web surfers looking for Brookfield's "MovieBuff" products who are taken by a search engine to "westcoastvideo.com" will find a database similar enough to "MovieBuff" such that a sizeable number of consumers who were originally looking for Brookfield's product will simply decide to utilize West Coast's offerings instead. Although there is no source confusion in the sense that consumers know they are patronizing West Coast rather than Brookfield, there is nevertheless initial interest confusion in the sense that, by using "moviebuff.com" or "MovieBuff" to divert people looking for "MovieBuff" to its web site, West Coast improperly benefits from the goodwill that Brookfield developed in its mark.

Using another's trademark in one's metatags is much like posting a sign with another's trademark in front of one's store. Suppose West Coast's competitor (let's call it "Blockbuster") puts up a billboard on a highway reading—"West Coast Video: 2 miles ahead at Exit 7"—where West Coast is really located at Exit 8 but Blockbuster is located at Exit 7. Customers looking for West Coast's store will pull off at Exit 7 and drive around looking for it. Unable to locate West Coast, but seeing the Blockbuster store right by the highway entrance, they may simply rent there. Even consumers who prefer West Coast may find it not worth the trouble to continue searching for West Coast since there is a Blockbuster right there. Customers are not confused in the narrow sense: they are fully aware that they are purchasing from Blockbuster and they have no reason to believe that Blockbuster is related to, or in any way sponsored by, West Coast. Nevertheless, the fact that there is only initial consumer confusion does not alter the fact that Blockbuster would be misappropriating West Coast's acquired goodwill. We conclude that the Lanham Act bars West Coast from including in its metatags any term confusingly similar with Brookfield's mark.

Registration of a domain name for a web site does not trump long-established principles of trademark law. When a firm uses a competitor's trademark in the domain name of its web site, users are likely to be confused as to its source or sponsorship. Similarly, using a competitor's trademark in the metatags of such web site is likely to cause what we have described as initial interest confusion. These forms of confusion are exactly what the trademark laws are designed to prevent. Accordingly, we reverse and remand this case to the district court with instructions to enter a preliminary injunction in favor of Brookfield in accordance with this opinion.

## Points for Discussion

1. Both Brookfield and West Coast use the Web to sell their services, and the court sees this as evidence that their businesses are highly similar, thus likely to cause customer confusion. Suppose that neither company were involved in e-commerce. Would it make sense for a court to point to the fact that both a plaintiff and a defendant company sell their wares in the old-fashioned, "brick and mortar" way as itself an indication of possible customer confusion between the two?

2. By using "MovieBuff" as a metatag, West Coast Entertainment lured Web surfers likely searching for Brookfield's services to their own Web site, a practice the court here disallows. Suppose that this usurping of a metatag did not involve two commercial competitors but instead the Web sites of a prominent politician and of an interest group seeking to air widely its criticisms of that political figure. Should the U.S. media law system's elevation of political speech over commercial speech

mean that the dissidents should have a right to lure the unsuspecting Web surfer to their own Web site, which might be in the form of a biting parody of the politician's own Web site?

## ■ *A&M Records v. Napster*

### 239 F.3d 1004 (9th Cir. 2001)

*Judge Beezer:*

Plaintiffs are engaged in the commercial recording, distribution and sale of copyrighted musical compositions and sound recordings. The complaint alleges that Napster is a contributory and vicarious copyright infringer. The district court preliminarily enjoined Napster from engaging in, or facilitating others in copying, downloading, uploading, transmitting, or distributing plaintiffs' copyrighted musical compositions and sound recordings, protected by either federal or state law, without express permission of the rights owner. We entered a temporary stay of the preliminary injunction pending resolution of this appeal.

Napster has designed and operates a system which permits the transmission and retention of sound recordings employing digital technology. In 1987, the Moving Picture Experts Group set a standard file format for the storage of audio recordings in a digital format called MPEG-3, abbreviated as MP3. Digital MP3 files are created through a process colloquially called "ripping." Ripping software allows a computer owner to copy an audio CD directly onto a computer's hard drive by compressing the audio information on the CD into the MP3 format. The MP3's compressed format allows for rapid transmission of digital audio files from one computer to another by electronic mail or any other file transfer protocol.

Through a process commonly called "peer-to-peer" file sharing, Napster allows its users to: (1) make MP3 music files stored on individual computer hard drives available for copying by other Napster users; (2) search for MP3 music files stored on other users' computers; and (3) transfer exact copies of the contents of other users' MP3 files from one computer to another via the Internet. These functions are made possible by Napster's MusicShare software; Napster provides technical support for the indexing and searching of MP3 files, as well as for its other functions, including a "chat room" where users can meet to discuss music, and a directory where participating artists can provide information about their music.

A first-time user is required to register with the Napster system by creating a user name and password. If a registered user wants to list available files stored in his computer's hard drive on Napster for others to access, he must first create a user library directory on his computer's hard drive. The user then saves his MP3 files in the library directory, using self-designated file names. He next must log into the Napster system using his user name and password. His MusicShare software [available from Napster's Web site] then searches his user library and verifies that the available files are properly formatted. If in the correct MP3 format, the names of the MP3 files will be uploaded from the user's computer to the Napster servers. The content of the MP3 files remains stored in the user's computer.

Once uploaded to the Napster servers, the user's MP3 file names are stored in a server-side library under the user's name and become part of a collective directory of files available for transfer during the time the user is logged onto the Napster system. The collective directory is fluid; it tracks users who are connected in real time, displaying only file names that are immediately accessible.

To search the files available from Napster users currently connected to the network servers, the individual user accesses a form in the MusicShare software stored in his computer and enters either the name of a song or an artist as the object of the search. The form is then transmitted to a Napster server and automatically compared to the MP3 file names listed in the server's search index. Napster's server compiles a list of all MP3 file names pulled from the search index which include the same search terms entered on the search form and transmits the list to the searching user.

[Or], the Napster user creates a list of other users' names from whom he has obtained MP3 files in the past. When logged onto Napster's servers, the system alerts the user if any user on his list (a "hotlisted user") is also logged onto the system. If so, the user can access an index of all MP3 file names in a particular hotlisted user's library and request a file in the library by selecting the file name.

To transfer a copy of the contents of a requested MP3 file, the Napster server software obtains the Internet address of the requesting user and the Internet address of the "host user"(the user with the available files). The Napster servers then communicate the host user's Internet address to the requesting user. The requesting user's computer uses this information to establish a connection with the host user and downloads a copy of the contents of the MP3 file from one computer to the other.

Plaintiffs claim Napster users are engaged in the wholesale reproduction and distribution of copyrighted works, all constituting direct infringement. Secondary liability for copyright infringement does not exist in the absence of direct infringement by a third party.

Plaintiffs must satisfy two requirements to present a prima facie case of direct infringement: (1) they must show ownership of the allegedly infringed material and (2) they must demonstrate that the alleged infringers violate at least one exclusive right granted to copyright holders [by U. S. Copyright law]. Plaintiffs have sufficiently demonstrated ownership; as much as eighty-seven percent of the files available on Napster may be copyrighted and more than seventy percent may be owned or administered by plaintiffs. Plaintiffs have shown that Napster users infringe at least two of the copyright holders' exclusive rights: the rights of reproduction and distribution. Napster users who upload file names to the search index for others to copy violate plaintiffs' distribution rights. Napster users who download files containing copyrighted music violate plaintiffs' reproduction rights.

Napster contends that its users do not directly infringe plaintiffs' copyrights because the users are engaged in fair use of the material. Napster identifies three specific alleged fair uses: sampling, where users make temporary copies of a work before purchasing; space-shifting, where users access a sound recording through the Napster system that they already own in audio CD format; and permissive distribution of recordings by both new and established artists.

Napster users are not fair users. The "Purpose and Character of the Use" factor focuses on whether the new work merely replaces the object of the original creation or instead adds a further purpose or different character. In other words, this factor asks whether and to what extent the new work is "transformative." Downloading MP3 files does not transform the copyrighted work. Courts have been reluctant to find fair use when an original work is merely retransmitted in a different medium; reproduction of audio CD into MP3 format does not transform the work.

This element also [concerns] whether the allegedly infringing use is commercial or noncommercial. Direct economic benefit is not required to demonstrate a commercial use. Rather, repeated and exploitative copying of copyrighted works, even if the copies are not offered for sale, may constitute a commercial use. Napster users engage in commercial use of the copyrighted materials largely because (1) a host user sending a file cannot be said to engage in a personal use when distributing that file to an anonymous requester, and (2) Napster users get for free something they would ordinarily have to buy.

[With respect to] the Nature of the Work [element], works that are creative in nature are closer to the core of intended copyright protection than are more fact-based works. Copyrighted musical compositions and sound recordings are creative in nature; [this] cuts against a finding of fair use under the second factor.

As to the Portion Used, while wholesale copying does not preclude fair use per se, copying an entire work militates against a finding of fair use. File transfer necessarily involves copying the entirety of the copyrighted work.

[Concerning the] Effect of Use on Market, the proof required to demonstrate present or future market harm varies with the purpose and character of the use. Napster harms the market in at least two ways: it reduces audio CD sales among college students and it raises barriers to plaintiffs' entry into the market for the digital downloading of music. Having digital downloads available for free on the Napster system necessarily harms the copyright holders' attempts to charge for the same downloads.

Napster contends that its users download MP3 files to "sample" the music in order to decide whether to purchase the recording. Napster argues that the district court: (1) erred in concluding that sampling is a commercial use because it conflated a noncommercial use with a personal use; (2) erred in determining that sampling adversely affects the market for plaintiffs' copyrighted music, a requirement if the use is noncommercial; and (3) erroneously concluded that sampling is not a fair use because it determined that samplers may also engage in other infringing activity.

The district court determined that sampling remains a commercial use even if some users eventually purchase the music. We find no error in the district court's determination. The record supports a finding that free promotional downloads are highly regulated by the record company plaintiffs and that the companies collect royalties for song samples available on retail Internet sites. Free downloads provided by the record companies consist of thirty-to-sixty second samples or are full songs programmed to "time out," that is, exist only for a short time on the downloader's computer. In comparison, Napster users download a full, free and permanent copy of the recording.

Napster further argues that the district court erred in rejecting its evidence that the users' downloading of samples increases or tends to increase audio CD sales. The district court, however, correctly noted that any potential enhancement of plaintiffs' sales would not tip the fair use analysis conclusively in favor of defendant. We agree that increased sales of copyrighted material attributable to unauthorized use should not deprive the copyright holder of the right to license the material. [Consider] the example of the film producer's appropriation of a composer's previously unknown song that turns the song into a commercial success; the boon to the song does not make the film's simple copying fair.

Napster also maintains that space-shifting is a fair use. Space-shifting occurs when a Napster user downloads MP3 music files in order to listen to music he already owns on audio CD. [But whenever we have accepted this argument in prior cases] the methods of shifting did not also simultaneously involve distribution of the copyrighted material to the general public; the time or space-shifting of copyrighted material exposed the material only to the original user [such as from a hard drive to a portable MP3 player]. Conversely, it is obvious that once a user lists a copy of music he already owns on the Napster system in order to access the music from another location, the song becomes available to millions of other individuals, not just the original CD owner.

We find no error in the district court's determination that plaintiffs will likely succeed in establishing that Napster users do not have a fair use defense. Accordingly, we next address whether Napster is secondarily liable for the direct infringement under two doctrines of copyright law: contributory copyright infringement and vicarious copyright infringement. We first address plaintiffs' claim that Napster is liable for "contributory" copyright infringement. Traditionally, one who, with knowledge of the infringing activity, induces, causes or materially contributes to the infringing conduct of another, may be held liable as a "contributory" infringer. Napster, by its conduct, knowingly encourages and assists the infringement of plaintiffs' copyrights.

Contributory liability requires that the secondary infringer know or have reason to know of direct infringement. The district court found that Napster had both actual and constructive knowledge that its users exchanged copyrighted music. The district court also concluded that the law does not require knowledge of specific acts of infringement and rejected Napster's contention that because the company cannot distinguish infringing from noninfringing files, it does not "know" of the direct infringement. It is apparent from the record that Napster has knowledge, both actual and constructive, of direct infringement. The district court found actual knowledge because: (1) a document authored by Napster co-founder Sean Parker mentioned "the need to remain ignorant of users' real names and IP addresses since they are exchanging pirated music"; and (2) the Recording Industry Association of America informed Napster of more than 12,000 infringing files, some of which are still available. The district court found constructive knowledge because: (a) Napster executives have recording industry experience; (b) they have enforced intellectual property rights in other instances; (c) Napster executives have downloaded copyrighted songs from the system; and (d) they have promoted the site with screen shots listing infringing files.

[However], we depart from the reasoning of the district court that Napster failed to demonstrate that its system is capable of commercially significant noninfringing uses. If a computer system operator learns of specific infringing material available on his system and fails to purge such material from the system, the operator knows of and contributes to direct infringement. Conversely, absent any specific information which identifies infringing activity, a computer system operator cannot be liable for contributory infringement merely because the structure of the system allows for the exchange of copyrighted material.

We nevertheless conclude that sufficient knowledge exists to impose contributory liability when linked to demonstrated infringing use of the Napster system. Napster has actual knowledge that specific infringing material is available using its system; it could block access to the system by suppliers of the infringing material, [yet] it failed to remove the material.

We turn to the question whether Napster engages in vicarious copyright infringement. In the context of copyright law, vicarious liability extends to cases in which a defendant has the right and ability to supervise the infringing activity and also has a direct financial interest in such activities. Napster's future revenue is directly dependent upon increases in userbase. More users register with the Napster system as the quality and quantity of available music increases. [Thus] Napster financially benefits from the availability of protected works on its system.

The district court [also] determined that Napster has the right and ability to supervise its users' conduct. We agree in part. The district court correctly determined that Napster had the right and ability to police its system and failed to exercise that right to prevent the exchange of copyrighted material. Napster's reserved right and ability to police [its own system, however, is limited] by the system's current architecture. As shown by the record, the Napster system does not "read" the content of indexed files, other than to check that they are in the proper MP3 format. The files are user-named and may not match copyrighted material exactly (for example, the artist or song could be spelled wrong).

The district court correctly recognized that a preliminary injunction against Napster's participation in copyright infringement is not only warranted but required. We believe, however, that the scope of the injunction needs modification in light of our opinion. Specifically, we reiterate that contributory liability may potentially be imposed only to the extent that Napster: (1) receives reasonable knowledge of specific infringing files with copyrighted musical compositions and sound recordings; (2) knows or should know that such files are available on the Napster system; and (3) fails to act to prevent viral distribution of the works. In crafting the injunction on remand, the district court should recognize that Napster's system does not currently appear to allow Napster access to users' MP3 files.

> *Editor's Note:* On remand, the district court amended its injunction so as to demand that Napster remove from its system MP3 files corresponding to specific songs within three days of being notified by the copyright owner of its claim.

## Points for Discussion

1. The financial interdependence between radio stations and owners of copyrights in musical works is governed by a federally imposed "compulsory licensing" plan, wherein the copyright holders may not withhold the right to play songs on the radio, and radio stations pay a blanket fee to copyright clearing houses that then, in turn, distribute the funds to the copyright holders. Should such a system be devised to govern the relationship between record companies and companies such as Napster?

2. As you likely know, there also exist on the Web mechanisms for "peer-to-peer" sharing of MP3 files that, unlike Napster, do not involve a central clearinghouse of data. Should you, as an individual purchaser of a CD, have an affirmative right to make copies of it and give those copies to a friend? How about a hundred friends? Should that right extend to placing an MP3 file corresponding to a song from a CD on the Web for *anyone* to copy?

*Notes*

# *Notes*

*Notes*

*Notes*

# Notes

*Notes*

# Notes

# Notes